Sex, France, and Arab Men, 1962–1979

Sex, France, and Arab Men, 1962–1979

TODD SHEPARD

The University of Chicago Press
Chicago and London

The University of Chicago Press, Chicago 60637
The University of Chicago Press, Ltd., London
Published 2017
Paperback edition 2021
Printed in the United States of America

30 29 28 27 26 25 24 23 22 21   1 2 3 4 5

ISBN-13: 978-0-226-49327-5 (cloth)
ISBN-13: 978-0-226-79038-1 (paper)
ISBN-13: 978-0-226-49330-5 (e-book)
DOI: https://doi.org/10.7208/chicago/9780226493305.001.0001

Library of Congress Cataloging-in-Publication Data

Names: Shepard, Todd, 1969– author.
Title: Sex, France, and Arab men, 1962–1979 / Todd Shepard.
Description: Chicago ; London : The University of Chicago Press, 2018. |
    Includes bibliographical references and index.
Identifiers: LCCN 2017033937 | ISBN 9780226493275 (cloth : alk. paper) |
    ISBN 9780226493305 (e-book)
Subjects: LCSH; Sex—France. | Prostitution—France. | Arabs—France. |
    Algeria—History—Revolution, 1954–1962.
Classification: LCC HQ18.F8 S447 2018 I DDC 306.70944—dc23
LC record available at https://lccn.loc.gov/2017033937

♾ This paper meets the requirements of ANSI/NISO Z39.48-1992
    (Permanence of Paper).

CONTENTS

Sex Talk and the Post-Algerian History of France

The object of my history is, to some extent, the imperialist colonization inside European space itself. How forms of domination over people or over certain categories of individuals were established and how they made the functioning of Western societies, modern societies, possible.

—Michel Foucault (1978)[1]

Algerian questions—and answers—made the sexual revolution French. This book is a history of how and why, from Algeria's independence from France in 1962 and through the cultural and social upheaval of the 1970s, highly sexualized claims about "Arabs" were omnipresent in important public discussions in France, both those that dealt with sex and those that spoke of Arabs. Two phenomena became enmeshed: the ongoing consequences of the Algerian war (1954–1962) and the so-called sexual revolution—which in roughly those years grabbed public attention and rapidly changed how sex was evoked, lived, and (far more slowly) legislated, even as it also provoked critique, activism, and resistance. To understand each of these things, it is necessary to analyze them together. The fight for sexual liberation is usually explained as a US and European invention. What this juxtaposition of the war's aftermath and "revolution" renders visible is that it also developed out of the worldwide anticolonial movement of the mid-twentieth century.[2]

1. "La scène de la philosophie," in Dits et écrits, t. 3 (Paris: Gallimard, 1994), 571–595; 581; "The Stage of Philosophy, A conversation between Michel Foucault and Moriaki Watanabe," Translated by Rosa Eidelpes and Kevin Kennedy, New York Magazine of Contemporary Art and Theory 1: 15 (2014); http://www.ny-magazine.org/PDF/The_Stage_of_Philosophy.html.

2. On the centrality of anticolonialism to the so-called sexual revolution, see Henry Abelove's pioneering text "New York Gay Liberation and The Queer Commuters," in Deep Gossip

"An Algerian Harvest": In 1967, this was the title the newspaper *Le cri du monde* (The World's Lament) gave to critic Xavier Grall's assessment of the fall season's new literary novels. Grall expressed the hope that his selection might offer the French public an opportunity to gain some perspective on "the physical and moral drama of the [Algerian] war." There were, he noted, "easily a dozen titles I could cite," but the one he focused on was Pierre Guyotat's just-published *Tombeau pour cinq cent mille soldats* (A tomb for five hundred thousand soldiers). Grall fretted that the book gave too much importance to the war's violence. Yet he embraced what he took to be its greatest insight: "It remains true that the Algerian war had something notably erotic about it." Guyotat—like Grall, a French veteran of the conflict, but one who had been imprisoned for desertion in 1962—had written an enigmatic note to himself in early 1967 to describe the manuscript that became *Tombeau*, which more acutely raises some of the issues at stake in post-1962 France: "decolonization and 'de-eroticization.'"[3]

With this coupling, Guyotat gave voice to the hope that the mid-twentieth-century tide of decolonization had laid low not just European colonialism, but the foundations on which, as subsequent scholars detail, Orientalist erotic fantasies (and nightmares) had long flourished. His controversial 1967 novel, through its excess and experimentations, forces attention to how the mixture of violence and desire exploded during the Algerian war. That admixture aimed to exaggerate and disable, through a process he named "de-eroticization," what had made this recent history so sexual—an ambition it could not possibly achieve. This conflicted past is what Grall's commentary tames into "something notably erotic." Both men's statements are compelling because they give evidence of how quickly familiar sexualized claims about Arabs reemerged in the aftermath

---

(Minneapolis, MN: University of Minnesota Press, 2005), 70–88. This book focuses on an elongated chronology of what French historian Michelle Zancarini-Fournel terms "the '68 years"; see, Michelle Zancarini-Fournel, "Conclusion," in *Les années 68: Le temps de la contestation*, ed. Geneviève Dreyfus-Armand, Robert Frank, Marie-Françoise Lévy, and Michelle Zancarini-Fournel (Paris: Complexe, 2000).

3. Unless otherwise noted, all translations from the French are by the author. Xavier Grall, "Une moisson algérienne," *Le cri du monde* 13 (December 1967), 52–53; Pierre Guyotat, *Tombeau pour cinq cent mille soldats, sept chants* (Paris: Gallimard, 1967); the citation is from his work notebook, collected in Pierre Guyotat, *Carnets de bord, v. 1 (1962–1969)*, ed. Valérian Lallement (Paris: Lignes & Manifestes, 2005), 200. On Guyotat, see Catherine Brun, *Pierre Guyotat, essai biographique* (Paris: Flammarion, 2015). Grall was the author of an essay on French draftees during the war, *La génération du djebel* (Paris: Du Cerf, 1962), along with many other texts.

of Algeria's independence. Their choice of terms also accurately signals the intensity with which this happened.[4]

The year 1962 was not a definitive break point between before and after. Yet claims and presumptions that the end of French rule in the Maghreb (Morocco and Tunisia had regained their independence six years before Algeria) was exactly such a rupture—as well as the significant developments that supported such arguments—fashioned what came after. This is why the category of "post-decolonization" is useful. Post-decolonization, invocations of sex, and Arabs now primarily described people, relationships, and events located within France even as they always also referenced Algeria. Until the end of the 1970s, another key difference with other variants of so-called sexual Orientalism was that the focus of most assertions was on men rather than women and, in that context, masculinity rather than effeminacy. These discussions churned through a class of evidence that scholars largely ignore, which I refer to as "sex talk": diverse references to sex, sexual morality, deviance, and normalcy in publications, archived documents, and visual sources. Sex talk expanded dramatically in these years, thanks to growing demands for sexual liberation and the transformative power of consumer capitalism.

The post-decolonization grammar of sex talk changed contemporary France. The claims ranged from fascination to reprobation. In a 1962 study, essayist Edouard Roditi asserted that "it is usually agreed in France that Arabs have been gifted with greater manliness than us," which the author linked to their more "primitive" social organization. The tension this quote highlights between "gifted" and "primitive" aptly announces the contradictory ways that assertions about Arab men moved over the following years. What remained constant, however, was an affirmation of stark difference, which opened some possibilities even as it closed more.[5] Many scholars

4. Extensive analyses and descriptions of sexual and gender practices or erotic tastes were one of the forms of "science," of research and truth claims about "the Orient," that, as critic Edward Said first proposed, tell us more about the society that produces them—i.e., "the West"—than about the people they claim to explain. Edward Said, *L'Orientalisme: L'Orient créé par l'Occident* (Orientalism), trans. Catherine Malamoud (Paris: Le Seuil, 1980). Throughout this book, the term "Arab(s)" usually appears unmarked, except when it is placed in parallel with other problematic categories or its use demands particular attention. Still, as the work of Said and others demonstrate, it is always a problematic term; this book details various reasons why it mattered to actors at the time.

5. Edouard Roditi, *De l'homosexualité* (Paris: SEDIMO, 1962), 330–331. Sigmund Freud had written much on the binarism of primitive vs. neurotic; see, e.g., his 1915 "Reflections upon War and Death," in *Character and Culture*, ed. Philip Rieff (New York: Collier Books, 1963), 107–133.

have claimed that until the 1990s French public debate avoided grappling with the racism and dehumanizing violence that marked the Algerian war as well as colonial and post-decolonization France. Yet attending to sex talk reveals that many French people could and did debate racism and the suffering that colonialism and decolonization inflicted.[6] It thus maps out important connections between two conversations that have drawn much scholarly attention in recent years, yet which too often ignore each other: histories of empire and histories of sex.

Over the course of the 1960s and 1970s, many critics rejected the accusations of sexual perversion leveled at Arab men in France. Maghrebi authors were particularly attentive to this multipronged assault. In *Les ambassadeurs* (The Ambassadors), the Tunisian director Naceur Ktari offered a crude summary of some of the key stereotypes at play. This 1975 feature-length film starkly depicted the difficulties faced by the "immigrant workers" who had become such a visible feature of contemporary France. It was directly inspired by an October 1971 murder in the poor and heavily Maghrebi Goutte d'Or neighborhood in Paris. Djellali Ben Ali, a fifteen-year-old Algerian, died at the hands of Daniel Pigot, the jealous and racist concierge in his building. Pigot was convinced that the boy had slept with his wife. One scene depicts a group of concerned "French" inhabitants who have gathered together thanks to the activism of a far-right (and *vieille France*) hotel owner. Stirred to anger, they list the problems they have with the behavior of their Arab neighbors; all relate to sex:

MAN: They follow our women and are ready to rape them . . .
WOMAN: They are all faggots . . .
MAN: In any case, they'll sleep with anything, even goats . . .
WOMAN: There are several that come on to me . . .

As this book confirms, this almost comical mélange of seemingly contradictory actions and inclinations captures the intensity and depth of ambient prejudices.[7]

Some radical critics, however, drew other lessons from claims about

6. Benjamin Stora, *La gangrène et l'oubli: La mémoire de la guerre d'Algérie* (Paris: La Découverte, 1991); John Talbott, *The War without a Name: France in Algeria, 1954–1962* (New York: Alfred Knopf, 1980). For a challenge to this view, see Raphaëlle Branche, *La guerre d'Algérie: Une histoire apaisée?* (Paris: Seuil, 2005), 20–21. While the French government did not officially accept the designation "Algerian war" until 1999, it appeared regularly in French sex talk throughout the 1960s and 1970s.
7. For reports on similar claims, see, e.g., Katia Kupp, "Le plongeon dans la Goutte-d'Or: 'Les ambassadeurs,'" *Nouvel observateur* 649 (18 April 1977), 78.

supposed differences between Westerners and Arabs. Note, for example, that Roditi's 1962 essay twinned descriptions of Arab and "Muslim" societies as "primitive" with the qualification "less neurotic." Indeed, it paralleled what he characterized as their healthier approach to masculine sexuality with that of ancient Greece. The French-born (Turkish-Jewish) American literary and art critic did so to an end: he meant to critique recent antihomosexual laws in France. Other writers had somewhat different purposes. After May 1968—when protests by leftist students, transformed by a general strike that shut down the country, seemed to open a new era of revolutionary change and brought new issues and arguments into left-wing and wider discussions—celebrations of Arab men as a source of political inspiration increased among many left-wing commentators. Leftists spoke of a liberatory freedom and forms of political action particular to "Arab" or "Maghrebi" actors and militants. France, the West, and those who worked for "revolution," they claimed, could learn from this model. The fact that the Algerian National Liberation Front (FLN) had led one of the few violent uprisings that forced an unwilling colonial power, France, to hand over sovereignty made Algeria especially important. After 1962, some admirers called Algeria "the Mecca of revolutionaries." In stark contrast to the static hierarchies associated with "Oriental despotism"—a term taken from Hegelian and Marxist analyses and the model that structured sexual Orientalism—French activists across the "'68 years" cherished the "Arab revolution" as an alternate fantasy, one of radical possibilities (figure 1).[8] With the virtual disappearance of such claims by the end of the 1970s, the period this book analyzes came to a close.

The public conversation about sex and Arabs stretched far beyond the far left. The active interest of right-wing voices in these questions indeed reminds us that such recriminations against Arabs did not simply emerge full-born from popular prejudices or historical precedents. Efforts to advance reactionary political claims rehearsed, stoked, and spread decidedly pernicious attacks. In November 1978, after multiple showings on the art-house cinema circuit, Ktari's *Les ambassadeurs* appeared as the centerpiece of one of France's most popular primetime television shows, *Les dossiers de l'écran* (Reports from the big screen). In response, the editor-in-chief

8. On "Mecca," see Jeffrey James Byrne, *Mecca of Revolution: Algeria, Decolonization, and the Third World Order* (Oxford: Oxford University Press, 2016). On the central role of "despotism" in sexual (especially homoerotic) Orientalism, see Joseph A. Boone, *The Homoerotics of Orientalism* (New York: Columbia University Press, 2014). The emphasis on political lessons was what differentiated this from other "Islamo-" and "Arabophile" arguments that were typical of all forms of Orientalism (just as philo-Semitism always shadows antisemitism).

Figure 1. "The Arab Revolution. Problems. The State of Affairs. Perspectives."
This 1975 cover image for a special insert in the Trotskyist weekly *Rouge* was
one of numerous far-left celebrations of the Arab world as new revolutionary "homeland." See *Le Cahier Rouge New Series* 3. Supplement to *Rouge* 305
(June 1975); permission to reproduce graciously provided by Rouge/RaDAR.

of *Minute*, a far-right weekly, offered an alternate depiction of the "concerned" French men and women whose meeting the Tunisian director had staged.[9] The writer ironically defended "those Frenchmen so profoundly abject that they are incapable of joyously embracing the transformation of their neighborhood into a Casbah." François Brigneau evoked "those heartless Frenchmen so full of themselves that they dislike the stench of Arab cuisine filling their streets, the noise of Arab music, the presence of an overly large Arab minority taking up the seats of the school their children attend." He added one final element to this chain of stereotypes, and it was the most important: the rejection by "those Frenchmen" of what Brigneau termed "the vigor of Arab sexuality."[10] The wry tone presented each element in this list of worries as comprehensible, even self-evident. Most of his concerns focused on the external, on infringements on French sensibilities and senses. Yet this last, right after he summoned the image of "children," located the problem as a difference in kind, a threat inherent to "the Arab man," which menaced intimate boundaries, French families, and the nation.

The supposed sexual threat that "Arabs" posed to "the French" was foundational to post-1962 far right efforts to re-enter mainstream discussions. All the important elements in this fringe of French politics had embraced the defense of French Algeria until the bitter end. To this end, many had supported a terrorist group, the Secret Army Organization (OAS), that from early 1961 used deadly violence in both Algeria and France in an effort to overthrow the government of Charles de Gaulle. Few repudiated such choices, which had deeply discredited the far right. Their attempts to reestablish a foothold in French political institutions would have to wait until after 1979—when the National Front (founded in 1971) began to win some seats—but their efforts to insert an argument about Arab men and sex into public debates had immediate and durable purchase, and laid the groundwork for electoral success.[11] This helps explain why, post-

9. At an earlier point in the film, Ktari shows an immigrant ripping down a poster for *Minute*, which had "Dehors les Algériens [Algerians out]!" in large block letters.

10. François Brigneau, "Haro sur les 'anormaux,'" *Minute* 867 (22–28 November 1978), 8–9. On the central role of "the abject" in mid-twentieth-century far-right activism in France, see Sandrine Sanos, *The Aesthetics of Hate: Far-Right Intellectuals, Antisemitism, and Gender in 1930s France* (Stanford, CA: Stanford University Press, 2012).

11. This success was exactly what the radical-right theorist Alain de Benoist termed "metapolitics," his summons for extremist activists to focus on altering the terms used to describe society rather than waste their time fighting more immediate struggles, which they would lose. He played a key role in the development of such attacks, and was the most influential founder of the Nouvelle Droite. See Anne-Marie Duranton-Crabol, *Visages de la nouvelle droite: Le GRECE et son histoire* (Paris: Presses de la Fondation nationale des sciences politiques, 1988).

decolonization, accusations of sexual deviance resonated in virtually all the other social and political registers in which anti-Maghrebi sentiments played out, whether these entailed charges of criminality, high birthrates, parasitism, barbarism, "smells," "noises," or the like.

Was There a "French" Sexual Revolution?
Local and Global Histories

Public debates deployed sex and sexuality in ways that offered the French people a chance to assess, evoke, and even to analyze histories and memories of French Algeria, the war, and empire. To map the potent intersections of empire and sex, each chapter of this book explores one key public debate. These focus successively on the far right, gay liberation, debates about prostitution and so-called social Catholics, the "sodomy vogue" of the 1970s, and how the question of rape shaped far left and feminist politics. This history provides a new perspective on the "French" sexual revolution.

Recently, historians have struggled to bring detailed cultural histories into dialogue with wide-lens global histories: this book offers one model. In broad terms, the French sexual revolution and French controversies about sex in the 1960s and 1970s can be fruitfully mapped onto a transnational chronology of crises and evolutions, a global movement that produced clear parallels in other countries (in the United States, Germany, and the United Kingdom, for example). Yet, as this book shows, what was particular here—what made these controversies "French" rather than "Western" or "late modern"—were the central roles that invocations of Arab men and Algeria played in them and the ways that such invocations altered the contours and, at key moments, the substance of debates about contemporary sexuality.[12]

What follows does not fully explore the divisions between diverse far-right currents; the focus of primary source research was on the 1960s, when those who in the 1970s would become associated with the Nouvelle Droite and/or the Front National, along with "nationalistes" (those who embraced the European nation) and "nationaux" (those who cared only for the French nation), were all deeply intertwined, notably around "Algeria." For a focus on the conflicts and divergences of the far right, see Jean-Yves Camus and Nicolas Lebourg, Les Droites extrêmes en Europe (Paris: Seuil, 2015). On the Front National's first electoral victories, see: Françoise Gaspard, A Small City in France: A Socialist Mayor Confronts Neo-Fascism, trans. Arthur Goldhammer (Cambridge, MA: Harvard University Press, 1995).

12. On the sexual revolution, see esp. Beth Bailey, Sex in the Heartland: Politics, Culture, and the Sexual Revolution (Cambridge, MA: Harvard University Press, 2002); Dagmar Herzog, Sex after Fascism: Memory and Morality in Twentieth-Century Germany (Princeton, NJ: Princeton University Press, 2005); Frank Mort, Capital Affairs: London and the Making of the Permissive Society (New Haven and London: Yale University Press, 2010). On the need to "regionalize" the

The Erotics of Algerian Difference

What I term "the erotics of Algerian difference" allowed French men and women to grapple with the unstable boundaries of nation and identity in the post-decolonization moment. During the Algerian revolution, anti-colonial activists, most of them Maghrebis, engaged issues of sex and gender that would be at the heart of the sexual revolution. Their arguments against torture or in response to French claims about the "Islamic veil" made clear that sexual norms, too, were colonial in nature, even as the larger struggle they were part of offered analyses and arguments to challenge them. The influence of these arguments on subsequent French discussions makes the post-1962 erotics of Algerian difference somewhat distinct from the longer history of sexual Orientalism, of which it is a part. Sexual liberationists, notably "homosexual revolutionaries" and feminists—such as Catherine Deudon, a photographer and writer, who in 1974 blamed "hetero colonialism" for ongoing lack of attention to lesbian concerns—had proved attentive students; extreme right activists, in turn, were harsh and early critics. The crucial context was immigration, and discussions of the erotic relationship of France and the French to Algerian men shaped claims and framed disagreements between the right and the left. To misuse Freudian terminology, all engaged the unspoken question of whether the libidinal links between Algerian men and the French were to be repressed through demonization, or cathected through emulation or objectification.[13]

Talk of sex and desire helped French observers think through post-1962 relationships, real as well as imagined, between Algeria and France and between Maghrebis and French people. Decolonization, many had presumed, would shrink connections. Somewhat surprisingly however, international links between Algeria and France seemed to grow more important

---

history of the sexual revolution, see Dagmar Herzog, *Sexuality in Europe: A Twentieth-Century History* (Cambridge: Cambridge University Press, 2011), 133; see also the essays in *Sexual Revolutions*, ed. Alain Giami and Gert Hekma (Basingstoke, UK: Palgrave Macmillan, 2014). For an impressive social history of "love, gender, and sexuality" in post-1945 France that marvelously re-examines the "French" sexual revolution on the ground, see Régis Revenin, *Une histoire de garçons et de filles: Amour, genre et sexualité dans la France d'après-guerre* (Paris: Vendemiaire, 2015), esp. 16–19.

13. On how the Algerian revolution set the stage for the sexual revolution, see Todd Shepard, "'Something Notably Erotic': Politics, 'Arab Men,' and Sexual Revolution in Post-Decolonization France, 1962–1974," *Journal of Modern History* 84 (2012), 80–115; and Todd Shepard and Catherine Brun, "Introduction: Guerre des sexes, politiques du genre," in Brun and Shepard, eds., *Guerre d'Algérie: Le sexe outragé* (Paris: CNRS éd., 2016), 11–26. Catherine Deudon, "Le colonialisme hétéro," *Actuel* 38 (January 1974), 15–16.

rather than less after the war of independence. In 1973 and 1974, the so-called Arab oil embargo sparked much criticism, as (mainly Arab) states in the Organization of Petroleum Exporting Countries (OPEC) sought to persuade other countries to support Arab demands against Israel by leveraging access to oil. The unexpected economic crisis, which began to preoccupy French commentators at just that time, intensified negative reactions. Together, these events seemed to explain the new prominence of anti-immigrant arguments and their anti-Arab valence. Both were visible in a series of government decisions from the 1972 Marcellin-Fontanet circular, which drastically increased legal limits on the rights of immigrant workers, to the July 1974 circular that "suspended" the immigration of all workers and members of their family. In this context, innumerable commentators consistently turned to sex to evoke, assess, or castigate Franco-Arab connections. Of course, there was no obvious relationship between the economics of oil supplies and sex. As this book demonstrates, the economic context nevertheless intensified the circulation of sex talk about Arabs, which was already dense with meaning, and helped certain arguments crystallize.[14]

Most such sex talk concerned Algerian or "Arab" men, in part because the vast majority of the large numbers of Algerians in France were young men.[15] Public debates and, even more clearly, classified government assessments after 1968 make clear what numbers or the usual "universal" categories do not: Most French discussions about "immigrants" or "immigrant workers" in general—categories that, empirically speaking, included women, girls, boys, and men from countries such as Italy, Portugal, and Spain as well as those from the Maghreb and other former colonies—focused on Algerian men. A 1976 study commissioned by the French prime minister's office, titled "The Motivation of French Reactions toward Immi-

14. Yvan Gastaut, "Français et immigrés à l'épreuve de la crise (1973–1995)," *Vingtième Siècle: Revue d'histoire* 84 (2004), 107–118; Fausto Giudice, *Arabicides, une chronique française* (Paris: La Découverte, 1992). Michael Seidman describes how demands for sexual liberties emerged among French students in 1962 just as Algerian independence was won, and states that debates about racism and "colonial" immigrants were crucial factors in the shape their protests took; see Michael Seidman, "The Pre–May 1968 Sexual Revolution," *Contemporary French Civilization* 25 (2001): 25–41.

15. In 1962, Algerians constituted 85 percent of France's North African (presumed or "culturally") Muslim population of about 410,000; in 1970 their part had declined to around 75 percent. At that time, the number of "Muslim" noncitizens in the country was over 800,000 and counted approximately 608,000 Algerians (the largest group of immigrants, ahead of the Portuguese) but also 143,000 Moroccans and 89,000 Tunisians. The overwhelming majority were male manual laborers, but the proportion of women and children had actually increased since 1962. See Ethan Katz, *The Burdens of Brotherhood: Jews and Muslims from North Africa to France* (Cambridge, MA: Harvard University Press, 2015), 217.

grant Workers," reported that the people interviewed all distinguished between "immigrants" and "foreigners." The second term, "which connotes difference, is applied most particularly to Maghrebis, so that people say: 'A Swiss is not foreign; a Spaniard is a bit more when you think about it; an Arab, are you kidding!'"[16] One of the key priorities the research institute proposed to the government was in fact "to transform the immigrant from North Africa into a foreigner like the others."[17] Even within this category, Algerians stood apart. A 1971 police report submitted to the Ministry of the Interior claimed that, "as it concerns Algerians . . . the reports we have are unanimous." Among their French neighbors, "the expressions they adopt range from fear to distrust to diffuse hostility and a priori rejection." A 1973 report to the prefect of the Rhône Département was even starker: "The reactions that are currently out in the open amply demonstrate that the autochtone population is growing ever more reticent in accepting this foreign population, which is to say the North African population, above all the Algerian [population]."[18] Nor do the overwhelming percentages of men among them (although lower than among contemporary South Asian immigrants in Britain, for example) fully explain why the long-standing Orientalist obsession with "Muslim women" was so much less central during the '68 years than was talk of Arab men.

Most important was how successful anticolonial critics had been in positioning the "revolutionary" or heroic Algerian man as the embodiment of (universal and true) manliness, a figure who had confronted the overwhelming force—and the sadistic unmanly tactics, notably torture—of France, and freed his nation and family from colonial oppression. The prestige and aura of this figure, now only a historical memory in France, fashioned political thought in the 1960s and 1970s. On the world stage, the talismanic importance that Gillo Pontecorvo's 1965 film *The Battle of Algiers* (with its insistent depictions of potent semi-nude Algerian male bodies) and the "Algerian" writings of Frantz Fanon achieved in "Third

16. Insitut Pierre Bessi, "Motivation des Français à l'égard des travailleurs immigrés: Test de Moyens d'Actions" (Paris 7 April 1976), 15, in Centre des archives contemporaines des Archives nationales de France, Fontainebleau, France, hereafter CAC: 19960405/11.

17. Insitut Pierre Bessi, "Motivation des Français à l'égard des travailleurs immigrés: Resultat de la recherche d'idées" (Paris 22 March 1976), 22, CAC: 19960405/11.

18. Jacques Pélissier, "Evolution de la population étrangère dans le région Rhône-Alpes" (Villeurbanne, 15 June 1973), 4, in CAC: 19930317/16. On numbers, see Katz, *The Burdens of Brotherhood*; on the United Kingdom, see Ian R. G. Spencer, *British Immigration Policy since 1939: The Making of Multi-racial Britain* (London, 1997), 19; on shift from invocations of "families" before 1962 to talk of "young men," see Amelia Lyons, *The Civilizing Mission in the Metropole: Algerian Families and the French Welfare State during Decolonization* (Stanford, CA: Stanford University Press, 2013), conclusion.

Worldist" and leftist circles—for example, among the Black Panther Party in the United States—amplified the effects of wartime debates (figures 2 and 3). In addition, whereas the other emblematic figure of Algeria's resistance, the "veiled woman," remained definitively not French (in large part because of its association with Islam), anticolonial and Third Worldist representations of the heroic Algerian man staked their claims on the same ground that French voices considered their own, namely (necessarily masculine) universalism. For some, such as post-'68 leftists, this meant that Arabs could be models and allies. For others, first and foremost far-right

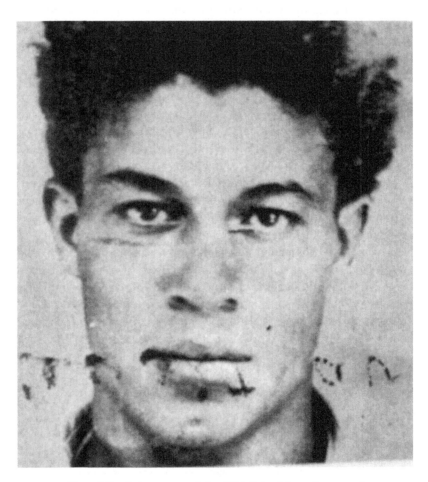

Figure 2. Revolutionary masculinity: "Ali la Pointe" (nom de guerre of FLN fighter Ali Amar [1930–1957]). Police photograph; reproduced by courtesy of *L'Humanité*, Paris. All rights reserved.

Figure 3. Revolutionary masculinity: Brahim Haggiag as
Ali la Pointe in *The Battle of Algiers* (1965).

activists, this meant that the need to reject both such claims and an Algerian presence on French territory, alongside or with French people, could appear quite pressing. Both contributed to how immigration, and Arab immigration above all, became an important political topic over the course of the 1960s and 1970s.[19]

By the end of the 1970s, most on the left had become too wary of invoking Arab men as models. Numerous controversies had made leftists too concerned about the many complications such references implied. Subsequent efforts to think about the politics of coalition, intersectionality, or the like ignore these earlier discussions, which invoked similar terms. Yet the far right continued to talk about sex and Arabs to advance their agendas, and proved equally adept when "Islam" and "the Muslim woman" reemerged as crucial references. What disappeared around 1979 was an intense conflict between certain French people about different ways that connections between "Arab men" and "sex" could be understood. On one side were those who argued that, precisely because of their specific history—a history in which French colonialism and anticolonial resistance had played crucial

[handwritten marginalia: "why?"]

[handwritten marginalia: "1979; turning point in thinking about 'Arab men' and 'sex'"]

---

19. On French republicanism, universalism, and gender, see esp. Joan W. Scott, *"Only Paradoxes to Offer": French Feminists and the Rights of Man* (Cambridge, MA: Harvard University Press, 1996). Judith Surkis incisively analyzes how the "scandalous" trials of Djamila Bouhired and Djamila Boupacha reworked visions of "Algerian femininity." See "Ethics and Violence: Simone de Beauvoir, Djamila Boupacha, and the Algerian War," *French Politics, Culture, & Society* 28 (2010), 38–55.

roles—Arab men offered the solution to a variety of French problems. On the other were those who argued that Arab men were emblematic of all the problems that Arabs continued to wreak on France and the French. The first perspective has faded. The second, much evidence suggests, has become even more influential. But looking back, it is clear that the claim by numerous scholars that the French forgot the Algerian war until the early 1990s is false. What has been forgotten was how much the Algerian revolution shaped France's sexual revolution and, more broadly, its history.[20]

Against (French) Vanilla History

This book relies on sex talk as evidence, and seeks to historicize it with as little voyeurism and as little prudery as possible. It does so to show how much specific histories shaped how sex was lived even as sex, in turn, shaped what it meant to be French, "Arab," or Franco-"Arab" in France. Not just any history, but very difficult, recent, and threatening histories of empire: their striking effects emphasize how necessary it is to analyze both the history of sex and how sex changed history. Multiple chapters of this book explore the damaging efficacy of efforts to assert that links between sexual acts (which included sodomy, rape, and venal sex) and identities (never just sexual or sexed, but also racialized, national, and even class) are natural, essential, and unchanging—without history. Others chart the risky possibilities opened up through attempts to think about the same acts and identities historically and politically, and why and how these efforts faded from view. Some do both.

Both wide-ranging sources and specific methodological choices anchor the multiple challenges this history poses to extant understandings of the sexual revolution and of the 1960s and 1970s more broadly. I focus on debates that had widespread public resonance, and on discussions that have been central to existing scholarship on the sexual revolution. My interpretations attend more to the exemplary—the oft-repeated, the seemingly self-evident—than to the exceptional. Diverse types of sources inspired them. In addition to archived government documents, I explored print media (periodicals, pamphlets, and books) and numerous fictional works. These diverse sources were drawn from numerous archives, from police archives in Paris and Marseille to the French national archives, personal papers, and the archives of leftist, gay rights, and feminist organizations, as well

---

20. On French discussions of the "Arab boy" in the 1990s, see Nacira Guénif-Souilamas and Éric Macé, *Les féministes et le garçon arabe* (La Tour d'Aigues, France: Éd. de l'Aube, 2004).

as those of authors and publishing houses. Audiovisual sources, both fictional and nonfictional, proved crucial. Alongside Ktari, films such as *The Last Tango in Paris* (1972), *Diabolo menthe* (1977), and *Dupont Lajoie* (1975) receive extended attention. So, too, do the documentaries of Carole Roussopolous and the archived programs of state television. Certain scholarly books produced in France do double service as both guides to analysis and as revelatory primary sources; these include Edward Said's *Orientalism* (1978/1980), Alain Corbin's *Filles de noce* (1978), Michel Foucault's *Histoire de la sexualité*, volume 1 (1976), Tahar ben Jelloun's *La plus haute des solitudes* (1975), Gilles Deleuze and Félix Guattari's *Anti-Oedipe* (1972), and Edgar Morin's *La Rumeur d'Orléans* (1969).

This history book, it must be emphasized, is also a product of the context in which it was researched and written. To clarify: Ongoing developments in France and the United States have underscored the significance of certain earlier discussions that, although important at the time they first appeared, now seem to have disappeared from popular and scholarly memory. Since 2012 in France, the far-right National Front has repeatedly been described as the most popular political party in the country. Its assertions about the threat that inhabitants with ties across the Mediterranean and to "Islam" pose to France are central to its success. Contemporary claims that misogyny and homophobia uniquely characterize Maghrebis and Islam have taken on particular importance in campaigns by certain intellectuals and politicians to normalize arguments the far right first articulated. It is clear that anxieties about the intersection between sexual difference, sexuality, and Frenchness continue to trouble many French people deeply. Similar concerns are rife in other Western societies (see, e.g., Donald Trump).[21] What follows here, then, is a "history of the present" in the Foucauldian sense. It challenges current histories of what mattered in France between 1962 and 1979 by paying attention to how "categories of contemporary debate that now appear inevitable, natural, or culturally necessary" coalesced short decades ago. The disjunctions with the present are particularly disturbing in part because many of the actors in current French discussions were also involved in this earlier history, either as individuals and or as social groups. This history of the present approach drew me to many sources that other historians have ignored.[22]

21. On the veil, see esp. Joan Wallach Scott, *The Politics of the Veil* (Princeton, NJ: Princeton University Press, 2007); on the debates provoked by the Marriage for All law, see Camille Robcis, "Catholics, 'the Theory of Gender,' and the Turn to the Human in the French Gay Marriage Debates: A 'New Dreyfus Affair'?" *Journal of Modern History* 87, no. 4 (2015), 892–923.

22. Editors, "Introducing *History of the Present*," *History of the Present* 1, no. 1 (2011), 1–4.

This is clearly the case with one particular focus of research, which might be termed "Maghrebi perspectives." People of Maghrebi descent are key actors now in French developments. They were in the 1960s and 1970s, too, which makes it odd that most history books ignore or ghettoize them—an aspect of what I term "vanilla history." The sources proved rich: they included studies, articles, books, films, and videos created by men and women who identified in various ways as Maghrebi. My work likewise draws on numerous personal advertisements and letters to the editors of newspapers and magazines, whose authors were presumed, perhaps inaccurately, to be "Arabs" or "Berbers" living in France. Throughout the period under examination, growing numbers of Maghrebis (notably from non-elite milieus) published and expressed themselves in writing and film. Algerian, Tunisian, and Moroccan independence had offered new arguments for why people linked to these countries should be heard (and new educational possibilities that gave many greater access to larger audiences). Another reason for the growing number of such sources was that the years after 1968—as French historians have incisively identified—became the era of the witness.[23]

By the early 1970s, the testimonial was in season. Again and again, in publications ranging from books by respected publishers to gay liberationist journals and porn magazines, from feminist monthlies to mainstream newspaper articles in scholarly as well as leftist publications, Arabs, Algerians, Maghrebis were incited to speak and were offered the opportunity to do so. The need to hear from witnesses rather than merely experts came to seem necessary to many.

Vanilla histories of the West erase the importance of people of color; vanilla histories of sex pretend that its multiple valences and diverse forms are best ignored. This book rejects both choices, even as it shows why they are linked. My study repeatedly demonstrates the striking degree to which the "immigrant" or "Arab" perspectives that made it into print or onto the screen were framed in terms of sex and sexuality. Over the course of the 1960s and 1970s, to speak as "Arabs" in French, or to be talked about, involved, and seemingly required, entering into a dense thicket of talk about sex and masculinity. Two theorists whose work in those years placed questions of sex, love, and sexuality at the heart of social critique help to make sense of this summons. In 1971 Roland Barthes wrote, "Social censorship is not found where speech is hindered, but where it is enjoined." And power,

23. See, e.g., Annette Wieviorka, *L'ère du témoin* (Paris: Plon, 1998).

as Foucault persuasively demonstrated in *The History of Sexuality*, volume 1 (1976), now worked primarily through the injunction to speak of certain things, rather than via repression.[24] Repeatedly, Maghrebis who could participate in French discussions had to testify about sexual topics. This can appear self-evident when one reads their published "voices." The archives of French publishing houses, however, flesh out this suspicion. Systematically, referees and editors bolstered their arguments to each other that readers were eager to hear the "voices" of "Arab men" with assertions that those texts these experts recommended for publication were ripe with sex.[25]

That is also why a larger context is needed to analyze French evidence that people from North Africa produced. The literary critic Gayatri Chakravorty Spivak used the 1973 Foucault-Deleuze conversation cited above to begin her exploration of the question "Can the subaltern speak?" Her answer was no, because the statements of subalterns—those on the margins or seemingly outside of social life—are recorded in the same language that shores up the society that oppresses them; to be legible, its grammar is still at work in even the most unorthodox or marginal utterances. Joan Wallach Scott, similarly, maps out the limits of how too many historians interpret the "experience" of the marginalized.[26] My research on the many "Maghrebi" witnesses who spoke in 1970s France takes up the insights of Spivak and Scott. The evidence nonetheless suggests that the ways in which Maghrebis themselves invoked Arabs and sex do tell us much, and about more than their "identities." So, too, with claims made by women and self-identified homosexuals (many of them feminists, gay liberationists, or sexual revolutionaries). Yet to assess such evidence and arguments requires a bigger canvas. As a number of critics have noted, exoticization and racial fetishism have marked numerous discussions among (French) feminists and male homosexuals. It is also true that attention to "Maghrebi" perspectives can reveal truer stories. To limit oneself to such insights, however, misses

24. Roland Barthes, *Sade, Fourier, Loyola* (Paris: Seuil, 1971), 130; also *Sade, Fourier, Loyola*, trans. Richard Miller (New York: Hill and Wang, 1976), 126 (translation altered); Michel Foucault, *The History of Sexuality*. Volume I: *An Introduction*, trans. Robert Hurley (New York: Pantheon Books, 1978). See also Tiphaine Samoyault, *Roland Barthes* (Paris: Seuil, 2015), 604.

25. See, e.g., Claude Durand, "Paul Flammand" (23 January 1973), in IMEC: Fonds Le Seuil [SEL] 3743.6; Monique Lebas, "Note de Monique Lebas à la comptabilité" (Paris 23 August 1973), 1, in IMEC: HAC 8745 Fonds Hachette Livre: 5GE.

26. Gayatri Chakravorty Spivak, "Can the Subaltern Speak?" in *Marxism and the Interpretation of Culture*, ed. Cary Nelson and Lawrence Grossberg (Urbana: University of Illinois Press, 1988), 271–313. Joan Wallach Scott, "The Evidence of Experience," *Critical Inquiry* 17, no. 4 (Summer 1991), 773–797.

the bigger story. What this book shows is that, post-decolonization, even people in France who thought of themselves as being free of Maghrebi connections lived and thought with Algerian accents.

The first four chapters of this book focus on minorities (far right activists, gay liberationists, gay French men, Maghrebi authors) in order to sketch out the discursive and political context for how and why the Algerian revolution and its aftermath informed sex talk in France. The first two chapters focus on the far right between 1962 and 1968, a political movement that encouraged efforts to establish clear distinctions between "the French" and "Arabs" in order to separate them. Through sex talk, writers and activists analyzed and bemoaned French defeat at Algerian hands, but also—notably through the idea of Algerian men as sex criminals who menaced post-1962 France—shifted from a defense of "French Algeria" to a fight against an "Algerian France." Chapters 3 and 4 analyze how 1970s gay liberationists and the newly visible gay world inverted these fears as they embraced the post-decolonization presence of Arab men in France. The next five chapters show in concrete detail how the erotics of Algerian difference informed 1970s debates about three issues critical to broad publics and diverse constituencies: prostitution and "white slavery," sodomy, and rape. The conclusion signals how 1979 French debates about the Iranian revolution helped displace these earlier discussions, which opened space for evocations of the "Muslim woman" to return to center stage.

This book shows that the reason why so many people in general spoke about sex and Arab men in the 1960s and 1970s was because of foundational problems in French politics, which Algerian independence crystallized. Although key aspects of what made the period distinct have since disappeared, the claims embedded in these stories still resonate clearly in current debates in France and elsewhere. This history helps explain why.

ONE

The Far Right and the Reinvigoration of Sexual Orientalism in Post-Decolonization France

Vice undoubtedly played a larger role than even oil in what concluded with the capitulation of Evian.

—André Figueras (1962)[1]

Between 1962 and 1968, it can seem, the longstanding erotic fascination of the French for Algerians had faded. But this seems true if one attends only to evidence from the vast majority in France who met Algeria's independence—after thirteen decades of French occupation—with acceptance, relief, joy, or indifference. On the far right, things looked different, as writers, theorists, and activists fixed on the upheaval around sex the conflict had catalyzed, and sought to make sense of it. In their read, it was sexual trouble that explained what they saw as political problems; sexual abnormality set the stage for the collapse of France's "natural" domination of Algeria. As the end of French Algeria approached, most intensively at the moment of Algerian independence and then over the course of the 1960s, people in the "national/nationalist camp" rehearsed claims about sexual acts, sexualized humiliation, and lust to explain how France had lost Algeria and what lessons must be learned. They homed in on "deviant" masculinity, with assertions about the aberrant hypermasculinity of "Arabs" and the decadent effeminacy that had made the French unable to defeat them. They also sought to use such references to advance their ultranationalist political agenda. This meant rewriting the history of French Algeria, French

1. The Evian Accords, which the French government and representatives of the Provisional Government of the Algerian Republic agreed to on 19 March 1962, put an end to their conflict and established a process that quickly led to Algerian independence. André Figueras, *Les origines étranges de la Ve République* (Paris: Les presses du Mail, [July] 1962), 166.

imperialism, and the Algerian war in order to make the healthy virile leadership they claimed to incarnate seem urgently necessary for France in the aftermath of Algerian independence.

In the last years of the Algerian war, when the long-standing (if retrospectively odd) French consensus that "Algeria is France" had finally shattered, the far right joined with others to defend the claim. Ultranationalists, en masse, enthusiastically embraced the argument that all people born in Algeria were fully French. This meant that not just the "European" and Jewish minorities but the large "Muslim" (Berber and Arab) majority, too, were *français à part entière* [completely French]. Far right voices adopted whole cloth antiracist arguments central to French republicanism—and historically anathema to their political family—in order to keep Algeria within the French Republic. On the one hand, such affirmations sought to give depth to the fact that, legally, both Algeria's territory and its people were French. On the other, they aimed to deny that Algeria was a colony or that racist colonialism had rendered French promises about the inclusion of Arabs and Berbers in the French nation unbelievable to most.[2] The failure of such arguments to prevent independence helps to explain the intensity and contours of the racism that followed. Too many subsequent commentators blame repatriates—the pieds noirs, people of "European" or Jewish backgrounds who left their native Algeria after independence and resettled in metropolitan France—for spreading the virus of racism in post-decolonization France. The Algerian framing of post-decolonization French racism and far-right ideology, however, is far more complex. It was not "transferred" onto French soil around 1962, pace Benjamin Stora. It developed there, stoked by unresolved paradoxes linked to the failed republican project of French Algeria and its disappearance. Claims about gender and sex, and especially about manliness and virility, anchored and shaped novel formulations of longstanding fears.[3]

After 1962, new racist arguments seemed necessary to explain the defeat of the French Algeria cause and to move beyond it. These arguments can appear to be a simple recalibration of old xenophobic reflexes, which at various points since the mid-nineteenth century had targeted "alien" groups—most obsessively, Jews—as enemies of France. The primary target,

2. On these paradoxes and how they intensified at the end of French Algeria, see Todd Shepard, *The Invention of Decolonization: The Algerian War and the Remaking of France*, 2nd rev. ed. (Ithaca, NY: Cornell University Press, 2008).

3. See esp. Benjamin Stora, *Le transfert d'une mémoire: De l'"Algérie française" au racisme anti-arabe* (Paris: La Découverte, 1999).

now, was the Arab, the Algerian, and the Muslim—although the latter category would prove less central until after the Iranian Revolution of 1979. Proponents of the new anti-Arab racism presumed that the Algerian revolutionaries' victory over France, ongoing tensions between the two countries, and the growing number of Algerians living in metropolitan France were factors that made this enemy different, more threatening. Two themes were crucial and linked: "invasion" and sexual crimes. Both emphasized the ongoing intimacy of French-Algerian connections as sources of danger. These propelled far-right militant warnings that the Arab threat was an existential danger to their nation.

After the Algerian war, the French ultra-right fringe reached its lowest point of influence ever. It ebbed even more than it had after 1945, when links to the Nazi occupiers, the Vichy state, and collaboration had led to prison terms for many activists and discredited the movement in the eyes of most French people.[4] Ideologically, those who remained on the far right—and, most important, those who had recently joined their ranks, almost all drawn by their commitment to "French Algeria"—accentuated this movement's long-standing anti-Marxism and its post-1940 anti-Gaullism. What was new was an intense focus on what they identified, in the words of historian René Chiroux, as "the threat posed by . . . the rise of peoples of color," whom previously they had merely despised or denigrated.[5] This included a disdainful fixation on the leaders of newly independent states ("N——r Kings," in their jargon) and an emotional investment in the struggles of white supremacist regimes in South Africa and Rhodesia and in the defense of Portuguese colonialism and US segregationism. Such language summoned what can be thought of as a "white international" to stymie the course of world events. The January 1965 cover of *Europe-action*, a monthly journal published from 1963 to 1966 that had great influence in the far-right milieu, warned that "In Africa, It's OPEN SEASON on Whites," with a photo of a miserable-looking, disheveled, and barefooted blond girl as illustration (figure 4). One aspect of the fight most engaged them, however: to stop Algerian immigration. (Indeed, the same 1965 cover also

4. On the much quicker reintegration of politicians associated with Vichy and collaboration, see Richard Vinen, *Bourgeois Politics in France, 1945–1951* (Cambridge: Cambridge University Press, 1995).

5. René Chiroux, *L'Extrême-droite sous la Ve République* (Paris: Librairie générale de droit et de jurisprudence, 1974), 87. Until at least the 1930s, French far-right discussions presumed that Africans and North Africans were at once inferior to and manipulable by their French and European betters; see esp. Sanos, *The Aesthetics of Hate*, 194–244.

Figure 4. "In Africa, It's Open Season on White People."
Europe-action 25 (January 1965), front cover.

announced a story that supposedly revealed the power of "The FLN in the South of France.")[6]

The ultranationalist right quickly qualified their fight as resistance to "the Algerian invasion of France." This became the most important struggle

6. *Europe-Action* 25 (Janvier 1965).

in what they saw as a larger war to defend French identity, a campaign that had to be pursued not only in print but on the ground.[7] Until the events of May 1968, the far left and, more broadly, the French media and main-stream politicians paid little attention to the country's large numbers of non-European immigrants. Yet right-wing extremists had paid much attention. The periodical *Europe-action*, along with a small but energetic activist group with the same name, played central roles. In the midst of the 1965 presidential campaign, activists from Europe-action organized multiple and sometimes violent public demonstrations around the motto "Algerian immigration: stop" (figure 5). The theme of "the Algerian invasion of France" was first turned into a rallying cry in the pages *Europe-action*. The revue was home to a cadre of ideologues (Alain de Benoist, Dominique Venner, Jean Mabire), whose incendiary ideas served both to renew far-right doctrine and, later, to produce what became the "Nouvelle Droite."[8] It was a fundamental shift in emphasis, notably in how it presented Arabs as more worrisome than Jews. In 1967, the former editor of *La libre parole* (the antisemitic newspaper founded in the late nineteenth century by Edouard Drumont), Henry Coston approvingly noted that *Europe-action* "has vigorously denounced the invasion by foreign elements that it judges dangerous for public peace and health," even as he regretted that "they have broken with those 'obsessed by the Judeo-Tibetan Hydra.'"[9] While many on the far right and elsewhere in France continued to fixate on a supposed Jewish menace to French society, other elements were now absorbed in racialized fears about Algerian immigrants.[10] (Many fully embraced both forms of xenophobia; François Brigneau of *Minute*, for example, had joined the collaborationist Milice in 1944 and continued to vilify Jews even as he campaigned against Arabs.)

7. Francis Bergeron and Philippe Vilgier, *De Le Pen à Le Pen. Une histoire de nationaux et des nationalistes sous la Ve Republique* (Paris: Dominique Martin Morian, 1985), 52.

8. Jean-Christian Petitfils, *L'Extrême Droite en France* (Paris: P.U.F., 1983), 109; *Europe-Action* 22 (October 1964). On the birth of the Nouvelle Droite and its links to *Europe-Action*, see Duranton-Cabrol, *Visages*; also, Stéphane François and Nicolas Lebourg, "Dominique Venner et le renouvellement du racisme," *Temps présent* (23 May 2013), http://tempspresents.com/2013/05/23/dominique-venner-renouvellement-racisme-stephane-francois-nicolas-lebourg/, accessed 5 October 2014.

9. Coston, "Europe-Action," in Coston, *Dictionnaire de la politique française*, vol. 1 (Paris: Publications Henry Coston/Librairie Française, 1967), 730; Coston's quotation is from *Europe-action bulletin* 113 (1966); see Pierre-André Taguieff, "La stratégie culturelle de la Nouvelle Droite en France, 1968-1983," in *Vous avez dit fascismes?* ed. Antoine Spire (Paris: Montalba, 1984), 13-152, 26.

10. Richard Vinen, "The End of an Ideology? Right-Wing Antisemitism in France, 1944-1970," *Historical Journal* 37, no. 2 (1994), 365-388.

It was the post-1962 reduction of "Arab" masculinity to "hypervirility" that grounded far-right efforts to prove that this group was more threatening than other supposed menaces, past or present. "Invasion" emphasized "mass" action, which took up far-right arguments against refugees in the 1930s, but was different from the dense register of antisemitic claims, which obsessed over the dangers posed by Jewish individuals and

Figure 5. "Soon There Will Be One Million of Them."
Europe-action 22 (October 1964), front cover.

the transnational networks they supposedly maintained. Specifically, the "Arab invasion" topos, with its emphasis on brutish male lust, marginalized fantasies of seduction, which antisemitic certainties that "the Jew" was both effeminate cosmopolitan and rapacious beast foregrounded. (It differed in similar ways from the other most important French trope of aberrant masculinity, which presented religious Catholics, too, as effeminate, rapacious, and in fealty to foreigners.)[11] This new bête noire, usually depicted as male and lust-driven—and in ways that obfuscated the politics of French-Algerian histories even as they drew on anger and resentment about French "humiliation"—proved remarkably compelling to ever-growing numbers of French people.

From "Masculine Humanism" to the the Crisis of Masculinity

The far right's own fixation on manly strength and virility helps explain their post-Algerian obsession with the masculinity of both "Arabs" and "the French." To explain the defeat in Algeria, they presented the former as deviant and dangerous and the latter as emasculated. The first target of these extremists was other ("white"/"European") French men. This was particularly visible among self-defined "national/nationalist" youth groups, who insistently mocked the "dubious" masculinity of other youth movements. A 1966 photo montage published in *Cahiers universitaires*, a journal edited by men who would become key figures in the Nouvelle Droite, celebrated "Parisian students tired of seeing the Latin Quarter invaded by a horde of hairy and repugnant 'beatniks.'" They "made the decision to establish . . . a select committee for immediate haircuts. . . . Vigorous hands thus took up scissors and considerably refreshed the scuzzy mops of several beatniks who appeared to be of the male sex." While in 1944 it was women accused of "horizontal collaboration" with male enemies whose heads had been shaved ("les tondues") by anti-Nazi and anticolloborationist mobs, here a neofascist organization targeted the hair of French men who had failed to embody the rightist radicals' vision of manliness.[12] An August 1969 report from the Prefecture de police described how "physical force . . . is a

11. On the parallels between French warnings about Jewish and Catholic male effeminacy, see Ari Joskowicz, *The Modernity of Others: Jewish Anti-Catholicism in Germany and France* (Stanford University Press, 2013). After the Enlightenment, claims about the aberrant effeminacy of religious Catholics developed most widely among "free thinkers" and on the left. Yet it also had an important place among proto–Nouvelle Droite thinkers and activists.

12. On "les tondues [shaved women]," see Fabrice Virgili, *La France virile: Des femmes tondues la Libération* (Paris: Payot, 2000).

priority for militants" of the new and youthful far-right group Occident. Its members "need to inspire fear" while their embrace of "violent fisticuffs aim to prove that the movement physically matters." The choice of words—"vigorous hands," "violent fisticuffs"–emphasizes building solidarity through a hyperphysicality that can be deployed towards violent ends. Occident would come to be known as a group that fetishized "manly," militant behavior, seeing it as preferable to an indulgence in the feckless pursuit of theoretical concerns. Yet, as several scholars have convincingly demonstrated in discussions of interwar fascist movements across Europe, including Nazism, to take such self-presentation at face value misses the mark.[13] Far-right agitation was girded by theory, and the quest for manliness seemed to offer one way into larger discussions. Affirmations of biological "truths" about masculinity seemed well -suited to legitimate other ideological claims.

Dominique Venner was a long-time far-right militant who had fought with the paratroopers in Algeria (1954–1956), had been imprisoned for his ties to the OAS (1961–1962), and had then launched *Europe-action*. He proposed an ideology that he named "masculine humanism" in *Pour une critique positive* (written and circulated in 1962, first published in 1964). The text aimed to do for the post-Algerian far right—the "nationalist revolution," as the author and others characterized their struggle—what Lenin's "What is to be Done?" (1902) had offered to Russian Marxists. In Venner's vision, true manliness was the only embodiment of the truly human. It thus could anchor an authoritarian and racist program to "save" France and Europe.

For this far right, sexual liberation was the newest danger that threatened the "white race." A 1965 cover story in the extremist *Révolution européenne* hints at how worried many in the milieu were: "Homosexuality, eroticism: What they are is weapons against white peoples."[14] Thus, to respond to this particular alloy of enemies, it was necessary to rejuvenate certain superior men so they could defend the "race." "Masculinism," argued Venner, needed to be the foundation of ideological renewal because, in his tendentious reading of the scholarship, "five percent of individuals, sociologists admit, are deeply perverted, insane, vice-ridden." Like moral-

13. Jean Bertolino, *Les Trublions* (Paris: Stock, 1969), 122; Joseph Algazy, *L'Extrême-Droite en France de 1965 a 1984* (Paris: Harmattan 1989), 61.

14. Marcel Savane, "Exploitation de l'érotisme contre les peuples blancs" [on the cover: "Une arme contre les peuples blancs: L'érotisme," *Révolution européenne* 8 (15 August–15 September 1965), 4–5.

izing sexologists since the late -nineteenth century, certain eugenicists, and fascist and Nazi theorists, he identified such people as meriting punishment, perhaps elimination. "At the far other end, one can observe a similar proportion of men who, naturally and in a developed way, possess particular qualities of energy and self-sacrifice that predispose them to serve the community, which is to say to lead it." A new far right, Venner proposed, needed to focus on exposing how "democracies, which have installed the reign of scheming and of money, are largely under the control of" the perverted. In turn, "the Nationalist Revolution will need to get rid of the first and bring the second to power."[15] Venner and many of his ideological brothers embraced paganism. Yet their concerns resonated with key Catholic far-right thinkers, such as the Belgian moral philosopher Marcel de Corte, a Maurrassian and counterrevolutionary. Their dedication to enforcing clear distinctions between people focused most on divisions between men and women. Their writings, however, spent much space bemoaning indifferentation—the modern insistence that, socially, all people are fundamentally the same, rather than divided into distinct groups that must be hierarchically ordered—and this connected them tightly to more explicitly racist theorists. De Corte's contribution to one of many early 1960s efforts to renovate far-right thinking, this one in *Ecrits de Paris*, began with the affirmation: "1—Our century quite clearly is not that of definition. It wallows in the vague, the unclear." He claimed that "the art of definition, which is essentially objective, has been lost." Instead, "everywhere it has been replaced by what I crudely and directly call 'logical masturbation.'" The overarching metaphor he chose emphasized the causal role so many on the far right assigned to sexual perversion and gender deviance. "Contemporary philosophy is homosexual from the bottom to the top: the other qua other is banished and only the other as me is recognized. . . ."[16] Such affirmations would later develop into key anchors for the arguments

15. Venner, "Pour une critique positive," *Europe-action* 5 (May 1963), 3–80. The longer original essay was first distributed in July 1962 (see "Editorial," *Europe-action* 5 (May 1963), 2.

16. Marcel de Corte, "Une définition de la droite," *Ecrits de Paris* 228 (July–August 1964), 74–79. On de Corte, see Francis Balace, "Les maurrassiens belges après 1945," in *Charles Maurras et l'étranger, l'étranger et Charles Maurras: L'Action française—culture, politique, société*, vol. 2, ed. Olivier Dard and Michel Grunewald (Bern: Peter Lang, 2009), 67–96, esp. 80–86. Belgium played a key role in French far-right discussions across the 1960s, as many French activists lived in exile north of the border because of their pro-OAS criminal activities. Still, far-right francophone discussions in Belgium were as contentious and divided as they were in France. Here I indicate one shared theme, rather than assert contiguity of thinking between Venner and de Corte.

of French scholars who vilified late-1990s government proposals to legalize domestic partnership (the PACS) as a way to offer state recognition of same-sex couples. In 2012 and 2013, leaders of the mass movement to stop the extension of civil marriage to same-sex couples popularized such claims that legal reform threatened to destroy the very foundations of human civilization, and were helped by journalists and public intellectuals who uncritically echoed them. In the 1960s, however, they were part of a vigorous post-decolonization discussion on the far right about how to save "European peoples" from imagined enemies.[17]

The binary of healthy virility versus a disturbing sexual perversion was foundational for the modern ultranationalist French far right, which had emerged in the late nineteenth century. Yet this theme had grown in importance over the course of the twentieth century. Since the interwar period, far-right analyses of "the French people" wavered between two deeply gendered visions. The most durable proposed that the French were troublingly feminine. When ultranationalism crystallized during the pre-1914 Third Republic, its leaders and thinkers shared the certainty that social psychologist Gustave Le Bon and others articulated vis-à-vis the new role of "the masses" (of mass politics and mass publics). They conceived of "the people" as dangerous, as defined by feminine irrationality, and so requiring great men and manly elites to lead them.[18] The second vision emerged only after 1918, when certain elements of the French far right began to entertain the idea that a "masculinization" of the people was possible. As the historian Kevin Passmore shows, these activists shared the right-wing "identification of a corrupt contemporary France with a 'tart' given over to luxury, impulsive behaviour and fantasy." Yet some, Passmore argues, represented themselves as "the agent[s] of national regeneration," and proposed the "masculinization of people" as their project. This was new. As Sandrine Sanos suggests, in her history of the far-right literary circle that included Louis-Ferdinand Céline, the role of the racialized French empire was critically important to arguments that Frenchmen could be remade as manly. Both possibilities—the need for manly elites and the remasculin-

17. On the PaCS debate, see *Au-delà du PaCS: L'Expertise Familiale à l'épreuve de l'homosexualité*, ed. Daniel Borrillo and Éric Fassin, 2nd ed. (Paris: PUF, 2001). To understand the evidence from these far-right claims about "masculinity" and "manliness," the work of gender theorists is necessary. See esp. Judith Butler, *Gender Trouble: Feminism and the Subversion of Identity* (New York: Routledge, 1990).

18. On Le Bon et al, see Andreas Huyssen, "Mass Culture as a Woman: Modernism's Other," in Huyssen, *After the Great Divide: Modernism, Mass Culture, Postmodernism* (Bloomington: Indiana University Press, 1986), 44–64.

ization of the French—continued to be debated on the right-wing fringe. Both, however, required a "virile" elite to guide the French.[19]

Throughout the 1930s and into the 1960s, and well into the present, the possibility of a far-right-led masculinization of the people, whether through Venner's "masculine humanism" or by other means, remained less convincing to most on the extreme right than the long-standing celebration of a virile avant-garde. Sympathetic to the latter position, interwar writer Drieu La Rochelle understood "the mediocrity of the average man" as indicative of a society "enslaved to its desires," which made it incapable of "manly force." *The Centurions*, the 1960 Jean Lartéguy best-seller that focused on paratroopers in Algeria, was one popular version of this vision, with its depiction of a small group of valiant warriors undermined by French society. With Algerian independence, this vision of an effeminate and decadent France unable to defend its manhood, its men, or its women became even more convincing to many on the far right.[20]

A War over Manliness? History versus Fantasy

Such disdain had reached a fever pitch in summer 1962, as Algeria became independent. Numerous far-right reports on the French handover of Algeria to the troops of the FLN depicted French weakness, unchecked by Gaullist effeminacy, as opening the doors to uncontrolled "oriental" perversion. A subsequent article in *Europe-action* summarized some of the claims. "We will never know the number of people kidnapped . . . sent off to Police headquarters or bordellos . . . tortured, raped—even the young men—their throats cut, disemboweled, then incinerated, most in the furnaces of Turkish baths." The paratroopers and other valiant men who had defended French honor and virility had been betrayed. Those who turned their backs on these heroes, many on the far right suggested, were driven by perversion.[21] In July 1962, one well known commentator, André Figueras, admitted that there was reason to think that French economic elites had forced independence so as to seize new opportunities in Algeria. Yet he

19. Kevin Passmore, "Class Gender and Populism: The Parti Populaire Français in Lyon, 1936–40," in *The Right in France*, ed. Nicholas Atkin and Frank Tallett (London: IB Tauris, 2004), 183–214; Sanos, *The Aesthetics of Hate*. See also, e.g., Caroline Campbell, *Political Belief in France, 1927–1945: Gender, Empire, and Fascism in the Croix de Feu and Parti Social Français* (Baton Rouge: LSU Press, 2015).

20. Michel Dobry, *Le mythe de l'allergie française au fascisme* (Paris: Albin Michel, 2003), 212; *Les centurions* (Paris: Presses de la Cité, 1960).

21. Georges Bousquet, "L'Armée," *Europe-action* 2 (February 1963), 8.

insisted that "vice undoubtedly played even a larger role than oil in what concluded with the capitulation of Evian." Such claims proved quite convincing among far-right audiences.[22]

After 1962, however, some on the far right still embraced the belief that, if properly guided, the French people could be (re)masculinized. These ultranationalists described a growing popular awareness that the Algerian defeat had aggravated an ongoing crisis of masculinity. In the 1950s, many who discussed the emergence of *"le cadre"* [the middle manager] as a new intermediate type of masculine ideal (between the "bourgeois" and the "proletarian") understood this development as symptomatic of a larger "crisis." Cultural critic Kristin Ross identifies "decolonization," and notably the Algerian revolution, as the phenomenon that precipitated the recognition of this crisis.[23] Other critics claim that the war and, more specifically, obsessive French representations of instances of nationalist sexual violence against French troops helped create a "crisis." Psychoanalyst Bernard Sigg, for example, argues that "the cultural clash of a monogamous European colonialism and a traditionally polygamous Islamic society encouraged an unprecedented explosion of sexual—and especially homosexual— violence" in French literature. Such causal links, which rely on unverified claims about forms of FLN violence, echo arguments that far-right propaganda rehearsed during and after the war. All these interpretations suggest that, during and after the conflict, the constant circulation of images and stories of emasculation, sexual violation, and genital mutilation supposedly suffered by French forces destabilized French self-definitions vis-à-vis masculinity.[24]

The French in those years arguably did witness a crisis in masculinity. Such crises are quite constant in the modern West, as recent scholarship recognizes. The argument that men embody masculinity in opposition to women, who embody femininity, is at once profoundly fragile—so blatantly in contradiction with the lives and actions of so many people—and yet crucial to multiple forms of modern social control and organization. It thus functions through endless crisis, as actors reposition claims and turn to new sources to stabilize them, paradoxically renewing and redefining assertions that gender difference is natural and self-evident. What is dubious

22. Figueras, *Les origines*, 166.

23. Kristin Ross, *Fast Cars, Clean Bodies: Decolonization and the Reordering of French Culture* (Cambridge, MA: MIT Press), 1995.

24. See, e.g., Raphaëlle Branche, "La masculinité à l'épreuve de la guerre sans nom," *Clio* 20 (2004), 111–122. Philip Dine, *Images of the Algerian War: French Fiction and Film, 1954–1992.* (New York: Oxford University Press, 1994), 142, 191.

is that Algerian violence was the cause of the "crisis" in post-1962 France. How French actors combined images of violence and assertions about masculinity to speak of the war and French defeat was more important.[25]

One particular image—the emasculation of French male victims—has been central to French discussions, both during the war and in literary and scholarly depictions ever since. Its relationship to real violence is tenuous. Between 1958 and 1959, French military authorities, historian Jacques Frémeaux notes, "recorded . . . five hundred throat cuttings, with the cadavers frequently then mutilated (emasculation for men, disembowelment for women)." During this period, Algerian forces killed some six thousand French soldiers and perhaps one thousand civilians.[26] Emasculations, that is, touched at most 4 or 5 percent of the dead; yet this horrific symbolic attack on virility came to typify French descriptions of all Algerian violence. Literary scholar Catherine Brun, who identified this motif, offered a convincing reading for why it circulated so widely: "Emasculation cuts off the possibility of analogy, of exchange, of dialog." This symbol works "'to polarize' and naturalize what separates [Algerian from French] so that, as the moment of mutilation renders undeniable, the difference could justify a combat to the death between 'Us' and 'Them.'" Loosely sourced but much reiterated references to emasculation offered a violent affirmation of nonresemblance between two groups that, over the course of the conflict, according to French law, were citizens of the same French nation. "'Cutting off balls' in the end works to render unthinkable, forever and ever, the very idea of *relationship* [*rapport*]." This, Brun's reading of French evidence and French interpretations makes clear, explains why endless rehearsals of such stories of emasculation proved so necessary. The French failure in Algeria, these proclaimed, resulted from Algerian inhumanity: their incapacity to be like the French, and the danger that they posed to the French, the blatantly sexual nature of which rendered it so threateningly intimate.[27]

25. On this question, see Scott, "*Only Paradoxes to Offer*" (1995); Judith Surkis, *Sexing the Citizen: Masculinity and Morality in France, 1870–1920* (Ithaca, NY: Cornell University Press, 2006).

26. Catherine Brun, "Guerre couilles coupées," in *Guerre d'Algérie: Le sexe outragé*, ed. Catherine Brun and Todd Shepard (Paris: CNRS Éditions, 2016), 141–159; Jacques Frémeaux, *La France et l'Algérie en guerre 1830–1870, 1954–1962* (Paris: Économica, 2002), 234–235. For overall numbers, see Benjamin Stora, *Algeria, 1830–2000: A Short History*, trans. Jane Marie Todd (Ithaca, NY: Cornell University Press, 2001), 109.

27. Brun, "Guerre couilles coupées" (2016).

From Victimizers to Victims

It was exactly this claim—that no further *"rapport"* between "Algerians" and "French" could be risked—that all of the angry remnants of the French far right sought to prove after 1962. What those writers grouped around *Europe-action* needed to analyze, following Venner, was why they had failed to keep Algeria French and how it was that, in this failed effort, most on the French far right had come to insist that "Algerian Muslims" were wholly French. Together, they argued, these two strategic failures explained why their political family now found itself even more isolated than it had been at the end of World War II. Insisting that Algerians and French were two wholly distinct peoples who needed to be kept apart, they posited, would reconnect their movement to the people they claimed to embody. Sex talk was the richly instrumentalist language these far-right thinkers latched onto.[28]

Over the course of the 1960s, the primary tactic that such writers and activists deployed was to demonstrate that in Algeria there had been a war over masculinity—who had "the balls," and so on—and that de Gaulle, and thus the French people, had been found wanting, to the humiliation of France. Those (such as Venner) who worked to reinvigorate French masculinity drew on the deep repertoire of Orientalist thinking to present Algeria as a woman who had needed French domination. In spring 1968, Jean Mabire, Europe-action activist and far-right writer (and disciple of Drieu), published *Outlaws*, which celebrated the paratroopers as virility incarnate, fighting in a world cut off from women, and in a very sexualized and thus dangerous relationship with Algeria. His characters took control of Algeria, directly and bodily, for France. "He felt his stomach and his thighs heavy against the earth, as if to possess it. The soil was warm. He thought of lovemaking. Then he thought of his country." Nothing suggests that this was supposed to be comic. Rather, just as Lartéguy had claimed in his wartime novel *The Centurions* (1960), Mabire's book proposed that it was the failure of French leaders to pursue similar sacrifices inspired by patriotic virility that had betrayed the paratroopers.[29]

Such invitations to focus on questions of sex and gender worked not to encourage a reoccupation of "lost" Algeria, but to mobilize French people to defend France against Algerianization—as if to taunt citizens into

28. See Dominique Venner, *Pour une critique positive* (Paris: Saint-Juste, 1964); Shepard, *The Invention of Decolonization*, ch. 3.

29. Jean Mabire, *Les Hors-la-loi* (Paris: Robert Laffont, 1968), 149.

imagining the dire consequences should such efforts fail. In early 1968, the weekly magazines *Minute* and *Rivarol* published articles that enumerated how horrible things were in independent Algeria, reminding readers of how much better life had been—for the Algerians themselves, of course— under French rule. The Algeria they described, post-French and therefore suffering, had a female face. In January a *Rivarol* journalist, in his review of a special issue of the left-leaning journal *Cahiers pédagogiques* dedicated to "the French language in the Maghreb," highlighted a discussion of a "deeply troubled adolescent Muslim girl" confronted, in the reading *Rivarol* gave the article, "with an Orient that now imposes its overarching tyranny in even the most minor element of [women's] daily lives." This led the journalist to conclude: "We now find ourselves at the edge of a new reign of darkness in the Maghreb." In late March, a front-page article in *Rivarol* headlined "The Misery of the Algerian Woman" announced that "her life will consist of only suffering and deceptions" (figure 6). Inside, two pages focused on the "harem slaves" who, "at least in Algeria are not eunuchs, but Algerian women . . . who find themselves, six years after independence, in a state of oppression unknown since the [French] conquest." As with so much ultra-right language in this discussion, the qualification "harem" sought to repurpose critiques of Western colonialism—of slavery, of colonized victims—into attacks against Arab men. That is, these summons to masculinize "the French" through the reaffirmation of male authority were grounded in outraged attacks on a masculinized Algeria. Theirs was a bad form of masculine domination, the argument went, while that which the extreme right proposed for France was good (for women above all, of course).[30]

What France had brought, such far right arguments insisted, was a well-ordered gender system that protected women. While citing the testimony of the Algerian feminist Fadéla M'Rabet, author of *La femme algérienne* (The Algerian Woman, 1965) and *Les algériennes* (Algerian Women, 1967), who had always linked her struggle for women's rights to anticolonial nationalism, *Rivarol* chided her because she "forgot to state that, under French rule,

30. E.g., Georges Bousquet, "Le 13 mai, après dix ans . . . *Hors-la loi, Expiation, Révolte: Terminé!" Rivarol* 904 (9 May 1968), 8–9; "Algérie Algérienne," *Rivarol* 890 (11 February 1968), 7; "Six ans après Evian: Misère de la femme algérienne," *Rivarol* 897 (21 March 1968), 1, 3–4. *Rivarol* first appeared in 1951, with the goal of rehabilitating those associated with the Vichy government and/or accused of collaboration. Its subtitle was *Hebdomadaire de l'opposition nationale*, later amended to *Hebdomadaire de l'opposition nationale et européenne* to encompass the growing distinction between "nationals" and "nationalists." The more "theoretical" monthly *Ecrits de Paris* has been owned by *Rivarol* since 1951. *Minute* was founded in 1961, with the goal of defending French Algeria and rejecting the leadership of Charles de Gaulle.

Six ans après Evian :
misère de la femme
algérienne

Juchée sur son âne, cette petite Algérienne sourit à son destin. Elle ne sait pas encore que sa vie ne sera que souffrance et déception.

Figure 6. "Six Years after Evian: Misery of the Algerian
Woman." *Rivarol* 897 (21 March 1968), 1.

the abusive situation she describes, which has led to a wave of suicides, was unknown." The article offered a whitewashed historical description of gender relations in Algeria in which "French authorities were always available to help out, as were French families, who naturally played the role of women's guardians." This was because men ran these families and "their paternalism had much to recommend it." It also outlined the reforms that followed from May 1958, which showed, in the critic Gayatri C. Spivak's formulation, "white men protecting brown women from brown men." Highlights of those reformist efforts were the nomination of Nafissa Sid-Cara as secretary of state in the Michel Debré government; the "unveiling ceremony" of "13 May" [*sic*]; the Feminine Solidarity Movement which Mme. Massu, wife of the military commander in Algiers, established. Subheads within the article—"Women in Chains," "Arab Racism Says No to Mixed Marriages," "Single Women in Danger"—dramatized M'Rabet's statements about the elevated number of rapes in Algeria and made clear the article's tacit theme: The situation of Algerian women revealed the menace that newly liberated Algerian men now posed.[31]

The far right was torn about who to hold responsible: de Gaulle and the Gaullists, defined by "female" cowardice; or Algerians, whose animal maleness now threatened all of France. One author suggested that during the Algerian War, the FLN had been kept "on the other side of our frontiers," but that now, "thanks to the Gaullists, even the Mediterranean does not keep them out"—which implied that the Gaullists had chosen to lose a winnable war and that their "choice" left France vulnerable to victimization by Algerian men.[32] Beyond the confused logic, the charge also revealed the ongoing tension between far-right visions of the French people as either, by definition, mired in female irrationality or able to be masculinized. If the former was the case, an elite corps of true men was needed to lead them; if the latter, news of supposed affronts at the hands of Arab men might reinvigorate them.

Anti–de Gaulle attacks reached their height with false reports that Algeria's leader, President Houari Boumédiène, had been invited to visit Paris. According to François Brigneau, writing in *Minute*, the imminent state visit had not yet been confirmed because the *"fellagha"* (bandit; a pejorative term for pro-independence fighters during the war) leader "wants [to parade down] the Champs- Elysées." Because "de Gaulle gives everything away," there could be little doubt that "he will reopen our frontiers to the Arab invasion and welcome the dictator of Algiers into Paris."[33] Brigneau then let his imagination run wild. "The scene is easy to envision," he wrote. "A morning in spring. 11 a.m. From the Concorde to the Etoile, a light breeze rustles the green and white standards attached to the flagpoles, abutting the tricolored flags." The symbols of the Algerian and French Republics, that is, share the symbolic center of the French capital, and columns of men march through "in the form of a V—V like theft [*vol*], rape [*viol*], violence, vindictiveness—the motorcycles lead the parade." Brigneau turns the banality of diplomatic pomp and circumstance into a beachhead offered by France for Algerian aggression to seize new ground. "The prime

31. On these developments, notably on the "unveiling" of 16 May 1958, see Shepard, *The Invention of Decolonization*, ch. 7. Spivak, "Can the Subaltern Speak?" 297.

32. Liliane Ernout, "André Morice: 'La seule indépendance possible pour notre pays . . . ,'" *Rivarol* 891 (8 February 1968), 4–5.

33. *Minute* 310 (7–13 March 1968), 8–10.

minister [of Algeria] arrives in front of the Tomb of the Unknown Soldier. An emotional moment that definitively seals the death of French Algeria and the birth of Algerian France."[34] In its displacement of French humiliation out of Algeria and into "Algerian France," the article echoes with an ongoing effort to educate the French public in the lessons some on the far right had drawn, an attempt to channel and reorient the emotion of "nostalgeria" onto the current reality of a France "invaded." It is not the far right that is bitter and vengeful because of the loss of French Algeria; independence itself, he proposes, unleashed the bitterness and violence of Algerians onto France.

The theme that *Europe-action* had launched, envisioning "the Algerian invasion of France," was constantly repeated and then grew in intensity during the presidential campaign of Jean-Louis Tixier-Vignancour in 1965—although it did not break into larger discussions beyond far-right circles. In 1964, when Tixier-Vignancour—the man who had provided legal representation to Raoul Salan (a French army general who had gone underground to lead the OAS, and who had been in prison since 1962) and other OAS activists—discussed in the pages of *Minute* his decision to run for presdient, he explained: "While we were partisans of French Algeria, we do not support Algerian France[, t]his invasion of France by a swarm of ne'er do wells, failures, disease-carriers. . . ."[35] Articles published in anticipation of the tenth anniversary of May 1958 relayed these same concerns. In the conclusion to her interview with André Morice, a former Socialist politician and defender of the French Algeria cause, Liliane Ernout asked rhetorically if "tomorrow, the situation in France will be any better . . . than it is in Algeria?" She did not make clear whether the Algerians in France or the Gaullists in power would be most responsible for this "Algerianization" of France.[36]

34. François Brigneau, "Le défi de Boumedienne: Il veut les Champs Elysées," *Minute* 310 (7–13 March 1968), 8–10; "Cette Algérie qui va de Dunkerque à Marseille," *Minute* 227 (4 August 1966), 12. Boumédiène's official title was "president of the Revolutionary Council," which can be translated as either "president" or "prime minister" in French (e.g., president of the council, a title that was changed to "prime minister" by the French Constitution of 1958).

35. *Minute* (24 March 1964). The thesis of the "fear of immigration-invasion-colonization of France by the colonized" had existed since the 1930s and 1940s, See Guy Pervillé, "Antiracisme, décolonisation de l'Algérie, et immigration algérienne en France," *Cahiers de la Méditerranée* 61 (2000), 121–130. In an analysis that relies exclusively on examples related to Algerians, Yvan Gastaud has analyzed what he sees as a more general phenomenon of "the foreigner, source of insecurity, an always present claim." Yvan Gastaud, *L'immigration et l'opinion en France sous la Ve République* (Paris: Le Seuil, 2000), 479–480.

36. *Minute* (24 March 1964); Ernout, "André Morice."

Algerians as (Sexual) Criminals

In their campaign to warn their fellow Frenchmen about the dangers that
the Algerian "invasion" posed to their country, far-right periodicals in the
1960s systematically associated Algerians with criminality. In one odd and
telling instance, an article about a German murderer loose in France, the
author put the blame on the large number of . . . "North Africans." Without
explaining the connection (although the choice was certainly symptomatic
of far-right efforts to erase histories of the Occupation as well as those of
empire), the author hastened to add, "I am in no way trafficking in racism:
it is a statistical fact." He added that "it would be a good thing, in my hum-
ble opinion, if an official census of delinquents on French soil be established, which listed them nation by nation." Such a census, he maintained,
"would help everyone think about what's happening." Dominique Venner
had already theorized this proposal in the pages of *Europe-action*. He had
called for depictions that showed "Europeans" as "victims" of Algerian aggressions, rather than "as it used to be, as the aggressors," which would also
work to show that "the nonwhite races threaten French society."[37] While
in its first year *Europe-action* had focused on the demographic threat (notably the danger of "métissage"), by 1964 its writers had developed a list
of specific physical aggressions that Algerians inflicted on French people.
In an editorial, Venner evoked the specter of a post-independence onrush
of Algerians into France, to warn that "these gentlemen who are arriving
at an ever quickening pace bring, in the place of gifts, their illnesses, their
vermin, and their vice." The last element helped explain the others and
became ever more central.[38]

Sexual crimes held pride of place in this far-right campaign (figure 7),
a clear difference from previous far-right campaigns against "the Jews," the
"*métèques*" (foreigners), or the like, where the theme had been present but
marginal. Such an approach relied on language and certainties that Orientalist commentators had elaborated over the nineteenth and early twentieth
centuries, and which, since at least the 1920s, French journalists, academic
experts, and law-enforcement officials had invoked to warn of the dangers

37. "Le Palais: Pas de chance, ou pas de poigne!" *Rivarol* 893 (22 February 1968), 2. On
Venner, see Harvey Simmons, *The French Front National: The Extremist Challenge to Democracy*
(Boulder, CO: Westview Press, 1996), 47. For examples, see, e.g., Dominique Venner, "Nous
sommes coupables!," *Europe-action* 24 (December 1964), 3.
38. Dominique Venner, "Bientôt ils seront 1 million," *Europe-action* 22 (October 1964), 3.

Figure 7. "Wanted: Mohammed el-Prick, born in Algeria, living in France.
This man is dangerous! Liable to kill! Rape! Steal! Plunder! etc., etc. To
find him, you won't have to look very far . . . all around you, there are
700,000 just like him!" *Europe-action* 22 (October 1964), back cover.

that Algerian migrants posed to France.[39] What is noteworthy, however, is that affirmations that Arab men embodied animalistic sexual excess were more than just long available ideological crutches or far-right verbal tics: they reflected a well theorized set of tactics which the small group of far-right young men associated with *Europe-action* had defined and worked to convince other journalists and politicians to pursue. The unprecedented marginalization of far-right activists in France added urgency to this campaign. They repeatedly and enthusiastically deployed the "Arab invasion" tactic over the course of the 1960s.

In early 1968, an editorial in *Minute* relaunched the campaign, with the proclamation that "the Algerian colony has set up camp," and summoned the weekly's journalists and readers "to expose the dangers posed by this invasion, which is now growing in leaps and bounds." The first example it gave was from "rue de Bagnolet (20th arrondissement of Paris): Mohand I., 30 years old, grabs Mlle. Micheline S. by the throat and tries to rape her. . . ." Letter writers quickly responded to the editorial's summons. They produced not only numerous other examples of Algerian criminal deviance, but analyses of why this was allowed to happen. In a response published under the title "The Brothers Have a Right to a Reduced Fare," from M. P. (Draguignan), the author complained about the judicial leniency shown to "a North African" charged with "attempted rape with a threatening weapon." He explained that "an FLN leader, while speaking in Tunis [during the Algerian war], said that 'France is a bitch nation, which will resist the male for a while, but always ends up giving in.' He was, it pains me to say, correct." Another *Minute* article, this one published in early May and entitled "Now That's Cooperation, My Friend [*mon'zami*]," first reproduced an editorial from a Dijon daily which claimed that "every day, young girls and women are being harassed by North Africans," before revealing the story of "another North African with an overly developed sense of sociability, who accosted two young soldiers the other evening in Nancy in order to involve them in a very special form of cooperation." ("Cooperation" was the term the French government used to describe the various forms of

39. On this language, see Tahar ben Jelloun, *La plus haute des solitudes: Misère sexuelle d'émigrés nord-africains* (Paris: Seuil, 1977), 8; Frantz Fanon, "Le 'syndrome nord africain' (1952)," in *Pour la révolution africaine: Ecrits politiques* (Paris: François Maspero, 1964), 13–25; and Emmanuel Blanchard, "Le mauvais genre des Algériens: Des hommes sans femme face au virilisme policier dans le Paris d'après-guerre," *Clio: Histoire, femmes et sociétés* 27 (2008), 209–22. On its development during the 1930s, see Neil MacMaster, *Colonial Migrants and Racism: Algerians in France, 1900–1962* (London: Macmillan, 1997), 132–135; Ralph Schor, *L'opinion française et les étrangers en France, 1919–1939* (Paris: Publications de la Sorbonne, 1985), 126, 165–66.

assistance it claimed to offer to poorer countries.) A March article in *Rivarol* made the homosexual insinuations a bit clearer, drawing attention to "the large number of Algerian 'tourists' who cruise the dark streets and public gardens of Paris." The assertion that Algerians were violating the rules of French hospitality was linked with suggestions that they both augmented and benefited from sexual deviance in France.[40]

In connecting Algerian men to rape, sexual harassment, and homosexual promiscuity, far-right journalists worked to substantiate a larger, traditional argument: Only the French national/nationalist camp embodied a normal and healthy manliness capable of defending the French from their perverted enemies. Ultranationalist activists expressed particular outrage that French law—as a result of the March 1962 Evian Accords, which French officials had negotiated with Algerian nationalists in order to end the Algerian war—authorized Algerians to enter, live, and work in France (liberal possibilities that could be revoked for certain individuals, under defined conditions). Ultra-right arguments again and again insisted that healthy connections between French people—and most importantly, between men and women—depended on maintaining natural and necessary divisions—between normal and abnormal, healthy and perverted, French and Algerians—all of which the growing numbers of Algerians present in France actively undermined. The invaders' most potent weapons, far-right writings suggested, derived from their uncontrollable sexual lusts. Who, then, was responsible for such decadence, this debasement of French masculinity, the Algerians or France itself? The far right media could not decide. The former appeared as oversexed—not "male" in the noble sense such activists attributed to (true and French) men, but animal, whereas France was overrun and governed by those who sought to let the country respond as a "bitch." This ambivalence was key, for it encouraged proponents of both to opine extensively on the topic of Algerian deviance.[41]

From 1962 until early 1968, however, such arguments had failed to advance any of the primary goals of those who made them. The first of those goals was to replace depictions of Algerians victimized by French colonialism with understandings of Arabs as victimizers of innocent French people.

40. François Brigneau, "Le défi de Boumedienne: Il veut les Champs-Elysées," *Minute* 310 (7 March 1968), 10; M. P. (Draguignan), "Les frères ont droit au tariff reduit," *Minute* 311 (14 March 1968), 18; "Ca, c'est social mon'zami," *Minute* 319 (9 May 1968), 11; Georges A. Bousquet, ". . . Et le fellagha Medeghri a eu les honneurs de l'Elysée," *Rivarol* 895 (7 March 1968), 2.

41. Georges Aubert, "Editorial: 'Le Mâle et l'Effort,'" *OAS Information* 4 (Bône, 20 December 1961), in Service historique de la Défense, Vincennes, France (hereafter, SHD): 1H/1735/1.

This reversal would make it possible, they strategized, to reconnect the far right to the broad mainstream of the French right. The rightist government instead continued to encourage immigration, notably from Algeria, and to provide limited social services to immigrants; right-wing politicians continued to avoid any connection with public figures or political movements that had been linked to the OAS or too closely to French Algeria; far-right politicians continued to see their extremely small electorate shrink. This caused far-right arguments about "invasion" and "sexual crimes" to grow more shrill, rather than to fade. In spring 1968, these xenophobic efforts gained new traction even before the "events of May '68" allowed post-Algerian reactionaries to reposition their existing claims, develop others, and, most important, make their arguments—and their members—more beguiling, in order to draw other French people to their side.

TWO

May '68, "Arab Perversion,"
and Anti-Arab Racism

By mid-1967, the small world of the French far right was abuzz with discussions anticipating May 1968. It published books and polished arguments that aimed to take advantage of all of the coming publicity to advance far-right arguments. It did not expect what actually happened, of course: the stunning, fast-moving, and seemingly revolutionary upheaval that began early in that month, which saw student protesters join up with striking workers in the public spaces of Paris and beyond, thereby shutting down the country. That "May '68" is a decidedly left-wing story, with a key role for de Gaulle. What ultranationalists had been waiting for, instead, was the ten-year anniversary of May 1958, when pro–French Algeria crowds in Algiers and their allies in the armed forces toppled the Fourth French Republic and brought Charles de Gaulle back to power. The approaching anniversary intensified the already rote references to the Algerian war that peppered their deliberations.[1]

Yet these far-right conversations were roiled by a preoccupation with many of the "leftist" concerns that would explode into public consciousness through the events of what became known as "May '68": the pressing need for radical change, an attachment to spectacular forms of protest and politics, the insistence that de Gaulle's rule had stultified the nation,

---

1. Numerous books appeared that catalyzed far-right bitterness. Among the most important were ex-general (and '61 putschist) Maurice Challe's *Memoirs: Atonement*, by Pierre Laffont (ex-deputy from Oran); *Outlaws*, by novelist and ultranationalist thinker Jean Mabire; and, the most well known, *The Sons of All-Saints' Day*, the first volume of Yves Courrière's incredibly popular and politically driven history of the Algerian war. More than one million copies were sold of the four volumes of *La guerre d'Algérie: Les Fils de la Toussaint*, vol. 1 (Paris: Fayard, 1968); *Le Temps des léopards*, vol. 2 (Paris: Fayard, 1969); *L'Heure des colonels*, vol. 3 (Paris: Fayard, 1970); and *Les Feux du désespoir*, vol. 4 (Paris: Fayard, 1971). See Branche, *La guerre d'Algérie*, 20–21.

the belief that there was still time for French initiatives to change Europe and the world, and a certainty that questions of sex and gender mattered deeply. These concerns were also rife with references to Arab men. Oddly enough, far-right discussions in 1967 and early 1968 also focused on institutions that would be key sites for the May "events" around Paris: Nanterre University and the Odéon Theater.

Torn between "Nostalgeria" and "the Arab Invasion"

What had been true since at least 1962 remained the case in 1968: the far right was traumatized by Algeria. Yet what the discussions brought into view was how conflicted this agitated coterie of activists and writers was about why they should bring up Algeria and Algerians. Most sought to keep the Algerian war alive through shared memories, acrid recriminations, and tendentious comparisons between the upheavals of 1954–1962 and current events. They remained bitter at what they saw as an unnecessary French defeat and at de Gaulle, whose actions and allies, in their view, had lost the war, but who, maddeningly to them, still ruled France. Some, however, focused their efforts on identifying Algerian immigrants as a current danger to France. The actual events of May 1968 both highlighted the tensions among participants and allowed the second approach to emerge more prominently. That is, far-right reactions to "May" advanced the efforts of the small group of theoreticians who over the course of the 1970s would come to be known as the Nouvelle Droite. This French new right pivoted from bitter pining for the lost province (often termed "nostalgeria") toward a focus on the Algerian "invasion" that, they argued, threatened France. Public debates that linked sex, violence, and politics made this happen.[2]

Periodicals such as *Minute, Rivarol,* and far-right newsletters depicted current French leaders as lacking the manly vitality necessary to have won the war or to defend France now. A steady stream of allusions to anti–"French Algeria" acts during the war were tied to unsavory intimations: close personal connections between French public officials and Arabs and

---

2. On trauma, see esp. Dominick LaCapra, *Writing History, Writing Trauma* (Baltimore: Johns Hopkins University Press, 2001). On proto-Nouvelle Droite theorization, see esp. Anne-Marie Duranton-Crabol, "La 'Nouvelle Droite' entre printemps et automne, 1968–1986," *Vingtième Siècle: Revue d'histoire* 17 (1988), 39–49; Tamir Bar-On, *Where Have All the Fascists Gone?* (Aldershot, UK: Ashgate, 2007). On "nostalgérie," see Lynne Huffer, "Derrida's Nostalgeria," in Patricia M. E. Lorcin, ed., *Algeria and France, 1800–2000: Identity, Memory, Nostalgia* (Syracuse, NY: Syracuse University Press, 2006), 228–246, 230fn6.

"Blacks." Most emblematic were constant descriptions of de Gaulle that began to focus less on his "crimes" against fellow Frenchmen (which, extreme-right activists were certain, he had committed during World War II, the war's-end "purge" of collaborators, and then the Algerian War), and instead portrayed him as being in bed with Algerian leaders, as well as leaders from across francophone Africa. When *Rivarol* referred to President Houari Boumédiène as de Gaulle's "colleague from Algiers," the implication of deviant masculinity was clear to loyal readers: if in 1962 France had abandoned its naturally dominant role and submitted to the FLN, this was because the country's leaders were driven to submit themselves to other, more brutish non-French men. As a pro-OAS publication put it in 1962, de Gaulle had "sold off Algeria" to the FLN in "obedience to his invert's neuroses [female needs in a male body], which commands him to give himself over to the male." It invoked, as extreme-right thinkers did so often, the language of science, here of psychology, to offer clear diagnoses of sickness and organic deviance to tar opponents. The editorial was at pains to make clear that by "male," it did not mean man, an equal, but instead something more bestial, "despite the fact that the latter [the male/FLN] has only the sexual attributes, in the absence of the psychological ones." In addition to the litany of accusations against de Gaulle and his "lackeys" in France, numerous other articles anticipating the anniversary detailed the supposed incompetence and barbarity of those who now governed Algeria.[3]

In February and March 1968, this general theme of Algerian deviance profiting from and accentuating French decadence was developed at length in a series of articles in the French press on that symbolically significant site of Fifth Republic policies: Nanterre University.[4] Student radicals there who demanded greater sexual liberty (a campaign that began in March 1967

3. Aubert, "Editorial: Le Mâle et l'Effort"; Georges Bousquet, ". . . et le fellagha Medeghri," 5; Jean Bourdier, "Mauriac a aussi péché par omissions," *Minute* 311 (14 March 1968), 13. For an explanation of how the far right described de Gaulle as devirilized and homosexual, as well as for a broader discussion of the ways in which representations of sex, sexuality, and gender were central to the far-right response to May 1968, see Todd Shepard, "L'extrême droite et 'mai 68': Une obsession d'Algérie et de virilité," *Clio: Histoire, femmes et société* 29 (spring 2009), 35–55.

4. On the far right and masculinity, see Carolyn Dean, *The Frail Social Body: Pornography, Homosexuality, and Other Fantasies in Interwar France* (Berkeley: University of California Press, 2000); Sanos, *The Aesthetics of Hate*, and Mark Meyers, "Feminizing Fascist Men: Crowd Psychology, Gender, and Sexuality in French Antifascism, 1929–1945," *French Historical Studies* 29 (2006), 109–142. For details of Franco-Algerian accords concerning immigration, see Jacques Simon, *L'immigration algérienne en France de 1962 à nos jours* (Paris: L'Harmattan, 2002), 229–232; and Laure d'Hauteville, "Algériens: Feu la liberté de circulation," *Plein Droit* 29/30 (1995), 87–89.

and would lead to the 22 March Movement in 1968) had focused media attention on what was happening on the outskirts of Paris, within the recently completed US-style campus. (Their most well known member was the charismatic French-German-Jewish redhead "Dany" Cohn-Bendit, who would become tightly linked to "May '68.")[5] Far-right Cassandras of the "Arab invasion" jumped into this discussion about sex and upheaval to insert warnings of Algerian male deviance into the story. At least four different publications, all of which repeated the same "facts," linked the new university's "crisis" to Algerian perversity: the blame for what was described as widespread prostitution and drug use could be placed, on the one hand, on the largely Algerian inhabitants of the surrounding *bidonville* (shanty-town) and, on the other hand, on Algerian students. The weekly *Rivarol* appears to have published the first article linking the "crisis" to Algerian sexual perversity: "Here is how a witness describes the 'campus' of Nanterre. 'Drugs, orgies, invasion by those from the *bidonvilles*. . . . Above all, prostitution (female students, prostitutes who've arrived from outside, with no difficulty whatsoever, 'to work' for bidonville North Africans).["6] Subsequent articles in other periodicals gave increasing space to the Algerian "cause" of Nanterre's problems: the non-far-right (although pro–French Algeria/OAS) newspaper *Combat* followed up with a February 14 "exposé," which begins: "Strange things are taking place at the university complex that was supposed to be the pride of the [Fifth Republic]. Narcotics, prostitution, pederasty." *Combat* pointed out (inaccurately) that "25 percent of dorm residents are foreigners, with the majority from North Africa. Many of the latter, as their fellow students will admit, lack sexual maturity and think of women as servants who specialize in 'knob polishing.'" Whereas the courteous young French man respected women, North Africans "have no limits. In the cafeteria, they interrupt girls to ask their characteristic question: 'What do you think of mixed marriages?'" While the question was reported so as to shock readers, even worse was that "the response sets the stage for what happens next, and the infrequency of the 'commodity' means that sometimes the 'prey' will have multiple appetites to satisfy. . . ." This was a reference to gang rapes, another recurring motif of far-right anti-Arab vituperation; this stereotype reemerged around 2000, when anecdotal claims about gang rapes in public-housing projects (*la banlieue*) sparked a media frenzy. As police reports from the late 1940 through the 1970s

5. See Michael M. Seidman, *The Imaginary Revolution: Parisian Students and Workers in 1968* (New York: Berghahn, 2004), 44–47.
6. Marcel Signac, "Après les bagares [sic] de Nanterre: Un abcès a vider: Les 'campus,'" *Rivarol* 890 (11 February 1968), 12.

make clear, while claims that Arab immigrants were particularly prone to rape and sexual violence were constant in French media and political discussions, official statistics proved the opposite. Once the disproportionate number of young men in this group was taken into account, the rates were similar or inferior to those of the general population. Chapter 8 of this book explores this question at length.[7]

Not only were Algerians considered dangerous, but their abnormal masculinity was said to corrupt those around them. *Rivarol*'s use of the term "invasion" emphasized the deeply sexual metaphor at play. The "Arab invasion" meant Arab men penetrating French people of all kinds as well as French spaces. The repetitive list of dangers made this clear: prostitution and the traffic in white women (*la traite des Blanches*), rape, homosexuality, pederasty. The February article in *Minute* affirmed that the surrounding Arab neighborhoods had encouraged the establishment of "networks of student pimps" who "lend their rooms, for a small fee, to Pigalle prostitutes who come 'to work' the *bidonville* clientele at a leisurely pace." Whereas *Combat* had vaguely invoked "pederasty" with no elaboration, the article in *Minute* focused on it in a section subtitled "Fans of Arab Boys." The description starts from the perspective of "those living in the dorms . . . their rooms look down on the *bidonville*, and they witness the constant traffic of debonair gentlemen, looking slick and shady at the wheel of their sports cars. The 'fans' are on the lookout for Arab boys, whom they pick up and then drop off before night falls." The analysis, however, did not stop there. Instead, the author linked sexual deviance to political dissidence, implicitly invoking radicals' much discussed embrace of student demands for sexual liberty: "Certain students, known for their avant-garde ideas but characterized by their abnormal morality, were quick to follow suit: while the ways of our Lord are sometimes mysterious, those of Karl Marx and Mao are pretty straightforward. They, in turn, began inviting little brown-skinned lads into their bedrooms." Note the wholly circular logic: the presence of "little brown-skinned lads" catalyzed the students' "abnormal morality," which had led them to their "avant-garde ideas," and transformed it into acts of sexual deviance, which further cemented their ties to "Arab boys."[8]

7. François Cazenave, "Nanterre en folie: An III du complexe universitaire," *Combat* (14 February 1968), 8–9. Key to the media discussion early in 2000 was the film *La squale* (Fabrice Genestal, dir.: 2000). See also Samira Bellill and Josée Stoquart, *Dans l'enfer des tournantes* (Paris: Gallimard, 2003).

8. Signac, "Après les bagares [sic]," 12; Pierre Grégoire, "Il s'en passe de belles au campus de Nanterre!" *Minute* (29 February 1968), 12–13. On *Combat* and its history of pro-French Algeria politics, see Anne-Marie Duranton-Crabol, "*Combat* et la guerre d'Algérie," *Vingtième siècle: Revue d'histoire* 40 (1993), 86–96.

While the left and the Gaullist government remained silent—rendered cowardly, according to far-right critics, by their "Arabophilia"—it was left to right-wing radicals to tell the truth: "Everyone at Nanterre tries to hush up certain activities of the North Africans. Fear reigns. Several co-eds, too caught up in their commitment to the decolonization of peoples of color, found themselves at parties of a very special kind, just the girl and numerous Algerian men." The implication of gang rape or orgiastic debauchery was once again unavoidably clear. Here, though, the responsibility of French anticolonialists is also visible, a theme that would mushroom around "May." "After the séance came to an end, the threats came out: 'Shut your trap!'"[9] In March 1968, the royalist magazine *Restauration nationale* warned that "the extension of expanded liberties [at Nanterre or the University Lille-Annapes] will quickly lead to anarchy, to systematic orgies. . . ." Through such warnings, far-right activists presented the dangers posed by leftist campaigns for sexual liberation as being closely linked to those posed by the "Arab invasion." They also bemoaned the willingness of the insufficiently right-wing Gaullist government to let the plague spread. Another royalist newspaper, *Aspects de la France*, suggested that "the moral order, which the Fifth Republic and its leader support, gets along easily with the giant disorder constituted by the participation of student agitators at Nanterre in *la traite des blanches*." The writers asked what could stop "these sexually obsessed foreigners." Other far-right publications would take up the same claims, but the force of events would resituate the far right's deployment of the "Algerian reference."[10]

May 1968

It was during the "events of May" themselves that the far right's anti-Algerian campaign both blossomed and took root among a larger public. The far-right press impatiently awaited the collapse of the Gaullist regime, and most predicted that it would come through upheaval. Pierre Dominique of *Rivarol* had suggested in early March that either "a general strike" or "an insurrection" would develop out of (in either case) Algerian origins.[11] Responding to a March 1968 editorial in *Le Monde*, "A Bored Coun-

9. Grégoire, "Il s'en passe de belles."

10. Grégoire, "Il s'en passe de belles"; *AFU* 131 (March 1958), cited in Jean-Paul Gautier, *La Restauration nationale: Un mouvement royaliste sous la 5e République* (1958–1993) (Paris: Syllepse, 2002), 85; Pierre Chaumeil, "Scandale à Nanterre," *Aspects de la France* 1,011 (8 February 1968), 12; *Le Crapouillot* 3 (nouvelle série) (summer 1968), 28.

11. Pierre Dominique, "Les exigences du Salut public," *Rivarol* 895 (7 March 1968), 16.

try," *Minute* mocked the "tears" editorialist Pierre Viansson-Ponté shed "for a 'little France reduced to little more than a hexagon." In the *Minute* editorialist's view, "When for years one has campaigned to abandon French lands. . . . one doesn't then come complaining about the banality of our national destiny." The loss of Algeria had led to a "little France," easily abused.[12]

As soon as the events of May began, far-right journalists saw dark causalities in the problem of Algeria. Some references were predictable: the weekly *Lettre confidentielle*, for example, informed its readers in early May that "a mysterious North African in charge of pro-Chinese subversion in Europe" had manipulated French students and provoked the street demonstrations. While the determination to identify a conspiracy is unsurprising, the claim stands out because it involves an "actual," if nonexistent, Algerian.[13] Far more typical, however, and more interesting, was the shifting of focus in the references to Algeria: from recriminations concerning the history of 1958 or 1962 or warnings about Algerians in France, most on the far right now compared what was going on to the Algerian war, and in particular to pro-French Algeria activism during the war. A surprising number saw in the May events the resolution of certain crises that the "defeat" of French Algeria had provoked.[14]

The episode that provoked the most intriguing links with Algeria was when student protestors took over Paris's Odéon Theater and used the famed Latin Quarter institution to hold extensive public discussions. It was not the speeches that leftist intellectuals gave that drew far-right attention, nor their calls to change the world, but the location: for ultranationalist commentators the Odéon had become perhaps the most vivid and demeaning monument to what they saw as the humiliation of defeat in Algeria and the accompanying decadence that had destroyed the army and devirilized the Nation. In 1966, the Odéon, a publicly-run space, had

---

12. "*Le Monde*: Un pays qui s'ennuie," *Minute* 312 (21 March 1968), 12.

13. See Maurice Bardèche and François Duprat, "La Comédie de la Révolution: Mai 1968," special issue of *Défense de l'Occident* (June 1968), 49–52. In the months following May, the far-right activist and historian François Duprat and Maurice Bardèche—the brother-in-law and defender of the fascist French writer Robert Brasillach, who was executed for collaboration after the liberation of France—would attempt to impose "the East German connection" to explain the events.

14. On how the authorities dealt with foreigners during the event, see Daniel Gordon, "'Il est recommandé aux étrangers de ne pas participer': Les étrangers expulsés en mai–juin 1968," *Migrations Société* 88 (July–August 2003); Seidman, *The Imaginary Revolution*, 247–248. See also "Les mesures pour maintenir l'ordre" (Paris, 24 June 1968), 2, in CAC: 19800273/61, which included a list of nationalities; by the far the largest number of foreigners expelled between late May and late June were Algerians (32 of 183; 22 Germans made up the second largest group).

staged a production of a play by Jean Genet. The writer had gained wide renown in 1949, when French intellectuals campaigned to void his condemnation to life in prison because of the brilliance of his novels; in 1952 Jean-Paul Sartre made the man he qualified as "homosexual, traitor, and thief" the subject of a six-hundred-page study, *Saint Genet, Actor and Martyr*.[15] The play was *Les paravents* (*The Screens*), in which the French Army in Algeria offers the setting and the manifest topic for a radical meditation on Genet's great themes, among them homosexuality, prostitution, and criminality. The central characters are the peasant Saïd; his mother, Warda, who is a prostitute; and a number of French soldiers. According to many who attended, the Odéon staging of the play's sexual motifs was at once intense and forthrightly non-normative: The casting had all the actors take on both male and female roles, and many, whatever sex the character, simulated anal sex on stage. In *Figaro littéraire*, the Catholic and Nobel Prize–winning novelist François Mauriac worried about the disastrous effects the play might have on French youth, with its erasure of any distinction between "good and evil." The entwined themes of sex, eroticism, and the dangers of emasculation that had tormented the far right since the Algerian war all surged forth. In conversation with Mauriac, Thierry Maulnier—author, Académie Française "immortal," and a man with long-standing ties to the far right—sought to reassure him: "A bourgeois society has handed over the stage of its theaters to . . . something like a permanent revolution, which has thus been rendered more or less inoffensive and emasculated." Responses like these reflect what a mistake it would be to reduce a play like *Les paravents* to a purely political reading. Yet in 1966, according to the British cultural critic Timothy Mathews, this "play was presented [in the press] as a diatribe against France." Far-right activists seized the stage.[16]

The Odéon Theater: From Genet to the "*Enragés*"

The campaign against Genet's play brought a new generation of ultranationalists into open conflict with de Gaulle's government about Algerian questions. This time, questions of masculinity, sex, and deviance were front and center—just as they had defined the war, at least in histories proposed

15. Edmund White, *Genet: A Biography* (New York: Vintage, 1993).

16. François Mauriac, *Bloc Notes*, vol. 4, *1965–1967* (Paris: Seuil, 1993), 221, cited by Herman Lebovics, *Mona Lisa's Escort: André Malraux and the Reinvention of French Culture* (Ithaca, NY: Cornell University Press, 1999), 141. On Maulnier, see Sanos, *Aesthetics of Hate*, 63–154; Timothy Matthews, *Literature, Art and the Pursuit of Decay in Twentieth-Century France* (Cambridge: Cambridge University Press, 2005), 157.

by Venner, Mabire, Larteguy, de Benoist, and their "brothers." The play opened on 16 April 1966, and protests that aimed to close it down began on Friday, 29 April 1966. The group that soon took the most active part in the protest was the thuggish and youthful Occident. For members such as Alain Madelin (who with his future wife attended almost every staging) and Patrick Devedjian, daily protests against the play both consolidated the camaraderie of this extremist movement and helped convince them of the benefits of "spectacular" politics. Their constant efforts to disrupt the play—which, after large public demonstrations outside, culminated with dead rats and tear gas thrown onto the stage—brought this small group almost as much media attention as their embrace of street violence, and allowed activists to relive the fight for French Algeria.[17] As in their earlier efforts to keep Algeria French, far-right groups failed in their campaign to stop the play's run. When he was presented with a request by members of his government's majority to strip the Odéon Theatre of all public funding, Minister of Culture André Malraux refused. Yet his strong public defense of the theatre's right to produce Genet's play gave new definition to far-right claims that governmental Gaullism was in bed with far-left efforts to destroy France.

This, then, was the context in which far-right observers watched left-wing students' mid-May 1968 take-over of the Odéon. Transfixed by the hated Gaullist regime's humiliation, the far-right press unanimously saluted the event. Jacques Massannes in *Aspects de la France* remarked that "if this mishap were not an episode of the bloody tragedy our country is experiencing, one would have to smile, one would say that Jean-Louis Barrault and Madeleine Renault [codirectors of the theater] have reaped what they sowed." For François Brigneau, in *Minute*, "the Odéon occupied by ['Dany'] Cohn-Bendit . . . seems less shocking to me than the Odéon occupied by Barrault." The notorious Nazi collaborator and antisemite Lucien Rebatet went the furthest, announcing that "last week's student take over of l'Odéon was the type of announcement that filled me with joy." The occupation should be interpreted, these journalists argued, as an inevitable response to the desacralization that de Gaulle's ministers had authorized, and to the meaninglessness of French culture that Gaullist France had produced. "During four years [de Gaulle] bled dry an Algeria he meant to deliver up, eager to drop his pants," Rebatet wrote, meaning that the French president had offered himself sexually to the FLN. "He has done it again,

17. Frédéric Charpier, *Génération Occident: De l'extrême droite à la droite* (Paris: Seuil, 2005).

first seeking to bleed dry the Latin Quarter. . . ." France under de Gaulle, Rebatet continued, "could no longer be thought of as normal." Aided by the events of May, other reactionary writers would seek to redirect this fixation away from de Gaulle as the cause of French perversion, and to focus instead on Genet and his ilk.[18]

Most on the far right were more troubled than intrigued by the ongoing upheaval, yet all were pleased that would-be revolutionaries had taken the Odéon away from Genet. The bigger point was that students had won victories against the Gaullist regime that the marginalized far right had identified as necessary but had been unable to achieve on its own. Yet hostility toward the events quickly displaced early empathetic reactions, as far-right "unmanly" journalists presented the student "fanatics" as both buffoons and a danger; protesters indeed, it was their fundamentally unmanly "buffooneries" that menaced France, threatening further devirilization. Rather than continue to focus on the Gaullist regime as the primary danger, most on the far right turned their attention to other internal enemies: the Communist Party, as always, but especially the perverted cohort of leftists eager to sap the nation's ability to defend itself (and its women) from the Arab invaders.[19]

"Our Angry Twinks"

Assertions about masculinity and sex made it emphatic that the problem stemmed from a sissified left. May '68, far-right voices proclaimed, was not a real revolution but an effeminate farce. Ironically, the key evidence they evoked was the absence of left-wing violence. The context was "nostalgeria." In every venue, far-right commentators compared May '68 to proFrench Algerian activism, with its embrace of OAS violence. Others compared the police response in May 1968 to what pro–French Algeria youth had confronted in Algiers—or, indeed, in Paris—at the end of the Algerian war. As *Rivarol* proclaimed, still mocking: "We are no longer back in the day when those bad Algerian colonists filled the streets to defend their shocking privileges! The barricades they put up were rotten, whereas those of the students are beautiful and good barricades, worthy of those of 1848 [when Paris demonstrators precipitated the collapse of the monarchy]

18. Jacques Massanes, ". . . Ce qu'on ne vous dira pas ailleurs: Jeudi 16 mai—je suis des vôtres!" *Aspects de la France* 1,027 (23 May 1968), 2; François Brigneau, "'Anticommunistes, je vous ai compris,'" *Minute* 321 (6 June 1968), 6–7; Lucien Rebatet, "Les beaux draps," *Rivarol* 906 (23 May 1968), 3. On Rebatet, see esp. Sanos, *The Aesthetics of Hate*.

19. "Il faut en finir avec la chienlit des Cohn-Bendit!" *Minute* 318 (2 May 1968), 5.

and 1944 [when an uprising in Paris helped drive German forces from the city]! . . ."[20] The most obvious difference—in a comparison that even some Gaullist politicians made—was the leftists' alleged lack of patriotism. Yet critics also found the leftists wanting in terms of revolutionary ability and vigor. One headline contrasted them: "Ten years after the tricolor [blue-white-and-red] May Thirteenth, a red tide unfurls over the boulevards."[21] The different colors of the two moments signaled a difference in content: French patriots had been serious and dedicated, while May's students were just having fun. As *Rivarol* put it in the middle of May: "French Algeria activists [in 1958] crossed the Mediterranean," while in 1968 "the fanatics [*enragés*] hardly dared to cross the Boul' Mich [the main thoroughfare of the Latin Quarter]." The far-right activist and historian François Duprat would later make this claim more explicit as he narrated how the movement had ended: "The 'revolutionaries' of May and the Communist Party, who were briefly tempted to take direct action, practically fainted once General de Gaulle gave one energetic speech [on television, 30 May]. To vanquish the OAS, it took thousands of arrests, hundreds of condemnations, hundreds of deaths as well." France had sacrificed the manly men of the OAS and now, predictably, it was the unmanly men who sought to take advantage of the decadence that resulted.[22]

The far right's obsession with sexual difference powerfully shaped their response to May '68. To render visible the leftist movement's "failure" to be suitably virile, the far-right press printed multiple images of female protesters. Women almost never appeared as themselves responsible, which reflected the certainty that only manly men were capable of positive action. Rather, depictions of female protesters aimed to explain, as captions and accompanying articles made clear, the movement's inability to act like true revolutionaries, like real men. The front cover of the 16 May issue of *Rivarol*, for example (figure 8), presents a beskirted young woman on top of a burned-out car; the caption mockingly proclaims that "a cutie complains . . . she has a blister; the car has been roughed up as well." The text also highlights another leitmotif of far-right representations of the events, which was the supposed failed masculinity of leftist men: the young

20. "L'action des 'étudiants en colère' se situe dans le droit fil des fastes libératoires," *Rivarol* 905 (16 May 1968), 2. On OAS violence, see Shepard, *The Invention of Decolonization*.

21. René Saive, "Dix ans après le 13 mai tricolore, la marée rouge déferle sur les boulevards," *Le Crapouillot* (new series) 3 (summer 1968), 9. The comparison resonates with how the French right-wing press responded to the far-right riots of 6 February 1934; see Kevin Passmore, *The Right in France from the Third Republic to Vichy* (Oxford: Oxford University Press, 2012), 295.

22. Georges Bousquet, "D'un 13 mai l'autre [sic]," *Rivarol* 905 (16 May 1968), 6; Duprat, *Les mouvements d'extrême-droite en France depuis 1944* (Paris: Albatros, 1972), 3.

"Quand les peuples cessent d'estimer, ils cessent d'obéir"

16 MAI 1968 — No 905

HEBDOMADAIRE DE L'OPPOSITION NATIONALE
REDACTION, ADMINISTRATION, 354, RUE SAINT-HONORE, PARIS (1er)

France : 2,00 F.

"Rivarol" et... David Rousset vous expliquent

pourquoi et comment De Gaulle est l'allié «objectif» des enragés de Nanterre

DE DIEN-BIEN-PHU A GAY-LUSSAC...

Rééditant le geste de J.-P. Duprey, héros du folklore sacrilège des anars, les « enragés » avaient profané et souillé la tombe du Soldat Inconnu.

Une délégation d'anciens combattants d'Indochine et d'Algérie a tenu, le 8 mai, à réparer cet outrage en déposant, sous la conduite de Roger Holeindre, une gerbe en l'honneur des morts de Dien-Bien-Phu.

Pendant ce temps, au Quartier Latin, une mignonne se fait plaindre, sous l'œil désabusé de son compagnon (bien peu secourable) : elle a une bosse au pied. La voiture, elle aussi, est cabossée.

Mais les tracts provocateurs font état, dès lundi, de... huit morts ! Pourquoi pas le massacre de la rue d'Isly ?

(Photos ADNP et Régis Galbrun)

Figure 8. *Rivarol* (16 May 1968), front cover.

woman in the photo is said to complain "as her bored companion (who's unfit to help her in any case) looks on." The sexes were too similar, which made true manliness and female submission almost impossible.[23]

In the first week of May, in contrast with the pro-French Algeria "men" of 1958–1962, *Rivarol*'s editorial picked out the word that would be taken up across the far-right press: "twinks" (*minets*): "our angry twinks," "the twinks of Nanterre," "Marcusian twinks." Descriptions of student leaders "Dany" Cohn-Bendit, Jacques Sauvageot, and Alain Geismar focused on their "Shetland and Cashmere sweaters." An article reproduced a letter to *Le Monde* that described the same young men—the "hotheads" of Nanterre—as "dandys." Their ability to get university professors to support them revealed that both students and professors "revel in sadomasochism." *Rivarol* wrote two weeks later, in reference to "teachers" who joined in with the student upheavals: "We believe that they can be diagnosed (like the case of comrade [Louis] Aragon) in terms of the sadomasochism that so excites today's trendy intelligentsia." "Except for what's noted on their ID Card," wrote Rebatet when he sought to discredit the students who had

23. *Rivarol* 905 (16 May 1968), 1. On Gaullist politicians use of such comparisons during "May," see Shepard, "L'extrême droite," 52–54.

taken over the Odéon, "what youthful attributes does this horde still possess?" The reader was instructed that, while legally male, in reality "these beardies, the lice-ridden mops . . . these little bitches one wouldn't touch with a stick" were under the sway of France's "pedants of decadence"—Sartre, Blanchot, Barthes, Lacan—who manipulated them through "verbal perversion." "Perversion," even more than intellectualism, was presented as the primary threat. One odd parallel construction dismissed them as "our wolf cubs with big ideas—and teeth sawed off by years of intellectual comfort," in opposition to the "wolves" of the . . . S.S. The celebration of the German Nazi Party's armed police, infamous for its role in the Shoah, anchored this warning about failed masculinity.[24]

Through these insistent presentations of the protestors as either women or (mainly) devirilized, unnatural, and womanly men, far-right journalists set the stage for the shift from "nostalgeria," with its attendant fixation on de Gaulle and his "regime" as responsible for French decadence, to a different source: a new generation of leftists. This reframing allowed far-right journalists to connect French leftists to the larger "Algerian" danger and "Arab invasion" which, they proclaimed, worked to transform France into a "bitch nation," and a mongrel one at that. An early June report in *Minute*, "Genet Has It Bad for the Redhead," described the writer's visit to the occupied Sorbonne and told of "how Genet swooned at 'the power this boy [redhead and student leader Cohn-Bendit] exudes,'" before noting that, "in the redhead's absence, he found other Sorbonne twinks to his taste: 'Joy is pumping through my body,' he confided . . . 'It's just so pretty, to see all these young men rebelling.'" No longer satisfied to see the students occupy "Genet's theater," here *Minute* drew on Genet's reputation to define the students in terms of homosexual perversion: "Let's hope that the 'young men' of the Sorbonne had enough tact to erase the slogan that the most conformist among them had spray-painted on the walls: 'Students, don't let yourself be *enc—* [sodomized].'" Like the "Arab boys" of Nanterre, the activists both attracted perverts and spread deviance. The article ended with an adamant return to the far-right's Algerian fixation—and Genet's: "The '*enragés*' must have writhed in delicious agony; Jean Genet already had revealed the secret source of his political opinions in a *Playboy* interview: 'Perhaps if I hadn't gone to bed with Algerians I might not have been in

24. "De Berlin à Nanterre, en passant par Nantes: L'internationale universitaire de la contestation," *Rivarol* 903 (3 May 1968), 5; Georges Bousquet, "D'un 13 mai l'autre [*sic*]," 6; "La peste est entrée dans Paris! . . . ," *Rivarol* 906 (23 May 1968), 2; "A chacun son boche!" *Rivarol* 905 (16 May 1968, 2–3; "L'action des 'etudiants en colère'," 2–3; Rebatet, "Les beaux draps," 3. The far-right press frequently identified the PCF-aligned novelist Aragon as a homosexual.

favor of the FLN.'"[25] It was a particularly clear example of the new far-right eagerness to link students, Arabs, and perverts.

"Sexual Racism" Moves beyond the Far Right

A few recent studies of "May '68" compellingly examine how Algerian references shaped and served activists on the so-called new left that had begun to emerge during the Algerian war and that the uprising made newly prominent: various strands of left-wing radicalism that distanced themselves from what they described as the institutionalized and limited politics of the main left-wing parties, and most especially France's Communist Party (PCF) and Socialist Party (SFIO). Such leftist students and writers repeatedly sought inspiration in the Algerian revolution. It was one of the exemplary victories that the forces of progress and justice had won against international imperialism, capitalism, and the power of the French government.[26] During these same months, however, far-right journalists and activists also looked to Algeria. They did so in order to incite Orientalist fears of contamination and to link leftist calls for revolt and revolution—sexual or other—to an Arab invasion. No matter that they had supported *Algérie française* (French Algeria); only their politics could stop, they proclaimed, a "*France algérienne* (Algerian France)."[27]

What distinguished this far-right deployment of extant Orientalist stereotypes was that, in the intense rush of "May '68," ultranationalist efforts directly targeted leftist arguments based in solidarity and *tiers-mondisme* (Third-Worldism). This rhetoric allowed a supposed French fifth column (of "twinks" and their ilk) to displace the unmanly Fifth Republic as the traitors who, the far right warned, were opening France up to invasion.

---

25. "Genet en pince pour le rouquin," *Minute* 321 (6 June 1968), 20; "Interview: Jean Genet," *Playboy* 11 (1964), 45–53.

26. On Algerian "inspiration" and May '68, see esp. Daniel A. Gordon, *Immigrants and Intellectuals: May '68 and the Rise of Antiracism in France* (Pontypool, UK: Merlin Press, 2012) and Kristin Ross, *May '68 and Its Afterlives* (Chicago: University of Chicago Press, 2002), which both map the geneaology and complexity of the French new left. They detail, for example, how some elements of this new left joined in the early-1970s negotiations that subsumed the SFIO (officially, the French Section of the Workers' International) and other groups into a new Socialist Party (PS), led by François Mitterrand. While it is necessary to speak of a French "new left" despite the many divisions and differences that traversed this constellation, it is not useful to capitalize the term. This is in part because both PCF and SFIO (and, subsequently, the PS) explicitly defined themselves in relationship to Marxism, which made new-left relationships to them different than those between new lefts in places such as the United States, Britain, or Germany, where the main center-left parties were non-Marxist.

27. On "la France algérienne," see, e.g., François Brigneau, "Le défi de Boumedienne. . . ."

Notably, the far right latched onto leftist arguments for sexual liberation, which the writers identified as foundational to the May '68 movement, in order to link proponents of "revolution" to the Arab danger that supposedly menaced France. Their writings charged that the new left militants, like the Algerians whose revolution they so admired, were themselves perverted savages or, at best, the effete accomplices of the Arabs. In either case, they threatened the nation.

At the very moment when "May '68" gave enormous visibility and renewed energy to a left-wing summons for "sexual liberation" as well as to "revolution," key elements of the isolated yet agitated far right turned to their ready-made lenses, which linked both to Algerian threats. Such interpretations of what was at stake and of how to respond proved very attractive to many people in France. This included at least some who were well positioned in government. Shortly before the presidential election of June 1969, which de Gaulle's resignation had precipitated, an unsigned "Very Private Note to M. le Président Georges Pompidou Concerning the National Education System," argued that "the French people voted against anarchy and specifically against anarchy in the domain of education" in the June 1968 legislative elections. De Gaulle had called the snap vote in order to regain the upper hand from the protesters, yet it was the campaign led by then Prime Minister Pompidou that consolidated the right wing's victory. The conservative coalition's slogans for the first round of the June elections, as the writer Bernard Brillant notes, made it possible for the right to put aside the divisions the Algerian war had imposed: the words "liberty" and "democracy" were defined as emblematic of all anticommunists (small "c" or PCF), and this allowed candidates previously rejected as pro-OAS to be welcomed back into the "republican" fold.[28] What had most concerned those who voted for order, the "Very Private Note" affirmed, was the "leading role played by the most privileged youth and those from the Third World" in the May events.[29]

The far right per se remained isolated and ineffective. Yet its ideological claims seemed to be gaining traction. A June 1968 article in *Rivarol* directly linked the Gaullist "Power's" urgent need to conclude "a 'tainted union' with the troublemakers they had been persecuting" (i.e., former support-

28. Bernard Brillant, *Les clercs de 68* (Paris: PUF, 2003), 105. The most visible far right/ Gaullist alliance was on display during the 30 May 1968 march on the Champs-Elysées; see Shepard, "L'extrême droite et 'mai 68.'"

29. "Note très confidentielle à M. le Président Georges Pompidou sur l'éducation nationale" (13 May 1969), 16, in CAC 19800273/254.

ers of the OAS) to an announcement that the government had decided "to impose limits on Algerian immigration."[30] The far right press greeted this and other "anti-Algerian" decisions by the government as victories, payback for their May '68 efforts. In late May and June 1968, the decision by many of its members and voices to work in tandem with Gaullists and others on the mainstream right to isolate the far left had made their voices louder. Georges Pompidou's "rightward swing," much remarked in the lead up to the late June 1968 elections, reflected this; his subsequent departure from the prime ministry (July 1968) seemed to many commentators to confirm the post-de Gaulle possibility of right/far-right *retrouvailles* (reunion).

Discord between Gaullists and the extreme nationalists did not end, yet "an impression of complicity between the far right and the Gaullist regime took within public opinion." Scholars have sought to explain the new complicity. Jean-Christian Petitfils, historian of the extreme right, privileges the sidelining of "Algerian nostalgias." The far-right journalists and essayists Francis Bergeron and Philippe Vilgier extend the chronology of "May '68" to include de Gaulle's withdrawal from public life in 1969, which allows them to argue that "all of the themes tied to *Algérie française* (amnesty [for pro-OAS activists who were either prisoners in French jails or in exile because of outstanding arrest warrents], Eurafrica, anti-Gaullism) were no longer in play," and so explain the changing alliances. Such interpretations are substantively wrong; different themes linked to French Algeria took the place of those that had divided conservatives from the ultranationalist right. These themes, which linked anti-Arab racism and fear of sexual liberation, proved widely appealing to both. The post–May '68 downgrading of right versus far-right tensions over other aspects of the heritage of the Algerian war made them usable.[31]

Many Gaullists and others on the mainstream right quickly began to

30. "Rien ne va plus entre l'Algérie et la France," *Rivarol* 910 (20 June 1968), 3. On the renewal of far-right and rightist connections, see Seidman, *The Imaginary Revolution*, 221–224. On government statements on immigrants, disease, immorality, and crime, see, e.g., "Colloque Rhône-Alpes sur la Migration algérienne: Conclusions générales—Dimanche 15 octobre 1967," in Centre d'accueil et de recherche des Archives nationales de France, Paris, hereafter CARAN: F/ 1A /5015. On restrictions on immigration, see Rabah Aissaoui, *North African Political Movements in Colonial and Postcolonial France* (New York: Palgrave Macmillan, 2009), 160–165.

31. Chiroux, *L'extrême droite*, 171; Petitfils, *L'extrême droite*, 121; Bergeron and Vilgier, *De Le Pen*, 100. Numerous other questions continued to divide the far right from the mainstream right.

adopt the sex-drenched language and terms of anti-Algerian racism that ultra-right thinkers had elaborated since 1962—and because of 1962.[32] For the ultranationalists, the emergence of "May '68" as a compelling explanation for what they claimed was the "devirilization" and decadence of France (in the place of de Gaulle) allowed a redefinition of their doctrine so as to make such claims more acceptable and appealing to the French right writ large—and to others as well. Who had allowed Arabs to humiliate and violate France? The shift in blame from emasculated Gaullists to unmanly leftists helped set the stage for an outpouring of French anti-Algerian racism.

The Post-May Revival of Anti-Arab Racism

By the summer of 1969, as historian Joseph Algazy maps out, there was "a surge of anti-Arab racism."[33] Around Paris, numerous sites where Algerian immigrants were known to gather were the target of a series of terrorist attacks. A November 1969 article in *Le Monde* reported: "Over the course of four months, from 28 May to 27 September [1969], fifteen attacks— including seven in one night—have been carried out in the Paris region, targeting cafés owned by North Africans or buildings where Algerian workers live."[34] In his analysis of what helped produce the new "racist climate," Algazy notes the emergence of local groups of "inhabitants," such as a group in Peronne (the Somme) who in "1969 organized themselves into a Committee to Keep France for the French (CFAF), and proceeded to distribute tracts warning of the 'clear danger'" that, the group argued, was represented by "'the presence in France of 3,200,000 undesirables, notably Arabs, Blacks, Slavs, and Portuguese known for their dubious morality and weak professional qualifications,'" which the CFAF blamed for "the reemergence of diseases, notably venereal."[35] In *Le Monde*, Jean-Maurice Mercier pointed to the brutal "Affaire de Crespin [Nord]," in which two young girls "eleven and twelve years old . . . were discovered assassinated on Sunday 24 August 1969." Newspaper accounts were quick to point out that the girls had been raped. "Several people interviewed by the police affirmed that on that day an individual 'of North African appearance'—that's the

32. For a description of how Gaullist politicians and journalists quickly adopted this language, see Aissaoui, *North African*.

33. Algazy, *L 'Extrême-Droite en France*, 72.

34. Jean-Maurice Mercier, "'Hitler avait raison': Des attentats contre des cafés nord-africains aux souvenirs de nazisme," *Le Monde* (23 November 1969).

35. Algazy, *L'extrême-droite en France*, 73–74.

usual euphemism— had been noticed near the site of the crime." Mercier noted that "a composite drawing was even worked up based on these 'testimonies' and the individual in question remained the number-one suspect until the day—Wednesday, 27 August—when a 45-year-old father of a family with no Mediterranean roots whatsoever admitted to committing the crime." Alongside the link to sexual crime, Mercier's article also noted that "the prostitutes around Pigalle who reject any client 'of Mediterranean appearance' are more and more numerous." Mercier qualified this as part of a newly virulent "'sexual racism.'"[36]

A 1970 note for a government study group asserted that "French opinion is quite strongly concerned about foreign criminality." The report blamed this in large part on "fear of competition at once economic (which exists) and sexual (largely mythical)." In a public response to the very study from which this note drew, a center-right senator also linked "a quite serious problem that we don't speak about enough, that of security" to questions of the sexuality of Algerian immigrants. "Can we ignore the physical needs of men in the prime of their youth, when a sex life is the most important element of life between the ages of 18 and 30?"[37] For a number of observers at the time, such reactions resulted directly from far-right activism. A 1971 report titled "Lyon Confronts Racism?" recounted that "'Algerians, get out!' the slogan of *Minute*, has received, in Lyon . . . a favorable echo." The welcome went far beyond Lyon.[38]

Anti-Algerian violence also grew dramatically in these years. An incident that generated much attention took place in the Goutte d'Or neighborhood of Paris on Wednesday 27 October 1971, when a fifteen-year old boy of Algerian origin, Djellali Ben Ali, died from a bullet to the neck after a fight with the concierge of his building. The event quickly sparked what the historian Michelle Zancarini-Fournel terms "an unprecedented mobilization around the situation faced by immigrant workers." The historian details how "the Goutte d'Or became, in a few short weeks, a new site of struggle" with the involvement of philosophers Michel Foucault and Giles Deleuze and writers Jean Genet and Claude Mauriac, among others.[39] What leftist groups targeted explicitly was the racist nature of the crime.

36. Mercier (1969); see also AFP et AP, "Un cultivateur, père de 5 enfants est l'auteur du crime de Crespin," *L'Impartial: Feuille d'avis des montagnes* 28, 119 (28 August 1969), 1.

37. Michel Massenet, "Les problèmes posés par l'immigration etrangère en France," *Séance du 4 juin 1970 de l'Academie des sciences morales et politiques*, 239–260, 249, in CAC: 19960405 /1.

38. Vincent Lalu, "Lyon à l'épreuve du racisme? Après Paris, la plus forte concentration d'étrangers," *Combat* (6 December 1971), 10.

39. Michelle Zancarini-Fournel, "La question immigrée après 68," *Plein droit* 2 (2002), 3–7.

Their explanations, however, were more specific. They highlighted how sexual paranoia had driven the concierge to kill. As a report from the recently launched far-left Agence-Presse Libération (APL) described it, "The concierges [M. Daniel Pigot and Mme. M] were unmarried. According to the neighbors' testimony, Mme. M 'is a loose woman'; 'she goes out with everybody.'" The crucial detail, according to Mme. M's neighbors, was that "she prefers to choose her lovers among the North Africans; [Pigot] is exasperated." What happened then resulted in the young Djillali being killed as a sexual rival, despite his innocence. "Back to the jealous concierge. . . . He goes after Djillali, the youngest male in the building, who never touched his woman, but who is an Arab." For APL, the causes of this murder derived from post-1962 far-right campaigns, and their "Algérie française" inspiration: "Let those nostalgic for the OAS take note: there will no longer be racist crimes that are not revenged, not in the 18th [arrondisement of Paris, which included the Goutte d'Or], not elsewhere!"[40] This did not stop anti-Algerian violence, however, which spiked again around Marseille in 1973 and would continue in subsequent years.

The success of the "Arab invasion" argument—notably, how it displaced the focus of far-right vituperations from Gaullists to leftists—allowed earlier fantasies about a war over manliness to be significantly revised. From 1962 until 1968, certain ultranationalist writers and fellow travelers asserted that the loss of French Algeria was the primary sign of the supposed unmanning of the French, perhaps even its cause. After 1968, they asserted instead that the war over masculinity between Arab men and Frenchmen was still being waged. France was the new front. It was necessary to look to the lost battle for French Algeria to learn crucial lessons.

"The Mass Arrrival of North Africans . . . Encourage[d] This Upsurge of Homosexuality"

Male homosexuality, in far-right accounts, explained much. In 1978, after emphasizing that French fears of "the vigor of Arab sexuality" were reasonable, *Minute* editorialist Brigneau then suggested a "New [book] topic for [openly gay author Jean-Paul] Aron: on the importance of the penis in FLN propaganda." The editorialist winkingly linked this explanation of

40. "Mercredi 27 octobre, le jeune Dejallali Benali, 15 ans et demi . . . ," *Agence Presse Libération [APL] informations* 68bis (4 November 1971), 2, 3, 5, in Bibliothèque de la documentation internationale contemporaine, Nanterre, France, hereafter BDIC (fonds Assia Melamed) F delta rés. 696/22/1–3.

France's humiliation in 1962 to his suggestion that Aron's sexual life currently involved Arab men. His insistent hint was that male homosexual desires and acts had allowed Arab sexuality to assault France. Several months later, a far-right activist on trial in Toulouse for an armed attack on several men in a local park made the connection a bit differently. When asked to explain why he had carried brass knuckles, he responded, "Because I have already been attacked by Arabs and leftists." He had used the weapon, however, for what the newspaper termed a "faggot hunt" ("la chasse aux pédés"). This link between far left, "Arabs," and (male) homosexuals was telling.[41]

The far right continued to invest multiple and contradictory assertions about Arab male sexual deviance, as subsequent chapters in this book will explore. Yet persistent efforts, which grew after 1968, to link the supposedly dangerous sexuality of Arab men to homosexuality proved particularly successful. Such claims drew directly from arguments that had consolidated in far-right discussions over the 1960s. A 1965 article in *Rivarol*, for example, warned its readers that "if it proves true that the number of homosexuals continues to grow, they will become a 'social phenomenon,' a 'social fact,' and thus will become the focus of all the usual do-gooders . . . just like the readers of Mme. [Françoise] Sagan, the minions of 'Massa' ['*Môssieu*' Ahmed] Ben Bella, and the fans of Jonny Halliday [*sic*]." The article described those responsible for attempts to counter the oppression faced by homosexuals as being linked to Algeria and the far left, such as a "university professor, at once distinguished, progressivist, and pro-fellagha." It asserted that homosexuals had helped destroy French Algeria, with the affirmation that "the cuddles of saint [Jean] Genet helped liberate Algeria (the FLN took its share of the financial results of his 'lovemaking')." These homosexuals, the author argued, were supported by the Gaullist government, notably by former prime minister "Michel Debré, aka Fidèle [Fidel/loyal] Castrated," and their shared goal was, to the author's horror, "the progressive erasure of sexual difference," and nothing less. "No more difference of sexes whatsoever! Liquefied, at last, the neuroses! . . . We're plunging head-on into such nauseating extravagance."[42] Such arguments would take on new force in subsequent decades, most visibly around the *Manif pour*

41. Brigneau, "Haro"; "Toulouse: La chasse aux pédés," *Libération* (31 March–1 April 1979), 20.

42. Etienne Lardenoy, "Vers les temps meilleurs par l'homosexualité sociale," in *Rivarol* 751 (3 June 1965), 10.

tous of 2012–2014.[43] In 1970, a right-leaning scandal sheet, which sought to explain the growing talk of homosexuality in France, tied it to how "after the Liberation [1945], the mass arrival of North Africans . . . encourage[d] this upsurge of homosexuality."[44] No evidence supports this interpretation.

It also would be a mistake to think that far-right rhetoric and maneuvering alone allowed such claims to resonate rather widely in French discussions. This was due in large part to the new post-1968 political context, which the sexual revolution had fashioned. After decolonization (and after the Shoah), antiracist arguments had more potency than ever before, notably in comparison with the interwar period. Antiracists harshly critiqued the marginalized far right and its claims about "Arab men," notably those linked to sex. This debate was new. The next chapter explores "this upsurge," specifically the radical gay liberation movement, which roiled the already incendiary French scene in early 1971. Many members of that movement, in ways that seemingly echo far-right arguments, invoked erotic bonds between Arab men and homosexuals. They did so, however, to advance what this new movement deemed a revolutionary struggle, to remind French people about the continuing importance of their country's imperial past, and to celebrate the Maghrebis' still-ongoing anticolonial resistance.

43. On the *Manif pour tous*, see esp. Robcis, "Catholics"; Camille Robcis, "Liberté, Egalité, Hétérosexualité: Race and Reproduction in the French Gay Marriage Debates," *Constellations* 22, no. 3 (2015), 447–461.

44. Georges Valensin, "Le comportement de l'homosexuel," *Le crapouillot* 12 (August–September 1970), 27–40.

THREE

The Algerian Revolution and Arab Men
in the Fight for Sexual Revolution

You see, when one takes, for example, the uprisings of homosexuals in the United
States and compares them to the massive uprisings that can happen in a Third
World country where people as we speak are dying from hunger . . . it can seem
ridiculous [to compare], but I would say no, it is not ridiculous. . . .

—Michel Foucault (1979)[1]

After May 1968, and in a worldwide context where demands for sexual
liberation became more widely discussed, arguments that fingered North
African men as a key cause of "perverse" sexual activity took on new importance in France. The far right used many such claims to advance racist
arguments, to spark fears of an "Arab invasion" driven by out-of-control
lusts. Their goal was to make French people more amenable to the type
of regime they espoused, through the displacement of recent histories—of
Nazism, fascism, and collaboration as well as of the OAS—that had discredited such projects. A December 1972 program on the public radio network France-culture, which interviewed the proverbial Parisian taxi driver,
gives some measure of their success. It indicates the renewed attention
in these years to claims that linked French decadence and Algerian male
deviance:

Q: Sir, excuse me, can I ask what you think about homosexuals?
A: The who?

1. Michel Foucault, interviewed by Farès Sassine, "Il ne peut pas y avoir de sociétés sans
soulèvements" (August 1979); originally published in Arabic, French version in *Revue Rodéo* 2
(2013), 34–56. See also Sassine, "Foucault en l'entretien," 30–33 online at http://fares-sassine
.blogspot.fr/2014/08/foucault-en-lentretien.html, accessed 17 May 2016.

Q: Homosexuals.

A: Oh! Homos, well, you know . . . *merde* [damn], they're fags . . . queers [. . . .]
We don't like 'em, that's for sure. We had to deal with Algeria, now the homos; we're not going to take it anymore! *Algeria > Gays (the next problem)*

A bit later, in response to a follow up, the taxi driver explained:

A: Yes, of course, the foreign influence is obvious, all those *bougnoules* [dirty Arabs] wandering around Paris; they say they're here to work but what they love is to get [*bleep*]. . . . If the French government doesn't start to limit foreign immigration, well, faggotry is just going to become even more widespread. Take my word for it.[2] *faggotry is the Arabs' fault.*

The sentiments this taxi driver expressed had a long history, yet the context that produced them was very recent and quite different. For in these same years, others also drew political lessons from claims that linked homosexuality in France and Arab men. Some contemporaneous French activists made clear that making "faggotry . . . even more widespread" was something they dreamed of. They, like the far right, linked these developments to male Arab immigrants, but the interpretations they proposed differed starkly. What is remarkable in these years is not just the repetitiveness of far-right arguments, nor their stridency. It is that they were part of a larger political conversation, the existence of which largely explains their new popularity.

Even though ultranationalist activists since 1962 had emphasized such links, it was proponents of sexual liberty—many of whom spoke in terms of a revolution—who had launched the public debate that produced this radio interview. Indeed, some on the left responded in ways that broke quite dramatically from previous left-wing movements. This transcript, for example, appeared in a far-left publication that mocked it rather than disputed it. Such responses dropped the usual argument that to find the perverts, one should *chercher la droite* (look to the right)—for left-wing parties had long argued that sexually abnormal behavior resulted from right-wing authoritarianism, bourgeois decadence, or the like. Writers and activists associated with a new organization, the Homosexual Front for Revolutionary Action, which went by its French acronym, FHAR, argued that the politics of "perversion" would open up new possibilities for political action.[3]

2. Transcription in "Ceux qui nous aiment bien," *L'antinorm* 2 (1973), 5.
3. On the FHAR, see Michael Sibalis, "L'arrivée de la libération gay en France: Le Front Homosexuel d'Action Révolutionnaire (FHAR)," *Genre, sexualité & société* 3 (2010), 2–17; Julian

The Post-Decolonization Grounds for
Revolutionary Homosexual Action

It was through public evocation and exaltation of sex between male Arab immigrant workers, most particularly Algerians, and "French" and "European" homosexual males that the FHAR most aggressively advanced its claim to be at the vanguard of revolutionary action. In April 1971 the "Maoist Spontex" group Vive la Révolution handed control of the twelfth issue of its magazine *Tout!* to members of the FHAR. The magazine's first issue had appeared in September 1970, and the monthly had already become France's most widely read and distributed leftist periodical, with a circulation of about fifty thousand. In it, the FHAR militants printed a more complete version of the statement by Genet that a far-right weekly had cited in 1968, and which he originally had made in *Playboy*: "Perhaps if I hadn't gone to bed with Algerians I might not have been in favor of the FLN. That's not so; I probably would have sided with them anyway. But perhaps it was homosexuality that made me realize Algerians are no different from other men."[4] The quotation was splayed diagonally across part of the magazine's centerfold, in the midst of articles, collages, and headlines. In June 1968, *Minute* had truncated it in an attempt to intimate that the student militants of May '68, like Genet, were driven by unnatural lusts rather than by rational politics. The extended quote, published in *Tout!* at the center of four pages of calls for revolution and sexual liberation, read quite differently. Here, Genet's remarks suggested that revolutionary political understandings and actions could result from thinking about sexual connections—such as that between the French writer and his Algerian lovers—because they established bonds between types of people whom oppressive social structures at once defined as wholly distinct (repressed homosexuals and colonized Algerians) and worked to keep apart. FHAR-associated militants embraced such claims.[5]

Jackson, *Living in Arcadia: Homosexuality, Politics, and Morality in France from the Liberation to AIDS* (Chicago: University of Chicago Press, 2009), 184–194; Frédéric Martel, *The Pink and the Black: Homosexuals in France since 1968*, trans. Jane-Marie Todd (Stanford: Stanford University Press, 1999), 20–48.

4. Already, months after 1968, a literary critic celebrated how Genet's *Les paravents* and its homoerotics allowed France to think about its Algerian trauma: "This symphony of noises and odors, of knobs and holes, and the war, that grandiose organ, this erotic Eden, for one makes war as one makes love: rebels and legionnaires, Algerians and para[trooper]s, each fascinated by the other." Gilles Sandier, "Un théâtre d'agression," *Magazine littéraire* 27 (March 1969), 10–15.

5. This reading draws from Jean-Paul Sartre's formulations, e.g., *Saint Genet, comédien et martyr* (Paris: Gallimard, 1952). On the publication of *Tout!* and subsequent scandal, see esp.

During its less than three years of existence (1971–1974), the FHAR shared with others on the new left—in France and elsewhere—a reliance on what it saw as the joined struggles of anticolonialism and antiracism that had gained such purchase on public debate as well as political organizing and action in the post–World War II era.[6] It is no coincidence that the initial group of "revolutionary homosexual" activists—overwhelmingly women—had found inspiration in the inaugural issue of *Tout!* The new periodical included a translation of imprisoned Black Panther Party leader Huey Newton's "Declaration in Support of the Just Struggle of Homosexuals and Women," which had been released in the United States just one month earlier (August 1970; Genet later claimed that he had convinced the Black Panthers to release this statement). Newton's text addressed his Black Panther comrades, the group he had helped found in 1966 that "saw black communities in the United States as a colony" and which had "declared themselves part of a global revolution against American imperialism."[7] Newton offered an extended explanation for why male disdain, disgust, and fear of male homosexuals, and of women more generally, were structurally similar to racism. It is also telling that, after a group of FHAR women engaged in their first public action in March 1971, they registered with the authorities under the name Humanitarian Anti-Racist Front (Front humanitaire anti-raciste, or FHAR) rather than Homosexual Front for Revolutionary Action.[8]

References to the Black Panthers, like those to the inspirational model of the US Gay Liberation Movement, remind us of how much trans-Atlantic exchanges shaped the sexual revolution—notably radical same-sex sexual activism—and the new left in France. The second issue of *Tout!*, for example, devoted its centerfold and multiple other pages to the Black Panther

Ron Haas, "Guy Hocquenghem and the Cultural Revolution in France after May 1968," in *After the Deluge: New Perspectives on the Intellectual and Cultural History of Postwar France*, ed. Julian Bourg (Lanham, MD: Lexington Books, 2004), 175–200.

6. For a particularly useful examination of this in the West German case, see Jennifer Ruth Hosek, "'Subaltern Nationalism' and the West Berlin Anti-Authoritarians," *German Politics and Society* 26 (2008), 57–81. On the importance of "third-worldism [*tiersmondisme*]" in France around 1968, see Ross, *May '68*, esp. 80–100. On the postwar context and antiracism, see Todd Shepard, "Algeria, France, Mexico, UNESCO: A Transnational History of Anti-Racism and Empire, 1932–1962," *Journal of Global History* 6 (2011), 273–297.

7. Joshua Bloom and Waldo E. Martin. *Black against Empire: The History and Politics of the Black Panther Party* (Berkeley: University of California Press, 2013).

8. On the name, see Sibalis, "L'arrivée de la libération gay en France," 4; "Hubert Fichte Interviews Jean Genet," *Gay Sunshine Interviews. vol. 1*, Winston Leyland, ed. (San Francisco: Gay Sunshine Press, 1978), 93. On the foundational importance of anticolonialism for 1960s American gay radicalism, see Abelove, "New York City Gay Liberation."

Figure 9. Still from the shooting of "Royal Opéra," the fourth part of the 1979 experimental film *Race d'Ep*, directed by Lionel Soukaz in collaboration with Guy Hocquenghem. Initial flirtation scene between the young Frenchman and "the American." According to Soukaz, he had not sought permission to film in the bar, which was not explicitly gay. Interestingly, the Maghrebi man who inserted himself between the two actors to order a drink had no link to the production; he was a customer. In this still photo of the shoot, he is third from left; Piotr Stanislas is fourth and Hocquenghem fifth. Image and permission to reproduce graciously provided by Lionel Soukaz.

Party, through writings, photos, and visuals.[9] A much discussed document of French gay liberation, Lionel Soukaz's 1979 multipart film *Race d'Ep*, captures this influence in its fourth volume, which is organized around the erotic-romantic depiction of the encounter between a French gay man, played by the philosopher and former FHAR spokesperson Guy Hocquenghem, and a blond American, played by Piotr Stanislas. Their story begins at a bar that, if not explicitly gay, is tense with men exchanging glances (several played by former members of the FHAR, such as Gilles Châtelet, Copi, and Michel Cressolle). Their subsequent *flânerie* through Paris intersects with a visual history of a gay male past in which the United States plays a central role. What to make, however, of the Maghrebi man who steps between the white French and American men as they try and connect at the bar (figure 9)? Or of the film's poster, which depicts a Maghrebi or métis man in the arms of a white man, his arm raised (figure 10)? His

9. See Jackson, *Living in Arcadia*; Françoise d'Eaubonne, "Le FHAR, origines et illustrations," *La Revue h* 2 (1996), 18–30. On the importance of the US (especially New York City) reference in the 1970s development of gay French commerce, see Dennis Altman, *The Homosexualization of America: The Americanization of the Homosexual* (Boston: Beacon Press, 1982), 217.

Figure 10. Poster for the 1979 experimental film *Race d'Ep*, by Lionel Soukaz in collaboration with Guy Hocquenghem. The image is from Guy Hocquenghem, *Race d'ep! Un siècle d'images de l'homosexualité* (1979); permission to reproduce graciously provided by Lionel Soukaz.

hidden right hand either—the emphatic title that envelops it and his gaze suggest—points toward some horizon or is clenched in the fist of radical solidarity.

Learning from Arabs

Attention to the trans-Atlantic current has obscured the central role of anticolonial movements and colonized peoples of color in making the sexual revolution. As in the case of *Race d'Ep*, however, these post-decolonization foundations emerge clearly when the archives are examined more closely. With sexual revolutionaries, the evidence is everywhere. The most significant antiracist and "Third Worldist" touchstones in FHAR-ist writings, bar none, were images and descriptions of Algerian men, which were frequent. In 1978 a pseudonymous author mockingly claimed that, around the FHAR and "among the avant-gardes," "not a scrap of pseudo-sexolutionary writing didn't speak of Arabs, as if to hug close an FLN they never knew."[10] Although dismissive, this quote nicely captures the insistent effort of a number of sexual revolutionaries to invoke revolutionary Algeria in order to link their struggle to anticolonialism and tiers-mondiste paradigms. It tells us more than do more recent analyses that limit themselves to often well-founded critiques of what, in 1980, the feminist writer Emmanuèle de Lesseps termed "the designation of members of oppressed groups as sexual objects . . . the fixation of homosexuals on 'the Arab man.'"[11] Through this reference, FHAR writers made explicit the role of the Algerian revolution in defining the French new left. More broadly, the diagnosis also opened up analyses about "the fixation" of *French people* "on 'the Arab man,'" which de Lesseps's examples elide (she paired sexual or sexed groups with racialized groups: "homosexuals"/ "Arab men" and "white women"/ 'Black men"). In "Trois milliards de pervers: La grande encyclopédie des homosexualités" ("Three Billion Perverts: The Big Encyclopedia of Homosexualities,"

10. Emou, "Deux monographies parallèles qui parfois se coupent . . . L'amoureuse et la sexuelle, l'hétéro-éros et l'homofaber," *Recherches* 35 (Nov. 1978), 249–264.

11. Emmanuèle de Lesseps, "Sexisme et racisme: 'Ce n'est rien, c'est une femme qui se noie,'" *Questions féministes* 7 (February 1980), 95–102, 101. For more recent (and very insightful) analysis of fetishization and eroticized objectification of Arabs in French and Western homoerotic or gay discussions, see Joseph Massad, *Desiring Arabs* (Chicago: University of Chicago Press, 2007). For critiques of FHAR racism, see, e.g., Mekki Bentahar, *Les arabes en France* (Rabat: Société Marocaine des Editions Réunis, 1979), 155; Gary Genosko, "The Figure of the Arab in 'Three Billion Perverts,'" *Deleuze Studies* 1 (2007), 60–78; Maxime Cervulle, "French Homonormativity and the Commodification of the Arab Body," *Radical History Review* 100 (2008), 171–179.

Figure 11. From "The Arabs and Us," the longest of the four sections of "Three Billion Perverts: The Big Encyclopedia of Homosexualities," the March 1973 special issue of *Recherches* edited by FHAR militants. The militants "appropriated" an image that had been published in the January 1972 issue of the (male) nudist magazine *Olympe*. It accompanied an article by George Lamy entitled "Voyages," which recounted Lamy's visit to the "outskirts of the desert" in the Algerian Sahara, and described the boy as "Mohamed, who is sixteen. His dream: to become a professional guide." See *Olympe* 45 (January 1972), 12–14.

1973), another special issue produced by members of the FHAR, this one of the academic journal *Recherches*, the central section was entitled "Arabs and Us" (figure 11). In one article, "20 Years of Cruising," the author dated his political awareness to the Algerian revolution, reminiscing: "I became Algerian; I am Arab Algeria. If they lose, I'm out of luck; if they win, I, too, could triumph. . . ." As in this example, these texts identified Algerians as comrades in struggle and as models for action, exaggerating arguments that were widespread on the French far left.[12]

During the 1970s, militants in the FHAR and other same-sex sexual radical groups drew parallels between their oppression and that suffered by

12. "Vingt ans de drague," *Recherches* 12 (1973), 53–60; 57. This special issue of *Recherches*, edited by members of the FHAR, was given the title "Trois milliards de pervers: La grande encyclopédie des homosexualités"—in references, usually shortened to "Trois milliards de pervers." In this book the special issue is referred to as "Three Billion Perverts," the English translation of its shortened title.

North African immigrants. "We feel deeply the solidarity of the oppressed that links us with Arabs," as *Tout!* 12 proclaimed. They often followed the very common usage on the French new left of the category "racism" to describe any form of oppression. At other times, though, there were more careful efforts. As part of their critique of medical institutions, for example, one FHAR flyer cited the Hôpital St.-Louis, in Paris, to argue that it was a place that "conjoined anti-Arab and anti-fag racisms."[13] In 1972 the leftist journal *Partisans* brought together a round table on "experiences of repression." A gay male participant relied on a comparison with Arabs to convince others that anti-homosexual insults in the "popular classes" merited critique rather than just empathetic understanding. "It's connected to the anti-Arab racism of the working class. Many French workers react similarly to Arabs: 'They are here to take our jobs!'"[14] Several years later, when a member of a gay liberation group in Lyon sought to assess the meaning of three recent murders of gay men in his city, he insisted that "these three murders clearly fill me with fear. I live like an immigrant, who has just learned that three of his fellow believers [*corréligionaires*; i.e., Muslims] have been murdered." Another man suggested that "in the parallel you draw with the immigrant struggle, that which most matters . . . is the collective decision to speak out." It was the situation that Arabs faced in France, and the politics they had developed in response to that situation, that these gay activists drew on.[15]

French leftists relied more generally on similar references to "Algerians," "Arabs," and "immigrant workers" for inspiration. They modeled their action on both the Algerian revolution and the struggle of immigrant workers in present-day France: the ability to organize, and their ability to win struggles against "imperialism" and "capitalism." Of course, leftists often founded such parallels on seemingly hasty assumptions. A third man in the Lyon discussion quickly reminded the others of the limits of the analogy. "To move beyond this comparison, all the immigrant workers in France are oppressed and exploited, but not all the queens! In addition, when you're an immigrant, it's there on your face, which is not necessarily the case when you're a queen!"[16] The specific situation of Algerian men in France, their history of revolution and their confrontation with post-

---

13. Text from *Tout!* 12 reproduced in FHAR, *Rapport contre la normalité* (Paris: Champs Libres, 1971), 104; FHAR, "Appel aux médecins" (n.d.), in BDIC: (fonds Daniel Guérin) F delta 721/15/1, 1–2.

14. "Répression vécue-Table Ronde," *Partisans* 66–67 (July-October 1972), 137–149.

15. GLH-Lyon, "Dossier: Identités," *Interlopes*, 3-4 (Autumn 1978), 4–46.

16. Ibid., 10.

decolonization racism, was exemplary. Arab responses could be models without wholesale cooptation, or so it could seem.

Yet in the texts produced in the FHAR moment by its members or in dialogue with their arguments, representations of Algerian and North African men assumed a significance that went far beyond admired models for revolutionary action. Insistent claims about homoerotic and sexual interaction between those categorized as homosexuals and others categorized as Arab men (always represented as two wholly distinct groups) grounded specific claims about the revolutionary stakes of "revolutionary homosexual action." These spoke directly to the questions of class and "race" that, for diverse aspects of the French left, raised questions about the revolutionary potential of any politics anchored in sexuality.

Some texts merely sought to explain what exactly "revolutionary homosexual action" added to the larger struggle; they invoked sexuality as revelatory of larger tensions that others ignored. References to Arabs here buttressed claims that sex was a crucial question for radicals. In his introduction to Newton's "Declaration in Support of the Just Struggle of Homosexuals and Women," which he also had translated, the young Vive la Révolution militant and philosopher Guy Hocquenghem drew the attention of French leftists to the context within which the Black Panthers took action. He took this opportunity to introduce readers to the gay liberation movement. In the United States, Hocquenghem claimed, "it is above all within the revolutionary movement that they [activists in the new gay rights movement] have played a key role." What they contributed to the revolutionary struggle, he argued, was "criticizing the sexist division of roles, calling into question the bourgeois norms still prevalent among 'revolutionary militants.'" With feminists, "they have brought to decisive completion the cultural revolution" which had been "begun by groups of women within the movement."[17] Two years later, the philosopher Félix Guattari proposed a similar interpretation, which emphasized same-sex sexual radicals' ability to identify previously unrecognized forms of oppression. "From 22 March [the Nanterre University group, which included Cohn-Bendit] until today, via the FHAR and the MLF [Movement for the Liberation of Women], militancy has exploded outwards," as new domains of struggle and politics had been identified. What was new was that they concerned "all the power dynamics that control daily life, [and revealed] the struggle by the desir-

17. Hocquenghem, untitled introduction to "Déclaration du camarade H. P. NEWTON ministre de la défense du Black Panther Party pour soutenir la juste lutte des homosexuels et des femmes· pour leur libération," *Tout!* 1 (September 1970), 7.

ing multiplicity against statist normalization."[18] Such claims for the importance of sexual politics all relied on the novel importance of the category "sexual misery" in 1970s discussion.

"Sexual Misery" and the Revolution

Numerous groups and intellectuals of varying political stripes diagnosed "sexual misery"—which resulted from the absence of sexual satisfaction—as one of the chief ailments of modern society. The mid-twentieth-century German Freudo-Marxian theorist Wilhelm Reich had originated this diagnosis. In a 1931 text, which first appeared in a French translation in 1972, he had argued that "sexual misery in authoritarian, patriarchal society is a result of [the society's] intrinsic sexual negation and suppression." This combination "creates sexual stasis, which in turn begets neuroses, perversions, and sexual crime." The solution, he proposed, was clear. It was necessary to create a "society that has no interest in sexual suppression," which will "necessarily be free from sexual misery." Those who fought for sexual liberation, and many of their contemporaries, too, embraced the diagnosis and pursued the remedy.[19]

In fall 1966, the left-leaning journal *Partisans* put out a special issue on the theme "Sexuality and Repression," which included articles by some of the most important theorists and critics who became associated with the "sexual revolution," as well as a set of studies that examined the sexual conditions faced by women and youth. All used Reich's definition to insist that the key problem was "sexual misery."[20] That same autumn, the Situationists of Strasbourg—made up, like the Paris-based group that inspired them, of a small number (four) of assertively subversive activists drawn from avant-garde artistic movements—published and distributed a brochure, *On the Misery of Student Life*. Written by the young Tunisian revolutionary activist Mustapha Khayati, it paralleled "sexual misery" with economic, political, psychological, and intellectual forms of misery and caused a national scandal.[21] (Khayati's previous writings, let us note, had focused on the revo-

18. [Félix Guattari,] "Après la saisie du numéro spécial de Recherches" (undated), 1, IMEC: GTR 58.29/Fonds Félix Guattari.

19. Wilhelm Reich, *L'Irruption de la morale sexuelle: Étude des origines du caractère compulsif de la morale sexuelle*, trad. Pierre Kamnitzer (Paris: Payot 1972), 33–34. See Bourg, *From Revolution to Ethics*, 195–196, which includes English translation.

20. *Partisans*, "Sexualité et répression," 32–33 (October 1966); Alain Giami, "Misère, répression et libération sexuelles," *Mouvements* 20 (2002), 23–29.

21. Internationale situationniste de Strasbourg, *De la Misère en Milieu Etudiant: Considérée sous ses aspects économique, politique, psychologique, sexuel et notamment intellectuel et de quelques*

lutionary possibilities in Algeria; he quit the Situationist International to join a Palestinian revolutionary movement.) Around May 1968 and after, sexual misery grew in popularity as a category of analysis both in new-left statements and more widely.

For those who argued that the fight for sexual revolution was crucial to any struggle to radically change society, the concept revealed connections between struggles anchored in seemingly specific claims. When, in the aftermath of May '68, militant activity in favor of "immigrant workers" grew in strength, the theme appeared frequently.[22] In 1971, to take two examples, the immigrant-rights organization Groupe d'information et de soutien des travailleurs immigrés (Group for Knowledge and Support of Immigrant Workers, or GISTI) warned of "the sexual repression of which the immigrant, who is a man between 25 and 45, is a victim" and an Algerian sociologist asked whether "many of the immigrants, whether bachelors or married, who are unaccompanied, are condemned to painful affective solitude, which will unfailingly lead to social maladjustment, sometimes with serious consequences?"[23] This is why FHAR writings invoked sexual misery: to insist that their struggle placed the group at the forefront of "the revolution." Because "our sexual relations are by definition the negation of certain social relations that constitute patriarchy and capitalism," as one 1971 text proclaimed, revolutionary homosexuals were singularly situated to articulate what, in a 1972 interview, FHAR members described as "the sexual misery from which we all suffer, homos, women, blacks, Indians, immigrants, proles, high schoolers, youth, the insane. . . ."[24] In their use of the language of sexual misery, FHAR arguments rung with claims widely

moyens pour y remédier (Strasburg: l'IS, 1967). I have altered the usual translation; see *On the Poverty of Student Life: A Consideration of Its Economic, Political, Sexual, Psychological and Notably Intellectual Aspects and of a Few Ways to Cure It* (New York: Situationist International, 1967).

22. On how the immigrant question became so important in post-1968 France and on the far left, see Zancarini-Fournel, "La question immigrée après 68"; also Xavier Vigna, "Une émancipation des invisibles? Les ouvriers immigrés dans les grèves de mai-juin 68," in *Histoire politique des immigrations (post)coloniales, France, 1920–2008*, ed. Ahmed Boubeker and Abdellali Hajjat (Paris: Amsterdam, 2008), 85–94.

23. CIMADE Gisti, "Etude du GISTI sur les foyers pour travailleurs migrants" (July 1971), 14, in CAC: 19870056 /20; Ali Salah, *La communauté algérienne: Etude sur l'immigration algérienne dans le département du Nord, 1945–1972* (Paris, Editions Universitaires/ Lille, 1973), 172.

24. Yves Frémion and Daniel Riche, "La parole au Fléau social, groupe n. 5," *Actuel* 25 (1972), 8–9. Sexual misery was a theme that engaged numerous "French" commentators in these years; e.g., see Roger-Pol Droit and Antoine Gallien, *La réalité sexuelle: Enquête sur la misère sexuelle en France* (Paris: Robert Laffont, 1974); Ben Jelloun, *La plus haute*; Alain Corbin, *Les Filles de noce: Misère sexuelle et prostitution* (Paris: Aubier Montaigne, 1978); Edouard Glissant, *Le discours antillais* (Paris: Présence africaine, 1981).

accepted among an increasingly large circle of French cultural commentators as well as left-wing critics.

Sex Acts and Political Lessons

Far more precise and quite exceptional FHAR claims emerged in very explicit evocations of specific sexual acts and encounters. Representations of Arab men played a central role in the formulations of the FHAR. *Tout* no.12 presented a petition, which made this role clear: "We are more than 343 sluts. We've been buggered by Arabs. We're proud of it and we'll do it again. Sign and circulate this petition. Will the *Nouvel observateur* publish it??? And discuss it with Arab Comrades" (figure 12).[25] The two "first person" stories on this centerfold, which accompanied the petition (in addition to the Genet quote about the FLN), also detailed erotic encounters with Arabs. In one of the stories, an "under-age fag" detailed his first, quite unpleasant sexual encounter with a man, identified as "the Arab." In the other, the author recounted his resistance to young men who violently attacked solitary men they supposed to be seeking sex in public bathrooms. After a first encounter, in which, thanks to his help, the victim escaped with only "two black eyes," five "delinquents" waited outside the urinal, insulting any single man who came by. Then "an Arab appears: the same insults, he calls them pieces of shit and I joined in with him yelling, 'You little racist shits, you want to trap us so you can get off on your hate.'" The episode ends with: "The Arab pulled out a knife when one of them tried to jump us. They fled."[26] The intersection in this story of "the knife" and the "public urinal" presented the special relationship between Arabs and "homos" as sexual—both of the story's heroes, it is suggested, are there for the same reason—and both are dangerous. The former, of course, was a symbol at once phallic and deeply linked to French fantasies of "Arab barbarism," while the latter had a homoerotic charge and a reputation as a site for sexual encounters between men ("Many of us cruise here," as an article reminded readers of *The Report Against Normality*, a book that came out a few months later and included versions of the texts in *Tout!* no. 12).[27] A notice that described the publication of "Three Billion Perverts" in the center-left weekly *Nouvel observateur* highlighted the foundational role of

25. From the centerfold of *Tout!* 12 (1971). The text parodied the famous "Manifesto of 343," which, the previous month, French feminists had published in the weekly magazine *Nouvel observateur* in support of abortion rights.

26. "Vie quotidienne chez les pédés," in *Tout!* 12, 6.

27. FHAR, "Ce n'est qu'un début: Notre vocabulaire," in FHAR, *Rapport contre la normalité*, 2.

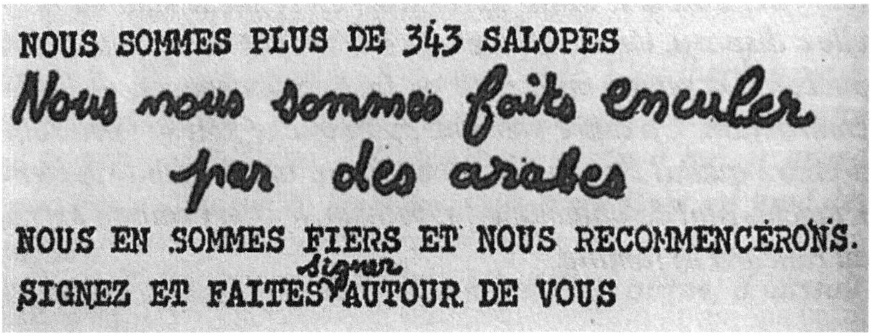

NOUS SOMMES PLUS DE 343 SALOPES
Nous nous sommes faits enculer par des arabes
NOUS EN SOMMES FIERS ET NOUS RECOMMENCERONS.
SIGNEZ ET FAITES *signer* AUTOUR DE VOUS

Figure 12. This late April 1971 FHAR "petition" parodied the famous 5 April
1971 "Manifesto of the 343" circulated by French feminists fighting to legalize abortion in France. Reproduced from Front homosexuel d'action révolutionnaire, *Rapport contre la normalité* (1971); first published in *Tout!* 12 (April 1971).

this dangerous relationship between homosexual and Arab men, which
"push[es] the contradictions inherent in manliness and repression to the
breaking point, as emblematized in this sentence: 'They [Arab men] fuck
us, but them, they're the ones who are oppressed.'" This article, like others, presented this erotico-political relationship as threatening, above all,
to those who oppressed both groups.[28]

A 1976 short story by Hugo Lacroix suggests the potency of this claim
about the politics of homosexual sex in France that involved Arab men. It
recounts how "anonymous hands felt up narrator number 2 during rush
hour" in the Parisian Métro, and then reverses the usual direction of the
political charge, to suggest that antiracism leads to sexual liberation. In Lacroix's telling—"1 time out of 2, it's 1 [one] Arab who did it, so you shrink
in, you don't want to start a race riot"—the leftist political injunction to
support "immigrant workers" allowed some of these instances of sexual
molestation to become moments when repressed desires broke free: "Or at
least that is the argument your brain comes up with to just let it happen."
Erotic contacts or relationships between men thus allowed these Arab and
homosexual men new opportunities to escape from the trap of sexual misery, whether it was imposed by "bourgeois" or "feudal" repression or by
racist social oppression.[29]

In these texts, Arab men embodied political agency and analysis, which

28. *"Trois milliards de pervers,"* Nouvel observateur 439 (9 April 1973), 19.
29. Hugo Lacroix, "Columbarium néon," *Cahiers critiques de la littérature* 2 (December
1976), 45–55.

homosexual connections made available to other French people. The author of "Twenty Years . . ." not only argued that "everything about my homosexuality can be linked to this history" of the Algerian war; he claimed that his obsession with "[cruising] the toilets of Arab bistrots" was part of "this history." In a much publicized 1972 magazine article linked to the public debate that FHAR actions had sparked, the philosopher and FHAR member Guy Hocquenghem recounted his own homosexuality to the readership of *Nouvel observateur*. He noted that, as an adolescent, "I was a little Rimbaud who needed it, a minor looking to be taken advantage of" by an older man. Yet, to explain how he became aware of this, he spoke of politics, and how it had led him to men. "It was in 1962, the era when the Algerian war was coming to a close. The trees of Paris were covered with little posters: 'We torture in Algeria.' On the photos, there were nude Arab men."[30] His excitement and his outrage, he claimed, together made him the man he now was, homosexual and "revolutionary." If Genet relied on sex to recognize the need to extend his political vision to Algerians, here the ways in which Arab masculine sexuality circulated in France created political understanding.

Within the FHAR, this focus on sex with Arab men contributed to the quick disengagement of most female members, even those who had done much to launch the group. It also crystallized concerns that others in the group had raised about masculinity and effeminacy among men, through discussions about sexual roles. In 1972, Guy Hocquenghem tried to explain why "the girls" had left the group, and made this particularly explicit. "They were tired of men whistling at them in the streets," he claimed. "To which the fags responded that they asked only for that: that they be whistled at, that someone"—a manly man—"grab their ass," as if they were women. "This was the reason" that "they went to Morocco or Tunisia," Hocquenghem claimed. Historian (and former FHAR member) Marie-Jo Bonnet put it differently, with the argument that women left the FHAR because they saw its male activists as being too intrigued by gendered sexual roles, of "top [*actif*]" and "bottom [*passif*]." It was precisely these discussions that were ripe with references to Arab men, which male activists claimed were profoundly political. The groups's reframing of the abortion-rights manifesto ("of the 343") aptly signaled how the "Arab" focus obscured lesbian concerns and alienated women activists. A rather quick split between gay male and lesbian "liberationists" was not specific to France. Here again,

30. Guy Hocquenghem, "Je m'appelle Guy Hocquenghem. J'ai 25 ans . . . ," *Nouvel observateur* 374 (10 January 1972), 32–33.

however, a phenomenon that occurred wherever the sexual revolution took hold was contoured through references to "the Arab man."[31]

Getting "buggered by Arabs" and being willing to come out about it signaled the "revolutionary homosexual" claim to have a unique understanding of the experience of racism and a unique connection to Arabs. The activists presented the resultant relationships as self-evidently far more meaningful than the connections with "immigrant workers" that other self-proclaimed revolutionaries affirmed. Arabs were central to these stories because this reference worked in terms of both identity and ideology. In terms of identity, it focused attention on acts and connections, on the power of libido, rather than on deeply anchored biographies. This focus helped to collapse boundaries between a tiny minority who did these things (homosexuals) and the large majority who, like them, suffered from "sexual misery." Ideologically, sex acts and desire not only linked "homos" and "Arabs," but connected "revolutionary homosexual action" to other forms of revolutionary politics.[32]

The multiple implications of the Algerian reference were much noted in responses to *Tout!* no.12, both from those who embraced the revolutionary potential of the FHAR and from others who highlighted the dubious ideological implications of sex talk about Arabs. One letter from a self-described homosexual published in *Tout* no.13 argued that "no struggle against racism can avoid dealing with us." Also published was a letter from the well-known Trotskyist intellectual and historian of the working class Daniel Guérin, who announced that he was adhering to the FHAR and signing the manifesto "We have been Buggered by Arabs," and added, "All my life, I have practiced a solidarity with Arabs based on shared op-

31. Guy Hocquenghem, "La parole au fléau sociale: Groupe n. 5 du FHAR," in *Actuel* 25 (November 1972), 9; Bonnet's statement cited in Fréderic Martel, *The Pink and the Black*, 46. While there has been limited scholarship on the history of French lesbians in the 1970s, Tamara Chaplin is at work on a study that includes this period. See also Sylvie Burgnard, "Se regrouper, se rendre visibles, s'affirmer: L'expérience des mouvements homosexuels à Genève dans les années 1970," *Genre, sexualité & société* 3 (2010); and the oral history project that anchors Françoise Flamant, *À tire d'elles: Itinéraires de féministes radicales des années 1970* (Rennes: Presses Universitaires de Rennes, 2009).

32. "20 ans de drague," *Recherches* 12 (1973), 56. "Coming out of the closet" was central to the ideology of the US Gay Liberation Front activists from whom the FHAR drew explicit inspiration, yet this metaphor was not used in their publications. Their embrace of similar self-revelatory tactics made explicit the nonessentialist and political nature of early-1970s arguments for this approach. "A small group from FHAR," for example, insisted that "anyone who wants to be part of FHAR must find a way to make public his/her revolutionary homosexuality." Quelques uns du FHAR, "Bilan," *Tout!* 16 (1971), 5.

pression. *Salut* and long live our liberation!!"[33] In parallel, others on the far left who insisted that Vive la Révolution had left the revolution behind when it turned its biweekly over to the FHAR, focused their critique of Vive la Révolution's betrayal on the special issue's representations and eroticization of Arabs. In its analysis of *Tout!* no. 12, the Trotskyist journal *Lutte Ouvrière* asked "how it is that people who claim to be revolutionaries came to edit a newspaper with contents no better than the graffiti found on public urinals." Editors relied on the Genet text to anchor their argument that sexuality, repressed or not, did not offer a basis for revolutionary politics. They invoked two groups associated with the "wrong" side of the Algerian war to assert: "Happily for Genet, he did not fall in love with a Messaliste [another nationalist faction, here defined as reactionary] or with a [French army] *para*[trooper]. Imagine the political problems he would have faced!"[34] A letter to *Tout!* that denied that "fags" formed a revolutionary class also castigated the sexual dynamic between homosexuals and Arabs that so many articles in the periodical's pages had celebrated. Its authors added that "to make mention of mainly Arab *enculeurs* [buggerers] (*ou enculés* [or buggered]) acts to maintain racist ideas such as 'All Arabs are *pédés* [fags],' and in a moment like this when there's a large-scale racist campaign raging, that just adds fuel to the fire."[35] A far more sympathetic article in the leftist *Politique-hebdo*, "Erect Revolutionaries?," anchored its critique— "Where it verges on the ridiculous is in the 'theoretical' parts of the book, with the idea that homosexuality in and of itself is revolutionary"—with examples from *Tout!* no. 12 in which Arab men were central. "Genet . . . the provocation of the so-called manifesto . . . it's brilliant . . . but they make a mockery of themselves. It mixes up two universes, two totally different languages." On one side was sex, "the language of the erotic, a closed-off world of pure expenditure, with no greater goal." On the other, in its references to the FLN and Arabs, the author distinguished "a sociopolitical language." But this very synthesis was exactly what anchored FHAR proposals for radical action, the homosexual revolutionaries' version of "The personal is political" (a slogan that French feminists had imported from the United States a few months previously).[36]

33. *Tout!* 13 (1971). On Guérin, his relations with FHAR, theories of sexuality, and revolutionary struggle, see esp. David Berry, "'Workers of the World, Embrace!': Daniel Guérin, the Labour Movement and Homosexuality," *Left History* 9 (2004), 11–43.

34. François Duburg, "*Tout!* Ou rien?" *Lutte ouvrière* (4 May 1970), 13.

35. 2 copains du SR—19è, "Courrier des lecteurs: Pédés riches, pédés pauvres," in *Tout!* 14 (1971), 2.

36. Gabriel Glazounov, "Révolutionnaires par la bande ? Suffit-il de se faire sodomiser par un Arabe pour être Marxiste-léniniste?" in *Politique hebdo* 6 (nouvelle série) (1971), 26. The

Same Struggle! Arab Intersections in French Radical Politics

Worrying evidence about growing anti-Algerian racism, which had resulted in numerous murders and attacks on Algerian-linked institutions in France, helps explain why the FHAR's Arab references became such a lightning rod for far-left criticism. Indeed, one letter to *Tout!* stood out because, as the author explained, "I couldn't care less about those 350 sluts who were mounted by Arabs. Everybody gets off however you can, and love has neither frontiers nor a homeland." What seems to explain its publication, and what made it so exceptional, was that the author, although he identified himself as a "simple worker" drawn to the far left, was "not at all in agreement with you about the constant support you give to immigrants, in particular to Arabs." With arguments that repeated those widespread in the far-right press, he insisted that France and modern civilization, unlike "love," needed stark boundaries. This meant pushing Arabs outside them. For most on the far left, however, it was necessary to recognize Algerian differences and also to stand in solidarity with them, on both sides of the Mediterranean. As much-repeated slogans suggested ("*Même combat!*" [Same struggle!]), revolutionary politics meant fighting for a revolutionary Third World and alongside "Third World" immigrant workers in France; against imperialism, racism, and other forms of oppression.[37]

The racism Arabs suffered in France contributed to leftist certainty that this category of people mattered politically. The political potential of the "Arab masses" motivated leftists' concern about the FHAR's Arab "*enculeurs (ou enculés)*." An RG (domestic intelligence) report put together in the weeks after May 1968 made this very clear. In its description of a "panorama of the far left that does not depend on the PCF," it was the Algerian war that allowed a non-PCF "far left" to emerge, which "the Vietnam war [between the United States and its allies and the forces in favor of North Vietnam] has accentuated."[38] Here again, the FHAR's Arab obsession made explicit the centrality that Algeria and Algerians continued to play in French definitions of what it meant to be French and the impor-

---

first use of the slogan "The personal is political" in French was in Carol Hanisch, "Problèmes actuels: Éveil de la conscience féminine. Le 'personnel' est aussi 'politique,'" in the special issue "Libération des femmes: Année zéro," *Partisans* 54–55 (July-October 1970), 61–64; see discussion in Pauline Delage, "Après l'année zéro: Histoire croisée de la lutte contre le viol en France et aux Etats-Unis," *Critique international* 70 (2016), 21–35.

37. Anonymous, "Nos lecteurs . . . : NON la France n'est pas raciste," *Tout!* 15 (1971), 2.

38. Direction Centrale des Renseignements Généraux (RG), "Panorama de l'extrême gauche ne dépendant pas du PCF" (24 June 1968), 1 and 2 n CAC 19800273/61, "Evènements de juin-juillet."

tance of sex in these discussions. Many on the far left were frustrated by what they claimed was the "quietism" of French workers, often equated with working-class support for the "revisionist" PCF. Foucault pushed this assessment to the extreme when he exclaimed to the writer Claude Mauriac in April 1976, "The proletariat does not want revolution. It's just as simple, just as implacable as that." Most leftists did not go this far, and held out hope that the working class could be mobilized; but they looked to other groups, notably more specific groups of workers, to catalyze revolution. Arabs in France seemed to offer a promising constituency.[39] A 1972 tract by the Commitee for the Defense of the Rights and the Life of Immigrant Workers helps make sense of why leftists thought this. It asserted that "in the last two years hundreds of Arabs have been assassinated by racist gangs under police protection." Yet the long history of oppression at the hands of French authorities, in France and across the Mediterranean, had fashioned a culture of resistance, to which they now appealed. "May the power of Arab workers rise up, those who fought colonialism during the Algerian Revolution, and . . . confront the same criminal police on French soil." The tract referenced the recent intervention in public debate of "one hundred French intellectuals" (among them Jean-Paul Sartre) in order to call for an "antiracist force on the model of the 121"—that is, like the 1960 manifesto signed by Sartre and 120 others in support of "*insoumission*" (conscientious objection) as a way to resist French violence and imperialism in Algeria.[40] A 1971 report from "A Small Group of Militants" informed their comrades that "immigrant workers make up nearly half of the industrial proletariat, the most exploited half, directly or indirectly. It is thus in the short term the most revolutionary part of the proletariat in France." A number of scholars rightfully point out that post-1968 discourse around "immigrant workers" was particularly invested in their status as "workers." Yet their status as Arabs also mattered greatly. For French leftists, the exceptional revolutionary potential of Arabs had multiple sources.[41]

39. Claude Mauriac, *Mauriac et fils: Le temps immobile* (Paris: Grasset, 1986), 235. Michael Scott Christofferson offers a compelling description of how, in the early 1970s, many on the far left shifted away from a commitment to "the working class"; see *French Intellectuals against the Left: The Antitotalitarian Moment of the 1970s* (New York: Berghahn Books, 2004).

40. "Comité de Defense des droits et de la Vie des Travailleurs Immigrés." Reproduced, with the claim that the tract was also published in Arabic on the verso, in "Intolérable! Sartre veut soulever les arabes: Sous un faux prétexte, un appel à la révolte des Nord-Africains en France," *Minute* 558 (20 December 1972), 9.

41. Un petit groupe de militants travaillant depuis un an avec des travaillurs immigrés, "La question des travailleurs immigrés" (Paris, n.d. [ca. 1971–1972]), in BDIC: Fonds Cahiers de mai/Immigrés; F delta rés. 578/8/travailleurs immigres 1968–1975, 1–10. See, e.g., Gordon, *Immigrants and Workers*.

As heirs of the Algerian revolution, Arabs in France appeared as natural allies for a new-left movement that constantly situated itself in reference to that struggle. For example, in Carole Roussopoulos's 1973 documentary *Lip 1 Monique*, which presented to French viewers the ongoing strike by workers at the Lip watch factory in Besançon, the opening scene shows an encounter between striking workers, barricaded around the factory, and CRS troops in full body armor advancing on them across a lightly wooded field. As some of the striking men throw rocks, loud voices fill the soundtrack: "You weren't so clever in Algeria, eh? . . . You weren't so clever in Algeria. Did you have to deal with 'em like this, eh? Bah, yeah, tell me who was there, you!" The strikers presented themselves as revolting Algerians, and identified their police special-forces opponents as the same men who had been defeated by the FLN and had brought shame on their country.[42]

The constant reiteration of the term "Arab" in leftist lingo, that is, cannot be reduced to the erasure of North Africa's rich ethnic and linguistic makeup, whether Berber, Jewish, or the like. The word rang with invocations of the "Arab Revolution" (figure 1), a 1970s concept that connected the heritage of the Algerian revolution to the current urgency of the Palestinian struggle as well as to Nasserism, the struggle in the Western Sahara, and ongoing intra-Algerian debates. French leftists worked to tie this global movement to local conditions in France. Many "bourgeois" leftists had been motivated to action by the ongoing Vietnam War. Yet it was far-left support for the Palestinian cause that finally drew "working class" militants toward leftist radical action and opened doors in immigrant neighborhoods—the Goutte d'Or in Paris, most famously—to far-left campaigners. The Comité Palestine described the mobilization after the murder of fifteen-year-old Djillali Ben Ali as that of "all those who are aware of racist oppression, all those who struggle together, French and immigrants in the factories, those who protected the Algerian people against the OAS and colonialism. . . . We marched up to Djellali's [*sic*] house." They had joined together, another tract claimed, "at the Goutte d'Or," in a crowd of "four thousand that marched with the flag of the Palestinian revolution and the flag of the Algerian revolution."[43] Both the Mouvement des travailleurs

42. *Lip 1 Monique* (dir. Carole Roussopoulos, 1973). A key reference for many new-left claims of worker quietism (and the role supposedly played by communist parties in this development) was Herbert Marcuse, *The One-Dimensional Man: Studies in the Ideology of Advanced Industrial Society* (Boston: Beacon Press, 1964). See, e.g., Tariq Ali and Susan Watkins, *1968: Marching in the Streets* (New York: Free Press, 1998), 210. For a critique of this argument, see Seidman, *The Imaginary Revolution*, 254–256.

43. Tract: "Où en sont les comités Palestine depuis la campagne anti-raciste sur Djeillali?" (n.d.), 2, in BDIC (fonds Immigration en France): F delta rés. 705/1/dossier 3.

Arabes (Movement of Arab Workers, or MTA) and the Comité Palestine organized to accentuate the former;[44] a quote from Palestine Liberation Organization leader Yassir Arafat, who identified France as a crucial terrain for the Arab Revolution, appeared on membership cards for the Comité Palestine.[45] Meanwhile, internal discussions in organizations such as the Cause du peuple (People's Cause) and the Gauche prolétarienne (Proletarian Left) excitedly reported that Algerian immigrants, who had mobilized to support the Palestinian struggle, were both willing to draw lessons from the Algerian revolution and able to understand how they could apply these global terms to local struggles in France. As one tract put it, "From the initial insight that 'we have the right to support the Palestinian Revolution,' we engaged revolutionary practices . . . [that] allowed Arab workers to gain a larger perspective."[46] For these leftists, the Arab revolution offered the prospect of radical change migrating to France and beyond.

This relationship between leftists and immigrants was at the heart of a report that André Postel-Vinay signed just three days after the newly elected president of the republic, Valéry Giscard d'Estaing, nominated him as secretary of state in charge of immigrant workers in the government of Jacques Chirac. It was a summons for the government to opt "for an immigration policy." He warned his colleagues that "the two million foreign workers who live in often miserable conditions in France have begun to become aware of their economic importance, of the mass they constitute, and of the forces [in society] with which they can ally." He shared the view of leftist organizations, which was that they were largely responsible. "In France," he wrote, "this coming-into-consciousness had been stimulated by a very active propaganda campaign, frequently the responsibility of extremist groups." He noted that "these groups consecrate a big part of their activism to the indoctrination of immigrants," and judged that "their activism turns out to be very efficient." His argument to his fellow ministers would have warmed the heart of leftist activists of various stripes: "Our unstable

44. On Vietnam, see esp. Ross, *May '68*, 80–100. Comité palestine—Sécours rouge 18è—Des habitants anti-racistes, "Tract: NOUS SOMMES DES MILLIERS PRETS A NOUS BATTRE POUR ECRASER LA BETE RACISTE" (late 1971), in BDIC (fonds Assia Melamed): F delta rés. 696/22/3. See Aissaoui, *North African*, 155–160. He notes that the MTA drew more Moroccans and Tunisians than Algerians. Camille Robcis notes that attendance sheets for Gauche prolétarienne cell meetings contained growing numbers of Maghrebi names from 1971 to 1973 (communication with author).

45. BDIC (fonds Immigration en France): F delta rés. 705/1/3.

46. See, esp., Abdellali Hajjat, "Les comités Palestine (1970–1972): Aux origines du soutien de la cause palestinienne en France," *Revue d'études palestiniennes* 98 (2006), 74–92. See also *L'enterrement de Mahmoud Al Hamchari* (dir. Carole Roussopoulos and Paul Roussopoulos, Vidéo Out, 1973).

and troubled society might well perish from a new 'May 68,' if this one had the support of a sufficient mass of foreign workers." This assessment mirrored the goals proclaimed by new-left revolutionaries, although it erased "Arab" agency. The note's threatening depiction of the political risks that the immigrant "mass" could or did pose would set the stage for the government's decision, weeks later (July 1974), to "suspend" all economic immigration.[47]

The hopes of French leftists that they had identified a new revolutionary constituency helps to explain their intense concern for currying support among Algerian immigrants. It was a key element of another question the radicals found crucial: how to gain the trust of workers. As a 1970 leftist tract called "Down with Imperialism" explained, the French government did all in its power "to avoid connections among immigrants themselves and connections with French workers so as to crush any possibility of union and revolt."[48] Such analyses informed the urgent concerns that leftists expressed about the FHAR's talk of sex with Arabs. This, they were sure, would alienate both Arab and French workers. An article by members of Vive la Révolution, which asked "Was our last issue antiworker?," defended the organization's willingness to publish the writings and images of the FHAR. Still, one militant noted, "It's really tough to show up in front of a factory and try to get people interested in [buying a copy of] *Tout*"—an action that involved "yelling 'Ask for issue no. 12 of *Tout!*, [in which you can] read our articles 'Fags and the Revolution' and 'I have been buggered by an Arab!'" The militant emphasized that such a sales pitch "can even get you in trouble. . . ."[49] In the same issue, the Maoist group also published a cartoon (figure 13) that offered a clear explanation of why the FHAR's struggle merited its support. The cartoon presents each of three categories—Arab, leftist, homosexual—as an obvious target for violent state repression, depicted in the form of two helmeted CRS officers. It thus suggests why the "faggot" needs to be accepted as being similar to members of the two other clearly "revolutionary" groups. The security officers have clubbed the "faggot" unconscious, although the victim could just as well have been an "Arab" or a "leftist." The cartoon presumes that the

47. Andre Postel-Vinay, secrétaire d'État auprès du ministre du Travail, chargé des travailleurs immigrés, "Pour une politique d'immigration" (31 May 1974), 1, in CAC: 19960405 /1. See Sylvain Laurens, *Une politisation feutrée: Les hauts fonctionnaires et l'immigration en France* (Paris: Belin, 2009), 217–219.

48. Collectif Parisien pour le 21 février, "A bas l'impérialisme" (February 1970), 1, in BDIC (fonds Vive la Révolution/Archives Françoise Picq): F delta rés. 612/16.

49. Christian, ouvrier du livre, "Notre dernier numéro est-il anti-ouvrier?" *Tout!* 13 (May 1971).

Figure 13. "Arab or leftist?" "Faggot." The figures represent officers of the
Republican Security Companies (CRS), the French riot police (among other
functions). Cartoon taken from Front homosexuel d'action révolutionnaire,
Rapport contre la normalité (1971); it first appeared in *Tout!* 13 (May 1971).

three "revolutionary" groups are wholly distinct, and also offers a reading
of the FHAR's arguments about the link between "faggot" and "Arab" that
had been trumpeted in the previous issue of its periodical. Yet while the
cartoon focuses on the formal aspects that link the three groups—shared
and state-sanctioned oppression—it ignores the content that, the FHAR
claimed, connected the three: sex.

It was not evident to everyone, however, that talk of sex—and homosexual sex in particular—would alienate either workers or Arabs. Sex radicals argued that sexually explicit language would bring the left closer to
the people, as it spoke to the heart of their lives and concerns. As Guattari
described in a text he wrote in 1974 to explain the importance of publishing "Three Billion Perverts": "To speak of sex is to come in contact with
the real practices of the masses: Pont de Clichy [an outdoor cruising area

in a neighborhood of Paris associated with Maghrebi immigrants], night-clubs, bistrots, it could be anything, and it's in no way just fags. Our universe has no limits. Ass-fucking, jacking off, these are everybody's sexual problems."[50] In a discussion of FHAR militants that appeared in the section of "Three Billion Perverts" titled "The Arabs and Us," one "M." sought to explain the politics of his connection with "the Arabs": "When I was a [leftist] militant, they told us that meant going into the working class and building relationships with young workers." The FHAR argued that sex created political relationships.

What was missing from other leftist groups, "M." argued, was a willingness to name these relationships and thus any ability to understand how they worked: "And I already had relationships with [young workers] who were drenched in eroticism, although nothing was stated." He explained that "basically [the party] asked us to seduce them into a relationship, to come onto them for the organization." He then sought to contrast that with the sexual relationships he had with young Arab workers: "But then with Arabs, at a hotel, it was something real, not just seduction camouflaged as politics."[51] The seeming crudeness of FHAR militants' descriptions of sex, according to this type of analysis, would allow real and meaningful political relationships to coalesce.

As some leftist responses to *Tout!* no. 12 had warned, the right-wing press proved eager to elaborate on any connection between homosexuals and Arabs in the most negative terms. As had been the case around May 1968, such references titillated readers at the same time as they insisted on the dangers that Arabs posed to France. An April 1973 article in *Le Figaro* titled "The Risks of Marching," for example, mocked the "freaky connections that emerge. . . . Young men, their eyes done up and their cheeks powdered, shoved the FHAR's newspaper into the hands of immigrant workers, as the latter chanted slogans, only one of them discernible: "*Même combat!* [Same struggle!]" In the FHAR committee newsletter that reproduced the article, a printed comment above it asked, "And why not?" In the far-right *Minute*, a mocking summary of *Tout!* no. 12 described the issue as "full of touching revelations about the services Arabs render to the sons of Sodom." Yet if some on the left were worried about how any mention

50. [Guattari], "Après la saisie."
51. This was consistent with a larger contemporary critique among leftists of the Communist Party's handling of sexual questions. See, e.g., François Delpla and Jean-Gabriel Foucaud, "Les communistes français et la sexualité (1932–1938)," *Le Mouvement social* 91 (April-June 1975), 121–152.

of homosexuality would alienate "Arab workers," the Arab influence drew far more concern on the far right. In *Minute*, the response to the FHAR's invocation of Arab men was straightforward: "In this domain, and perhaps others, reverse colonialism is at work."[52]

Rather than deny the stereotypes or to pretend that the smutty jokes were not about them, the FHAR's characteristic tactic was to embrace and reinterpret them. Arabs and homosexuals, its argument ran, did what time-honored folklore and pontificating experts repeatedly had established. This was a form of *détournement* (diversion), a tactic associated with the avant-garde revolutionary group the Situationist International and theorized by Guy Debord. As the historian Patrick Cardon explains the practice, "Something that, a priori, is banal can become something that brings the lies to light: all it takes is displacing it from one social context to another, from its original place to one that allows its critique to emerge."[53] In FHAR writings, "Arabs" and "fags" were perverts, but the definition of perversion was historical and political, part of wide-ranging efforts to control and limit what people could do with their bodies and other people. All people suffered from these harsh restrictions on whom they could connect to and in what ways, restrictions that alienated them from their desires. In 1974, with the world population reckoned at roughly three billion, the special issue of *Recherches* identified "Three Billion Perverts." Guattari described the publication thus: "It's the product of three billion individuals whose life experience of sexuality is marginal to the norm, a norm that itself can only be abstract. There is no healthy sexuality." There was only "perversion."[54] Certain people, however, blatantly violated the rules. Some—FHAR's sex radicals pointed to revolutionary homosexuals—suffered for their transgressions, yet supposedly also came to recognize their need for and pleasure in them. Their confrontation with what this meant provided the grounds on which political insight into how power worked and how it could be resisted became possible.

52. Jean-Pierre Mogui, "Les hasards du défilé," *Le Figaro* (10 April 1973); reproduced and commented on in *L'antinorm* 3 (1973), 13. Right-leaning and "popular" broadsheets also continued to give extensive coverage to murders and other crimes that involved "Arab" immigrants and homosexuals; see BDIC (fonds Daniel Guérin): F delta 721/15/3; "Le Front rose se met au Fhar rouge," *Minute* 475 (19 May 1971), 12.

53. Patrick Cardon, "Histoire d'une revue: *Le Fléau social* (1972–1974). Le mariage des situs et des pédés" (1999), http://semgai.free.fr/contenu/textes/p_Cardon_Fleau_social.html, accessed on 25 October 2014. On Debordian *détournement*, see, e.g., Anselm Jappe, *Guy Debord*, trans. Donald Nicholson-Smith (Berkeley: University of California Press, 1999), 48–73.

54. [Guattari], "Après la saisie."

The Revolutionary Politics of Arab Sexual Misery

To explain the supposedly widespread incidence of Algerian men in France having sex with French men, male sex radicals pointed to the "sexual misery" of immigrants in France. They also took up the Orientalist certainty that "Maghrebi" culture facilitated such sexual encounters. In their telling, the former was indicative of how the existing order limited the human potential of all people. They presented the latter as another way in which North Africa could serve as a model for French liberation—notably when Arab men confronted life in France, for it allowed them to find escape routes from sexual misery that challenged French sociosexual orthodoxy. Rather than simply being victims of the sexual repression from which all exploited people suffered, they rebelled. The ways in which racism and ongoing colonialism exacerbated their sexual misery rendered this form of capitalist oppression more visible to them, and less acceptable. In rebelling against it, they opened connections with suffering homosexuals, and this made it possible for homosexual "revolutionaries" to come to new understandings about repression and revolution. In a move that several outside commentators at the time identified as novel, a number of FHAR writings targeted neither "the West" nor the Orient, but "Judeo-Christian civilization" and "Judeo-Christian religion" for their repressive and destructive approach to sexuality.[55]

The positive references of the FHAR to the Arab world rehearsed claims typical of various "homophile" organizations. The founders of this earlier transnational movement had adopted this desexualized term to advance their embrace of "normality" as the grounds from which to question social restrictions on same-sex sex and sexuality, and to work with existing authorities to reform them. In the 1950s United States, for example, the homophile magazines *One* and *Mattachine* published numerous articles that urged Western societies to learn from the more liberal attitudes toward sex in Muslim and Arab countries. "In some respects the Orient . . . [is] ideal for the gay element," the inaugural issue of *One* announced; a 1958 article tied a similar claim to references to the Algerian revolution and Lawrence

---

55. For FHAR critiques of "Judeo-Christian" civilization and religion, see, e.g., the FHAR flyer "Le FHAR répond à la Déclaration écrite du 18 octobre 1971 de Roland Castro" (October/ November 1971), in BDIC (fonds Daniel Guérin): F delta 721/15/1, 1–2; Guy Maës and Anne-Marie Fauret, "Homosexualité et socialisme," *L'Antinorm* 1 (1973), 3–5. For claims that the use of "Judeo-Christian" was novel, see Gabriel Glazounov, "Opprimées oppressantes: Le livre de l'oppression des femmes," *Politique hebdo (nouvelle formule)* 6 (1971), 20.

of Arabia.[56] A 1964 French study celebrated "how Islam adopted such a different attitude toward homosexuality than Christianity did." Unlike both Jews and Christians, the author proclaimed, "Among the Arabs, the evolution developed in the direction of more indulgence and an adaptation to the actual mores of peoples who converted to the Muslim faith."[57] In January 1954, the first issue of *Arcadie*—a French "homophile" monthly that sought to elevate and desexualize discussions about homosexual men and women—centered around a short story by the well-known right-wing essayist and novelist Roger Peyrefitte titled "The Little Arab Boy." Subsequently, *Arcadie* regularly ran articles about Arabs and North Africa. The inspirational impulse behind such discussions was flagrant in the opening lines of one of a series of 1955 articles on "Aspects of North Africa," which reassured readers that "it is rather difficult to talk of the 'homosexual problem' in North Africa because there practically is no problem."[58] In the mid-1970s, *Arcadie* published a celebratory nine-part series on "Arab Civilization and Masculine Love," one indication of the ongoing attraction this rose-colored vision exercised.[59]

Against a Glorious "Homophile" History

Like other groups of the post-1968 new left, the FHAR harshly rejected the generation of activists that came before, both in the name of a more forceful radicalism and through an embrace of new forms of political action that foregrounded spectacle and personal testimonial. As soon as it was born in the early 1970s, the FHAR had positioned itself in loud opposition to the assimilationist, anti-flamboyant homophile movement, which the organization Arcadie had embodied in France. The former seminarian André Baudry had started Arcadie in 1953, and its eponymously titled magazine quickly established a durable public presence. The group's Parisian club, a space that welcomed expert discussions and members-only meetings as well as weekly dances, had played a crucial role in reinforcing its network of homophiles, which included both women and, in greater numbers, men (there was not a separate homophile organization for women).

56. See David S. Churchill, "Transnationalism and Homophile Political Culture in the Postwar Decades," *GLQ* 15, no. 1 (2008), 31–66; Bruno Roger Vitale, "Arab Revolt," *One* 6 (1958), 1–9. On French homophile activism, see Jackson, *Living in Arcadia*.

57. Raymond De Becker, *L'Érotisme d'en face* (Paris: Jean-Paul Pauvert, 1964), 75.

58. Adrien Robert, "Aspects d'Afrique du Nord, Algérie," *Arcadie* 18 (June 1955), 17–21.

59. E.g., Marc Daniel, "La civilisation arabe et l'amour masculine. Partie III: Le Coran et l'homosexualité," *Arcadie* 255 (March 1975), 142–150.

These institutions, along with an annual gala dinner-debate, had allowed
Arcadie to build ties to influential authorities in the realms of religion,
medicine, law, and politics.[60] The women and men who set up the FHAR
were members of Arcadie, and they first discussed their plans at the club.
Yet intense criticism of Arcadie's conservative politics—its supposed embrace of gender and social cultural norms; its assimilationist agenda, which
took mainstream models of the family and of male and female behavior
as the norm; its eagerly cultivated ties with the Catholic Church and the
police; its pointed instructions to members about the need for discretion,
for blending in, and even for secrecy—justified the FHAR's claims to be
radically different.

Crucial to the FHAR's radical critique of its predecessors was its rejection of the quest to preserve and convey the "secret homophile past"—with
its golden ages, heroes, and martyrs—that had so obsessed Arcadie (and,
indeed, all other Western efforts to bring together so-called homosexuals
across the twentieth century). The FHAR mocked and rejected the work of
Arcadie to fabricate and distribute lists of famous (dead) homosexuals (in
1969, for example, the monthly magazine included reports on Louis Massignon, the renowned French "Islamologist," along with one on Lawrence
of Arabia)[61] as well as the group's sentimental efforts to explain important past relationships between men, or between women, as "homophile"
in nature. The clearest sign of this in FHAR-related texts was the virtual
disappearance of ancient Greece as a touchstone or symbolic reference—
although there were, on occasion, "Greek" images, notably in certain publications by groups associated with the FHAR. Homophiles had identified ancient Greece as a model of how truly advanced societies celebrated
same-sex attractions. They paid no attention to the fact that the Greek texts
they cited spoke only of love between elite males. In this, they adopted
late-nineteenth-century claims by commentators such as the Ango-Irish
playwright, writer, and homosexual martyr Oscar Wilde.[62] Such references
seemed too obviously elitist and male to most around the FHAR. They presented their interest in Algerian men, however, as a way to link their concerns about domination and masculinity with a political analysis of the

60. Jackson, *Living in Arcadia*.

61. Françoise d'Eaubonne, "Le cas de Lawrence d'Arabie," *Arcadie* 203 (November 1970),
548–554; Serge Talbot, "Louis Massignon et les saints apotropéens," *Arcadie* 205 (January
1971) 38–44.

62. On this phenomenon among US "homophiles," see Amy Richlin, "Eros Underground: Greece and Rome in Gay Print Culture, 1953–65," *Journal of Homosexuality* 49, no. 3-4
(2005), 421–461.

colonial history of France. Unlike in ancient Greece, the actions and agency of Arab men in the present against colonial, racist, and capitalist oppression appeared to make evocations of Arabs political.

Anticolonial Arabophilia?

In some ways, the FHAR's Arab fixation was in clear continuity with Arcadie, for its publications referenced Arabs often, and always represented them in sexually charged ways. What rendered it different from homophile writings, FHAR writers argued, was their effort to decolonize eroticized Arab references. They frequently identified anti-imperialism as foundational to their own ideology, which aligned them with most on the new left. Sometimes this meant self-consciously identifying their struggles with those who struggled against empire, just as they and others on the new left did in reference to antiracist politics. A 1972 tract explained, "WE, the homosexuals, are oppressed by bourgeois domination. The peoples of Indochina are oppressed by imperialist domination. Our liberation, like that of oppressed peoples, will take place in the frame of a political struggle against all forms of domination: ideological, political, imperialist, the domination of women, etc." Their anti-imperialism led "numerous FHAR comrades" to participate in the "commemoration of the tenth anniversary of the drama that cost the lives of eight people at the Charonne Métro station" in the last months of the Algerian war, when the police rushed a massive crowd protesting against the pro-French Algeria terrorist organization, the OAS. In the midst of that demonstration, some of the FHAR militants heard news that a twenty-three-year-old Maoist militant named Pierre Overney had been killed in a protest outside a Renault factory on the outskirts of Paris. They alerted the crowd and "came up with the slogan, taken up by a chorus of 1,500 people: Yesterday, CHARONNE, Today, RENAULT."[63] Unlike most leftists, however, their writings actively engaged the colonial politics of sex in France.

Numerous FHAR texts situated "European" Frenchmen's current sexual encounters with Algerian men in France in the context of histories of colonial domination and anticolonial resistance. An article in *Tout!* no.12 expressed regret that "everyone is stuck on the image of the old European fag getting off on little Arab boys." The sentences that followed went to the heart of the complex, vexed issue of the FHAR's attitude toward same-sex

63. "Au dehors!" FHAR no. 2 (1972), in IMEC: ABN 32.3 Collection Françoise d'Eaubonne/le FHAR.

erotic relations between "Europeans" and "Arabs": "Besides the fact that it was never as simple as that, let us note that, in France, it's our Arab friends who fuck us and never the reverse." The text then challenged the idea that this was just a stereotype, or that it reflected something inherent in either partner. "Isn't it obvious that this is a form of revenge, offered to them by us, against the Western colonizer?" Hocquenghem's version of anticolonial activism via sex was the most detailed. He argued that "between many Arab men and many homosexual men, there are desiring relationships that are unacceptable"—universally rejected not merely because they involved homosexual acts, but because they challenged and revealed the dense and violent history of racist imperialism. They were, that is, both desired and possible because of this history.[64] This history also, most importantly, made these "desiring relationships" so meaningful.

The continued significance of colonialism in France, such statements suggested, went far in explaining why French male homosexuals and Maghrebi male immigrants had different relationships to history and, therefore, different sexual needs. In a claim that had wide currency among 1970s leftists, one article published in "Three Billion Perverts" (1973) asserted that the Algerian war had given Algerians back their virility ("to be colonized is to lose some of one's manliness"). In turn, the FHAR argued that its embrace of effeminacy, of transvestism, of sexual "passivity," of "perversion," and its rejection of bourgeois morality at once directly challenged repressive norms on which patriarchy depended and made possible the connection forged with immigrant Arab men. As Arabs emerged from direct colonial rule of the Maghreb and into a post-decolonization racist society in France, and as "homosexual men" struggled with the weight of phallocratic oppression, their historically produced complementary desires made sexual connections more likely and mutually pleasurable. References to this unlikely couple functioned as empirical evidence of the acuteness of their analysis and the promise of their vanguardist vision.[65] Groups such as the FHAR could make "a [political] intervention that is not based on principled solidarity but on a relationship of desire." On this basis Hocquenghem insisted that now, in early 1970s France, such sex between "many Arab men and many homosexual men" opened up space for utopian politics.[66]

What Orientalist arguments—reframed by the far right for post-decolonization France—pronounced to be perversions typical and reve-

64. Hocquenghem, *La dérive homosexuelle* (Paris: Universitaires / Jean-Pierre Delarge, 1977), 109–110.

65. "Vingt ans de drague," *Recherches* 12 (1973), 55–60.

66. Hocquenghem, *La dérive homosexuelle*, 109–110.

latory of Arabs and Muslims, this FHAR discourse presented as the very grounds and model for radical politics. A left-wing politics of group difference, what Foucault termed "coalition politics" (yet here explicitly framed by the lessons of anticolonialism), becomes visible in FHAR writings.[67] It was possible, these arguments suggested, to recognize that different people had particular needs (sexual, among others) and struggles that were distinct from other groups of people because of history and politics and, at the same time, to make revolutionary connections (through sex as well as by other means). On the non-Leninist far left in the early 1970s, the code words that signaled this argument were "specificity," "autonomy," and "particularity." From this perspective, the Corsican and Occitan peoples, each fighting to maintain their culture against the French language, state and, society, had "specific" needs. Women's fight for equality and against misogyny was "specific"; even the industrial strikes by the Renault workers at the Flins factory or by the women of the Lip watch company had their "specificity," which could not be reduced to "the workers' struggle." The Mouvement des travailleurs Arabes (Movement of Arab Workers) highlighted its fight for the "autonomy" of "Arab workers" to direct their own struggles in France.[68] Yet all of these "particularities," many militants of the new left argued, were part of a joint struggle against oppression and capitalist exploitation. This was one of the ways in which new leftists distinguished themselves from the "Stalinists" (far-left commentators always put the "Communist" in the French Communist Party in quotation marks) and all other "reductive" Marxists who insisted that only class mattered. As Hocquenghem stated in defense of East Pakistan's 1971 revolt against West Pakistan, "Revolutionary analysis is universal in that its point of departure is the particular, and not when it refuses the particular as abnormal." As the reference to East Pakistan suggested, this vision of the importance of difference derived directly from new-left, notably "tiers-mondiste" analyses of the "revolutionary nationalism" that proponents identified as emblematic of anti-imperialist movements, especially in Palestine, Cuba, Vietnam, and Algeria.[69]

67. Foucault and Deleuze, "Intellectuals and Power." For the classic critique of Foucault's definition, see Spivak, "Can the Subaltern Speak?"

68. P. Mazodier (Salindres), "Nos lecteurs interviennnent: Comprendre la lutte des minorités ethniques," *Politique-hebdo (nouvelle formule)* 2 (1971), 3.

69. Guy Hocquenghem, "Vive le Bengale libre," *Tout!* 13 (May 1971); See Hosek, "Subaltern Nationalism"; and Bill Marshall, *Guy Hocquenghem: Beyond Gay Identity* (Durham, NC: Duke University Press, 1997), 6–8.

The Relationships of Coalition

In their effort to define their claims as political, even revolutionary, FHAR militants insistently pointed to what their sex talk about Arabs revealed about France's Algerian history. FHAR writings posited that their sexual relations with Algerian immigrants linked together two "specific" struggles—of immigrant Maghrebi workers and of homosexuals—and sharpened the revolutionary consciousness of each: through anticolonial sex, perhaps, but also through mutual recognition and assistance, which created relationships. There were boundaries, which history and politics had created, that required "autonomy," and yet it was revolutionary to make the *mutual* choice to connect across them. Since sex was political, sexual connections could build such coalitions. These arguments were part of something larger than gay politics. Their reveries suggested how crucial claims of meaningful difference between French and Algerians were both to French politics, on the far left as well as more broadly, and to ongoing efforts by French people to define themselves.

Left-wing accusations that such statements were deeply problematic (including numerous critiques published by other FHAR militants) closed down this discussion. Quite quickly after the publication of *Tout!* no. 12, voices aligned with the group expressed variations of the concern that others on the left had articulated. In early 1973, an article on "Arab bisexuality" that appeared in a FHAR-associated periodical, regretted that "ever since FHAR was formed, the 'Arab' question upset people each time we tried to raise it, became a taboo question, which provoked discomfort and avoidance." The pseudonymous author, Laboulu, recounted that "during a General Assembly that took place at [the University of] Vincennes on Monday, 4 December [1972] on 'sexual repression' . . . we witnessed the participants come to an agreement, in fact, to stop the debate, under the pretext that a meeting would be dedicated to [the 'Arab' question] 'later, some other day.'" In this author's analysis, the debate closed down because "this taboo"—against directly addressing "the question of 'Arabs'"—"has yet to be destroyed."[70] Yet others associated with FHAR challenged the presumption that what was at stake was a "taboo," and argued instead that "the question of 'Arabs'" had revealed profound problems in the group's analytic and political strategies. Deleuze described these problems straightforwardly in his contemporaneous "Letter to a Harsh Critic" (1973). "The text 'The Arabs and Us,'" he declared, is "even more oedipal than my daughter."

70. *Antinorm* 2, (February-March 1973).

A text published in "Three Billion Perverts" pinpointed the alienating effects of the publication of "an issue published about Arabs with no Arab [participation]."[71]

Ending the Discussion

The French left more broadly, French sex radicals, and the nascent gay rights movement all quickly moved away from engaging with the very explicit claims that FHAR publications made about how at least some French people enjoyed the Arab presence in France. Ironically, this silence reaffirmed the belief of some that racism was an uncomplicated and easily identified problem that could be avoided by ignoring the multiple registers and hierarchies through which difference functions. As President Georges Pompidou warned in September 1973, in the face of heightened racial tension and the murder of dozens of Algerian immigrants: "Let's not let France get dragged into a cycle of accusations of racism. Sometimes, just pronouncing the word summons to mind such ideas, and sometimes reality follows on from those ideas."[72] To speak about or fight against racism, in this view, was to contribute to it. The far right continued to link sex and Arabs to advance its agendas. Antiracist calls for silence failed to close this down. So did French men who identified as homosexuals, as the next chapter explores. There were plenty of references to Arabs in subsequent gay publications and debates. What was missing was any sustained effort to think politically about why "out" homosexuals felt it necessary to engage in this discussion, or to explore its history.

71. "Lettre à Michel Cressole," La Quinzaine littéraire 161 (1 April 1973), 17–19; reprinted as "Lettre à un critique sévère," in Deleuze, Pourparlers (Paris: Minuit, 1990), 11–23.

72. In Le Monde, (1 September1973), cited and translated in Aissaoui, North African, 188.

FOUR

Homosociality, "Human Contact," and the Specter of the Arab Man in the Post-'68 French Gay World

In fall 1979, the widely read French women's magazine *Marie-Claire* published an article in which, as in most issues, an anonymous woman told her story. "I Discovered His Homosexuality and I Married Him All the Same" recounted what its title promised—and a bit more. This coming-out narrative appeared just around the time the term and the concept had been imported to France (as "*le coming out*") from the United States. Yet the author's description of this revelation, which contained a very telling clause, could only have appeared in French. "P explained to me that he could no longer hide from me that which he had tried to hide: that he was a homosexual, that he loved Arab men."[1] What the quoted phrase asserts as self-evident—an association between (male) homosexuality and Arab men, one that perhaps hints at an equivalency—was yet another aspect of the erotics of Algerian difference that structured post-decolonization French discussions. In 1970s France, as in the sexual Orientalism of previous eras, explanations for this link varied, but almost all fixated on attributes imagined as inherent to Arabs—from perversion to open-mindedness, from lack of guilt to uncontrollable lusts—rather than questions of historical

1. (Propos recuilli par) Pierre Demeros, "Une femme raconte: J'ai découvert son homosexualité et je l'ai épousé quand meme," *Marie Claire* 325 (September 1979), 207–217. On "coming out" in France, see Michel Pollak, "Les vertus de la banalité," *Le Débat* 10 (1981), 132–143. The well known contemporary Spanish author Juan Goytisolo recounts in his memoirs that he made almost exactly the same declaration to his (French) wife in 1963: "It must be about a year ago [seemingly 1962] that I started to go out with Arabs and I needed a few weeks to recognize the evidence . . . that I was totally, definitively, irrevocably homosexual." He wrote the letter in Paris and in French. See *Realms of Strife: The Memoirs of Juan Goytisolo, 1957–1982*; trans. Peter Bush (San Francisco: North Point Press, 1990), 205; Bush's English translation cited here is based on the text in the 1986 Spanish-language memoir and not the French letter. Earlier, writer André Gide, among others, tied his own sexual discovery of male-male sex and his own homosexuality to Algerians.

context.[2] Although certain "revolutionary homosexuals" had invoked these connections to make political claims, proposing the Arab man as a source of radical solutions to French (sexual) problems, such efforts to think with this model faded quickly after the FHAR collapsed in 1973.

The specter of the Arab man loomed large in the much broader gay world that, beyond radical politics, emerged in 1970s France, made public through its bars, neighborhoods, magazines, films, pornography, sex shops, novels, community groups, and public intellectuals and given depth by the relationships it nourished, of love, friendships, and sex. This chapter explores how gay male discussions outside of the FHAR, most of which took place after the sharp rise and quick fade of radical gay liberation in France, continued to include a lot of Arab men, and why this sex talk mattered. Other perspectives also appear, offered by individuals who, as in *Marie-Claire*, kept the issue of homosexuality alive while declining to identify as gay. Maghrebi (male) commentators and authors were the most significant. Their interest in "gay male" sex talk about Arab men challenged claims from gay observers even as it also suggested the importance of the topic. After decolonization, that is, Maghrebi perspectives as well as Orientalist fantasies directly shaped how gay life and identities took shape in the crucible of the sexual revolution.[3] By the late 1970s, such tensions between explicitly "gay" and "Arab" depictions and explanations provoked a sharp division between some of the most audible gay voices. While a few invoked the Arab man to critique the emerging gay world and its relationship to the larger "hetero" word, others celebrated it, dismissing such arguments and the vision of the Arab man they relied on. Like the other public debates this book explores, this crisis produced no synthesis. Instead, the topic withered from view.

The Post-'68 Victory of the Hetero-Homo Binary?

The 1970s were a moment when, across the West, efforts to explain why certain males had sex with or desired other males grew in importance. The most well known of these efforts came from gay liberationists and their

2. Ideas about "the Orient" and male-male sex date back to at least the First Crusade, although they took on a new life in the late nineteenth century, with the emergence of a scientific discussion about homosexuality that coincided with the extension of French imperial rule over Algeria, Tunisia, and later Morocco.

3. This contribution has been missed by scholars such as Joseph Massad, "Re-Orienting Desire: The Gay International and the Arab World," *Public Culture* 14, no. 2 (Spring 2002), 361–385; or Jaspir Puar, *Terrorist Assemblages: Homo-Nationalism in Queer Times* (Durham, NC: Duke University Press, 2007).

allies, who urged lesbians and gays to "come out," to reveal their true sexuality, which militants argued would facilitate the struggle for social acceptance of homosexual people. This and other public discussions of same-sex sexual behavior increasingly fixed such acts and desires to homosexual identities, male and female. The idea was that the identities of most people are defined in fundamentally important ways by their attraction to members of the opposite sex, while attraction to those of the same sex defines the identities of a minority. Since the 1970s, however, certain scholars have challenged this view that "sexual identity" is an unchanging truth. These analyses tend not to focus on how specific individuals understand their attractions and emotions. Instead, historical research reveals that there have been enormous variations in the social understandings that determine how or even whether individuals try to interpret the meaning of their erotic attractions, or how they experience the erotic or affective acts and relationships they participate in or desire. These historical shifts in understanding also shape how contemporaries assess those acts and relationships. Such research reveals that sex and sexuality have histories, which change over time. Historian George Chauncey, in his influential *Gay New York* (1994), argues that "it was only between the 1930s and 1950s" that the view that all people were either heterosexual or homosexual became "the hegemonic way of understanding sexuality," at least in the United States. Until then, words such as "homosexual" existed, but in most discussions they referenced, as historian Margot Canaday puts it, "a perverted type whose perversion was defined primarily by gender inversion (mannishness in women and effeminacy in men) rather than by sexual behavior per se." Even in assessments of sex acts between men, she emphasizes, "it was that perverts wanted to be penetrated *like women*, rather than the fact that they had sex with men, that made them perverse." The novel definition of people in terms of their desire for members of one sex or the other gained considerable popular acceptance in the mid-twentieth-century United States. This "hetero-homosexual binarism" also encompassed women and, in subsequent decades, became pervasive and culturally important in multiple other so-called developed societies. In France, according to historian Régis Revenin, a similar shift took place in the 1960s. Chauncey's use of "hegemonic" suggests that it became impossible in such societies to have discussions about human sexual behavior without engaging with this argument. This dramatically shaped lived experience. As he explains in the US case, this meant that "men were no longer able to participate in a homosexual encounter without suspecting it meant (to the outside world, and to themselves) that they were gay."[4] This binarized vision set the stage for a newly visible gay world to emerge—one that resembles, in its key references, that which still exists today.

This hetero-homosexual binarism, some scholars suggest, largely squeezed out the strikingly plural forms of living, thinking, and managing sexual encounters that previously had made modern sexualities so "fluid and contingent," in the historian of Britain Frank Mort's assessment.[5] Starting in the 1970s, in France as in countries such as the USA and Germany, a number of scholars argue, activists who fought for gay and lesbian liberation advanced claims about human sexuality that did much to narrow contemporary thinking about sexuality. Many in the newly "out" gay world emphatically rejected the "closeted" past, and showed particular disdain for public attention to gender inversion. Before the post-'68 birth of "gay liberation," in their read, malignant stereotypes that reduced homosexuality to gender nonconformity ("mannishness in women and effeminacy in men," which in France was associated with effeminate male *tantes* and *folles*, and masculine female *jules* and *gouines*) had made it impossible for gay and lesbians to live fully human lives, much less "come out." In the 1970s, publications and statements by lesbians as well as gay men in the United States, the United Kingdom, Germany, and France celebrated sexual versatility and shared identities among sexual and romantic partners. All rejected the starkly gendered roles they associated with previous generations, notably the presumed connection that linked "masculine" to insertive sex acts, and "feminine" to receptive. Some militants argued

4. Chauncey, *Gay New York: Gender, Urban Culture, and the Making of the Gay Male World, 1890–1940* (New York: Basic Books, 1994), 13–14, 22; Margot Canaday, *The Straight State: Sexuality and Citizenship in Twentieth-Century America* (Princeton, NJ: Princeton University Press, 2009), 11, 11fn32 (emphasis in original). For post-1945 France, see esp. Régis Revenin, *Une histoire des garçons*, esp. 157–167. He notes that "starting in the 1960s . . . boys increasingly tended to place themselves in one or the other categories proposed by a sexual world that had come to be understood as binary" (160).

5. Frank Mort, *Dangerous Sexualities: Medico-Moral Politics in England since 1830*, 2nd ed. (London: Routledge, 2000), xxiv; for France, see also Revenin, *Une histoire des garçons*, 324. For an analysis of this earlier way of thinking about gender, sex, and identity in France, see Laure Murat, *La loi du genre: Une histoire culturelle du "troisième sexe"* (Paris: Fayard, 2006). Among the texts that anchored such historical work, see esp. Michel Foucault, *The History of Sexuality*; John D'Emilio, "Capitalism and Gay Identity," in *Powers of Desire: The Politics of Sexuality*, ed. Ann Snitow, Christine Stansell, and Sharon Thompson (New York: Monthly Review Press, 1983), 100–113; Eve Kosofsky Sedgwick, "Introduction: Axiomatic," in *Epistemology of the Closet* (Berkeley: University of California Press (1990), 1–65; Didier Eribon, *Réflexions sur la question gay* (Paris: Fayard, 1999); David Halperin, *How to Do the History of Homosexuality* (Chicago: University of Chicago Press, 2002).

that "liberated" homosexuals had to be sexually "versatile," to enjoy all forms of sex that homosexuality made possible.[6] Queer theorists and revisionist historians such as Chauncey, Canaday, Revenin, and Mort, in turn, have worked to recover the vibrant multiplicity that gay liberation helped push to the side.

The "Arab" Alternative to the Hetero-Homo Binary

The substantial role that "the Arab man" played in 1970s French discussions—especially those that emerged from within the gay world—troubles this story. The closet was not the only way of thinking sexual diversity. In the early 1970s, gay liberationists in the FHAR referenced Arab men to reject essentialized identities—for although their writings detailed seemingly static types of sexual relationship that linked "Arabs" (active *enculeurs*) and "homos" (passive *enculés*), they argued that this resulted from the historical conjuncture—from the continued importance, even post-decolonization—of colonial forms of domination and sexual repression, rather than revealing the truth about male "Arab" or "homo" sexuality. But that moment passed quickly. Across the era of coming out, the Arab man incarnated a different relationship between visibility, sex acts, and gendered identities than did the proud homosexual. The insistent linkage of Arab men to virility and sexual dominance, a particularity of sex talk in these years, framed these tensions. In the 1979 *Marie-Claire* article, the husband's Arab lover is also married. But while the Frenchman struggles to reconcile his wish to marry the woman he loves with his homosexual desires, the Arab lover has no such problems. This man appears to move easily from his wife's bed to that of his male lover—because, the article suggests, he plays the sexual role of the man in both. Gender, gendered roles, sex acts, and sexual identities lined up in ways that on the face of it escaped any easy division between heterosexual and homosexual. In 1970s French discussions, the Arab man embodied only one such arrangement: that of the manly man who sexually penetrated other people, no matter whom. This helps explain the striking absence of the effeminate Arab "ephebe," a staple of sexual Orientalism in other eras.[7] This was a different way of structuring conceptions of sexual pleasure and social identities, which tended to challenge gay liberationists' story of progress, of an escape from "the closet"

---

6. See, e.g., David M. Halperin, *How to be Gay* (Cambridge, MA: Harvard University Press, 2012), 55.

7. On the ephebe, see Boone, *The Homoerotics of Orientalism*, esp. 51–110; and Robert Aldrich, *Colonialism and Homosexuality* (New York: Routledge, 2008).

that was propelled by political activism. Or, more accurately, this French history raises key questions about existing historical accounts, which affirm that the post-'68 development of the contemporary gay world also ironically marked the triumph of hetero-homo binarism.

This is precisely why the Arab question offers new ways to think about this moment in the history of homo- and heterosexuality, in France and elsewhere. Social historical work on the United States after the June 1969 Stonewall Riots in New York City has begun to sap the claim that binarism became hegemonic among all people in that country. Still today, some scholars now recognize, multiple sexual cultures continue to coexist inside of Western nation-states, even if mainstream discussions ignore them. As was the case with Arabs in 1970s France, it was the persistence of racialized, religious, and post-decolonization identities and networks that anchored these minority sexual cultures, notably in the United States.[8] It was only in post-Algerian France, however, that, in the very years that it appeared on the larger public stage, the gay world was in a quite visible, sometimes tense dialogue about the coexistence of such a sexual culture. Which raises the question of why racialized and imperial questions have been ignored in histories of contemporary French homosexuality, given that after 1962 they were foundational.

Commentators over the course of the 1970s used references to the Arab man to raise questions about hetero-homo binarism. Renaud Camus, who became a literary celebrity in 1979, was a cheerleader for the new gay world, applauding the truth of this division and rejecting other ways of thinking about sexual identities. He dismissed the "Arab" and mocked "a flourishing tradition among homosexuals, above all those of a certain age, that celebrates Mediterranean sexuality: over there, they say, all men are like that." At the same moment, the FHAR-associated philosopher Guy Hocquenghem published *La beauté de métis* (The Beauty of the métis, 1979), a call for more connections, sexual among them, that crossed—and blurred—racial and national boundaries.[9] Such discussions questioned the centrality of consumerism and social class to a gay world more interested

8. George Chauncey makes this argument, notably concerning Latino and African-American communities. See his interview with Philippe Mangeot, "De l'autre côté du placard," *Vacarme* 26 (2004), 4–12. It is widely recognized that, across the era of coming out, certain iconoclasts rejected so-called binarism; in the US case, one well-known example is Gore Vidal (see, e.g., his "Some Jews and the Gays," *Nation* (14 November 1981), 489–97. This phenomenon is distinct from the persistence of minority sexual cultures.

9. Renaud Camus and Tony Duparc, *Travers. Roman* (Paris: Hachette, 1978), 127. "Tony Duparc" was a pseudonym Camus used to create the impression that the text had two authors; Guy Hocquenghem, *La Beauté du métis: Réflexions d'un francophobe* (Paris: Ramsay, 1979).

in new possibilities for public acceptance, love and mutual desire. By the end of the 1970s, this chapter shows, certain assumptions that had anchored widespread references to the Arab man in gay discussions became untenable. Rather than rethinking the Arab question, however, gay writers and commentators on French homosexuality largely stopped referencing it, except for titillation.

Copi's Tales of the New Gay World

During the 1970s, a growing number of fictional and nonfictional texts detailed the contours of the French gay world for readers, with explicit descriptions of who did what to whom and where. Of those focused on male homosexuality, many, perhaps most, included depictions of Arab men and noted their importance to gay life. These texts presented them as a group apart from *"les homos,"* yet in a binary relationship without whom—like "women," "lesbians," or "heterosexuals" (especially males)—the reality of the male homosexual could not be mapped. This is particularly visible in the dark and sparkling 1977 novel, *Le bal des folles* (The Fairies' Ball), by the exiled Argentine writer and cartoonist Copi ("My name is Raúl Damonte but I sign my books Copi," as the novel puts it).[10] In a move quite typical of the era, with its proclaimed openness to sex and its incitation for multiple truths about identity (and sex) to be shared with larger publics, the narrator, also named Copi, announces his need to "recount the homosexual social life of the era in St.-Germain[-des-Près, Paris]."[11] As the novel presents it, Copi's task is to write a novel for which his editor will pay him. The depiction of the period from mid-1960s until 1977 is rich with innumerable references to verifiable names, dates, and publications that align with what we know of Copi's own life and the France he lived in. The handwritten notebooks in which he first wrote and revised the text that became the novel offer additional depth and details.[12] The novel had some public success, in part because Copi himself was quite well known to theatrical and literary audiences and, as a cartoonist, to a much broader public. Copi was one of a remarkable generation of acerbic and leftist cartoonists ("Wolin-

10. Copi, *Le bal des folles* (Paris: Christian Bourgois, 1977), 52. Calder Publications (London) announced an English translation for 1999, which would have been titled *Drag Ball*. It never appeared.

11. Copi, *Le bal*, 16.

12. See David Wetsel, "Copi (Pseud. of Raúl Damonte; Argentina; 1941–1987)," in *Latin American Writers on Gay and Lesbian Themes: A Bio-Critical Sourcebook*, ed. David William Foster (Westport, CT: Greenwood Press, 1994), 116–121.

ski" and "Sempé," for example, are mentioned as colleagues in the first pages of the novel), his risqué "The Woman Who Sits" appeared weekly in the *Nouvel observateur*, and he had also—this was less widely known—penned cartoons for FHAR publications such as "Three Billion Perverts."[13]

To narrate the gay world, Copi needed interactions with Arab men, but their definitional role was always at once liminal, not fully part of this world, and deeply erotic. In the published text of the novel, the first two sexual encounters that the narrator details involve Arabs. Here again, the crude descriptions and the clearly framed distinctions between "Arab" and "homo" make these aspects of the text exemplary rather than exceptional. Copi's description of his encounter with the first man, "ugly and pretty old," in the downstairs bathroom of a cheap Parisian restaurant recounts both sex acts, where he plays one role and the man the other—"I blew him. He buggered me"—and the notable absence of any verbal exchange before, during, or after. Their exchange of glances—"He looked at me, I met his stare"—and then of clearer invitations—"I smiled a bit while also rubbing my zipper. He too grabbed himself, while looking very serious"—further discloses a world of shared signs and complementary pleasures that each player enters for distinct reasons and histories.[14] The second encounter with an Arab man, a taxi driver who brings him back and forth to the airport, also ends in a long and even more detailed sex scene in which Copi puts on a dress and then the man focuses wholly on "the buttocks." It begins, however, with the driver's question, "You like boys?"—which sets up the narrator's "And you, I asked him? He smiled into the rearview mirror." As Copi presents it, the answer appears beautifully clear and without evasion, even as it avoids any mention of gender, sex, or sexuality: "Me, I'm Moroccan."[15] *what . . .*

The published version of Copi's fictionalized history of gay Paris from the Swinging Sixties until the present (1965–1976) contains numerous other references to Arabs and North Africans. The notebooks that make

---

13. Copi, *Le bal*, 18–19. Wolinski was murdered in the massacre of the staff of *Charlie-Hebdo* on 7 January 2015 in Paris. These cartoonists, among others, were the subject of an exhibit at the BDIC in 1989–90. See Laurence Bertrand-Dorléac, "L'histoire croquée sur le vif," *Vingtieme siecle: Revue d'histoire* 27, no. 1 (1990), 110–111. In a 1978 article about an electoral list made up of gay rights activists, a far-right journalist noted that "one of the campaign's few merits . . . was to have uncovered a little-known side of the person who was for many years the star cartoonist for the *Nouvel observateur* and the idol of the intelligentsia: the Argentine Copi, who authored the poster of the [list] known as 'the faggots.'" See "Homos, mais pas élus," *Minute* 822 (22 March 1978), 3.

14. Copi, *Le bal*, 30.

15. Copi, *Le bal*, 47–51.

up the original manuscript, however, dramatize just how crucial such men were to his ability to map gay Paris. As in many of his archived manuscripts, the references to the Maghreb shrank dramatically as he wrote and revised *Le bal des folles*. What such revisions—the substantive cuts, handwritten corrections, and additions—suggest most obviously was how much the writer had to struggle to find other ways to mark spaces and encounters as queer, or even to define what it meant to be homosexual in Paris. In his writing, homosexuality always meant something more than just sex, and interactions between homosexuals ranged far beyond the explicitly sexual. Yet Copi's references to Arab men always made clear that homosexual sex did not mean that all partners were homosexual. They sometimes suggested that, at least in France, for homosexuals to have sex, Arab men were necessary.

In the manuscript, as in the published text, the chronology begins in 1965. Yet the notebook recounts that "he landed in Paris in 1965 when he was 18 years old and with only one idea in mind: meet some homosexuals." (In the book, it is the year "when I began to live publicly as a homosexual after having more or less hid it for quite a while," a rewrite that privileges the revelation of a preexisting identity over the productive role of interpersonal connections.)[16] He visits the most well-known homosexual hangouts and quickly picks one out, a "blond young man" whom he first sees "at café de Flore" and then "later, at Fiacre." He has found a fellow homosexual, but the encounter that sexualizes his entry into the gay world happens that evening, "at three in the morning," when he and the blond young man go to a late-night bar where "together they flirted with an Arab and brought him to a dark entryway." As the manuscript reveals, when Copi wrote a description of the Carrefour de Buci, his first impulse was to place "North Africans" there, before crossing it out and settling on "little twinks, badboys" (while in the published novel, only a subsequently added "transvestites" appears).[17] He also cut the narrator's reflection that "if I were younger I would probably have fallen in love with a Moroccan like so many other French fairies." Those who had more choices, that line suggested, chose to love men who themselves were neither homosexual nor French. The FHAR had pioneered arguments for the "right to be different" that challenged universalist ideas about left-wing politics and France. However, Copi's text was indicative of a "desire for difference," which em-

16. Copi, *Le bal*, 23.

17. Copi, manuscript "Le bal des folles"; cahier #1 (unpaginated and undated, ca. 1976–1977), in IMEC: COP 7/Fonds Copi; published in Copi, *Le bal*, 156.

braced multiplicity, in a direct challenge to the usual male-female binary that anchored universalist claims. Arab men, for him and many other openly gay male writers in these years, embodied this erotic politics of (Algerian) difference.[18]

Resisting "a Homosexuality That's at Last Wholly White"

Over the course of the 1970s, the willingness of writers such as Copi to reference their own homosexuality gave the wider French public increasing access to the gay world. This process also brought into view sharp dissension among gay critics about this so-called gay world, especially its dependence on a hetero-homo binarism. The gay world itself expanded substantially in these years, as new commercial institutions welcomed growing numbers of people willing to frequent gay bars or, at least, buy gay publications. Such developments led some gay observers to claim that this new publicity—this public "recognition" that alongside "heterosexuals" there were "homosexuals"—was destroying the long-standing coexistence of multiple modes of living and thinking about sexual contacts. The supposedly distinct sexual economy of immigrant men from North Africa served as the primary example.[19]

The most insistent critic was Hocquenghem, whose renown resulted from his 1972 "coming out," which the *Nouvel observateur* had published as "The Revolution of the Homosexuals." His public impact grew substantially when he became a columnist in the newspaper *Libération*, which Jean-Paul Sartre helped set up in 1971 and which was the most well-read forum for post-'68 leftist discussions in 1970s France. In 1976, Hocquenghem penned an article in *Libération* about the death of Italian filmmaker Pier Pasolini, who had died on the beach of Ostia, Italy, in November 1975. Pasolini's most recent films—*Arabian Nights* (1974), which he had shot in Yemen, and *Salò, or the 120 Days of Sodom* (1975)—had pushed to the extreme his long-standing interest in male bodies, in the willingness of rough young men—peasants, workers, and Arabs, among others—to enjoy sexual pleasures of all kinds, as well as his interest in the destructive, violent deca-

18. Copi, manuscript "Le bal des folles"; cahier #8 (unpaginated and undated, ca. 1976–1977), in IMEC: COP 7/Fonds Copi.

19. On the expansion of gay and lesbian venues in 1970s Paris, see Florence Tamagne, "Paris: 'Resting on its Laurels?'" in Jennifer V. Evans, Matt Cook, eds., *Queer Cities, Queer Cultures: Europe since 1945* (London: Bloomsbury, 2014), 240–260; Michael Sibalis, "Urban Space and Homosexuality: The Example of the Marais, Paris' 'Gay Ghetto,'" *Urban Studies* 41, no. 9 (2004), 1739–1758.

dence of bourgeois and aristocratic efforts to exploit such bucolic situations. Many observers blamed Pasolini's death on a sexual encounter gone wrong, with a seventeen-year-old male prostitute held responsible. Hocquenghem took the opportunity to bewail what he saw as the disappearance of the culture of the sexual outlaw—the man who pursued his desire for socially unspeakable sex with types of males whose marginality both allowed such connections and accentuated their desirability—which he blamed on the newly public gay world, both its commercial and political aspects. "Normalizing pressure works quickly," the philosopher asserted. The only place he saw ongoing resistance was "in the *banlieue* [France's suburbs, associated with public housing projects and "Arab" immigrants] or around Pigalle," and those who resisted were "queens obsessed with Arab men [*folles à Arabes*]. In any case the die is cast, which will lead to a homosexuality that's at last wholly white, in every sense of the term." Conventional and presentable ("vanilla," in my terminology) gay sex and lives, he asserted, depended on the exclusion of nonwhite men from the new gay world—especially Arabs, and what he defined as their different, edgier relationship to sex and male-male relations generally.[20]

In 1977 Hocquenghem again returned to this theme—that France was being divided into heterosexuals and homosexuals, destroying the more exciting complexity that previously reigned—in his review of *Le bal des folles* by Copi. He read it as a history of a vanished world. "In place of the Latin solidarity of queens, Spanish-flamenco queers, or big Arab-loving queens of the South of France has appeared the empire of Anglo-Saxonised homosex through liberationism."[21] In the manuscript for *Le bal des folles*, Copi had offered his own rather different analysis, which focused on how life in France changed "the Arab men" rather than on gay liberationists changing France. In two related scenes that he did not include in the novel, his character reencountered the Moroccan taxi driver "who had brought me on that round trip between Boulevard St. Germain and Orly [airport] almost ten years ago." In the first scene, on the run from the cops for murder (which he mistakenly thinks he has committed), the narrator "hopes that [the driver] won't recognize me. No, he's changed his style, he doesn't look in the rear-view mirror any more"—a change that, here, Copi connected to

20. On Hocquenghem and Libération, see Marshall, *Guy Hocquenghem*, 13–14; "Tout le monde ne peut mourir dans son lit," in Hocquenghem, *La dérive homosexuelle* [first published in *Libération*, 29 March 1976], 127–134.

21. "Invitation au délire," in Hocquenghem, *La dérive homosexuelle*, 142–144. Translation from Keith Harvey, *Intercultural Movements: American Gay in French Translation* (New York: Routledge, 2014), 85–86.

the man from Morocco's transformation "into a perfect Parisian." In the second scene, Copi tied the change to "family life," but not because family life had ended the taxi driver's "sexual misery." Rather, in the writer's telling, along with life in France, family ties have "embittered him."[22] What Copi shared with Hocquenghem was a sense of nostalgia, for a time when it was easier to have sex—notably, with Arab men. By which they mean men "of the people," workers who were socially marginal, unencumbered by French codes or perhaps just uneducated in them. The numerous "Arabs" who did not fit this description rarely appeared in gay writings in these years.

Returning the Gaze

In the 1970s, Maghrebi male authors and filmmakers, like their openly gay counterparts, had growing access to French audiences as their works— publications and films, fiction and nonfiction—won both distribution and attention. There seems to have been, remarkably, no overlap between the two groups. Yet a strikingly large percentage of French-language texts and films whose creators identified as Maghrebi commented on gay male attention to Arab men. They did so in multiple ways, although none were interested in exploring the heterosexual-homosexual binary as either a reality or a problem. Most gave evidence that suggested (just like Orientalist studies and French popular presumptions) that their roots were in a society where males having sex with males was rather common and not much frowned upon. All raised questions about the intersections between sex, gender, and power. Nearly all paid particular attention to how economics affected pleasures and desires. Their depictions reveal a clear shift between North African practices and what occurred in France, with interactions defined by money and material gain displacing those based on mutual (if distinct and complementary) sexual needs.

By far the most widely discussed books by Maghrebi authors published in France between 1968 and 1979 were by the Algerian novelist Rachid Boudjedra and the Moroccan writer Tahar ben Jelloun. Each writer emphasized questions of male sexuality, male sexual "perversion," and even male homosexuality. Their success gives some measure of how much the connection between male sexual "perversion" and North Africans intrigued numerous French people. In 1969 Boudjedra's first novel, *La répudiation*

---

22. Copi, manuscript "Le bal des folles," cahier #6, (unpaginated and undated, ca. 1976–1977), in IMEC: COP 7/Fonds Copi.

(*Repudiation*), appeared in France. Editors in his own country had rejected the manuscript, which was deeply critical of the existing Algerian regime ("the Clan") and of the sexually repressive Algerian society that allowed it to exist. It sold a stunning twenty-seven thousand copies in the first seven months.

In *Repudiation*, Rachid, an Algerian man, recounts his childhood to his French girlfriend, Céline, and places perversion at its center. Uncomprehending male fascination with women dominates the story, which presents Algerian society as tensely erotic and deeply misogynist; yet visible male desire for other men and boys is what the narrator relies on to make sense of the larger world he inhabits. It is Rachid's flight from grasping male hands—and a male sexual organ—in a hammam that precipitates both his incarceration for mental illness and his cogent condemnation of "the silence that will have to be observed so as not to trouble the certainties of a society anchored in its myths of purity and abstinence." His older brother Zahir, who committed suicide while still in love with an older Jewish youth, is the voice that, repeatedly in the novel, articulates what Rachid can only feel when confronted with the twisted interactions between men and women.[23]

In 1977, the Moroccan novelist Tahar ben Jelloun situated this vexed intersection between women and male homosexuality at the heart of his first nonfiction book, *La plus haute des solitudes: Misère affective et sexuelle d'émigrés nord-africains* (The Highest Solitude: The Emotional and Sexual Misery of North African Emigrants).[24] Like *Repudiation*, it was an unexpected best-seller, with some seventy-five thousand copies soon sold. Ben Jelloun claimed that these men suffered from a high incidence of impotence, which he linked to the fact that "the submission of women is . . . admitted in North African society," but also to the extreme importance that the performance of virility had for men from North Africa. Public performance of the sexual conquest of women was at the core, he argued, of how they defined who they were, their very subjectivity. (It would be a mistake to follow ben Jelloun's suggestion that this was specific to North Africa. Matt Houlbrook's analysis of interwar working-class male Londoners suggests that their definition of masculinity and self was quite similar. Revenin writes that for men in 1960s France, "bragging [about sexual encounters]

23. Rachid Boudjedra, *The Repudiation*, trans. Golda Lambrova (Colorado Springs, CO: Three Continents Press, 1995), 163–166.
24. *La plus haute.*

appears to be an essential element of the masculine habitus.")[25] This, for ben Jelloun, was why homosexual activity was so important for the men he interviewed, in the double sense of its relative frequency and its evocation, through a kind of aporia of negation, of deeper meaning: it was simultaneously one of the only sexual outlets available to them in France, and yet one that could not offer social legitimation. He saw nothing radical, merely more evidence of problems. As the anthropologist Paul Rabinow summarized, "The majority of the workers made it clear to Jelloun that whether or not they had homosexual relations was beside the point." It happened, and they did not see it as a big deal, but such acts were not "conquests." This meant that "they could not validate themselves to themselves whether or not they engaged in such mediated activity. Homosexual relations were not sinful, they might be a source of physiological relief, but they could not be a source of self-worth."[26] While the Arab men might find what was being discussed to be, to quote Rabinow, "beside the point," social scientists and their large French audiences were drawn to such narratives. The sociologist Juliette Minces, in her important 1973 study *Les travailleurs étrangers en France* (Foreign Workers in France), relied on Arab witnesses for her evidence. She concluded a discussion of the difficulties that immigrant workers in Paris faced due to sexual isolation with an allusive quote from one of her informants: "Luckily I found that one over there. At least when I feel too alone, then I sleep over there!" The author clarified what the man meant: "He had just pointed out his young neighbor and was immediately interrupted in Arabic by his companions. Of course, nobody was willing to translate what had been said." Such invocations of male homosociality tied tightly to homosexual acts entranced French audiences.[27]

In his first comic book, the Algerian-born French scholar and cartoonist Slimane Zeghidour (writing pseudonymously as Saladin) made clear that the performance of virility was very important in France, too. One cartoon (figure 14) emphasized how French disdain for Algerian homosociality, a disdain anchored in homophobia, denigrated the emotional needs of North African men in France. In one panel, two immigrants warmly greet each other; in the next, the homophobic response of passersby is to vilify

25. Matt Houlbrook, *Queer London: Perils and Pleasures in the Sexual Metropolis, 1918–1957* (Chicago: University of Chicago Press, 2005); Revenin, *Une histoire de garçons*, 148.

26. Paul Rabinow, "Book Review: Working in Paris," *Dialectical Anthropology* 3 (1978), 361–364.

27. Juliette Minces, *Les travailleurs étrangers en France: Enquête* (Paris: Seuil, 1973) 452.

Figure 14. Cartoon panel by Saladin (pseudonym of Slimane Zeghidour). From *Les migrations de Djeha: Les nouveaux immigrés* (1979), a collection of cartoons originally published in *Libération*. Permission to reproduce graciously provided by Slimane Zeghidour.

the men's warm homosociality. One cries: "Eeh!! Old lady . . . take a look at that . . . they sure lack decency, these savages, what a disgusting show! Pfff!!" A second warns: "Oooh!! This isn't ancient Greece, or Arabia, this is Paris. . . ." A third: "Oooh, what a pretty show! Oooh, Wilde." Zeghidour invoked two spaces or histories and one hero (the "martyred" fin-de-siècle Anglo-Irish writer Oscar Wilde) treasured by proponents of male-male love, but did so to demonstrate how French certainties rendered emotional contact between men out of bounds. A quote in a 1971 newspaper article titled "Lyon Confronts Racism" was typical of how such stereotypes entered more mainstream discussions: "'All the boys are homosexuals!' The school principal's remark meets the approval of the social worker who assists her," the journalist reported. "A portrait of the Algerian schoolboy as 'dirty, a vandal, lacking discipline' then follows." As we have seen, the stereotype was tenacious.[28]

28. *Les migrations de Djeha: Les nouveaux immigrés*, preface by Guy Bedos (Claix: La Pensée sauvage, 1979), 12. The book was a collection of cartoons that had first appeared in *Libération*. See also Lalu, "Lyon à l'épreuve du racisme?" 10. On the ongoing importance of such policing vis-à-vis "Maghrebi" males in France, see Nacira Guénif-Souilamas, "En un combat douteux: Concurrence pour la conformation sexuée des Français d'ascendance migrante et colonial," *Revue européenne des migrations internationales* 21, no. 2 (2005), 91–109.

Arab Writers on "French" Homosexuality

While ben Jelloun explored how French racism shaped the "emotional and sexual misery of North African emigrants," which included the disdain of potential female partners, he had little to say about how homosexuals viewed them. Many other Maghrebi commentators did, however. Boudjedra's third book, *Topographie idéale pour une aggression caractérisée* (An Ideal Topography for a Stereotypical Murder, 1974), takes place mainly in France, mostly in the Parisian Métro; French racism, chiefly the country's vicious mistreatment of Algerian immigrants, provides an overarching theme. In one critic's estimation, the sexual order "called into question here is the eroticism of Westerners rather than of Maghrebis"; this was a shift from Boudjedra's stance in earlier publications such as *Repudiation*.[29] Still, *Topographie idéale* also returns repeatedly to what are presented as limits, problems, in how Algerian men relate to women. In this description of France, unlike in Boudjedra's account of same-sex relations in Algeria, homosexual acts go unspoken, yet homosexual men somewhat paradoxically exist. The book follows an Algerian seeking to settle in France; if he did, the narrator explains, the immigrant would have to deal with "homosexuals on the prowl." Instead, he was murdered by racist thugs. The police officer investigating the crime opines that, to get eyewitness accounts of the man's Métro wanderings, "Find some faggot, it wouldn't surprise me if they tried to speak to him, them, they're always on the lookout for foreigners, they prefer 'em to locals for god knows what reason."[30] Boudjedra's characterizations of the (to follow Hocquenghem's line of argument) "Arabophilia" of French homosexuals are rather cutting, and quite distant from the thoughtful, even admiring depictions in *Repudiation* of homosexual acts and desires. What male-male eroticism offered in Boudjedra's Algeria was the grounds for an alliance with women to resist the horrors of patriarchy, an alliance that Boudjedra presents as impossible in France. As the literary critic Armelle Crouzières-Ingenthron notes, for Boudjedra, "in the absence of woman, subversion cannot exist, for she offers both its anchor and its motor."[31] Boudjedra's vision is opposed to male FHARist claims that homosexual men's interactions with Arabs rendered them indispensable to

29. Giuliana Toso Rodinis, *Fêtes et défaites d'Eros dans l'oeuvre de Rachid Boudjedra* (Paris: Harmattan, 1994), 77.

30. Rachid Boudjedra, *Topographie idéale pour une aggression caractérisée* (Paris: Denoël, 1975), 50, 184, 186.

31. Armelle Crouzières Ingenthron, *Le double pluriel dans les romans de Rachid Boudjedra* (Paris: L'Harmattan, 2001), 172.

any project for radical social change. He shared their arguments that sexual acts and interactions took on meaning because of context and history. Yet Boudjedra's novel targeted how, in contemporary France, such an erotic fixation worked to limit human interactions, in effect rendering any understanding of "the Arab immigrant man" more difficult.

Maghrebi Accounts of How France Changed Sex

The role of money—particularly as it shaped class status and consumerism—drew the attention of other Maghrebi commentators. In the middle of the Tunisian director Naceur Ktari's film *Les ambassadeurs* (1975), one scene mockingly depicts the efforts of an older French man to pick up three young Arab men. As in Boudjedra's depiction, Ktari offers a cutting depiction of French certainties that Maghrebi men are naïve, unaware of the sexual stereotypes about them. Ali (the "Djillali" character) enters a Place Pigalle bar, where he joins two of his friends at a table. They are chatting with a fifty-something man whom one of Ali's friends introduces to him as a "reporter." "Yes, on TV," the man specifies. He asks the three friends where they live, and when they tell him "Goutte d'Or," he responds, "Really, I've been wanting to film a story on this neighborhood. It's fascinating." This statement draws surprised shrugs from the young men. As the three friends stare at two beautiful young women, the "reporter" exclaims, "Ahh, we just can't hear each other here. Do you want to come to my place?" When they all go to the man's apartment, Ali wanders around, inspecting the objects on display: African masks, animal skins, musical instruments. The man's fascination for the exotic is clear. He admits that he's collected the objects in his travels, but quickly notes, "You know, for me, what matters to me, is that it's human contact." He then tells them about "my last story, it was on a transit camp here in France. There were a lot of Arabs there." Ali stares at the man, who explains how his work has helped raise public awareness about the "real situation these people suffer." Ali responds: "Y'know, all this stuff you're telling me, I could care less. What I want is, I want to live." The man asks what he means by "live well," and Ali responds, "Have cash, a beautiful car. . . ." In the background, the other two friends look through the reporter's closet. Rather than more items that fetishize the foreign or "human contact," the closet is full of high-fashion apparel, leather jackets, and expensive consumer items. After Ali speaks, one of his friends says, "Can we try them on?" even though each already has put on several items. As the reporter tries to get them to put the clothes back in the closet, one responds, with a wink and a smile: "Stop your blather, old man. We get it."

The other says, "If you want to be buddies, you'll let us choose, OK?" From free drinks to a few wardrobe additions beyond the reach of their meager salaries, the desire that drives them to put up with the reporter's come-ons, in Ktari's depiction, is inspired by economics and not eros, though also informed by good feelings. Their smiling recognition of what the reporter wants allows them to navigate this situation.

In testimonials published in the early 1970s of Algerian men who immigrated to work in France, the passage from Algeria to France alters the dynamics of same-sex sexual activity, as in Boudjedra's early novels, although less dramatically. In the Algerian childhood recounted in *Belka* (1974), an idyllic world is imperiled by perverts. "In the summer, we hung out on the wharf and the sea-pools. . . . Perverts would tempt kids of our age between the wharf's big cement blocks." The narrator, Belka, quickly adds that this happened "sometimes for a bit of bread and some chocolate," and that "they were really after the young bucks, those who looked like they'd come down from the mountains, bursting with health. The same clique hung out at the hammams and the public toilets."[32] Even back in Algeria, then, the (homosexual) quest for exotic (and naïve) masculinity was more compelling than the shared (and, again, supposedly naïve) desire that so transfixed many French commentators.

Belka's descriptions of what happened in France accentuate both sides of the equation. In his account of his time in a French prison camp with other suspected members of the FLN, he describes how he and his fellow prisoners put in place their own "police corps, which we named *la protection*." Its purpose was to defend the honor of the prisoners against French efforts to humiliate them: it "kept an eye on the whole camp 24/7 and came upon few infractions that might sully the dignity of the militants." One infraction, however, did occur somewhat regularly. "Homosexual misbehavior: the last case was uncovered at 3 a.m., when one member of a security patrol had a shoe hit his head while passing under a tree: the guilty parties had sought refuge up there, hidden in the leaves, to enjoy their vice. They were immediately presented before a special commission and sentenced to a beating."[33] The scene presents male-male sex as something expected, driven by lust, yet something that poses a danger for all Algerians—thus requiring punishment—because of French oppression. Ahmed's evocation of male-male sexuality in Algeria is somewhat different, resonant with Orientalist depictions that offer more reassurance to French

32. Mohamed Belkacemi, *Belka* (Paris: Fayard, 1974), 52.
33. Belkacemi, *Belka*, 338.

(or homosexual) readers. The author of *Une Vie d'Algérien, est-ce que ça fait un livre que les gens vont lire?* (An Algerian man's life; does that make a book that people will read?) focuses on Islam: "Anything that is beautiful, very beautiful and cherished, among us we say: 'God forbids it,' our religion bans it. So we don't do it, but we do horrific things instead." As in the cases of Boudjedra and ben Jelloun, the Maghrebi "dilemma" Ahmed describes concerns the relationship between men and women. "For example, you cannot look at a naked woman—it's banned by our religion—but if one day a guy is horned up and doesn't have a wife, he gets a boy. And he hides it." While all the Maghrebi authors describe male-male sexual contact as widespread, they offer various explanations as well as diverse judgments.[34]

When Belka settles into his life in Paris, he finally finds a name for "the homosexuals," those who spend time in the Goutte d'Or or Pigalle neighborhoods, in the same restaurants, cafés, and bars that he and other Maghrebi men frequent. "The whores and the homosexuals were disdained; they sat at separate tables, in a corner, when we were at the restaurant."[35] As in ben Jelloun's analysis, homosexuality and prostitution are linked. When Ahmed comes to France, as in Boudjedra's *Topographie idéale*, what he emphasizes is the fetishizing gaze of French male homosexuals. Of one he says, "He wanted me to ass-fuck him in the train station." His semipornographic description mirrors those of numerous French narrators, but with the emphasis entirely on how he is interpellated as a potential partner, rather than simply being potentially available. "There I was in the lavatory, I'm making sure I look good in a mirror, like this, and this guy, he's just there in the door of his toilet. He wanted me to come join him." This "first-person testimonial," of course, is highly mediated. Like others of the genre, editorial archives reveal the importance that publishers placed on such sexualized content. In 1972, the original referee who recommended publication of the manuscript that became *Une Vie d'Algérien* reassured its editor: "In the pages you have, sexual questions are not dealt with. They will be in what follows. The narrator himself says this could be an unending story, something like the *Thousand and One Nights* of an Algerian exiled in Paris and exiled from his country."[36] The opening lines of the book exemplify how almost all of the "testimonials" by Arab men published in French in these years used signs of deviant masculinity to draw in

34. Ahmed, *Une Vie d'Algérien, est-ce que ça fait un livre que les gens vont lire?* (Paris: Seuil, 1973), 113.

35. Belkacemi, *Belka*, 262.

36. Ahmed, *Une vie d'Algérien*, 138; FRB (François Régis Bastide), "Fiche de lecture PROJET de Marcel Marnat" (9 June 1972), 1, in IMEC: Fonds Le Seuil SEL 3721.2 Marcel Marnat.

potential readers. "My father, he messed up a lot of women. . . . And you'll see, he was a monster. I swear to you: he's a monster, a monster! And he was married to three women. You know, he stuck them in the house and locked them in. . . . A horrible man." Still, Ahmed's take on male homosexual desire, despite its scopophilic function, echoes with that presented in other Maghrebi perspectives.[37]

The testimony of another Algerian man—"based on an investigation by Ali Ghalem [the director of the film *Mektoub* (1970), also known as Ali Ghanem], co-signatory of this effort to correct the record"—this one in the context of a group letter he and others sent to *Libération* in 1977, opens onto all of these questions. It drew together an analysis of the daunting economy of desire that Arab men faced in France—desires that objectified them in league with structures that denied their own desires—and a critique of the power of economics. "French and Belgian heads of industry," this author discovered, "in league with the management of a young workers' hostel, came to 'hook up' with the residents, for whom the rules, it's important to note, banned any and all female visitors." Contemporary gay porn magazines fairly often evoked such hostels. In 1976 the gay glossy magazine *Hommes*, for example, interviewed José L, twenty-four years old, known as Carmen, a Parisian transvestite. She recounted that, until recently, "to go out dressed as women, my girlfriends and me, we went to the *banlieue*. We would sneak into a hostel for North Africans; it was *la nouba*, party time. They would hide us, because it was against the rules. They loved it, it was just crazy." Ghalem's investigation cast such fantasies in a different light, revealing how exploitation and oppression structured these spaces and possibilities.[38]

Selling "Human Contact"

In the same years as Maghrebi male authors found new publics—in the newly liberalized context of post-1968 and, somewhat later, Giscardian France—a newly public, highly visible gay media and cultural presence emerged.[39] In this more self-consciously gay and assertive environment, the Arab male held pride of place. Like the publishers of highly sexualized books by men from North Africa, the editors of gay magazines and the pro-

37. Ahmed, *Une vie d'Algérien*, 13.
38. Mustapha Djajam, Ali Ghalem, Mahmoud Zemmouri, Jean Duflot, Pierre Boiron, Jacqueline Narcy, "Courrier: Histoire d'un mec qui ne voudrait pas sombrer dans l'antiféminisme," *Libération*, (10 May 1977), 2. "Les hommes et les travesties," *Hommes* 25 (Spring 1976), 10, 46.
39. For the best historical analysis of this period, see Jackson, *Living in Arcadia*, 195–225.

moters of gay plays and productions seemed certain that Arab men would sell, much as they had in the 1950s, when, according to sociologist Andrée Michel, "delinquency . . . which in France is associated with North Africans, is highlighted by certain magazines when they launch their first issue."[40] Porn magazines provided the clearest examples, as the first issues of almost every one that targeted men who were attracted to other men (whether their titles were explicitly bisexual or homosexual) included articles about and pictures of Maghrebis, or of men identified as such. In December 1975, for example, the first issue of the magazine *Don* displayed an evidently very young North African as the centerfold, while in early 1978 the first article of the first issue of *Gay Magazine* opened with what was announced as a multi-episode series called "Chronicles: Brahim's Stories." No further episodes were published.[41] Arab men also appeared in key roles in commercial theatrical or variety shows that targeted gay men. The publicity around one such show in 1974, "Last Tango in the Jungle," drew attention to its Franco-Algerian star Jalil David[42] An interview with the playwright and director of the play *Model Boy* highlighted how the play's antihero "can't deal with being dominated (sexually) by a young Arab, and that is what provokes the drama."[43] It is worth noting that, in its first issue, *Nous, les hommes* magazine did something different: in a tactic quite similar to one used in the first issues of numerous pornographic magazines aimed at heterosexual male audiences, it was the Algerian war that provided the cover story. A veteran of the war, that is, was the model: "He's 32 years old and his name is Jean-Pierre. He tells us how to become a manly man, a tough guy."[44] During the 1970s, in sharp distinction with such cover stories, neither erotic stories nor pornographic photo spreads that appeared in commercial publications and featured Arab men ever directly referenced the Algerian conflict.

In numerous photos, interviews, and articles, pornographic magazines presented their readers with transparently Orientalist depictions of Arabs as open-minded and profoundly sexual. Arab men never appeared as homosexuals themselves. If they stood outside the heterosexual-homosexual binary because of an easy willingness to have sex with other men, their

40. Andrée Michel, *Les travailleurs algériens en France* (Paris: CNRS, 1956), 161. Although I had access to the archives of mainstream publishing houses, this was not the case with the archives of the porn magazines, which appear to have been destroyed.

41. *Don* 1 (December 1975), 42–43 ; *Gay Magazine* 1 (February 1978), 1–17.

42. "Dernier Tango dans la jungle," *In magazine masculin* 10 (April-May 1974), 34.

43. Andre Gauthiez, "Interview de Yves Jacquemard and Jean-Michel Sénécal," *In magazine masculin* 6 (August–September 1973), 26–28.

44. Jean-Luc Michel, "Dans la serie 'Les durs': Voila la PARAS!" *Nous, les hommes* 1 (1970), 1–5.

representations most often included a primary interest in sex with women. In buying such a magazine, the consumer gained access to a world where desire or pleasure, rather than money, explained why such males would sleep with men such as the reader.

In the interview that accompanied his nude photos in the gay porn magazine *In magazine*, the young Egyptian "Antonio" both defined his attitude to life in terms of "'Mektoub' . . . 'It is written [the word of God]'" and reminded readers, "In our countries, we're very precocious. And we don't have your prejudices. Love is so marvelous; why deny oneself and feel bad simply because of the sex of your partner. How ridiculous."[45] In a 1973 article in *Nous, les hommes* magazine, one of the first soft-porn gay magazines, the interviewer asked Saïd D., a Moroccan immigrant, "Are French boys more understanding than French girls?" Saïd D. replied: "Certain, yes . . ." Interviewer: "These friendships, were they ever sometimes, how can I say this . . . a bit interested for diverse reasons?" It was a question that seemed to imply money, but Saïd's published response focused only on the homosexual implications: "You want to ask if these guys wanted to sleep with me? Some, yes, others, no. It doesn't matter; in Morocco, we love to make love." It was for this reason, he suggested, that "we're not going to throw a hissy fit [*s'affoller* (sic)] if someone wants to do something with you that it's enjoyable to share. We don't make a big deal about it. Each person has a right to what pleases him." Whereas in *Belka* or Boudjedra, Islam was the source of problems in Maghrebi heterosociality, depictions in gay porn frequently presented it as a solution. The interviewer in this article asked Saïd D., "Do you think the Prophet said that [each person has a right to what pleases him]?" Saïd D. replied, "Mohamed said: 'The one being sought and the one who seeks are made of the same light.' Not bad, no?"[46] A subsequent issue gave one indication of how much such statements, and the photos that accompanied them, pleased readers of *Nous, les hommes*. "The interview with Saïd D. brought in an enormous number of letters," the editors noted. "We try to be objective in all domains. It's not always easy."[47] What the editors referred to was the insistent antiracist frame within which the article had introduced Saïd D., and which letter-writers had echoed.

The Spring 1973 article that introduced Saïd D. was entitled "North Africans," and it opened with the claim, "Young Arab men, there are hundreds all around us," before quickly urging the (presumably non-Arab)

---

45. "Les aventures du bel Antonio," *In magazine* 31 (February-March 1978), 37–40.

46. Robert de Sanits, "Les Nord Africains," *Nous, les hommes* 13 (Spring 1973), 10–12.

47. Moktar, algérien de Paris, "Courrier entre nous, les hommes," *Nous, les hommes* 16 (Winter 1973), 12.

reader to "take note of this: never, or almost never, is one of these young Arab men with a Frenchman." The article invoked the history of empire—"The French presence certainly did linger–at what a tragic cost—for more than a century in North Africa"—in order to regret that "the divorce, it seems, has not yet ended." The journalist addressed his readers: "Still, talk to an Arab: quite often you would be surprised by the subtlety of his judgment, his humor, and, above all, which is so very important"—and so often noted by gay male commentators—"by the open spirit that allows him so easily to forget all the problems our attitude has inflicted on him, with the aim of winning our friendship."[48] As in nonpornographic gay male writings, Arab homosociality offered both easy explanations for potential "human contacts" and a seemingly pure explanation for erotic fantasies. One reader wrote to say, "You cannot know how much I appreciated all that the young Moroccan worker, Saïd D., had to say. The good sense of his answers, his goodness when confronted with the indifference of our compatriots or worse, I found particularly moving."[49] Another reader recounted: "When I was a schoolboy, my best friend was Hamid, a little Arab boy. The marvelous souvenir that he left with me guards me from all racism towards North Africans." This letter writer "want[ed] to specify that I am heterosexual, which should give more weight to my letter!" This was a claim that strenuously sought to sustain the hetero-homo binarism that was so fundamental to the era, even as it strained credulity. Its assertion of greater authority resonated with ideas about Arab male sexuality as unbound by the constraints (of puritanism, self-control, neuroses, etc.) that supposedly channeled the desires of Westerners.[50] A letter from one Moktar, an Algerian living in Paris, in response to the interview with Saïd D., brought together the themes of homosociality and of desires free from the limits of the hetero-homo binarism. It did so with a sharp reminder that, in present-day France, such fantasies had human costs and were linked to social inequalities. "I would like to tell you frankly what I go through," Moktar wrote. "Even though I'm well educated in French, live in the home of a person who has a great situation, and am welcomed into the homes of well-regarded people, I feel that I am always held at a distance." Moktar noted the attitude of French women. "They say, 'You turn me on,' but never, 'I love you.' In a café I overheard one girl, talking about me, say: 'I

48. De Sanits, "Les Nord Africains," 10–12; 11.

49. EM, Paris -7e, "Courrier entre nous, les hommes," *Nous, les hommes* 14 (Summer 1973) 8.

50. NB, Cherbourg, "Courrier entre nous, les hommes," *Nous, les hommes* 16 (Winter 1973), 12.

want to do that little *bicot* [a pejorative for Arab] but I don't dare say so.'" Moktar then addressed the readers of the gay porn magazine more directly. "It's thanks to my French friend (he's kind of like my father, I'd say) that I learned about [your magazine] and the sympathy that appears (sometimes) in its pages for North Africans. Thank you. Friendly smile." He was, that is, a man interested in women who was "kept" by a man. His friendly letter offered proof of his openness to the homosexual implications of the announced homosociality. Indeed, he seemed to welcome at least some of them. This, along with the fact that the speakers who hurt him were described as women, rendered his effort to call attention to the racism he suffered publishable by a gay male magazine, if perhaps not wholly legible.[51]

The sentimental claim that "friendship" and "sympathy" were what linked Arab men and French homosexuals—and explained as well as demonstrated the supposed anti-racism of gay men (or, in the case of the author of one letter cited above, readers of gay porn)—intensified in tandem with the new gay commercial culture. Seeking a rationale that lay beyond mere mutual desire, the claim minimized the role of pecuniary factors as it sought to affirm desexualized and shared bonds. It was an argument that the "homophile" periodical *Arcadie* actively supported. A 1973 article coauthored by the founder and leader of Arcadie, André Baudry, insisted that "while there is certainly a discussion to have about the value of homophilia as a factor in bringing people together, it would be impossible to deny its importance in bringing the races together: even in the United States, homosexual groups are particularly 'integrationist' around this question. There probably is no other milieu where interracial friendships are more frequent than in homophile milieus." These connections, as this explanation makes clear, were quite distinct from the political reading that FHAR-aligned radicals had celebrated. In such a way were the bonds between "gay" and "Arab" men naturalized, which deflected any demand for political analysis.[52]

Sexual Tourism

In many gay magazines and publications, tourism, particularly sexual tourism, also represented opportunities to share encounters, to develop new forms of "human contact." The approach developed by the French Club Méd group—its *"gentils organisateurs"* and its promise of an escape from

51. Moktar, algérien de Paris, "Courrier," 12.
52. Marc Daniel and André Baudry, *Les homosexuels* (Paris: Casterman, 1973), 117.

the consumerist and work-obsessed West[53]—underwrote the descriptions of destinations well suited for French gay male tourists, and North Africa held pride of place. The charms of the Mediterranean were often simply highlighted, as in many of the picture spreads in semiporn magazines. In 1968, for example, the "nudist" *Olympe* introduced a feature thus: "Our May Apollo is Tunisian, noticed on the beach at Hammamet, Mhammed Boudhina, 18 years old."[54] In 1972, meanwhile, the magazine claimed, "At the edge of the [Algerian] desert we met Mohamed, a young Arab. . . . Mohamed is 16. His dream: to become a professional tourist guide." ("The Arabs and Us" section of "Three Billion Perverts" reproduced his pictures.)[55] As the historian Julian Jackson notes, Arcadie, which usually avoided discussions of Arab men in reference to male homosexual life in France (except for describing them as potentially dangerous when encountered in outdoor cruising areas), hosted multiple lectures in which Tunisia and Morocco were presented as being among "the last homosexual paradises." These accounts offered "detailed information on what to expect and what to avoid in North African sexual encounters."[56] They instructed their audience in no uncertain terms "about the economic reality behind these encounters." As *Arcadie* writer Maurice Chevaly explained in 1969, "However unpleasant it may be to say this, we need to recognize that our principal ally is poverty." Nonetheless, it was an argument—with its bracing acknowledgment of the potential for exploitation in erotic relations between French and Arab men—that rarely found its way into print.[57]

Several tourist guides that targeted gay male travelers, and spoke clearly about sexual opportunities, became widely available in the 1970s. The most notable were the yearly *Spartacus* guides, which presented descriptions in three languages, including French as well as English and German. The French gay press spoke of tourism, too. All the guides relied on well-known claims about North Africa to tempt their readers. A writer interviewed in *In magazine* responded, "What did I notice about Libya, where I was in fact the only tourist around? As is always the case with Islam, the incredible official puritanism, which is transgressed (and it's better like that) on every street corner."[58] A 1980 article on Algeria in the new English-only

53. See Ellen Furlough, "Packaging Pleasures: Club Méditerranée and French Consumer Culture, 1950–1968." *French Historical Studies* (1993), 65–81.

54. Jean Montceau, "Appolons et Vénus méconnus" *Olympe* 4 (May 1968), 30.

55. George Lamy, "Voyages," *Olympe* 45 (January 1972), 12–14.

56. Quote from talk in 1972; see Jackson, *Living in Arcadia*, 199.

57. Ibid.

58. "L'écrivain 'In': Frédéric Rey cherche un 'énarque' et un 'voyou' pour une future adaptation de son livre à l'écran," *In magazine masculin* 14 (January-February 1975), 40–42.

Spartacus monthly magazine claimed, "There is no need to bother listing specific bars as all bars have available men, and a promenade in any town produces quick action."[59] In its entry on Tunisia the yearly *Spartacus* guide for 1976 reported, "It is said that everywhere you go you can find young Arabs [in English in the text] who are friendly and available. Just ask, or flash a smile, but do be careful!"[60] North African men, such guides insisted, were not bogged down in questions of heterosexuality or homosexuality: it was a land of mutual (male) pleasure. That the men in question were of the "popular" (non-elite) classes was implicit.

There were, as well, regular references to the exchange of cash or gifts, yet the *Spartacus* guide insisted that this did not explain local male willingness to have sex with French men. It was either culturally specific or unnecessary. In Tunisia, it was "expected" that a small gift—that is money—would accompany the act, or so said the guides. Yet the 1976 *Spartacus* guide described Algeria as a country with a "friendly population. . . . The boys do not expect to be paid for having sex; it's a favor to them to make love with you. . . . After all, a woman costs 15 dinars." Although seemingly in direct opposition, both were directly linked to a claim about the supposed local culture around sexual roles. The 1977 edition stated, "Across North Africa and the eastern Mediterranean, you'll find the traditional heritage of bisexuality." It informed readers that men in this region "will assign you the traditional woman's role, which is to say that, for them, you are there for them, you are there to be penetrated and thus to fulfill their own sexual satisfaction."[61] The *Spartacus* guide (which began publication in Stamford, UK, in 1970 but quickly shifted to an Amsterdam base in 1972 to escape legal harassment) also offered some insight into the particular importance of Arab men for the French. In its 1976 listings for France, multiple bars and, more frequently, public cruising sites included the code word "Arabs" in English. For example, in the listing for the "old fort behind old city" in

59. "Algeria, an appraisal by one of our correspondents," *Spartacus: For Gay Men* 3 (December 1980), 23–25. On such guides, see Gordon Waitt and Kevin Markwell, *Gay Tourism: Culture and Context* (New York: Routledge, 2014), 65–70. For a history of homoerotically charged travel to the Mediterranean by European men, see Robert Aldrich, *The Seduction of the Mediterranean: Writing, Art and Homosexual Fantasy* (New York: Routledge, 1993), 162–185.

60. *Guide Spartacus* (1976), 565.

61. *Guide Spartacus* (1977), 56. Literary critic Ross Chambers, in his analysis of *Incidents*, a posthumously published text by Roland Barthes, notes that one of the stark differences between the gay cruising the author describes engaging in on the streets of Paris and in Morocco is the "striking deemphasis of commoditization in the touristic Moroccan text," even though Barthes is very clear that in Paris he pays. Ross Chambers, "Pointless Stories, Storyless Points: Roland Barthes between 'Soirées de Paris' and 'Incidents,'" *L'esprit créateur* 34, no. 2 (Summer 1994), 12–30.

Belfort and the Jardins, Ave. Ch. De Gaulle in Thionville, the word "Arabs" was accompanied by the codes "G" (largely gay), "R" (prostitutes frequent this site), and "AYOR" (at your own risk). The code "Arabs" did not appear in the guide's listings for any other European country.[62]

Economics and Desire

By the late 1970s, a more frank discussion of the question of money developed, which directly challenged presumptions that a "different" sexual culture was the main explanation for why some Arab men were willing to have sex with gay men while primarily desiring sexual contact with women. More gay male authors wrote explicitly about the interplay of sexual and economic misery as well as prostitution to explain why some North African males were willing to have sex with other males. In 1978, for example, a gay liberationist, in discussing the gay cruising areas of Lyon, spoke of "sexual misery on the wharves" where many men sought to have sex with other men. While many homosexuals, he recognized, were there because of their own "sexual misery," the situation was worse for "a big percentage of immigrant workers, who are fundamentally heterosexual but who have homosexual relations" because they had no choice.[63] In his much-discussed book *Les garçons de passe* (Call Boys, 1976), the *Libération* journalist Jean-Luc Hennig also linked the presence of so many young Maghrebi men among male prostitutes to "sexual misery." He offered a cultural analysis, which explained why some could be tempted into the trade: "It's a way to show off, to demonstrate your virility, like they say, to fuck the other guy." Yet the business demanded more than that. "At the start, they are offered the masculine role, but. . . ." It was this semi-imposed versatility that needed to be explained, and here "Maghrebi" culture—which supposedly focused on roles, on who penetrated whom—would not suffice. "There is first of all the basic need for sex," Hennig wrote, "with all of the sexual misery that ben Jelloun describes in *The Highest Solitude*."[64]

The late 1970s also saw growing, if still relatively infrequent, public indications that "*rapprochements*" on the basis of shared desires were possible: there were, on the one hand, Arab men willing to acknowledge their sexual "openness" and, on the other, some Arab men who identified themselves as preferring other men sexually. This was visible in the breathtak-

---

62. *Guide Spartacus* (1976), 172, 197.

63. GLH-Lyon, "Dossier: Identités," *Interlopes* 3-4 (Autumn 1978), 4-46.

64. Jean-Luc Hennig, *Les garçons de passe: Enquête sur la prostitution masculine* (Paris: Libres-Hallier, 1978), 62.

ingly popular "Sandwich" supplement to *Libération*, with its sexually open personal advertisements.[65] Among ads that clearly indicated that their authors were male and Maghrebi, many played with French fantasies of Arab sexual openness concerning the gender of possible partners. Many, notably, were in the controversial "Prisoners" section. Far more frequently than was the case with other prisoners, those who had Arabic/Berber names or identified as North African either expressed a willingness to hear from both men and women, or said nothing about the gender of potential correspondents. In 1979, for example, "Mohamed S." described himself as a "young man of Moroccan nationality" and wrote, "I wish to correspond with homos and women of any nationality." Meanwhile, "Young Berber, 20 years old," was "seeking out women or nice men who will write to him."[66] Yet a small number of Maghrebi authors of ads made clear that they sought the company of fellow male homosexuals. In January 1980, for example, "Lajimi" described himself as "Tunisian, 23 yo, brown hair, 70 kg, 1.73 [m], masculine, not bad, welcoming, looking for a guy between 18/22 years, handsome, well built, masculine, who loves durable friendship and more as well, for joint vacation in Tunisia and, if we get along, life together, no effeminates."[67] Murat, more ambiguously, presented himself as "Young 29 yo man, lkng for companion to travel to South Asia . . . homo preferred." Whether what these authors signaled were complementary needs (for sex or companionship) or desire for male company, all these ads manipulated codes that, precisely because of the ways in which they invoked Arab masculinities, were markedly French. This fluency proved difficult for most (other) French people, gay or not, to recognize; they remained too attached to "Maghrebi" difference, notably of Arab male desire as either naïve or uniquely polymorphously perverse.[68]

The Unimaginable Gay Arab

In his 1974 play *La tour de la Défense* (Skyscraper), Copi provided an unusually frank depiction of the exclusively homosexual desire of a young

65. For an insightful historical analysis of personal ads and queer identities in the Netherlands during the 1960s and '70s, see Andrew DJ Shield, "'Suriname—Seeking a Lonely, Lesbian Friend for Correspondence': Immigration and Homo-Emancipation in the Netherlands, 1965–79," *History Workshop Journal* 78, no. 1 (Autumn 2014), 246–264.

66. Mohammed Sabboui, "Taulard(e)s: Beaux yeux noirs," *Sandwich-Libération* 1 (1 December 1979), 29; Sam Ferhat, "Taulard(e)s: Jeune Kabyle de 20 ans," ibid.

67. Lajimi, "Messages: Vacances ensemble en Tunisie," *Sandwich-Libération* 6 (5 January 1980), 10.

68. Murat Duhem, "Chéri(e)s: Charter," *Sandwich-Libération* 7 (12 January 1980), 7.

and "masculine" North African man, and of the incapacity of the French people who desire him to accept that he is gay. "Micheline," a gay man who also likes to dress up as a woman, has fallen hard for "Ahmed," and seeks to tempt him into yet another sexual encounter via the flirtatious line "Oh, you're obsessed. You love ass that much?" What shocks, however, is Ahmed's response: "Me, that's all I like. I am not into women, I only like boys!" To this, Micheline can only respond, "He's crazy! Where are you from, you?"[69] The play also raises another fraught and important issue, which appeared intermittently in the research that grounds this book. Since the 1990s, activists and theorists have worked to distinguish analyses of "trans" identities from those defined by sexuality.[70] In this exchange, as in many of the frequent references to trans topics in his work, however, Copi presumes that his audience will collapse transsexuality, transgender, and transvestism into homosexuality. It is a presumption very typical of the era, with its embrace of the hetero-homo binary and concomitant challenge to understandings premised on gender inversion. Yet the particular attention Copi gives to an "Arab" sexual economy and its relation to the consolidation of binarism in France accentuates the erasure of any distinction between "trans" and "homo" in this exchange, which raises gender inversion ("You love ass that much?") in order to draw attention to the "real" sex of the object of desire ("I am not into women, I only like boys!"). What Copi highlights here—"He's crazy! Where are you from, you?"—is the great difficulty contemporary French thinkers faced in trying to understand that men defined as being Arab or from North Africa (especially men from the popular classes) could identify as gay, and could do so in reference to sexual object choice as distinct from gender identity. Still, even this more capacious representation of sexual self-positioning offers little explanation of how Ahmed's sexual choices are racialized. The erotics of Algerian difference summoned Arabs to speak, but within limited parameters.

Post-1968 discussions had great difficulty in taking the subjectivity of so-called Arabs seriously,—that is, to recognize that factors beyond the sociological ("the Arab man in France") shaped individual sexual choices. This had been evident in the discussions animating the FHAR, and it raised many questions about the antiracist claims of gay male activists. Yves Jac-

69. Copi, *Les quatres jumelles, suivi de la tour de la Défense* (Paris: Christian Bourgois, 1974 [1999]), 111.

70. See, e.g., Susan Stryker, "(De)Subjugated Knowledges : An Introduction to Transgender Studies," in Stryker and Stephen Whittle, eds., *The Transgender Studies Reader* (New York: Routledge, 2006), 1–17. In French discussions, see esp. Beatriz Preciado, *Testo Junkie: Sexe, drogue et biopolitique* (Paris: Grasset & Fasquelle, 2008).

quemard, who cowrote the play *Model Boy* (1973) with Jean-Michel Sénécal, drew attention to a different interpretation in an interview that the
co-authors gave to *In magazine masculine*: "How many supposedly liberal
Europeans, and homosexuals to boot, are convinced that the North Africans (whom they take advantage of) are nothing more than objects for
their pleasure?"[71] Although relatively uncommon, such texts probed the
relationship between gay men and Arab men to question why so many
presumed that these were two distinct groups, even amid assumptions
that privileged lines of communication existed between them. It was possible at the time to argue that extant Orientalist certainties, especially gay
male "Arabophilia," made it difficult for the objectified Arab men to express their own desires and pleasures, which concurrently could include a
wish to be recognized as gay. Yet almost no French commentators did so.
In a 1977 letter to *Libération* which catalogued a variety of ways in which
French sexual stereotypes affected Arab men, several Algerian men and
their French colleagues highlighted how "the supposed venality of the Arab
homosexual" damaged those who faced such assumptions. "Arabs also
have the right to find love in their difference," they pointedly reminded
readers.[72]

Renaud Camus against Hocquenghem . . . and the Arab

A little-noticed disagreement among openly gay intellectuals suggests how
the 1970s Arab question was pushed out of the center of French thinking about homosexuality. On one side of the debate were two openly gay
writers who had accompanied the FHAR and written in *Libération*, Hocquenghem (born 1946) and Hennig (born 1945); on the other side was
their contemporary, the novelist and critic Renaud Camus (born 1946),
who had spent the early 1970s working at éditions Denoël and published
his first novel, *Travers* (Off the Beaten Path) in 1978. Despite the reminder
that Djajam, Ghalem, Zemmouri, and others had offered, none of the
texts in question entertained the idea that Arab men themselves could
be homosexual. It was the place of the Arab man in French homosexual
life that concerned these writers as they staked out their positions on the
past, present, and future of the gay world. As was the case in FHAR discussions, the attention of these gay intellectuals to the Arab question seems

71. André Gauthiez, "Interview de Yves Jacquemard et Jean-Michel Sénécal," *In magazine
masculin* (6 August–September. 1973), 26– 28. Jacquemard-Sénécal was the pseudonym the
two authors signed to the detective novels they began to publish in 1976.
72. Djajam et al., "Courrier," 2.

to have facilitated the exclusion of women, heterosexual or lesbian, from their writings. This despite the ways in which so many male Maghrebi authors in these years joined questions of women to their reflections on male homosexuality.

In 1979, it was the preface by the literary critic Roland Barthes that originally excited discussions among Parisian intellectuals about the publication of *Tricks: 33 Stories*, by Renaud Camus. The young author had published two previous books and was the literary editor of the first "general" French magazine aimed at gays and lesbians, *Le Gai Pied*. Barthes, however, had kept his distance from gay politics and rejected "coming out," notably as concerned his own homosexuality. Yet his silence on this question, he recognized, had led him to miss opportunities to articulate novel forms of critique. Tiphaine Samoyault, Barthes's biographer, argues that the preface reflects his decision "to speak of the position of difference and marginality that [homosexuality] can make available for thinking differently." To speak of homosexuality allowed him to propose new ways to critique the existing order. His preface focused on acts, on sex, rather than on identities. *Tricks* itself, however, insisted on the connections between acts and gay male identity. The book recounted a series of sexual encounters (thirty-three in the first edition; by the 1982 edition, there were forty-five), all between men. What Barthes announced was the overture of a new era for sex, an age when ideological struggle could be left behind. Behold, he wrote, a text that contained "the most happily shared pleasures. . . . This book tries to speak of sex, in this instance, of homosex, as if that particular fight had already been won, and overcomes the problems such a project poses: in all tranquility." *Tricks*, Barthes suggested, signaled the end of gay politics and a new age of gay sex.[73]

The gay world that *Tricks* presents is full of masculine men who reject fixed roles; they are open to male-male sex acts and positions of all kinds. The shadow of the Arab man, however, troubles this textual monument to a gay world of uninhibited males, many of them very manly indeed, as they commit every possible sex act imaginable with other uninhibited men. The text has only a few references to "Arabs," but they are telling in what they disclose about this French gay intellectual's take on the place of Arab men in his gay world, and in France. One reference is in the only footnote, a long two-page footnote. It recounts an unpleasant end to an

73. Samoyault, *Roland Barthes*, 664. For Barthes, see *Roland Barthes par Roland Barthes* (Paris: Seuil, 1975), notably his well-known discussion of the "two H's: homosexuality and hashish" (58).

afternoon Camus spent in an outdoor cruising area (where men sought anonymous sex with other men) around Marseille. He discovers that his car has been vandalized, which leads him to recount how a local acquaintance, "a leftist teacher," suffered the exact same symbolic vandalism (the brake pedal of the car ripped off and placed so that passersby could see it; in French "*pédale*" is a pejorative word for gay). In the case of his acquaintance, the attack came after one of his students saw him leave a gay bar and informed other students. As Camus explains it, "they're little proles, and more than that, Mediterraneans." What this meant, he continues, is that they are "obsessed with every myth of virility and, especially, with homosexuality." It is, his teacher friend clarified, nothing like Paris, with its enlightened adolescent boys. These "Mediterraneans," he explains, "think of nothing but that—it's a veritable obsession. Their favorite insult, as soon as they hit eleven, twelve, or thirteen years of age, is '*Enculé!*' [a pejorative term for a man who has been sodomized]." The vandalism is one of only two incidents in the book that evoke politics or homophobia. The other happens in the United States, and results, to the shock of Camus the Frenchman, from white Americans learning that his American sexual partner is black.[74]

Camus carefully refers to the young Maghrebi teens he speaks of as "Mediterraneans," and this embeds them in a culture he sees as fixated on sexual roles, anathema to his vision of the new gay male world. In his previous book, Camus offered an extended reflection on "the old Mediterranean sexuality that some hold up as if it's a model." What he saw in this was "a sexuality of roles, rigorously defined once and for all, and never interchangeable." He rejected the limited and restricted nature of this proposed alternative. "For me, who dreams only of endless changes, of name, of faces, of bodies, of sex, of poses, of arguments, to be able to become another, and then another yet again!"[75] In *Tricks*, Camus gives a clear indication that his utopia offers no place for the practices he more usually associates with the sexual world of Mediterraneans. In *Tricks*, however, he assertively names it "Arab." In one of a number of stories in which Camus describes an encounter he had in a dark backroom—a commercial all-male space where men come to have sex, to be in the company of other men wanting and having sex. He writes that he placed his own hands "on the guy's ass," and that the other man "was roughly caressing my asscheeks, and then slid his finger between them." Camus immediately emphasizes,

---

74. *Tricks: 33 récits* (Paris: Mazarine, 1979), 189–190, 341.
75. Camus and Duparc, *Travers*, 128.

"I did the same thing between his." Sexual versatility, here as in so many post-Stonewall gay texts, was the ideal, with each person willing to take any sexual position. Into this encounter ("during this time") of shared openness and mirrored sexual interests, a foreign figure intrudes. "A fortysomething Arab had approached us, and suddenly I felt his completely stiff cock against my ass." It is the weight of an approach to sex he rejects entirely. "I pushed him aside with one hand," Camus says.[76]

Already, in 1978, Camus had detailed his argument that "the old Mediterranean sexuality" was a rejection of freedom. To critique "the celebration of Mediterranean sexuality that typified an earlier generation of homosexuals," he insisted that "what is forbidden is not less intense" in that model—"it's far more so." By this he meant that a focus on what people (men and boys) did, on acts, was less important than how they spoke about these actions in terms of identity. "These people cannot even conceive that they could be homosexual," he explained; "whatever [sexual] activities they engaged in with us, they never would admit what they were." Modern Western homosexuals had no lessons to learn from this approach, only lessons to give. What Camus particularly targeted was the failure of too many to recognize the power of a shared sexual identity. In "Mediterranean" mode, he wrote, "the homo-hetero is less important than the top-bottom couple."[77] His work proposed that the insult "enculé" came from this culture, from the repressive past. Like Barthes, however, he saw a future opening around him that consisted of "the most happily shared pleasures." It was the hetero-homo binary that made these pleasures possible, creating the gay world of bars, backrooms, and books like his. The strict difference between "homo" and "hetero" allowed for each group to revel in their sameness.

A contemporary review in Libération picked up on the oddly racialized fixation of Camus's analysis. Jean-Luc Hennig—gay liberationist, author of Garçons de passe—emphasized not freedom versus oppression, however, but sameness versus difference. In Tricks, according to the article, "cruising insistently appears as a homologous story. As an obsessional object, a rhetoric of repetition, an identifiable story." Hennig criticized Camus' celebration of sameness: "This is basically the polar opposite of the discourse of the métèque [alien] and the nomad, which Hocquenghem proposes in his La beauté de métis [1979]." Hennig was referring to a book that had been published a few months earlier. While its text did not focus on sex, its title was evoked in a key line: "Foreigner: it is with you that the most beautiful

76. Camus, Tricks, 59
77. Camus and Duparc, Travers, 128.

children are made: this explains the fury of racists and the puritanism of antiracists." This assertion spoke to both the insistence with which far-right ideologues had worked to end any possibility of Franco-Algerian *"rapports"* once French domination was no longer tethered to empire, and the haste with which leftists had fled from tricky efforts to think the erotics of Algerian difference.[78] Hennig highlighted the opposition between Hocquenghem and Camus. The previous year, Camus had critiqued Hocquenghem directly, specifically for his celebration of a "Mediterranean" sexuality "in which the act does not automatically produce its author as a homosexual, etc. To sum up, [Hocquenghem] does not hesitate to try and camouflage, with a well known sleight of hand, the most backwards-looking approach with an avant-garde one." In the reading Camus offered, Hocquenghem had gone so far as "to propose as a model exactly that which the entire movement has risen up to reject." Whereas Hocquenghem fought to put the brakes on the imposition of "a homosexuality that's at last wholly white," Camus embraced purity as a model for the future.[79] By 1979, Camus's disdain of Hocquenghem's vision seemed to some to reflect a new level of sexual freedom; it did reflect a seeming need among theorists of homosexuality to move beyond troubling conceptions of "the Arab man."[80]

Thinking Gay History beyond the American Model

The contradictory claims of Camus and Hocquenghem upend presumptions about identity politics or "communautarianism" in both French and "Anglo-Saxon" discussions. Hocquenghem would continue to defend radical politics in all domains until he died of AIDS in 1988. His career embraced the contradictions as well as the radical hopes that the FHAR had brought to the fore. He was the first French person to "come out" publicly, even as he became a sharp critic of the "normalization" of male homosexual life. He cared about his relationship to Arab men, and he thought that French male homosexuals as a group should care about theirs as well, because he thought that such connections went beyond any gay world, and opened up more possibilities. The ways in which this might limit possibilities for Arab men, either those who might want to define themselves as gay or those who did not, became a key theme in his later work.[81]

78. Hocquenghem, *La beauté*, 12.
79. Camus and Duparc, *Travers*, 127.
80. Jean-Luc Hennig, *"Tricks* de Renaud Camus (1)," *Libération* (14 March 1979), 10.
81. See Richard A. Kaye, "Writers: Guy Hocquenghem. A New French Connection," *Advocate* 406 (10 October 1984), 42–43, which discusses how Arab males and erotico-political

The career of Camus, which today continues to flourish, has been much more straightforward: since the 1990s, the gay literary phenomenon has emerged as one of the most influential theorists of French ultranationalism and racism, with a particular fixation on Arabs. His "Big Replacement" theory, which hallucinates that the "native white" populations of ever larger areas of Europe are being driven out and replaced by people with roots in sub-Saharan Africa and the Maghreb, has drawn the applause of a wide array of supporters, from influential voices in the French media to the most radical fringes of the far right. It derives directly from the "Algerian invasion" arguments that post-1962 far-right activists pioneered.

What the late-1970s dispute between Hocquenghem and Camus makes clear is that the fixation on Arab men they shared had emerged from gay liberationist discussions and, more broadly, from French discussions across the era of sexual revolution. Since then, however, one version of this interest has remained consequential. With *Tricks*, Camus participated in a broader erasure of the Arab question from considerations of how gay politics should develop. He believed in the primacy of sameness—of sexually versatile and virile men who had sex with similar men; of "native whites"— and *Tricks* suggests that a community composed of mirror images requires keeping people defined as different (or who embrace difference) out. These arguments set the stage for the fabrication of a vanilla gay past that made "coming out of the closet" seem the only political response possible. This displaced the anticolonial politics of the FHAR's gay liberationists, notably Hocquenghem, with his own sharp rejection of "a homosexuality that's at last wholly white, in every sense of the term."

The newly vanilla version of gay politics that Camus had championed also cast as backwards people who opted not to link the pleasures or relief they found in sex acts to a specific sexual identity. Evidence from the sexual revolution makes clear that the need to define a public homosexual identity was political, a response to a specific history. Yet this has become difficult to recognize. Instead, an evolutionary schema has come to seem obvious which proposes that coming out is the only possible result of the inevitable march of progress. Erasure of the Arab role in making a modern

---

relationships with Western males are central to Hocquenghem's *L'amour en relief* (Paris: Albin Michel, 1982), published in English as *Love in Relief*, trans. M. Whisler (New York: SeaHorse Press, 1986), and the short film Hocquenghem made with Lionel Soukaz, *Tino* (1985). See also Hocquenghem's last novel, *La Colère de l'agneau* (Paris: Albin Michel, 1986). See also Antoine Idier, "Les vies de Guy Hocquenghem: Sociologie d'une trajectoire à l'intersection des champs politiques, culturels et intellectuels français des années 1960 aux années 1980" (PhD thesis, Université d'Amiens, 2015), 201–202, 475–477.

gay identity in France is part of this comforting project. The trajectory of Renaud Camus, as the Conclusion makes clear, suggests that current racialized visions of "white" France draw from this gay myth.

Beyond Militant Minorities

In most accounts of the '68 years, the "coming out" of gays and lesbians onto the public stage—individually and, more important, as a visible element of the French people—is one of the clearest signs that sexual liberation either freed people to enjoy new possibilities or put an end to the reign of morality and discretion. This chapter shows how attention to the figure of the Arab man opens up perspectives on what changed and how that are more complex than good or bad, freedom or hedonism. After May 1968 there were militant groups, such as the FHAR, which advanced starkly radical claims that the only dangers linked to sex came from efforts to repress or limit it. After 1962, as previous chapters in this book have also assessed, certain far-right groups enflamed dark fears about the dangers that growing erotic liberties posed to the French, dangers which gained greater traction after '68. Yet what gave depth to the so-called sexual revolution, in France and elsewhere, were precipitous shifts in public opinion. For example, cross-sex erotic relationships outside of wedlock became widely accepted.

To understand this French history and measure the effects of its post-Algerian frame, it is not enough to focus only on groups that embraced or rejected "sexual revolution." It also is necessary to look to larger contemporary discussions about sex and society which touched broad publics and sparked much debate. The rest of this book does exactly that, to reveal how this era of unsettled boundaries nourished discourses that linked Arab men and sex and sexuality in France in ways that escaped the purview of militant or other engaged minorities.

FIVE

Prostitution and the Arab Man, 1945–1975: Algerian Pimps and the "Takeover" of the "Whores of France"

Brothels and colonies are two extreme types of heterotopia.

—Michel Foucault (1967)[1]

In an odd episode in the 1977 hit film *Diabolo menthe* (Peppermint Soda), Anne, the youngest of the two sisters at the center of the story, chats worriedly with her friends about *la traite des blanches* (literally, "the traffic in white women"; "white slavery" is the usual English-language equivalent, but the French term *traite* will be used here, because of its explicit gender and racial resonances). Anne warns her friends that many young French girls like themselves, who did nothing more than walk into a clothing store's changing room, were knocked unconscious, only to awaken and find themselves in North Africa, sold into prostitution. Her tale of the *traite*, a focus of public outrage since the mid-nineteenth century, includes all of the genre's key characteristics: innocent ("white") females hijacked into prostitution (often across borders) by men whom they hardly knew and yet had trusted, men who were most often (dark-skinned) foreigners. This is one of several dubious sexual truths the girls share among themselves. Seconds earlier, another girl has informed her friends, with her hands spread as far apart as possible, that an erect penis is "this long." Yet the film doesn't rely on the smiling disbelief of its viewers to deal with Anne's tale; she raises the subject again, near the end of the film, to tell her friends that her older sister has informed her that "there is no traffic in white women." Since 1978, when Alain Corbin published his pathbreaking history of

1. Michel Foucault, "Of Other Spaces" (trans. Jay Miskowiec), *Diacritics*, 16, no. 1, (1986), 27.

French prostitution, *Women for Hire*, contemporary historians repeatedly have confirmed this.[2] In stark contrast, since the lurid scenario apparently first emerged in the 1880s, and until today, public officials and opinion-makers have mobilized repeatedly to combat what they claim is an actual, pervasive menace, lumping together anecdotes to make the narrative seem at once credible and threatening. This tends to happen in eras when questions of boundaries are unsettled—between states, between types of people, and especially between men and women.

Fears about prostitution do not fit obviously into existing histories of the sexual revolution, which is why Anne's invocation of the *traite* is so odd. This is perhaps why such fears have received almost no subsequent attention. As *Diabolo menthe* signals, in the course of celebrating the joys of sexual liberation, there were wide-ranging public debates about various forms of prostitution in France in this era. To an astonishing extent, such talk drew links to Algeria and "Arabs." This chapter and the next map this phenomenon in order to ask how, in the post-decolonization era of sexual liberation, the racialized fears that had long been prominent in French discussions of prostitution became central to assessments of venal sex.

To understand why an Algerian-accented discourse of prostitution took on this role during the sexual revolution, this chapter starts at the end of World War II. It first reveals the important connections between dramatic shifts in how the French managed, on the one hand, prostitution, and on the other, the "end of empire," notably Algeria's war for independence, paying special attention to legal and institutional changes that would have durable effects. Then it plumbs the invention of the figure of the Algerian pimp. Between 1945 and 1962, and then after decolonization, this highly functional bogeyman became the object of public fascination and political fulminations—one identified by a surprising number of commentators as the driving force behind Algeria's liberation and then the "Arab invasion" of France. This burgeoning association between "pimp" and "Algerian" fed and was fed by a renewed fixation on the pimp as a danger to French society, notably its women. The next chapter focuses on an interlinking set of other narratives about prostitution which emerged after 1962, and which

---

2. Corbin, *Les Filles de noce*, 405–436; Judith Walkowitz, *Prostitution and Victorian Society: Women, Class, and the State* (Cambridge: Cambridge University Press, 1980). The most important analysis of how the "narrative" of "white slavery" consolidated and why it has proven so durably popular is in Judith Walkowitz, *City of Dreadful Delight: Narratives of Sexual Danger in Late-Victorian London* (Chicago: University of Chicago Press, 1992), 81–134. In addition, see esp. Molly Watson, "The Trade in Women: 'White Slavery' and the French Nation, 1899–1939," PhD dissertation, Stanford University, 2000.

So first they need gang and then they need prostitutes

turned around the supposedly insatiable lusts of Maghrebi men living in France as immigrant workers, and their need for prostitutes. These narratives suggested that France was playing a dangerous game in allowing such people on its soil. The end of the next chapter returns to post-1962 stories about the *traite*, which linked or synthesized these two sources of fear and loathing, pimps and clients, and catalyzed panic about male sexuality and male failures between France and Algeria, Europe and North Africa. Such panic spread through stories that focused on "white" women reportedly sent to North Africa and "Arabia," usually by Arab traffickers.

These claims circulated widely among French people. Still, they first blossomed in more confined circles, to which this chapter and the next pay particular attention: on the one hand, social Catholics, who were broadly on the left; on the other, the far right. The term "social Catholics" refers to a broad grouping of clergy and laity who in various ways worked to address "the social question"—the sharp inequalities that accompanied the growth of industrial capitalism and the material and moral suffering that ensued— through "Christian" public action, whether social work or politics.[3] Since the defeat of the Nazis, social Catholics had staked out public positions on decolonization and on racism that starkly diverged from those of the far right. During the Algerian war, social Catholics (along with "progressive" Protestants) had been critical of imperial abuses, open to dramatic colonial reforms, and eventually accepting of Algerian independence.[4] Then and, even more insistently, after 1962, they had emphatically condemned racism. Yet the far right and social Catholics shared a deep concern about developments around sex in post-1962 France—leaders of both groups talked urgently about the potential damage that "sexual promiscuity," shifts in public attitudes toward sexuality, and sexual "decadence" would surely cause—even if the reasons they gave and the ways in which they expressed such worries often differed. The anxieties they shared led writers and activists from these opposed groups to use similar warnings about the "Arab" shape of French prostitution to win the attention of larger publics. The lessons they hoped to impart were distinct: one group aimed to lead French people to moral renewal through religious revival, while the other

3. Social Catholicism in France emerged in the late nineteenth century; its clearest political echo was "Christian democracy," which in France had its greatest influence at the Liberation and after. On origins, see esp. Jean-Marie Mayeur, *Catholicisme social et démocratie chrétienne: Principes romains, expériences françaises* (Paris: Éditions du Cerf, 1986); on Christian democracy and other manifestations of social Catholicism in the twentieth century, see, e.g., *Les catholiques dans la République, 1905–2005*, ed. Bruno Duriez (Paris: Éditions de l'Atelier, 2005).

4. See Darcie Fontaine, *Decolonizing Christianity: Religion and the End of Empire in France and Algeria* (Cambridge: Cambridge University Press, 2016).

sought national renewal through racial pride. Yet there were fundamental affinities in their arguments. This is unsurprising since, alongside a durable connection to the Roman Catholic Church, they relied on shared statistics, claims, and references.

In the 1960s and '70s, both social Catholic and far-right talk of prostitution targeted the promiscuous sexual needs of French men and the moral relativism of French society, which winked at such activity, both defined as sapping French strength and morality. Deviant sex—the frequenting of prostitutes—was tied to trafficking with Algerians and Arabs, an "other" in a Christian world view, or quite simply the enemy in explicitly far-right discussions. These understandings emerged in the aftermath of World War II and took on new urgency during the Algerian war.

Writing Christian Morality into Laïc Law: "Social Plagues," Venal Sex, and French Empire, 1946–1960

After World War II there was a substantive shift in French discussions about the connections between prostitution and "North Africans," especially Algerians, even as they continued to echo with accounts of venal sex in "the Orient" that had thickened over the course of the nineteenth century. Following defeat in the Napoleonic wars, and in reference to the Maghreb, prostitution had become particularly salient in French versions of long-standing Western claims about "Oriental perversity." In the late 1820s, as historian Gillian Weiss shows, a novel fixation on the enslavement of "white" (European) women for sexual service in the Barbary states—"allusions to sexual violence and intimations of racial mixing," as Weiss writes—emerged as one of the most frequent arguments deployed by French writers who, with their insistent accusations against Maghrebi "barbarism" and "backwardness," set the stage for the 1830 invasion of Algiers.[5] After the occupation began, this argument faded from view, and broader claims that sex for hire was endemic, accepted, and necessary among North Africans reemerged. Such banter now reemphasized excitement and intrigue rather than horror or fear. Orientalist paintings, in which the street prostitute challenged the odalisque as favored subject; erotic postcards of Arab prostitutes; stories of boy prostitutes; stories of the women of Oueld Naïd, who traveled from their homes in the western mountains of Algeria to work as prostitutes in order to support their home

5. Gillian L. Weiss, *Captives and Corsairs: France and Slavery in the Early Modern Mediterranean* (Stanford, CA: Stanford University Press, 2011), 161–169.

villages—these were some of the evocations that, from 1830 on, circulated widely among French people. They were part of larger discussions that presented the Maghreb and its peoples as needing Western oversight, in part because of the aberrant sexual and gendered order that governed them, but which nonetheless also depicted various pleasures and titillations that might facilitate the work of governance.[6]

The post-1945 shift in discourse around Maghrebis and prostitution happened in lockstep with a dramatic reworking of French conversations about prostitution writ large. From 1791, during the French Revolution, until 1946, French law had been loudly silent about prostitutes, a state of "toleration" that left it up to municipal authorities to deal administratively with their existence. This changed when the Law of 13 April 1946 banned bordellos—termed *maisons closes* (closed houses) or *maisons de tolérance* (houses of toleration). Right after World War II, in December 1945, anti-prostitution campaigners convinced the municipal council of Paris to vote to close the bordellos, after a debate in which the councilor Marthe Richard took a key role. In late 1945 and 1946, a public press campaign that linked bordellos to the occupation and collaboration helped convince the National Assembly and government to make the Paris measure the basis of a national statute, which came to be known as the Marthe Richard Law. Many accounts, then and since, have described this law as the end of a "regulationist" system of prostitution in which prostitution was tolerated and regulated, although in ways meant to avoid official approbation. Under the "French system" so well described by Corbin, "regulationism" had meant that municipalities across France, including Algeria, required female prostitutes to register with the police and to submit to regular medical examinations; most had authorized bordellos, with the aim of obscuring the practice from public view by moving it off the streets as much as possible.[7] What the Marthe Richard law effectively eliminated was tacit official acceptance of the emblematic institutional home for this system. Although

---

6. On the French organization of prostitution in Algeria, see Christelle Taraud, *La prostitution coloniale: Algérie, Maroc, Tunisie (1830–1962)* (Paris: Payot, 2003); and Aurélie Perrier, "Sex in the Empire, 1830–1914," in "Intimate Matters: Negotiating Sex, Gender and the Home in Colonial Algeria, 1830–1914" (PhD dissertation, Georgetown University, 2014), 156–305. On the stories and images, see also Malek Alloula, *Le Harem Colonial: Images d'un sous-érotisme* (Paris: Slatkine, 1981); Boone, *The Homoerotics of Orientalism*.

7. See Lilian Mathieu, *Sociologie de la prostitution* (Paris: La Découverte, 2015), 24–27. Law 46-685 of 13 April 1946 leading to the the closure of houses of tolerance and a reinforcement of the fight against pimping, *Journal offficiel de la République française* (hereafter *JORF*) of 14 April 1946, 3138–3139; Corbin, *Les Filles de noce.* Like previous municipal decrees, these laws did not acknowledge the possibility of male prostitution.

its sponsors claimed that it ended regulationism, the key regulatory functions remained in place. The law now named them and assigned them to the police and hospitals: a companion law of 24 April 1946 reinstituted the social and sanitary registry of prostitutes that previously had been anchored in the bordellos by municipal decrees. French law now established a different form of regulationism: neoregulationism, which still allowed the police both to identify prostitutes (either through a declaration by an individual or without her consent) and to require all registered prostitutes to submit to regular examinations for venereal diseases.[8]

The end of regulationism came on 28 July 1960, when France became the last European country to ratify the 2 December 1949 "Abolitionist Convention" of the United Nations: the Convention for the Suppression of the Traffic in Persons and the Exploitation of the Prostitution of Others. Law no. 60–773 of 30 July 1960 inserted the convention into a broader law for the "Fight against Certain Social Plagues," which targeted alcoholism and "homosexuality" alongside prostitution. It also targeted "proxenetism," a status that, unlike the others, had always been, in post-Revolutionary France, a named object of legal repression and public reprobation. The law authorized the government to take repressive measures to combat these "social plagues."[9]

The constellation of measures imposed in 1960 was another powerful signal, this one institutional and legal, of how substantively the war over whether Algerians were French upended foundational sexual and gender norms in France. In his 1962 study *De l'homosexualité*, Edouard Roditi noted that the 1960 Social Plague Law was the first time that the category or the word "homosexuality" had been "spelled out in a French legislative text."

8. Law 48–1086 of 8 July 1948 on the detection and treatment of contagious venereal diseases (*JORF* du 9 July 1948, 6642). Christelle Taraud has shown that it was in the French colonies of the Maghreb, especially Algeria, that the "French system" hewed closest in practice to its stated goals. See Taraud, *La prostitution*.

9. Law 60–754 of 28 July 1960 Authorizing the Ratification of the Convention for the Suppression of Human Trafficking and of the Exploitation of the Prostitution of Another, Adopted by the General Assembly of the United Nations, 2 December 1949; Law 60–773 of 30 July 1960 Authorizing the Government to Take, Pursuant to Article 38 of the Constitution, the Measures Necessary to Fight against Certain Social Diseases; Ordinance no. 60–1245 of 25 November 1960 on the Fight against Pimping, *JORF* (27 November 1960), 10605; Circular of 25 November 1960 on the Suppression of Pimping, *JORF* (27 November 1960), 10610. Despite the fact that neither homosexual behavior and identities nor prostitution had been named in French law, all had drawn much police attention. While overconsumption of alcohol and "alcoholism" had been legally targeted, the "alcoholic" had not. Bertrand Dargelos, "Genèse d'un problème social. Entre moralisation et médicalisation: La lutte antialcoolique en France (1850–1915)," *Lien social et Politiques* 55 (2006), 67–75.

Roditi drew a direct link to ongoing French efforts to crush the Algerian revolution. He noted a parallel to the French Law of 29 July 1939, which—just weeks before Germany's antidemocratic and racist Nazi regime began World War II in Europe—targeted "social plagues" and sought to "increase the repression of vice" in order to show that context explained such juridical aberrations. The 1960 law, as Roditi pointed out, "came about at the very moment when, paradoxically, we promised to extend the quality of 'completely French' to some ten million North African Muslims whose sexual behavior is not always identical to that which our own Judeo-Christian tradition imposes." Roditi was struck by how extraordinary it was that an assertively secular (*laïc*) republic felt the need to "reassert, in legislative texts concerned with sexual crimes, moral principles and penalties that are only valid in one religious context." Historically, republican legislators had been hesitant to vote for laws that appeared to rely only on Christian morality or religious arguments, for reasons grounded in the French Revolution and subsequent republican struggles with the Catholic Church. Prostitution and homosexuality, which had long gone unnamed in post-1789 French laws, legislators now codified, so as to vilify and to authorize repression. Algerian nationalist challenges to existing conventions helped make this necessary.[10]

Roditi's powerful analysis of the social tensions that underwrote the 1960 antihomosexual laws has wider implications. Much has been said about how the 1960 "social plague" law catalyzed debate about homosexual rights, as activists targeted it as oppressive. Little has been said about how this same law was also a foundation for antiprostitution campaigns. This constellation of 1960 laws reveals how the Algerian revolution crystallized French concerns about sexuality and sexual behavior, fears about female sexuality as well as male.[11] These new laws targeted forms of sexual behavior that appeared alien or dangerous to family life and reproduction. In naming them, legislators also enjoined people to speak of them and, as Foucault theorized, made it possible to resist. This is particularly visible when these repressive laws are counterposed to the veritable revolution that, between 1964 and 1975, transformed French family law. As historians such as Camille Robcis show, legislators radically rewrote rules on "filia-

10. Roditi, *De l'homosexualité*, 110.
11. After 1945, such concerns shaped public debate and policies across the West; the French surrender during World War II and Vichy gave this transnational development a particular form in France. On larger trends, see Herzog, *Sex after Fascism* and *Sexuality in Europe*; and Bailey, *Sex in the Heartland*. On France, see esp. Revenin, *Une histoire de garçons*, 2–15; Richard Jobs, *Riding the New Wave: Youth and the Rejuvenation of France after the Second World War* (Stanford, CA: Stanford University Press, 2007).

tion" (legal links that codify paternal and maternal relationships), adoption, and the like that broke definitively with religious or other traditional references. How to explain this disjuncture? The 1960 reforms, which the Algerian revolution fomented, addressed individuals and deviant sexuality rather than the family. The debates around family law explicitly held Christian sources at a distance. Most important, from 1962 to 1979 it was sexual revolutionaries and other activists who placed questions of homosexuality and prostitution at the heart of public debate, whereas family law reforms saw legislators take the lead, with little public debate. This helps explain why social Catholics and others who failed to shape or block massive changes in French family law invested so heavily in the fight against prostitution (and, at other moments, homosexuality). It also makes clear how the 1960 laws framed key debates during the sexual revolution.

Decolonization and Algeria directly shaped the post-1945 French history of prostitution, although the historians of both questions have paid this little attention. At least through the late 1970s, the intersections between decolonization and prostitution continued to matter enormously, as the categories, rules, and public discussions around people involved in prostitution and around Arabs seemingly shifted in sync, and clearly were linked. Beyond dates, the laws and the debates that led to the end of regulationism also intersected tightly with the explanations and upheaval that decolonization engendered. These discussions saw renewed attention to the connections between venal sex, racialized differences, and the protocols of empire, which resituated the ways in which this association had been negotiated in previous decades. At almost every moment, these adjustments reinforced the importance assigned to this dark constellation.

Saving the Maisons Overseas . . . to Save Empire

Significantly, the government did not apply the Marthe Richard Law in Algeria. This fact emerged often in post-1962 debates about prostitution in France. From 1946 to 1962, it also drew much criticism from those fighting to "abolish" prostitution ("abolitionists"), people who had spearheaded the campaign to end regulationism. Abolitionists, and the many press accounts that relayed their concerns and claims, insistently linked Algeria or North Africa to French prostitution. In these years their arguments were constant: the continuation of regulated prostitution undermined French rule. What such critics never said, however, is what evidence from the period makes clear: complications linked to the end of empire were enmeshed with official hesitations about ending regulationism overseas and in the metropole. Until Algerian independence, the desire to combat anticolonialism trumped the call to repress prostitution. This explains the assertion, in one late 1960s "exposé," that "for a long time—*especially between 1946 and 1962*—it was possible to say that the courts were not harsh enough in the condemnations they handed down for pimping."[12] It was the triumph of anticolonialist demands for decolonization—specifically, Algerian independence—that allowed antiregulationist arguments to finally win the day in France.

After World War II, the credibility of explicit arguments both for empire and in favor of the regulationist approach to prostitution had collapsed. French authorities, in both cases, opted to change names and rewrite laws in order to hold onto the foundational aspects of the "French system." The 1946 Constitution transformed what formerly had been named "the empire" into "overseas France," and rechristened "colonial subjects" as "citizens," just as the April 1946 laws both ended regulationism and set up neo regulationism. In the aftermath of early 1960s shifts, both efforts appeared fruitless and hypocritical. Their effects, however, were substantial and require examination.

These twinned refittings came together perfectly in a set of 1947 government regulations fashioned in response to the Marthe Richard Law of 1946, which concerned the supposed needs of certain "French citizens from Overseas France." The technically specific language revealed some confusion. The constitution distinguished Algeria from Overseas France (it was, in the interpretation of most jurists, part of the metropole), and French laws had long asserted that all Algerians were French nationals, not colonial subjects. Yet the secret regulations made clear that "Muslim" Algerians were the main source of concern. That is, the inappropriate terms revealed that the text aimed to distinguish such men from other citizens, even if French law made this difficult. The goal was to make sure that, despite the ban in continental France, the access of this subcategory of "French citizens" to prostitutes could still be guaranteed, as well as regulated and surveilled, just as it had been previously. The racialized grounds of this effort were explicit.[13]

12. Dominique Dallayrac, *Dossier prostitution* (Paris: Robert Laffont, 1966), 133; emphasis added.

13. The Constitution of 1946 redefined all former colonies and protectorates as "France d'Outre-mer," (Overseas France); there was much disagreement among jurists about whether the Algerian *départements* were part of this, or part of the "metropole." All were also part of the new Union Française, which joined metropolitan and Overseas France. Since 1944, all people from Algeria were legally French citizens; like all other French citizens, they also now all had

These official Fourth Republic documents, which focus on the sexual needs and potential sexual partners of some Frenchmen, provide detailed evidence of how heavily racial thinking weighed on government decisions in the aftermath of the Shoah. Since the Third Republic began, French republicans had worked hard to keep references to "race," "religion," "ethnicity," or "origin" out of French laws and official regulations. Scholars of empire, or students of the governance of people of color in the metropole, have had difficulty identifying exceptions to this insistent formal colorblindness. One important recent study of "race" in contemporary France, for example, asserts its authority through the author's discovery of one single decree that explicitly references "race" and how authorities applied it in interwar French Indochina and in other colonies. It is telling indeed that this earlier decree concerned métissage—the children of "mixed race" couples, or what the racist language of laws in the United States, South Africa, and elsewhere termed "miscegenation"—which is to a say a question that renders corporeal certain fantasies about the intersection of sex, empire, and racial thinking. As the anthropologist Ann L. Stoler and others have detailed, such sexual questions were central to the consolidation of colonial categories, concerns, and rule, but in this study of métissage—as in almost all recent French scholarship on empire and race—the author does not explore this sexual foundation.[14]

Violating the Law to Protect the Race

These late-1940s governmental responses to the Marthe Richard Law were at once centered on the metropole and rife with invocations of race, ethnicity, and empire as well as of gender and sex. Other scholars have studied them, yet have avoided any consideration of what they suggest about republican governance and "race." Some military historians situate them in the context of histories of legalized prostitution, and limit their analyses to how these rules affected French soldiers (wink, wink, nudge, nudge). Others, who have explored how these explicitly racialized decrees affected prostitution outside the metropole, have focused only on their colonial implications, as if the history of "race," racism and, sex in France was reducible to the

"French Union citizenship," which also included Tunisians and Moroccans (each group also had its own nationality, so that they were not "French citizens").

14. See Emmanuelle Saada, *Empire's Children: Race, Filiation, and Citizenship in the French Colonies*, trans. Arthur Goldhammer (Chicago: University of Chicago Press, 2012). For Stoler, see, eg, *Carnal Knowledge and Imperial Power: Race and the Intimate in Colonial Rule* (Berkeley: University of California Press, 2002).

overseas colonial project, distinct from the history of France tout court. Yet they reveal much about French thinking in the 1940s, and they shaped the governance and the lives of people in France over the 1960s and 1970s—especially Arab people, who continued to find themselves positioned at the intersections of racism and colonialism even after decolonization.

A classified note dated 24 May 1947 made the racialized stakes particularly explicit. It concerned the existence "of Military Campaign Bordellos (BMC) on Metropolitan Territory." The Marthe Richard Law had made them illegal, along with other bordellos, which the note referenced when it spoke of "the numerous inconveniences the application of this measure poses as regards North African military personnel." It did this to preface its announcement that, in clear violation of the law, "the Ministry of the Department of War has agreed to reopen these establishments, *sous réserve d'une discrétion absolue* [on the condition that it be done in absolute secrecy]."[15] Previously, the existence of legal bordellos had been an obvious if tacit sign that the French government recognized the need (in terms of public health, the arguments went) to "regulate" prostitution. Now, the government embraced secrecy. It did so in order to continue authorizing regulated bordellos. But this was also a policy that enforced clear distinctions among its soldiers—between French "citizens"—on the basis of racialized origins and with the goal of limiting their sexual outlets to women of that very same "origin"—scholarship on French republicanism's supposed history of "color-blindness" nothwithstanding.

The BMCs were state-sponsored and regulated bordellos. Beginning in the nineteenth century, the French military had begun to organize such establishments for the benefit of its male personnel, though before 1914 their "organization," as historian Christelle Taraud puts it, "remains rather obscure."[16] Documents from World War I detail their existence both within the metropole and without, as well as the shuttering of those within the metropole in 1918. All the documents present the BMCs as a key aspect of efforts to "serve and protect" male military personnel. In subsequent

15. "Instruction confidentielle de l'EMA fixant le statut des BMC des unités nord-africaines stationnées sur le territoire métropolitain" (19 May 1947), and in SHD: 7U 572/10; and Circulaire n. 3107 du 24 mai 1947, in SHD: 6T/312; both cited in Michel Serge Hardy, *De la morale au moral des troupes ou l'histoire des B.M.C., 1918–2004* (Paris: Lavauzelle, 2004), 103; also cited by Raphaëlle Branche, "La sexualité des appelés en Algérie," in *Des Hommes et des femmes en guerre d'Algérie*, ed. Jean-Charles Jauffret (Paris: Autrement, 2003), 402–415. Branche cites it as a referent for the operation of B.M.C in Algeria, which is her subject; she does not explore its metropolitan implications. The most extensive discussion is in Christian Benoit, *Le soldat et la putain: Histoire d'un couple inséparable* (Paris: Pierre de Taillac, 2013).

16. Taraud, *La prostitution*, 341.

decades, however, most such efforts focused on a subset of these men. Over the course of the 1930s, when BMCs were reestablished in the metropole, and into the 1940s, extant instructions contained detailed references to the "color" and "race" of both the soldiers concerned and the women the military made sure were available to them. Which is to say that, despite the central role that fear of syphilis played in official explanations of French regulationism and especially of the need for BMCs, these military moves were tightly focused on the fantasmatic dangers of miscegenation and racial mixing (although the assertion that Arabs were syphilitic by nature was one element of racialized French early-twentieth-century medical knowledge).[17] What distinguished these earlier texts and decisions from those of 1947 was that they did not carry the signature of civil authorities. After World War II, to manage the pressing intersection between "race," empire, and sex, however, representatives of the French republic embraced racial categories that its constitution explicitly banned in order to circumvent a law its government had recently adopted.

The "confidential instruction" of 19 May 1947 that the 24 May note sought to explain is worth citing in full, because its affirmation of boundaries of gender, sexual, and racialized difference is so insistent. It outlined the operations of these "secret" BMCs.

I—The BMC is composed of a team of North African women, under the direction of a female contractor [*une concessionnaire*] of the same origin, which is made available exclusively to North African military personnel under the supervision of the Military Command.

II—The BMC is attached to a corps of troops or to a grouping of units that make up a corps that is stationed on metropolitan territory and made up of a majority of Algerian, Moroccan, or Tunisian military personnel. *The correspondence of nationality between the military personnel and the women must be respected.*

Military formations for which the number of North Africans does not justify the assignment of a BMC will be attached to a neighboring corps that has one.[18]

Almost as important as the need to guarantee that every "North African" soldier would have access to "North African" prostitutes, this note suggests,

17. On the importance of concerns about *"relations mixtes,"* see esp. Mathieu, *Sociologie,* 27; see also Benoit, *Le soldat,* 415. On syphilis, see Surkis, *Sexing the Citizen.*
18. Hardy, ibid. Emphasis added.

was the impulse to make sure that non-"North Africans" would not, at least in the metropole.

The "total secrecy" these notes summoned as a condition for this new version of tolerance did not pan out. Instead, a number of articles in the national press reported on the resulting bordellos (figure 15). All approved of the ministry's approach. One of the first articles appeared just months after the government's decision, in the true-crime weekly *Qui? Police*. It emphasized the racial nature of the operation, noting that the BMC at Camp Gallieni, in Fréjus, was "out of bounds for Europeans."[19] The mainstream press, too, covered them, and also focused on racialized distinctions between French soldiers. In March 1949, the weekly *Samedi-soir* published an article with the title "The Grunt [*troufion*] of '49 Respects Female Soldiers but the [Moroccan] Spahis Have Fatmas Back at Base." This framing of the story reassured readers that, since the institution of the Marthe Richard Law, (white) French soldiers had not become sexual obsessives and that, perhaps more important, no such risk had been taken with their Moroccan counterparts. It described the existence of "BMC (Translation: Military Campaign Boudoir [*sic*])" and reported from one in Senlis, which employed five women for the benefit of the 250 men of the 7th Spahis. Another article stood out, as its anonymous author asserted that the military had ignored civilian authorities to establish, "for the use of the North Africans of the Paris garrison," what the article named a "Clandestine Military Boudoir" (BMC in French) which "housed Mauresque boarders specially recruited to relieve their valiant compatriots." The others made clear that these establishments had been fully authorized.[20]

All the articles focus on recently imposed legal restrictions on houses of prostitution—the 1947 article quoted the "madam" stating that "since the shutdown we have to turn away candidates [for jobs as prostitutes]"—in order to explain the military's need to illegally establish these segregated BMCs. The media echo, however, reveals much more about a different and more important context: the post-1946 explosion of anti–North African racism. The proximate cause was the end of restrictions on the rights of "Muslim" Algerians to travel between Algerian and metropolitan departments or to settle and work in the metropole. (This was one result of the new status of citizenship that the 1946 Constitution had affirmed for all Algerians.)

19. Jean Nevers, "VII. Les filles à soldats de Fréjus," *Qui? Police* 62 (28 August 1947), 4–5.

20. "Le Troufion 49 respecte les soldates mais les spahis ont des fatmas à la caserne," *Samedi-soir* (12 March 1949), 8; "Les Boudoirs clandestins militaires," in "Voix de France et du monde," a special issue of *Le digest Français* (1948), 58–60.

Figure 15. "Clandestine Military Boudoirs," from "Prostitution 48," *Digest français* 4 (1948). All rights reserved (DR).

The racist press coverage that shadowed these shifts fixated on charges of sexual violence and deviance to define all "North Africans" as part of a menacing threat to France. A 1948 police investigation blamed criminals, notably those involved in "moral transgressions and proxenetism," for "discrediting all of their compatriots" in the "eyes of Parisians." Its assertion that the image of Algerians in the "eyes of Parisians" was tied to pimping, despite its odd causal claim, reveals how in the late 1940s newly pressing concerns about pimps impregnated discussions about Algerian newcomers.[21]

The figure of the pimp was newly visible in the very years that the tabloid press fomented public anxieties that newly arriving "Muslim" Algerians would threaten public order. The campaign in 1945 and 1946 that had led to the closing of the bordellos had relied on sharp denunciations of the exploitative inhumanity of the women and men who ran them. Many presented instances of collaboration between Nazi or Vichy authorities and the madams and other owners of the bordellos as telling examples.[22] In such arguments, prostitutes were simply victims, with no agency. To defend these poor women, a Communist journalist had written in late 1945, "They are the ones, the [brothel] owners, the procurers, who need to be eliminated." Now that the law no longer turned a blind eye to the "madams" and other managers of bordellos, the pimp, long a figure of disrepute (and of legal repression), emerged as the most efficacious figure to assume the role of soulless exploiter. Over the next several decades "he" also came to be described with growing frequency as Algerian. (Algerian prostitutes, on the other hand, were rare in public and police accounts.) The Algerian revolution, which intensified discussions of prostitution as a way to understand Franco-Algerian relations, brought this particular link to the fore.[23]

The Algerian Revolution and Prostitution

As soon as the Algerian nationalist FLN launched its war for independence, all sides sought to tar opponents with links to prostitution. The dispute about who was responsible for prostitution in French North Africa was

21. Le Dir. adjoint de la police judiciaire, "À M le Préfet de Police" (21 July 1948), 2, in Archives de la Police de Paris (hereafter APP): H/A 19.

22. Subsequent scholars, too, presumed that such wartime "collaboration" doomed regulationism. The historian Mary Louise Roberts has challenged this interpretation: she shows that the system, instead, was overwhelmed by the explosion of prostitution that the American occupation of France sparked—a story of American empire that the evidence here about persistent regulationism reinforces. See Mary Louise Roberts, *What Soldiers Do: Sex and the American GI in World War II France* (Chicago: University of Chicago Press, 2013).

23. Anne-Marie Richard, *Monde ouvrier* (29 December 1945), cited in Claire Laubier, *The Condition of Women in France: 1945 to the Present: A Documentary Anthology* (London: Routledge, 2003), 14. There has been no study of *souteneurs* or other pimps in French history. For a rather detailed explanation of legal measures that targeted *souteneurs* (and a polemical explanation for why they were so frequently applied), see "En quoi consistait avant 1946 le système français? 1-Tenanciers, rabbateurs, placeurs et trafiquants internationaux," in "Voix de France et du monde," *Le digest Français* (March 1946), 26–30; and Lucile Ouvrard, *La prostitution: Analyse juridique et choix de politique criminelle. Le livre* (Paris: L'Harmattan, 2000), 23–24n1–3.

long-standing and always seemed, if press coverage and other publications offer any indication, of great public interest. It had grown in intensity alongside the development of anticolonial activism in the Maghreb. In late summer 1952, for example, the Arabic-language Algerian nationalist newspaper *el-Kabas* "expressed great concern about prostitution," according to French officials. The Algerian journalists described the phenomenon as "the result of poverty, thus of colonialism." This campaign to stir people to action "does not look to the Administration" for solutions, the report said, "but to Muslims."[24] In 1954, the Moroccan author Driss Chraïbi published *Le Passé simple*, which depicts the hero's success in slipping into a "European-only" bordello and sleeping with all twelve of the "white" prostitutes. Chraïbi's depiction of the narrator, Driss, and his deceptions and joy, powerfully evokes the complex interplay of domination, fantasy, cowardice, and pleasure in the scenario. Such nuance (and self-critique), always rare, nearly disappeared when in the mid-1950s, both anticolonial struggle and antinationalist repression grew exponentially.[25] The Moroccan Istiqlal party, for example, sought to flex its power by driving prostitutes out of the medina of Khenifra; in February 1956, a small explosion targeted one "house of tolerance."[26]

The FLN announced a ban on prostitution and targeted pimps as soon as it emerged on the scene.[27] The group explicitly presented the commerce in prostitution as the product of French imperialism and those who participated, especially pimps, as objective allies of colonial oppression. During the war, pro-FLN propaganda sometimes denigrated Algerian women aligned with the French as being nothing more than prostitutes. In the most well-known example, the renowned writer and psychologist Frantz Fanon responded to the public "unveiling" of Muslim women on 16 May 1958 in the Forum of Algiers (part of the revolt and coup d'état that led to the collapse of the Fourth Republic) with the claim that the women had been dragged from whorehouses. More generally, however, pro-FLN writers

24. Service de liaisons nord-africaines. Cabinet du Gouvt. Général de l'Algérie, "Bulletin de la presse d'Algérie (questions musulmanes) no. 2251/NA/5 Période du 1 au 15 septembre 1952" (Algiers Sept. 1952), 5 in CARAN: 4AG/532.

25. Driss Chraïbi, *Le Passé simple* (Paris: Denoël, 1954). See Taraud, *La prostitution*, 354–356.

26. Ibid., 361.

27. According to Yacef Saâdi, the organization began the Battle of Algiers with several decrees to the population, including: "3/ Elimination of games of chance and of the ignominious exploitation of prostitution." See *Souvenirs de la bataille d'Alger: Décembre 1956–septembre 1957* (Paris: René Julliard, 1962), 82; Emile Dermenghem, *Le pays d'Abel: Le Sahara des Ouled Naïl, des Larbaa et des Amour* (Paris: Gallimard, 1960).

deployed the metaphor of prostitution to describe what French colonialism had done to all Algerians. In the first "sociological" study published in the name of the FLN, *L'aliénation colonialiste et la résistance de la famille algérienne* (The Resistance of the Algerian Family to Colonialist Alienation, 1961), the keystone chapter was titled "Prostitution." Its authors noted that "the prostitution that colonialism has instituted does not only affect women; the Algerian man, too, is affected; perhaps not in the same way, but with at least as much aggression and for at least as much profit." Sartre, after reading the manuscript, insisted that *Les Temps modernes* publish large sections of this synthetic rereading of existing scholarship. The philosopher's own work, of course, had repeatedly used prostitution to plumb the ways in which power worked—notably its racist and racialized forms— perhaps most explicitly in *La putain respectueuse* (The Respectful Whore, 1946), a play that focused on American antiblack racism.[28]

Abolitionists against Racism

What magnified discussions about Algerian prostitution was the government's decision to continue a regulationist policy based in legal bordellos in Algeria, even after the 1946 ban had taken effect in the metropole. This had led a small group of "European" French citizens in Algeria to target the policy. They claimed that it was the key factor that explained "Muslim" dissatisfaction with French rule. These antiprostitution abolitionists, led by the social Catholic Jean Scelles, rejected an argument that many other "Europeans" embraced: that Algerians—Arabs, Berbers, Muslims—were particularly tolerant of prostitution, or at least had a long tradition of accepting it. Although Scelles went as far as to claim that in "Kabylia [a Berber region east of Algiers] there is no such thing as prostitution," he usually made the argument that Islam banned the practice.[29] He often referred to a letter he had received in 1951 from the Grand Mufti of Algiers which read, "For us Mohammedans prostitution is one of the gravest sins."[30] The broader argu-

28. Saadia-et-Lakhdar [Salima Sahraoui-Bouaziz, aka "Saadia"] and Rabah Bouaziz [aka "Lakhdar"], *L'aliénation colonialiste et la résistance de la famille algérienne* (Lausanne: La Cité, 1961), 89; most of the book's contents were also published in *Les Temps modernes* 182 (June 1961), 1680–1734; and 183 (July 1961), 52–80. A new edition contains key information on the authors and the elaboration of this text; see "Présentation pour la réédition" (Algiers: Casbah éditions), 2014, 11–15.

29. Jean Scelles, "La psychologie des travailleurs manuels nord-africains en France," part 2, *Bulletin Auxilia* (March-April 1960), supplement, 4.

30. Jean Gabriel Mancini, *Prostitutes and Their Parasites* (London: Elek Books, 1963), 45.

ment was that French disregard for this supposedly central tenet of Islam largely explained widespread Algerian resentment of French rule.[31]

Over the course of the war, proponents of the abolition of prostitution repeatedly targeted the ongoing toleration of bordellos to criticize French rule in Algeria. As the *Le Monde* journalist Jacqueline Piaitier wrote in 1957, "These houses of . . . 'pleasure,' we know, have not been shut down in Algeria." She put the blame on racism, on those who deployed racist arguments—"The African temperament can be invoked to justify almost anything"—and those who benefited: "most notably the continued existence of bordellos reserved for Europeans only!" This was consonant with efforts by Scelles and his allies to move beyond religiously based arguments to show that the continued tolerance of organized prostitution in Algeria betrayed French republicanism and undermined French rule. Framed as antiracist, the fundamental claim—that the presence of prostitution was a clear sign that something was seriously wrong with those men associated with its practice—remained forthrightly grounded in religious morality.[32]

Pimps Rather Than Rebels?

French propagandists, too, linked their enemies to prostitution, with the same certainty that this association with immorality would discredit them. When the FLN emerged to contest French rule, pro-French commentators regularly sought to explain the role prostitution played in the group's existence. Unlike Scelles, they described its causal role as empowering bad men rather than producing humiliation and rage among Muslims. Such assertions encompassed the accusations that these "Muslims" were hypocritically betraying Islamic virtue and that such behavior was typical of all Muslims. One recurrent target was Ali la Pointe, nom de guerre of FLN fighter Ali Amar. In Gillo Pontecorvo's *Battle of Algiers* (1965), this local FLN leader appeared as a former small-time criminal and card shark who had escaped the sordid underworld life through the revolution. In one key scene, Ali confronts an Algerian pimp in the Casbah. He first orders him to submit to the FLN ban; when that fails, he kills him. French newspapers insisted that Ali la Pointe, like other such killers, had been a pimp; the pimps he and his comrades targeted were thus revealed as their competitors. As a 1971 article put it, he "was a former bad boy who had been a pimp in his

31. In other forums, however, Scelles regularly pointed out the devastating effects on Algerians of things like intense poverty, state violence, and European racism.

32. Jacqueline Piaitier, "La loi de 1946 a-t-elle porté atteinte à la prostitution? III: Les organisateurs du marché," *Le Monde* (5 September 1957).

British Algerian masculinity during war [margin handwritten note]

off hours."[33] The involvement of men like Ali la Pointe in the war was not an escape from this past: it was a continuation of their wrong and thuggish behavior. During the war itself—as well as in nostalgic recountings after 1962—this was just one aspect of a larger set of deeply Orientalist claims which presented Algerian masculinity and nationalism as brutish, overly aggressive, disdainful of women, and inhabited by a harem mentality. France, to the contrary, was a "modernizing" father who worked to free Algerian women from their culturally and religiously imposed chains.

A weightier (or at least more durable) charge claimed that Algerian pimps operating on the French mainland—the metropole—had in large part financed the FLN's struggle. This accusation appears to have first emerged in 1957, in the pages of a far-right magazine, *Rivarol*. As the left-wing literary magazine *Lettres nouvelles* mockingly summarized the "discovery": "The FLN has built up its war treasury through simply taking charge of the prostitution business, by eliminating French pimps. 'Except for a few hold outs, our guys have been pushed aside.'" Shortly thereafter, however, Paris deputy Jean-Marie Le Pen told the National Assembly that in "the 13th arrondissement, in my district . . . French metropolitan shopkeepers complain that efforts to extort money from them by Muslim organizations that camouflage themselves as pimps or common extortionists are going unpunished." He suggested that "extortion and the exploitation of prostitution bring in some one billion francs each month" for the rebels.[34] Just months before, the left-wing sociologist Andrée Michel recounted how the press had covered the first big crackdown by the Parisian police on the Algerian inhabitants of the Goutte d'Or—a poor neighborhood in the 18th arrondissement of Paris that was associated with both Algerian immigration and low-cost prostitutes—by transforming it into a crackdown against "pandering and drug trafficking." Michel criticized the fact that the newspapers made no mention of the "real reason, which was political [to fight FLN influence]." Their focus on supposed criminality rather than on FLN influence was particularly shocking because, as she noted, "the Ministry of the Interior had stated this [political target] clearly when it launched the campaign." Here as elsewhere, the media proved eager to reduce large and politically troubling developments to inflammatory talk about prostitution. Scholars have often done the same.[35]

33. "Des prostituées au Tribunale Grenoble," *Croissance des jeunes nations* 107 (1971), 85.
34. "Et pourtant, elle tourne," *Lettres nouvelles* 51 (July-Aug. 1957), 178; *J.O.R.F.* 100 de 1957 (12 November 1957), 4726. See also André Deslandes, *Le soleil gris* (Paris: Gallimard, 1962), 19.
35. Michel, *Les travailleurs*, 155.

French Prostitution and FLN Finances

There is evidence that money earned through prostitution did help finance the FLN, although the evidence is sparse indeed. Most historians of France rely on claims made in his memoir by Ali Haroun, former head of the Fédération du FLN in Paris. In Jean-Paul Brunet's exaggerated summary, prostitution "paid off big" for the organization.[36] While Haroun quotes from records in his private collection, scholars who rely on his claims, like Brunet, have not seen these records and cite no additional archival evidence. Other historians reference Djamila Amrane's oral history research, which the Algerian historian used to show that many Algerian prostitutes in France also actively participated in FLN activities even as they contributed money to the organization.[37] As the historian Marc André notes, these scholars, too, cite no archival evidence. His own research in Lyon departmental archives, however, does offer minimal evidence of such activity.[38] What is obvious is that both contemporary French discussions and later scholarship gave far more weight to the importance of prostitution in the funding of FLN activism than what had in fact been the case. More striking still is that such scholars make claims about prostitution without conducting any research into actual prostitution in France, even as they deploy claims about it to motivate their arguments about the FLN and Algerian immigration in France.

It was in September 1959 that warnings of a link between Parisian prostitution and the FLN reemerged in wider public discussion, beyond the confines of the far right. It did so through the efforts of the aforementioned Jean Scelles, a proven opponent of the far right. Scelles was a former anti-Vichy resistant (as a cofounder of Combat-Outre-Mer), counselor of the Assembly of the French Union (representing Algeria, 1951–1952), and social Catholic, inspired by Marc Sangnier. He had worked closely with the scholar Louis Massignon in a group they founded and presided over, the Christian Committee for Understanding France Islam, and in other initiatives for "Islamo-Christian understanding." The engagement that defined his later life, and which had already emerged as a central concern by the late 1930s, was the fight to eliminate prostitution. Scelles wrote to

36. Ali Haroun, *La Septième Wilaya: La guerre du FLN en France, 1954–1962* (Paris: Seuil, 1986), Jean-Paul Brunet, *Police contre FLN: Le drame d'octobre 1961* (Paris: Flammarion, 1999), 36.

37. Danièle Djamila Amrane-Minne, *Des femmes dans la guerre d'Algérie* (Paris: Karthala, 1994), 171–177; see, e.g., Lyons, *The Civilizing Mission*, 144.

38. Marc André, "Des Algériennes à Lyon (1947 à 1974)," (PhD diss., Université Paris-Sorbonne, 2014), 290.

Le Monde in the name of another organization he had founded in 1956, Equipes d'action contre la traite des femmes et des enfants (Action Teams against the Trafficking of Women and Children).

Scelles's op-ed article followed the interpretation offered by *Rivarol* and *Le Pen*, rather than that of Andrée Michel. It was written "in the wake of the shooting in the Châtelet neighborhood of Paris, which caused the death of one and injured six others, including a Moroccan prostitute"; it appeared under the title "Against the Slave Trade in Women." Scelles "reminded readers that, in Paris and in the provinces, gangs and pimps exploit prostitutes, either for their own pockets or to finance the rebellion."[39] The turn to claims developed on the far right would prove determinant. In 1960, the first article in the Scelles-aligned pamphlet "Solutions to the Prostitution Problem" was titled "North African Pimping and the Algerian Rebellion." Its subtitle proclaimed: "100 Million Francs Contributed to Terrorism!"[40] Over the course of the 1960s and 1970s, as he focused on the crusade to abolish prostitution in France and the world, Scelles, along with other social Catholic abolitionists—most of whom came from the left Christian milieu—played probably a greater role in nurturing and expanding vicious and racist French stereotypes about North African men than anyone not directly involved in far-right politics.

What is worth underlining in the 1959 *Le Monde* article is the claim that Algerian pimps controlled prostitutes in France and used some or all of the money this business produced to fund the FLN in its war against France. In the immediate aftermath of independence, multiple French newspapers quickly came to assert this as simple fact. The Gaullist-aligned *Paris-jour* proclaimed: "It is also true that prostitution, via the intermediary of nationalist pimps, had long nourished the [bank] accounts of the FLN."[41] The accusation usually suggested that the causal relationship might actually be the reverse: that the rebellion existed to allow Algerian pimps and criminals to extend their illicit activities. This theme recurred after Algeria won independence. In 1965 Georges Bidault presented French supporters of the FLN as the dupes of petty criminals. Bidault had led the National Council of the Resistance (against occupation and collaboration) at the end of

39. Jean Scelles, Equipes d'action, "Contre la traite des femmes," *Le Monde* (27-28 September 1959), 13.

40. Robert-André Vivien, "Le proxénétisme nord africain et la rébellion algérienne: 100 million de francs de contribution au terrorisme!" in *Solution au problème de la prostitution* (Lille: SLEL, 1960), annex xxi–xxiii, in Fondation Scelles/CRIDES 150.

41. Eric de Goutel, "Femmes à vendre: Le trafic de la honte. Ces Messieurs les proxénètes," *Paris-Jour* (28 November 1962), 9.

World War II, and had also served as French prime minister, but he was now living in exile because of his activities during the Algerian war. He had been the head of a new "National Council of the Resistance" aimed at overthrowing Charles de Gaulle and the Fifth Republic in the name of saving French Algeria and France. He mocked "the white knights of progress [who] turned themselves into unpaid middlemen for the most sordid forms of racketeering, prostitution among them." His assertion quickly escaped from the closed circuit of bitter supporters of the lost cause of Algérie française, to spread as fact among experts and activists seeking to inform the public about prostitution. The 1966 book *Dossier prostitution* (Prostitution File) claimed that "good year, bad year, it appears that French prostitution contributed several hundred million Anciens Francs [one to two million dollars] to arm the troops of [Algerian nationalist] Ferhat Abbas."[42] The book's author, Dominique Dallayrac, brought the point home with an extended interview: "Ahmed is Algerian. He arrived in France in 1959, sent as a representative of the FLN to collect the money that would fund terrorism and the rebellion. . . . Ahmed proudly calls himself the inventor of the 'shake-down offensive,' which [moved beyond North African pimps] and targeted pimps of all nationalities; 'Muslim virtue, whatever! Whatever it takes to get a flow of hot cash to those involved in the Djihad.'" The Muslim religiosity that, Scelles and others claimed, made Algerians so averse to prostitution was here revealed as a tool cynically deployed by devious "Arabs." As the 1960 abolitionist publication suggested, "Muslim virtue" was "probably . . . only given as a pretext." Dalleyrac, it must be noted, directly copied significant portions of this part of his book from the 1960 text, one signal both of the tight connections between the array of publications warning of an "Arab takeover" of French prostitution and of the non-existent research that anchored them.[43]

Defining Algerians as Pimps

Post-decolonization references to the participation of Maghrebis, notably Algerians, in the illegal organization of prostitution do have some anchor in police and official claims. In 1973, a police report affirmed that Algerians were responsible for most "foreign" criminality, "most particularly as it concerns morals charges and proxenetism," even as another contemporary

42. Georges Bidault, *D'une Résistance à l'autre* (Paris: Les Presses du Siècle, 1965), 262; Dallayrac, *Dossier prostitution*, 364.

43. Dallayrac, *Dossier prostitution*, 362; Vivien, "Le proxénétisme nord africain," xxi.

police report affirmed that only about 20 percent of charges for proxene-tism concerned foreigners.[44] A 1971 report by the prefect of police for Lyon rejected the claim that there was something that could be called a "foreign milieu" (the word here evokes an organized crime subculture), "insofar as it is widely used to explain the situation around prostitution, proxenetism, or the like, particularly in reference to North African delinquency." For Max Moulins, while "it is true that Lyonnaise prostitution depends heavily on this clientele," those North Africans who became pimps were "new arriv-als" who "must not, despite what it may seem, be thought of as profession-als and are, because of this relative lack of experience, very easy to arrest." It is an interesting recognition of the play of cultural capital, which might in part explain the seemingly large numbers of North Africans (in compari-son to their presence in the metropolitan population) who were arrested, condemned, and expelled. This leaves unanswered the key question of why the association was so tenacious.[45]

In the 1975 novel *La vie devant soi*, the young protagonist Momo, in his effort to understand his own Algerian origins, asserts that the very defini-tion of being an Arab in France is to be a pimp. Media discussions, rather than any reality, made such a fictional claim believable "in the eyes of Pa-risians." This novel's version of the claim also seduced the literary world: the popular novelist Romain Gary had published it under the pseudonym "Emile Ajar," a trick that was exposed when "Ajar" refused to accept the prestigious Prix Goncourt.[46] Police reports consistently affirmed that "North African pimps" made up a small minority of the overall total (with peaks of some 20 to 30 percent in police figures for certain localities), yet press and political discussions relentlessly portrayed Maghrebis as "con-trolling" French prostitution. A 1970 article about prostitution in Lyon highlighted several neighborhoods supposedly "wholly under the control" of the very "North African milieu" that the Lyon prefect would argue did not exist. "The Corsican *milieu* is on the decline, while the North-African

44. Dir. de la Réglementation; dir. gén. de la Police nat.; Min de l'Intérieur, "Note Objet: Problèmes posés par l'immigration étrangère—Projets de solutions" (Paris, 29 August 1973), 3; Anonymous, "Importance et nature de la délinquance étrangère en France" (Paris, 28 August 1973), 2; both in CAC 19960134/6.

45. Max Moulins, préfet du Rhône, "Note sur l'immigration étrangère dans le Rhône" (Lyon, 15 August 1971), 23, in CAC: 19860269/11. In both the national archives (e.g., CAC: 19960134/11) and the Archives départementales des Bouches du Rhône (Marseille; hereafter ADBdR), indications on individual expulsion orders do suggest that Algerians made up a plu-rality of expulsions for proxenitism.

46. Emile Ajar (Romain Gary, pseud.) *La vie devant soi* (Paris: Mercure de France, 1975), 42.

milieu is in the ascendant."[47] A 1966 article in the right-wing daily *Aurore* was typical, with its assertion that "40% of the pimps" who controlled Parisian prostitution were "North Africans. Parisians, Corsicans, Marseillais, Portuguese, Spanish, and Hungarians divvy up the remaining 60%."[48] In another study of prostitution published in 1961, the author affirmed that "35 to 40% of the knights of these ladies are North African, who aim to displace the men of the Isle of Beauty [Corsica]."[49] During a 1963 discussion in Marseille between members of the social Catholic abolitionist group L'amicale du Nid and "senior civil servants, judges, the police, social workers [from the Ministry] of Population," the civil servants reported: "Before in Marseille, the pimps were split between two clans: the North African clan, the Corsican clan." Recently, one "clan" had taken the lead: "The North Africans make up the largest part of the current pimp milieu (more than half)." Such made-up numbers anchored causal affirmations, which always reflected context more than evidence.[50]

Part of what allowed this certainty to consolidate were the diverse histories of how "North Africans" had "displaced" other pimps from the French market. They differed starkly over time, between those written when Algerians were legally French and those written when they were all presumed to be foreign, whatever their legal status. Before 1962, the claims varied quite widely.[51] Around 1950, the Paris police reported that "the Nord-afs came into conflict with Corsican and Marseillais specialists, who had established a privileged position" over the prostitution market. By late 1951, however, they reported that "there are currently no further incidents."[52] The man in charge of the judicial police in 1951 suggested that the "North Africans" did not have the criminal skills to hold onto their role in Parisian prostitu-

47. Jean-Pierre Besnard, "Spéciale Lyon: 'Une prostitution 'visible,'" in *Femmes et mondes* 9 (April-June 1970), 10–12.

48. *L'Aurore* [13 December 1966 article by Didier Leroux]; cited in Pierre Durban, *La psychologie des prostituées* (Paris: Librairie Maloine 1969), 148; Dallayrac, *Dossier prostitution,* 287, 300.

49. René Delpêche, *L'hydre aux mille têtes: Un document sur la prostitution à Paris* (Paris: Karolus, 1961), 117.

50. "Rencontre du 22 Novembre 1963 [entre L'amicale du Nid et hauts fonctionnaires de la Magistrature, la police, les Assistantes sociales de la Pop. à Marseille]," Marseille: Unpublished manuscript, November 1963), 1, in ADBdR: 38 J/1–93.

51. In the mid-1960s there were a number of articles that mapped out the new importance of pieds-noirs pimps, notably in Mediterranean cities, but these had largely disappeared by the late 1960s. See, e.g., Yvon Le Vaillant, "La guerre des gangs sur la côte: Mais à Nice, le milieu est souvent de droite," in *Nouvel observateur* (6 May 1965), 13–15.

52. La direction de la Police judiciare, "Le problème Nord Africain" (Paris, 22 November 1951), 14, in APP: H/A 19.

tion.[53] In his 1954 evocation of the prostitution business around Pigalle in *La physiologie de Paris* (The Physiology of Paris) (the 1965 re-edition layered on the more compelling title: *Paris en forme de Coeur* [Paris in the Shape of a Heart]), Armand Lanoux waxed poetic over the "rivalry between 'alumni groups' [*grands collèges*] from Algiers, Nice, or Corsica."[54]

Dallayrac's demographic history of recent conflict between pimps, however, typified post-independence recounting, which highlighted conflict and a stark difference between Europeans and North Africans: "Just yesterday . . . two groups monopolized the sidewalks: the 'Parigots' [Parisians] and the 'Mediterraneans' [Corsicans and Marseillais]. Today, two clans merit attention: the 'North Afs' and 'the metropolitans.' Between them, it's a daily struggle. . . ."[55] After 1962, the role of the war itself continued to balloon, even as commentators continued to invoke rumors and impressions more often than police statistics or research. In 1985 the historian Louis Chevalier would claim in a bluntly nonchalant racist tone that "North African pimps" had challenged "the Corsicans" for control of prostitution in the Goutte d'Or. The North Africans' conquest began, in Chevalier's telling, when certain pimps began "to stuff the rue de la Goutte d'Or and the rue de la Charbonnière full of tiny love pads." These Algerians worked "hand-in-hand with Algiers's North African milieu, thanks to the numerous relationships that traversed the Mediterranean, notably in terms of the exchange"—the *traite*—"in girls." Chevalier made the martial implications clear as he presented the takeover of the Goutte d'or as offering "a beachhead . . . for a veritable offensive that targeted Pigalle." The "Arab invasion" was a street-to-street affair, and manliness was the real battleground.[56]

The Failure of French Masculinity and the "Arab" Takeover of French Prostitution

Chevalier describes the intrusion of Algerian pimps into the Montmartre market as being unacceptable to the pimps who competed with them because it was an "affront to Corsican masculinity." Yet his pseudoanalysis

53. Raoul, dir. cab., "Objet: Prostitution Nord Africaine" (Paris, 10 August 1951), in APP: H/A 19, 2.

54. Armand Lanoux, *La physiologie de Paris* (Paris: Fayard, 1954), 51; 1965, 58–59; Armand Lanoux, *Paris en forme de Coeur: Physiologie de Paris* (Paris: Fayard, 1965).

55. Dallayrac, *Dossier prostitution*, 299.

56. Louis Chevalier, *Les Ruines de Subure: Montmartre, de 1939 aux années 80* (Paris: Robert Laffont, 1985).

and others like it participated in a post-1962 denigration of French manliness. Such accounts of the supposed incapacity of "French men" to master the Algerian males in their midst worked to summon French resistance and retribution. The previously cited 1960 abolitionist text explained that Algerian readiness to use violence had caused "the control of prostitution" to have "slipped from the hands of the 'Mediterraneans' into those of North Africans, especially those who originated in Algeria." The locals, in this telling, had lost because they had been unprepared to fight back with equal violence. In the 1970s, tales of conquest between "knights of the pavement" added indelible detail to fears of the "Arab invasion" that, first developed in the mid-1960s by far-right theorists, had moved into the pages of mainstream tabloids. There were no historical precedents for the colonization of a country by the poor foreign workers it had invited in, people who had little access to union membership, few political allies, no economic power, and at most the most basic of arms. Still, post-decolonization struggle between pimps in French cities had to mean something.

This talk of Arab pimps foregrounded the responsibility of French male clients of prostitution. In these discussions, French "johns" appeared as one source of the supposed "crisis of masculinity" which absorbed the French far right and many mainstream media sources as well. After 1962, in endless discussions of Algerian pimps taking over the French market and the many reminders of their FLN predecessors, those who frequented prostitutes emerged as sapping the nation's vitality on multiple levels. They had fallen to the level of animals, they had failed to be truly manly, and—in a real break from similar claims at other moments—they had contributed to the defeat of their country across the Mediterranean even as they continued to undermine its strength at home. Dallayrac's interview with Ahmed insisted on this point, and did so through aggressive racialization. The politics of the young man's activities did not stop when the "djihad" triumphed, at least in the quoted words of Ahmed: "I need vengeance [against France] and I am taking it out on French women. . . . Other Ahmeds, there's dozens, hundreds, there's a thousand. Bit by bit, they are going to get their bronze-colored hands on all the whores of France because what they need are men, and not pussies like those French men who couldn't even be bothered to try and hold onto their livelihood."[57] What was at play here was a series of widely deployed tropes in which the cruel Arab was defined

57. Dallayrac, *Dossier prostitution*, 362.

by hyper-virility—an excess of brute aggression and unbound libido that a number of far-right authors across the 1960s would explicitly term an "animal" maleness—while "his" (the cruel Arab's) success revealed the failed masculinity of French men that made this success possible.

These texts proposed that Algerian control of prostitution in France resulted from Gallic weakness—French men's inability to control themselves or respond to the Algerian threat—and that this had placed Algerian men in a position to control certain French women. In numerous non-abolitionist accounts, this takeover had resulted in a dramatic decline in the quality of the pimps when compared to a golden age of the "closed houses." As a 1969 study put it, "Today's pimp seems mainly to be a sordid, mediocre, or middling presence." The author, a certain Dr. Pierre Durban, unhesitatingly linked this to "the dramatic growth of the Arab element, which in Paris, at least, has outmaneuvered the traditional Corsican clan." The weakening of French men, in these analyses, hurt French women, namely prostitutes. Commentators directly linked "Arab" success to what Durban termed a "deep and ancestral contempt for women" (worse even than that of Corsicans, whom he and others also disdained, but whose success in the business of prostitution he explained as due to "a form of hyperpatriarchal civilization").[58] Such claims presented it as obvious that a deep appreciation of "la femme" (woman) had governed the success of earlier (French) pimps. No previous analysis or extant primary-source evidence supported them. What is striking is how the intense post-Vichy vilification of the "French" men and women who ran bordellos—as violent masters, brutal exploiters, and Nazi collaborators—disappeared. As the "Algerian pimp" absorbed all of the evil qualities, he whitewashed the dark French past, and specifically those who had incarnated it.

It is in abolitionist publications that one finds the most elaborate descriptions of the role of the independence struggle in altering the demography of French pimps. In 1978, a Catholic priest who worked with the "French Caribbeans in Paris" claimed that "before the end of the Algerian War, no one in the French West Indies knew what a panderer was." He did not argue, as Scelles had done with Kabylie, that prostitution was previously unknown. His thesis was that "over there, women would prostitute themselves as free agents." It was, however, "during the Algerian war" that "French Caribbean soldiers discovered organized prostitution."[59] In 1972 an abolitionist publication in Lyon published an investigative report that

58. Durban, *La psychologie*, 157.

59. Marcelle Leconte-Souchet, "Voyage à Travers le Paris des immigrés," *Femmes et mondes* 37 (April-June 1978), 11–15.

claimed to historicize the role of the local prefect and the police in overseeing prostitution since the Marthe Richard Law. The journalist Alain Sorel asserted that, since certain events during the Algerian war, French authorities had "wholly manipulated and controlled" what he called their "henchmen-pimps." He focused on Jacques Soustelle, a well-known anthropologist and, more important here, an ex-Gaullist politician from Lyon. Soustelle had been named governor-general of Algeria right after 1 November 1954, and had pursued a policy there of "integration"; he then had played a key role in the events of May 1958 and the subsequent return to power of de Gaulle, in whose governments he served between 1958 and 1961. He left to join forces with the illegal OAS, in protest against the decision by de Gaulle and others to accept Algerian independence. After independence he was in exile until, as part of de Gaulle and Pompidou's efforts to unite the right after the events of May 1968, he had benefited from amnesty. Each of these moments played a role in the dense claims Sorel made about pimps and political activism in Lyon and beyond.[60]

In Sorel's recounting of Soustelle's role in "16 May 1958, in Algiers," the key players were "pimps [who] brought whole trucks, carrying most of the prostitutes from the Casbah" in order to "amplify the number of people in the extraordinary scenes of fraternization between Europeans and Muslim that those nostalgic [for French Algeria] recount." This rehearses an argument made by Fanon and the FLN. (Like other French critics in the 1970s, however, Sorel did not cite allies of the FLN but General Jacques de Bollardière, who had been forced out of the French army after he criticized the use of torture during the war.)[61] Sorel turned back to Lyon to assert that in November 1959 Soustelle had called on one of his "pimp-'protegés,'" who then "came with a gang of henchmen he personally had recruited to stop a pro-peace demonstration that left-wing parties had organized." Yet again, "following the May '68 events in Lyon, the 'Milieu' made large numbers of prostitutes participate in the anti-leftist demonstration," which had brought far-right and Gaullist activists together. The durability of the Algerian connection, in Sorel's telling, explained much in the so-called Fetich's Club Affair, which centered on Lyon. Tellingly, the book that first brought the "scandal of Lyon" to public attention asserted that one of the pimps who played a central role, Hubert Sorba, "had been found guilty in 1961 of arms trafficking in favor the FLN."[62] I have found no evidence to support this claim,

60. Alain Sorel, "L'affaire de Lyon," *Femmes et mondes* 20 (January-March 1973), 14.
61. Ibid.
62. Jean Montaldo, *Les corrompus* (Paris: La Table ronde, 1971).

but it is of a piece with the "Algerian" references that crisscrossed this prostitution scandal. The next chapter sketches out some of these connections.

Conclusion

As this chapter has shown, the new attention to the category of pimps that the Marthe Richard Law instigated actually consolidated in the aftermath of Algerian independence, and its target was, first and foremost, "Arab pimps." Between 1946 and 1962, to fabricate and control Arab clients of prostitution, the French government embraced exceptional measures both in Algeria, by not applying the Marthe Richard Law, and in the metropole, by blatantly violating it. After Algerian independence, harsh new efforts to repress proxenetism coincided with public certainty that pimps in France were Algerian, and the same efforts stoked such beliefs. In 2000, Martine Costes, a social Catholic antiprostitution activist, noted that "from 1960 until today, legislators have endlessly sought to add a new verb, or sentence [to the law books], in order to hunt down the pimp wherever he may be." Costes pointed this out to highlight the inefficacy of such activism. It was inefficient in repressing prostitution, perhaps, but highly effective in tarring the types of men associated with pimping.[63] After decolonization, far-right theorists proclaimed that the lost war for Algeria was a fight over masculinity which was ongoing in the metropole. As this chapter has shown, very similar arguments—with similar words and frames—pretended to describe exactly such a battle raging over the control of French prostitutes.

The next chapter in this book begins by mapping the "scandal of Lyon," thus bringing into focus several key vectors that linked invocations of Algeria and claims about French prostitution after 1962. Those who brought this affair to light, like the French actors this chapter has focused on, came primarily from far-right or social Catholic perspectives. Although the "affair" involved no Algerian pimps, it revealed great public interest in questions about Arab clients. The chapter then turns to the emergence of a prostitute activism group—which began in Lyon in 1972, one unexpected effect of the "Fetich's Club Affair," and gained national attention in 1975—to analyze how claims about Arab clients and pimps together shaped the movement and its public reception. It ends by exploring why and how, after decolonization, a new set of claims about "the traffic in white women" was contoured by connections to Algeria, the Algerian war, and Arab immigration.

63. Martine Costes, "Préface," in Ouvrard, *La prostitution*, 13.

SIX

Prostitution and the Arab Man, 1962–1979: Prostitutes, Arab Clients, and "The Traffic in White Women"

There's a problematic that intrigues thousands of others [besides me], a search for connections that I pursue through bursts that I gather in my collection of notes. . . . Why the Arab male body, a body that women's servitude has shaped? Why prostitution? Does it not result precisely from what is happening sexually today and what is taking shape politically as a result of what is happening sexually?

—Pierre Guyotat (1973)[1]

Between 1968 and 1972, reports that Lyonnaise high society had been enjoying the hospitality of two luxury bordellos, le Fetich's Club and Les Écuries du Roy, sparked a string of revelations that drew national attention. A series of trials that began in November 1972 saw two top police officials jailed. These stories also led to the dismissal of the prefect of the Rhône Department, and the electoral defeat of a solidly implanted local deputy. What became known as the Fetich's Club Affair involved a murder and charges of police and political corruption, but it became a public scandal because it brought titillating details about prostitution—which concerned, most notably, the continued existence of (now illegal) bordellos and the pimps and madams who ran them—"to every home in France," as one account breathlessly put it. To fully map this saga's many intersections with the larger Algerian dynamics that structured French discussions of prostitution in these years, not to mention the saga itself, is not possible here. Yet attention to some of the connections will set the stage for this chapter's exploration of how these dynamics developed in new directions after 1962.

1. Pierre Guyotat, "L'autre scène," in *L'autre scène* 7 (Spring 1973), republished in Pierre Guyotat, *Vivre* (Paris: Denoel, 1984), 32–69.

All of those who leveled the accusations that drove the so-called Fetich's Club Affair, whether they were journalists, judges, or political activists, were tied to either the far right or social Catholicism. The primary accuser, Judge Etienne Ceccaldi, had tight links to both, since in 1960 he had been held in police custody for his ties to the OAS, and in 1964—"because of [his] experience in prison, no doubt" as he explained to one interviewer—he had become a "militant Christian." These dynamics resonated with the elements that structured the discussions of Algerian pimps and French politics explored in the previous chapter. Yet this scandal opened onto even wider discussions in 1970s France, which involved new actors and different aspects of venal sex.

None of the many published accounts of this affair make any effort to explain its extensive links with and echoes of the Algerian war. This is another example of how often French commentators have overlooked the importance of this context for understanding post-1962 France. In 1971, Jean Montaldo, a journalist for *Minute*, the far-right weekly, broke the story with his book *Les Corrompus* (The Corrupt), published by La Table ronde, a publishing house with tight ties to pro-French Algeria and far-right authors. What had drawn Montaldo's attention to the affair, in his telling, was a wholly peripheral case that took place in Lyon in December 1970, concerning an Algerian immigrant imprisoned on murder charges. Tahar Belamri confirmed his confession to the investigating judge, but then stated, according to Montaldo, "I don't understand your policemen. Why did they have to beat the soles of my feet? . . . And then, m'sieur judge, they tortured me. They put me through *la baignoire* [waterboarding]." The judge Chaumouton rushed to investigate these charges, which were ripe with echoes of the "events in Algeria," and he questioned the police commissioner who had overseen Belamri's arrest. Commissioner Javilliey, though cleared, lost his job, which allowed the Fetich's Club Affair to come to light.

Once the case of the tortured Algerian had removed Javilliey from power, another judge, Etienne Ceccaldi, was able to pursue his suspicions that the commissioner—along with other Lyon police officials and politicians, notably the Gaullist deputy Edouard Charret—had developed tight connections with the pimps and madams who ran a series of bordellos in the Lyon area. This was why, he claimed, they had stymied his investigation into an 11 December 1968 murder. It was Ceccaldi, it seems, who leaked the confidential legal files of this case, on which Montaldo based his book. Twenty-five-year-old Robert Hehlem, a known pimp, had died of a gunshot wound suffered while drinking at the Fetich's Club. The suspects were two other pimps who had brought the bleeding Hehlem to the hospital:

the Sorba brothers, Hubert and his younger brother Augustin—"lyrically nicknamed the cursed brothers of the Croix-Rousse (a neighborhood of Lyon)," as Montaldo put it. By 1974 two police officers, including Javilliey, had been jailed (although both were later cleared), and Deputy Charret's district, the Croix-Rousse, had voted him out of office.

Various published accounts linked all of these figures and their actions to the Algerian war. In his 1975 version of what happened, Javilliey gave further details of the torture charges. Belamri claimed he had been subjected to *"la barre"* (which in some descriptions from the Algerian war involved the "sodomization" of the victim with a metal bar; in others, it referred to being hung from a bar by bound limbs) and "electrocuted," the most emblematic form of torture used by French forces in Algeria. Javilliey also suggested that judges had invented the entire affair. One of the "madams" in the case, he recounted, had revealed the reason for such a fabrication when she told him that Ceccaldi had charged her to convey a message: "You tell Javielley to stop his campaign of vicious lies about the OAS. If not, things will turn out badly for him!"[2] What the commissioner termed "an old grudge," then, explained the whole affair. The extreme-right journalist Montaldo, Javielley wrote, was "a close friend of Mr. Ceccaldi," who himself had been imprisoned for ten days in 1960 on suspicion of aiding the OAS. Both Montaldo and Ceccaldi were pieds noirs. Javielley, that is, presented himself as a victim of pro-French Algeria rancor. Charret, too, had direct ties to "Algérie française," ties he had betrayed: though he owed his first entry into Lyonnais politics to Jacques Soustelle, he had rejected Soustelle's appeal to join him in quitting the Gaullist movement in 1960, in order to defend French Algeria. The lawyer who filed charges of defamation against Montaldo on Charret's behalf suggested that the far-right journalist "had vowed to bring Edouard Charret down" as a way to punish him for his betrayal of Soustelle, who in late 1968 had returned from exile to Lyon, and was again involved in Lyonnais politics. An unsourced account that came out before any of the trials reported that "the [far-right] opposition" charged that the Gaullist party in Lyon (UDR) had benefited from "money made from pimping." This rephrased far-right claims about the FLN, which had proven so convincing to social Catholic abolitionists as well as French journalists and subsequent historians. In addition, published reports linked Javilliey, Charret, the Sorba brothers, and Hehlem to

2. See Raphaelle Branche, "La Torture pendant la guerre d'Algérie," in *La guerre d'Algérie, 1954–2004: La fin de l'amnésie*, ed. Mohammed Harbi and Benjamin Stora (Paris: Robert Laffont, 2004), 381–402.

the Civil Action Service (SAC), a semilegal pro-Gaullist vigilante organization that developed out of the so-called barbouzes. This group of operatives, with secret support from members of the Gaullist movement and governments, had fought to crush the OAS through violence and other illegal means.[3] Then there was the claim that the pimp Hubert Sorba had been found guilty of arms trafficking for the benefit of the FLN. There seems to be no solid documentary evidence to prove any single one of the above accusations. What can be demonstrated is that all the accusations circulated widely, in every extant report, as if only references to France's bitter post-Algerian history could allow readers to make sense of this fantastic story of pimps, money, prostitutes, and the ways in which they corrupted politicians and the police.

Arab men in France played key roles in these narratives. The affair became public as an inadvertent result of claims that Tahar Belamri had been tortured. Then, the most widely reported initial responses focused attention on the link between poor Arab men and prostitution. This was despite the fact that no Arab individuals appeared to be involved in the story's high-end prostitution. The two prominent civilian authorities who later lost their jobs both quickly told the press that, despite the 1946 law, bordellos were a necessary part of contemporary French life. One explained this by the presence of Maghrebi immigrants. The *Nouvel observateur* used a quote as the title of its 1972 interview with deputy Charret: "The French people want the bordellos to reopen." In the interview, Charret explained: "I believe that the 1946 law—the famous Marthe Richard Law that banned bordellos—fixed nothing at all and needs to be rethought." While never-proven insinuations that Charret was "complicit with proxenitism" led to his defeat in the 1973 elections, this interview was one of a repetitive series of announcements by French politicians throughout the 1970s that it was necessary to "re-open the houses of prostitution." Almost none, however, went as far as Charret, who called for the establishment of "red-light districts. I am fully aware that this is a hypocritical and immoral solution," he proclaimed, "but if someone has another solution to propose, let him do so."[4] Instead, almost all proponents of legalizing bordellos anew drew

3. On the SAC, see François Audigier, "Le gaullisme d'ordre des années 68," *Vingtième siècle: Revue d'histoire* 116 (2012), 53–68.

4. Jean-Francis Held, "Les bordels de Lyon: Sous la pourriture 'normale,' un règlement de compte politique encore plus pourri," *Nouvel observateur* (21 August 1972), 26–27; Elisabeth Saint-Clair, "Edouard Charret: 'Les Français souhaitent la réouverture des maisons closes,'" *Nouvel observateur* (21 August 1972), 27.

directly from the arguments that Prefect Max Moulins laid out in the first press conference he gave about the Fetich's Club scandal. Moulins sought to explain that, despite the law, the existence of some illegal bordellos was inevitable. He noted, "Lyon is an agglomeration of 1.2 million inhabitants." He further remarked that this was a population "which includes a large number of bachelors." His explanation, however, depended on one crucial distinction among the bachelors: "Sixty thousand of them are North Africans." Whether the question concerned existing illegal bordellos or the idea of reopening the bordellos, the supposed threat posed by male Maghrebi immigrants provided the explanation.[5]

"Foreign Workers" and the Persistence of Prostitution

By the 1970s, the insinuation that North African immigrants living in France —a group made up overwhelmingly of single men, whether unmarried or unaccompanied by family—required prostitutes emerged as common sense. A 1968 article in *Le Monde*, which detailed how newly aggressive policing had led to the recent closing of "most" bordellos in the Paris area, warned readers that, despite such evidence, "we must not kid ourselves; the prostitution problem continues to flourish in Paris." As with all arguments that depend on common sense, there was no need for evidence: "What is necessary to remember is that the whole neighborhood around boulevard de la Chapelle attracts the foreign workers who all live as bachelors in Paris and the surrounding towns." By 1973 one televised nightly news program assured its audience: "It appears that in France, within the national territory, the clientele is shrinking [and] the remaining clients are mainly foreign workers or sailors or soldiers." Other contemporary discussions had much more to say about the first category than about the others.[6]

This argument had a long history, one with odd links to abolitionist campaigners. As early as the 1920s, the most important French organization fighting to abolish prostitution, and therefore to end the "regulationist" or "French" system of bordellos, gave public support to the idea that an exception could be made to meet the needs of "colonial" troops stationed in the metropole. After 1946, of course, this was what the government did (see chapter 5). In May 1959, the General Council of the Seine Department

5. Michel Castaing, "La prostitution aujourd'hui comme hier II: Un 'mal nécessaire' pour qui? *Le Monde* (15 March 1973), 10.

6. Kosta Christitch, "La lutte contre le proxénétisme à Paris," *Le Monde* (26 March 1968), 12; "Un flic et les prostituées," *Journal télévisé de 20h*, Chanel 2, 24 June 1973.

(Paris)—the same assembly that, inspired by Counselor Marthe Richard, had provoked the April 1946 Law through its decision to ban bordellos in Paris—had voted a resolution calling on the government to reopen "bordellos for the exclusive use of North African."[7] The vice president of that assembly, Robert-André Vivien, who had authored the resolution, emerged the next year in a different role: as a leading abolitionist author who wrote a pamphlet titled *Solutions to the Problem of Prostitution* (1960), published by a leading abolitionist publishing house. Marthe Richard herself had also joined the discussion about reopening bordellos; in a 1961 interview she remarked, "The ever growing number of North Africans spread among the urban centers of the metropole—whose sexual needs are particularly violent—have helped reshape the market for prostitution."[8] In an odd 1979 interview, Richard was presented as the adversary of a deputy who had called for reopening houses of prostitution, but she in fact agreed with him that Algerian workers had changed everything and that the situation needed to be rethought.[9]

Even as the law remained unchanged, such common sense shaped police activity. In general, police reports on prostitution presumed that, as a 1977 Marseille report put it, a high number of "immigrants" was "a factor that encourages prostitution."[10] In 1954, a police report defined the "clientele" that drew prostitutes onto Paris streets as being made up of "military, the physically ill, [and] North Africans,"[11] while another report from 1968 described "the influx of foreign labor, notably Blacks and North Africans," as one of the key factors that encouraged "growing and uncontrollable extension of clandestine prostitution."[12] A 1973 report stated that 450 of the approximately 800 prostitutes working in the city of Marseille did so in "la 'Cage' (Arab quarter) (1st [arrondissment])." How to respond to the situation, however, was far less clear. The 1973 report, which René Heckenroth, prefect of police in Marseille, wrote at the request of the Ministry of the

---

7. "Retours en arrière: Les initiatives depuis 1946," *Femmes et mondes* 45 (April-June 1979), 13.

8. Robert-André Vivien, *Solution au problème de la prostitution* (Lille: SLEL, 1960); "Les révélations de Marthe Richard," *Pan!* 2 (1971), 39–41.

9. "1-face à face Marthe Richard Joël Le Tac," *Il* 4 (January 1979), 2–6.

10. Lieut-Col. Vialet, commandant le groupement de Gendarmerie des Bouches du Rhône, "Prostitution no. 272/2" (Marseille, 21 January 1977), 3, in ADBdR 1650 W 1.

11. Georges Maurice, dir. général de la Police Municipale [Paris], "À M le Préfet de Police Objet: Prostitution féminine sur la voie publique Etat Major 2e bureau 2653" (6 December 1954), 5, APP: DB 412.

12. Claude Vallier, "Le nouveau danger des maladies vénériennes," *Tonus: Toutes les semaines au service du Corps médical* 341 (9 September 1968), APP: B/A 407, 2.

Interior, stated, "It is not advisable to impede prostitution or related solici-
tation in certain neighborhoods where a large number of foreign bachelors
live."[13] Yet in 1975 a report from a police officer subordinate to Heckenroth suggested the opposite, that "the presence of an immigrant population or the city's geographic situation (port) cannot be taken into account
to restrict the actions we might take."[14]

Immigrant Sexual Misery, Cause of Sexual Violence?

What are difficult to find, at least in the archives I have examined, are summons for the police to be stricter in the application of existing regulations
in such areas than in their approach to areas with smaller numbers of "immigrants." Instead, a number of commentators used claims about prostitution to call for a dramatic reduction in the number of "immigrants." At
the heart of this argument was the presumption that because of who they
were—single, young, and Arab men—they "represent[ed] a potential danger in terms of sexual violence," as the already cited 1973 police report
put it.[15] A senior civil servant who had long been involved in oversight of
Algerian immigration in the metropole gave a speech in June 1970 to the
Academy of Moral and Political Sciences, in which he noted, "It is not reasonable to want to have a policy that encourages immigration [*politique sys-
tematique de l'immigration*] if we hold onto the rigorous policy voted right
after the Liberation concerning the closing of certain houses [i.e., bordel-
los]." This desire was not reasonable because, he asserted, this combination
of policies had led to widespread fears among "women and young girls"
that they would be raped.[16] Rather than reverse the Marthe Richard Law,
Massenet suggested, it was necessary to restrict legal immigration severely.

Abolitionist groups repeatedly ventriloquized claims that sexual violence by "immigrant workers" could threaten French women. They did so
to reject arguments for reopening bordellos, which they insisted were premised wholly in this fear. One antiprostitution pamphlet summarized this
rather bluntly in a subtitle: "Foreign workers must have access to French
women, or all the good girls will be raped." Abolitionist critiques exposed

13. René Heckenroth, préfet délégué pour la Police, "À M. le ministre de l'Intérieur; Objet: Lutte contre le proxénétisme 137/CAB" (Marseille, 27 January 1973), 2 and 7, in ADBdR
1650/W/1.

14. Commissaire de la police, "Objet: Lutte contre le proxénétisme à M. le Commissaire
central adjoint chef de la sûreté urbaine de Marseille" (Marseille, 11 January 1975), 3, in
ADBdR 1650 W 1.

15. Heckenroth (27 January 1973), 7.

16. Massenet, "Les problèmes posés," 239-260.

what they claimed were the foundations of arguments like, "If we don't channel their sexual needs via new regulations concerning prostitution, imagine the threats they will pose to the honest girls of France (rapes, public indecency, etc.)!" A summary of the political implications was even more biting: "Since they might present a threat to public morality . . . it's important to channel their sexual impulses, which might degenerate"—not into rape or sexual harassment, but—"into revolutionary or social impulses." Such arguments for a return to "regulationism," the author affirmed, would force women into immorality in order to protect social peace: "It's of course up to women to take care of them!" One implication of such an argument was that neither "Arab men" nor "French women" would want to establish sexual connections, whether or not money was involved. Yet some did, as many other commentators insisted.[17]

The Fetich's Club Affair catalyzed abolitionist efforts. By 1974, evidence emerged that Prefect Moulins had been complicit in an aggressive effort to cover up official tolerance of high-end Lyonnais bordellos. Both leftist and abolitionist critics targeted the hypocrisy of the prefect's initial statements. As a journalist in the weekly *L'express* explained in early 1974, "The ex-prefect of the Rhône [Department] argued that prostitution offered a needed form of release for the immigrant workers who live in France without their family."[18] Already in 1972, an abolitionist pamphlet about the Fetich's Club Affair asked, "Why such tolerance?" It mockingly quoted Moulins's statement, which they interpreted to mean: "It would be good if the large number of bachelors among North African workers 'get their rocks off' with 'ladies of the evening,' so as not to rape 'our girls.'" Their critique was straightforward: "One little problem, however, is that the 'Fetich's Club' and the 'Écuries du Roy,' as a matter of fact—didn't let *Nord afs* [a pejorative reference to North Africans] enter." Although explicitly antiracist in tone, such propaganda repeated, ad nauseam and with no direct critique, assertions that Arab immigrants were sexually frustrated and thus prone to sexual violence. The only object of critique was the idea that reregulating prostitution was a way to respond to such a situation. To fight the mortal danger of prostitution, abolitionists eagerly circulated racist stereotypes. As had been the case during the Algerian war, these explicitly antiracist critiques of the Fetich's Club Affair insisted that links with prostitution dem-

17. Georges-Richard Mollard, "La prostitution en France, aujourd'hui: Un signe de mépris, un temps d'hypocrisie," *La revue nouvelle* 4 (April 1974), 712–726.

18. André Bercoff, "Prostitution: La lutte finale?," *L'express* 1175 (14 January 1974), 38–40, 39.

onstrated that those involved were bad people. Here, the target was men of influence. In these years, however, the same insinuations more often concerned Arab male immigrants.[19]

Maisons d'abattage, Misery, and the Market for Sex

There were, various reports revealed, far more bordellos in the Lyon area than just the ritzy Fetich's Club or the high-society Les Écuries du Roy. The Sorba brothers, for example, were co-owners of the Hôtel des Halles, which was what was called a *maison d'abattage* (butcher shop), a bordello "where immigrants line up in wait." In the 1979 televised debate between Marthe Richard and deputy Joel Le Tac, both agreed that the maisons d'abattage had introduced a new level of degradation into French prostitution. Le Tac remarked, "You know, what you said about the bordellos that cost five francs, that still exists in the Goutte d'Or neighborhood [of Paris], for the North Africans. I met one girl who did 120 tricks a day and that over the course of 12 hours."[20] Such depictions suggested that, to use Richard's terms, North African clients had "reshaped" the "market for prostitution," producing newly unsavory, dirty, and unerotic forms of the world's oldest profession.

The history of the sexual term *abattage* is unclear. In 1927, a book of reflections on "things seen" in French bordellos spoke of "charnel houses [*abattoirs*] of love," but this referred to the general phenomenon of the bordello rather than to a particular variant. By 1934, however, an author described "those girls who calculate that they have had relations with at least twenty thousand men each year" as working in "maisons d'abattage," and in the years after 1945 "maison d'abattage" as a term for bordello began to appear quite regularly. In 1946, the scandal sheet *Qui? Police* presented its readers with a history of the institution: "Maison d'abattage! A sinister name. . . . It goes way back, to 1913," when a bordello opened in "a horrific old building on the corner of boulevard de la Chappelle and the rue Caillié" (in the Goutte d'Or). It was in 1918, however, "when the war ended" and "Arabs in the thousands moved into the surrounding area," that the

---

19. Groupe d'informations sur la prostitution, "Le vrai scandale de Lyon," *Prostitution vérité / Antipaya* (*Femmes et monde* hors série 1972), 1. On this key one-off publication, see Lilian Mathieu, *Mobilisations de prostituées* (Paris: Belin, 2001), 40.

20. Marc Kunstlé and Jean-Claude Lamy, *Notre-Dame des Esclandres* (Paris: Presses de la Cité, 1973),191; "1-Face à face Marthe Richard Joël Le Tac," 2–6.

"maisons d'abattage" took root. It was this distinctive link to Arab men that propelled the term's popularity.[21]

By the late 1960s, the elements deployed to describe the maisons d'abattage were predictable and a largely Maghrebi clientele was the baseline. In a pro-abolitionist judge's 1959 study, the description of bordellos as places where the women "don't even leave the room they occupy as the clients line up on the stairs" divided the clientele into two groups who paid different prices. "At the time the tariffs were five hundred francs for North Africans and eight hundred francs for Europeans, who were a rare breed." The explanation of the different prices dripped with disdain. "The North-African client does not stay as long as the European. 'A *raton* ["coon," a racist insult], I get him off and out in five minutes,' one prostitute explained."[22] For *Le Monde* in 1968, these were "places where laborers from the Maghreb and Black Africa meet. In front of the specialized hotel, they get in line and wait to 'go up.' Each one comes back quickly and, quite often, gets back in the line." The explanation for why the maisons d'abattage existed was also widely shared. "The authorities choose to ignore it. 'All these workers live as bachelors,' they say, 'and that we can't just ignore.'" If France wanted this immigrant population, then maisons d'abattage were one result. Which conveniently allowed questions of sexual misery to displace larger questions of exploitation, insalubrious housing, and racism.[23]

The Goutte d'Or Neighborhood of Paris and Prostitution

Most discussions focused on the Goutte d'Or, in the Barbès neighborhood of the 18th arrondissement of Paris. In the 1978 documentary *A Saturday in the Goutte d'Or*, broadcast on Antenne 2 (the "second" French TV network), the camera pans over a streetmarket dominated by three-card monte tables. It pauses on a maison d'abattage: almost thirty men huddled around a door, with several women's voices audible from offscreen. One of the women proposes, "Three thousand" (i.e., thirty French francs); a second, "Two thousand." Then another woman says, "Move your ass; go up or go take a walk." A man aims to get some reaction out of her for free: "And

21. Jacques Roberti, *Maisons de société: Choses vues* (Paris: Fayard, 1927), 14. Léon Clément Bizard, *La vie des filles* (Paris: Grasset, 1934), 90; "On a fermé," *Qui? Police* [n.d.]1946, 14–15, in APP: B/A 408.

22. Marcel Sacotte, *La prostitution* (Paris: Buchet/Chastel, 1959), 79.

23. Kosta Christitch, "La lutte contre le proxénétisme à Paris: Devant les mesures répressives la plupart des hôtels ont décidé de fermer leur porte à la prostitution," *Le Monde* (26 March 1968), 12.

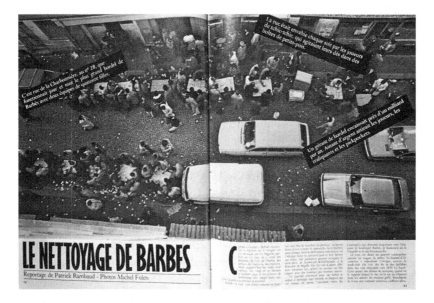

LE NETTOYAGE DE BARBES
Reportage de Patrick Rambaud - Photos Michel Folco

Figure 16. "The Cleanup of Barbès," from the inaugural issue of *Actuel: Le mensuel des années 80* (1979). The text on the left identifies the scene as 28, rue Charbonnière (Paris), "where day and night the biggest bordello in Barbès used to chug away with two teams of fourteen girls." The text at top right states, "The street was invaded every evening by shell game players, who shook their dice in cans of green peas." The bottom right text claims, "Each year, the manager of a bordello took in nearly one billion [old francs; i.e., ten million French francs, or about two million US dollars at 1979 rates]. That much money drew players, drug dealers, and pickpockets."

you, do you move your ass?" The narrator does not interrupt and there is no further explanation of what viewers are expected to know is the back-and-forth between prostitutes and potential johns.[24] In 1979, the first issue of *Actuel: Le mensuel des années 80* put the "clean up of Barbès" (the neighborhood that encompasses the Goutte d'Or) on its cover (figure 16)—and quoted "the owner of a Tunisian restaurant" who insisted, "Barbès is dead. There's no more women, it's dead." The journalist Patrick Rambaud claimed that until recently, "close to six hundred girls worked in twenty-one bordellos." They brought in "around fifteen billion in business each year."[25] To mention the Goutte d'Or almost always involved invocations of the post-

24. Yves Laumet, *Un samedi à la Goutte d'Or*, A2 (broadcast 29 May 1978).
25. Patrick Rambaud, "Le nettoyage de Barbès," *Actuel: Le mensuel des années 80* 1 (November 1979), 42–50, 114–117. In 1975, according to one study, 80 percent of the inhabitants of the area between le Boulevard de la Chapelle and the rue Polonceau and Jessaint were male. See Messamah Khelifa, "La Goutte d'Or," *Esprit* nouvelle série 3 (March 1979), 15–22; 17fn2.

1954 history of Algerians in France. For the far-left Agence-presse Libération, in a 1971 report on the murder of young Djillali Ben Ali, "This is
where the first networks in support of the FLN in France took root. This is
where very strong anti-racist and antifascist traditions took anchor."[26] In
Rambaud's telling, during the police operation to "clean up" the neighborhood, "the immigrants thought of the Battle of Algiers." The echoes of
arguments about Ali la Pointe and prostitution rung out sharply; those of
an "Arab invasion" were more muted.[27]

Yet militant memories were always intertwined with the neigborhood's
reputation for vice and filth. In the 1975 feature film *Les ambassadeurs*, the
Tunisian director Naceur Ktari depicted a group of three Maghrebi men
in Paris. One of the men tells the two others, "This is the Goutte d'Or . . .
shame of the Arabs." Another responds that if any "son of a whore tried to
film the goings-on. . . ." The one who spoke first remarks, in classic mise
en abyme, "He would be too embarrassed vis-à-vis his mother to put it on
film." As the third man heads off, the other two join a crowd of "Maghrebi"
men around the entryway to a maison d'abattage. As one man draws his
friend's attention to a blond woman, another woman smilingly says to one
of them, "Twenty-six francs." He ends up heading up with a darker-skinned
brunette instead. With this scene, Ktari, like so many Maghrebi artists and
commentators in these years, invoked French certainties about Arab men
(and their attachment to blonds) while subtly challenging them. Within
the smothering embrace that, as his film details, limited the options and
outlets for such people, to be seen and heard required meeting sexualized
expectations. Doing so could make it possible, however marginally, for an
artist to refocus the frame.

Ktari's film gave the most visually detailed description of maisons
d'abattage, yet many of the various efforts that brought "North African"
(male, often "immigrant") perspectives to the French public spoke of the
phenomenon. And if male "Maghrebi voices" did not volunteer their take
on the maisons d'abattage, they were asked. The sociologist Juliette Minces
quoted one such man: "If a guy is in need, he goes to Barbès, or another
place. He goes to the special places that they've opened just for that. With
police around and everything. . . . You just go and 'do your business' and

The article makes clear that the reference was to "fifteen billion" new French Francs, and not, as
might be expected, centimes.

26. "Mercredi 27 octobre, le jeune Dejallali Benali, 15 ans et démi . . ." Agence Presse
Libération (APL) informations no. 68bis 4 novembre 1971, 1, in BDIC (fonds Assia Melamed):
F delta rés. 696/22/1–3.

27. Rambaud, "Le nettoyage," 49.

you come back."[28] In the abolitionist *Femmes et mondes* magazine, a journalist noted, "It's awful to see these groups of men waiting in front of the hotel entry," and recounted how "a Maghrebi union activist" sought to respond. The activist's statement elicited sympathy for the immigrant men: "It's because they have the feeling that they can't resist any more, that their nervous system is at risk, which might possibly lead them to make some move they would regret." As such accounts attest, there was constant tension between explanations premised on "sexual misery" and those that lamented supposedly new forms of miserable sexuality. Both types of explanation invoked Arab men. Both drew links to the possibility of violence, especially sexual violence.[29]

The Prostitutes Speak

The debate about the maisons d'abattage also involved other female perspectives: those of prostitutes, almost all of them "French" (i.e., with no announced links to the Maghreb or other parts of Africa). No longer, as in 1945 and 1946, was the prostitute simply an object of concern. This change was in no way inevitable. It was instead part of a larger development that allowed numerous prostitute perspectives to gain a hearing. In the 1970s—the "era of the witness"—prostitutes, like "gay men" and "Arab men," spoke out. Two distinct groups of women grabbed much public attention: former madams, whose careers had spanned the 1946 "divide," and prostitute-militants, who positioned their profession in political terms. There were also many other prostitutes who had new access to the public record, and almost every one of them had quite a lot to say about Arab men.

In the mid-1970s, several books authored or "recounted" by former prostitutes or madams appeared to much acclaim. Most of these books proposed nostalgic recountings of the lost glories of "the French system." In the the post-Vichy discussions that set the stage for the Marthe Richard Law, madams appeared as vicious, violent, and exploitative. In the 1970s they were saucy ladies who dished about the past and then negotiated the subsequent ban on their business. In the book *One Two Two*, for example, Madame Jamet drew much publicity with her claim that the Nazi occupation, when her bordello was reserved for German officers, was "the

28. Minces, *Les travailleurs étrangers*, 450.

29. Marcelle Leconte-Souchet, "Voyage à travers le Paris des immigrés," *Femmes et mondes* 37 (April-June 1978), 11–15.

best time of my life."[30] This whitewashing—which presented the era as a time of commercial success, harmonious badinage, and sexual license—fit squarely into the mid-1970s "mode rétro" that, as scholars such as Henry Rousso have shown, looked back warmly at the Occupation. Yet this venal sex version was particularly dependent on new certainties that the Fetich's Club Affair had brought to the fore: that "the golden age of prostitution" in France had ended in 1946, and something much more sordid—that is, Arab—had taken its place.[31]

The most widely recognized act of prostitute agency in these years was the organized movement for the rights of prostitutes, which began in Lyon around 1972—as a direct result of the Fetich's Club scandal—before coming to national attention in 1975. As the sociologist Lilian Mathieu recounts, the "revolt" first took root in the summer of 1972, when a group of prostitutes sought to organize against a police crackdown that the Fetich's Club Affair had precipitated. The prostitutes failed utterly, notably in their effort to protect their right to operate safely as individuals. The most important Lyonnais newspaper asserted that the women were in no way free agents, but were wholly under male control: "Their 'boyfriends' kept them under watch, hats turned down over the eyes, parked in a car, making sure from a distance that things ran as planned."[32] This effort by the prostitutes did set the stage, however, for the remarkable success of a subsequent campaign.

In early June 1975, some one hundred prostitutes, led by a prostitute activist known as "Ulla," occupied the Church of Saint-Nizier in the heart of Lyon, and issued a series of demands. Over the next week, until the police forced them out, prostitutes in other French cities followed their lead and numerous organizations across France—both political groups and unions, both "new leftists" and feminists—debated their arguments and, in some cases, came out in support. Mathieu convincingly suggests that the prostitute movement's use of "new left" language generated this support. I would argue, however, that a more specific claim—that each prostitute was a free agent who worked for herself—better explained the new left enthusiasm for their cause. Meanwhile, the men involved in the trade—both the pimps and the clients—disappeared. As this chapter and the last have

---

30. Fabienne Jamet, *One two two (122, rue de Provence)* (Paris: Olivier Orban 1975).

31. On the mode rétro, See Henry Rousso, *Le Syndrome de Vichy de 1944 à nos jours* (Paris: Seuil, 1990), 163.

32. *Le Progrès* (26 Aug. 1972); cited in Lilian Mathieu, "Une mobilisation improbable: l'occupation de l'église Saint-Nizier par les prostituées lyonnaises," *Revue française de sociologie* (1999): 475–499; 477; 479.

demonstrated, in post-1962 France both figures (the pimp and the client) had been widely described as Arab. What also authorized the women involved—the leaders, the prostitutes quoted in the press and shown on film—to make these claims for individual agency was that they all were "French" (of "European" origin), and presented themselves as such.

As the movement developed, the prostitute-activists were repeatedly confronted with questions that concerned the role of pimps and, tightly linked with it, their own racism. In the documentary about the Saint-Nizier takeover that Carole Roussopoulos directed, "Ulla" made the argument quite clearly: "The political powers-that-be need the pimps . . . they need to find some, create some. . . . Beating up on prostitutes is just a pretext to create a need for pimps."[33] In a public discussion the following year between three women from the movement and university students in Lyon, the argument again surfaced, this time even more emphatically. The activists insisted that they were independent contractors and that there were no pimps involved. Claims to the contrary, they insisted, were part of a broader capitalist campaign to turn all relationships into economic arrangements. They, instead, sought to normalize the economic stakes of prostitution so that prostitutes, like everyone else, could have both economic and amical, human relations. "They deny the prostitute the right to have friendships," one said in response to the idea that she worked with pimps. "Why is it that in today's society we cannot accept that a prostitute can live with a man who offers her something different than what she finds on the streets? A bit of intimacy with someone." It was a plea for sexual agency, for the right of women to act sexually in different ways, with different people, for different reasons. We now know that the activists' argument was founded on some fundamentally inaccurate claims: pimps did play key roles. Yet the arguments of the activists' critics ignored the control that prostitute militants maintained over their own activism.

French authorities reiterated the explanation of prostitute activism that *Le Progrès de Lyon* had offered in 1972. As Minister of the Interior M. Michel Poniatowski argued on the TV show *Le point sur l'A2,*—"This whole affair has been organized by pimps."[34] In his extensive interviews with participants in the Lyon movement, Mathieu makes clear that while the prostitutes' assertions that there were no pimps involved was wholly erroneous, it was equally untrue that pimps controlled the movement. Mathieu cites

33. Carole Roussopoulos, dir., *Les prostituées de Lyon parlent* (Vidéo Out, 1975).
34. Michel Castaing, "Au Sénat: La commission des lois adopte plusieurs amendements tendant à renforcer la répression du proxénétisme," *Le Monde* (13 June 1975), 14.

one "leading figure of the movement" who told him, "The young women never would have been able to participate if their pimps hadn't given a sign." That is, certain women had the idea, but their ability to take action and mobilize other women required the agreement of "the pimps." While the prostitutes chose to tell an incomplete story, so as to depict themselves as having full agency, the police were so certain that these women had no power over their lives as workers that they, too, told inaccurate stories, denying the key role prostitutes had played in the mobilization.[35] This unwillingness to entertain the idea that women could make such choices about their bodies shaped internal police discussion in Marseille, one of the cities where prostitutes had mobilized on the model of Lyon. An early 1976 report on prostitutes and the fight to stop pandering noted "a new attitude, one defined by political demands," before immediately arguing that this was "more or less supported by the businessmen involved."[36] One year later, the report "takes note that the political movement of prostitutes and hotel owners . . . is nothing more than a memory." In this reading it was not the prostitutes, but the men who profited from them, who had determined the movement's messages. "Bit by bit the prostitutes stopped working with the businessmen, judging that the political spin the latter had tried to impose would hurt their interests."[37] What was depicted was cooperation between pimps and prostitutes, which preceded a decision by the prostitutes to end this cooperation in order to defend "their interests." Yet the police held tenaciously to a reading that presented only the choices made by "the businessmen" as "political."

The Movement of Prostitutes and Anti-Arab Racism

Talk of pimps directly challenged political depictions of the prostitutes' struggle premised on individual agency. This was because it linked the movement to "Arab" control of French prostitution, and it was in precisely this domain that the prostitute-activists' efforts to challenge such criticisms faltered. This became public in November 1975, when Ulla and "Sonia," the leaders of the movement in Lyon, held a meeting at the Mutualité auditorium in Paris. "Prostitutes from the Barbès neighborhood complain

35. Mathieu, *Mobilisations de prostituées*, 48.

36. C. Buissière, Préfet délégué pour la police, "Objet: Lutte contre le proxénétisme DD/AP- Poste 32.12 (Marseille, 24 February 1976), 5, in ADBdR 1650W/1.

37. C. Buissière, "Objet: Lutte contre le proxénétisme DD/AP- Poste 32.12 (Marseille, 21 Feb. 1977), 6, in ADBdR 1650W/1.

that they have been kept at arms' length from the movement," *Le Monde* reported, affirming that this effort to exclude was a direct reflection of the intraprofessional disdain for those who "went up" with immigrants. At the same meeting, Ulla further evoked a stark distinction between "independent" prostitutes and others, whom she linked to the men they dealt with. "If they close the hotels in Barbès," she told the meeting, "the immigrant clientele will leak out everywhere."[38] The activists worked to avoid any link to Arab men, as if this would sap public support for their claims to be taken seriously as independent political actors.

It was such developments that in spring 1976 led "a female student" to challenge the Lyon militants who spoke about the movement: "What is your position in relation to immigrant workers?" she asked, before immediately asserting: "You are racists." The first prostitute activist to respond rejected the argument, reaffirming that prostitutes' relations with clients (unlike with their "friends") were commercial. "Contrary to what you just claimed, it's literally false. . . . A prostitute prostitutes herself for monetary reasons only." Racism among prostitutes, she said, "plays a very small role." A second woman offered a different response: "Oftentimes some girls have been beaten up by Algerians, I'm sorry I have to say it. . . . There aren't that many girls who won't go up with immigrants and blacks. Those who won't go up are precisely those who have suffered abuse."[39] In the same conversation, of course, activist paeans to "friendship" and "intimacy" had been used to dismiss charges that the men they spent time with were pimps; the only abusive men the prostitute activists evoked were "Algerians." In each case, then, questions about Arab men troubled the female prostitutes' efforts to speak politically. Their efforts to distinguish themselves from men (pimps and clients) whom French people increasingly understood as Arabs led them to make arguments that depended on racist presumptions rather than on evidence.

There were many other published accounts of the lives of prostitutes that appeared in these years, both interviews and "tell-alls." All the women asserted that they and other prostitutes had agency—a claim that several

---

38. Br. F., "Le gala houleux de la prostitution: Trois mille personnes aux assises nationales," *Le Monde* (20 November 1975). Lilian Mathieu, who makes no mention of racism or anti-Arab questions in his study of the movement, offers an interpretation that, although developed to explain Ulla's response to transvestite prostitutes, also could be applied here: It is "an effort to keep out the most marginal groups." *Mobilisations de prostituées*, 86.

39. Mathieu, "Débat."

demonstrated through their rejection of Arab men. In her 1976 autobio-graphical narrative, former prostitute Jeanne Cordelier quoted a woman who explained that she had left one bordello and sought work in another because her job in the first one was "butcher's work [*abattage*]. Nothing but Arabs. Twelve hundred in one month."[40] Her statement went beyond the suggestion that there were different types of prostitution. It suggested that it was the category of clients, rather than just the conditions, that made one type of prostitution better than the other. Cordelier claimed that, in general, prostitutes had catholic appetites: "The girls had solid hips." But she cited one exception: "They only turned away *les bicots* [a pejorative term for Arabs]." In such conversations, what demonstrated the prostitutes' status as free agents was their choice of "French" clients, which served to affirm their own status as Frenchwomen. All described their forthright rejection of North African patronage, which offered reassurance to French readers. Prostitutes did want to have sex with certain types of men—French men, for example. In a conversation between two prostitutes that Cordelier re-counted, the first reassured the other that "Arabs aren't the only ones who want to hook up with a prostitute. I've seen good guys, too."[41] A 1969 ar-ticle in *Le Monde* maintained that the prostitutes of Pigalle in increasing numbers rejected clients who "look Mediterranean." The author of the ar-ticle attributed this rejection to "sexual racism" and the workers' miserable salaries.[42] In a six-part series of articles about prostitution that *Le Monde* published in 1973, author Michel Castaing noted, "Many prostitutes have chosen to no longer 'hook up with Arabs.'" In another publication, *One Two Two* (1975), a former madam describes setting up an unregulated bordello in the Les Halles neighborhood after 1946. "I wouldn't let either Arabs or Blacks in the door." This meant that her "biggest problem was with the Arabs. . . . The girls, *les Bics* [pejorative term for Arab], they just wouldn't do it with them. They would flee, lock themselves into the courtyard toilet."[43] In 1979, writing in *Actuel*, Rambaud described a scene in which one pros-titute yelled at another, "'Did you see Olga go up? She was with a rat!' Translation: an Arab. . . ." When her colleague minimized the problem, the woman insisted, "If Olga goes up with another rat, she's out of here! She'll never put a foot on this sidewalk again." A magazine article the next year

40. Jeanne Cordelier, *La Dérobade* (Paris: Hachette littérature, 1976), 78.

41. Cordelier, *La Dérobade*, 115, 391.

42. Jean-Maurice Mercier, "'Hitler avait raison. Des attentats contre des cafés nord-africains aux souvenirs de Nazisme," *Le Monde* (23 November 1969).

43. Castaing, "La prostitution aujourd'hui comme hier II," 10; Jamet, *One two two*, 257.

reported that "all the prostitutes insisted that they had never 'hooked up with' any Arabs or Blacks."[44]

French—Rather than "Prostitute"—Racism

What explained this, in Castaing's interpretation, was that "the myth of the 'threatening [*violenteur*]' Nord African is tenacious."[45] Other reporters, however, pointed to other johns as the primary source of racism. When Patrick Rambaud interviewed "a colossal girl" on the rue St. Denis who had told "a little Maghrebi man," "No, honey, you look too much the type [*t'es trop typé*; i.e., you look Arab]," he asked her, "Why did you blow off that guy?" She blamed "the fat guy coming out of the hotel across the way[.] If he had to pass an Arab on the stairwell, he'd never come back here. And that guy, he has big money."[46] A 1978 special issue of the abolitionist magazine *Femmes et mondes* (Women and Worlds) offered a more nuanced analysis "on the encounter between immigrants and prostitutes." What had inspired the idea of doing a special issue was that "we noticed among many of the latter strongly racist behavior," which the editors initially hoped to explain and, indeed, counter. "Then, however, we had to take account of the evidence we found: these women prostitutes are neither more nor less racist than the French collectivity in general: they are, in this domain, the mirror image."[47] The editors of *Femmes et mondes* also worried that the original focus of the special issue would contribute to a "form of brainwashing" that presented all "immigrant workers" as clients of prostitution (*"hôtels de passe"*). Since the mid-1960s, the magazine—and the abolitionist group that published it, L'Amical du Nid—had refocused on offering help to women and men who were prostitutes, and on countering publicly accepted stereotypes or falsehoods that surrounded prostitution. This, even as they remained committed to ending the practice of prostitution.[48]

Yet it was just such images—of lust-driven North African immigrants driving an increasingly visible and visibly miserable form of prostitution—that reappeared in many calls to reform prostitution laws. In 1975, André Jarrot, minister for the quality of life, suggested that "by taking radical mea-

---

44. Bercoff, "Prostitution," 40.

45. Castaing, "La prostitution aujourd'hui comme hier, II," 10.

46. Rambaud, "Le nettoyage," 114.

47. Christian Delorme, "Exploitation et solitude des immigrés: Introduction" *Femmes et mondes* 37 (April-June 1978), 4–6.

48. Ibid.

sures at the initiative of Marthe Richard, we made a mistake . . . we were not worried enough about the arrival of foreign workers."[49] Between 1973 and 1977, the Marseille prefecture of police included—with only small variations—a compelling set of claims in its biannual report on the policing of prostitution. It began, "Turning a blind eye to the prostitution trade is rather difficult"—suggesting that the officer who penned the report presumed that readers—fellow officers—had a shared certainty that prostitutes for North African immigrants should be tolerated or perhaps encouraged. This was not allowed by existing laws, but what made it most difficult, in his telling, was "the principle that all citizens are equal in relation to criminal law, and"—he emphasized—"the Marseille milieu has shown itself to be particularly sensitive about this principle." Equality of citizens was, of course, a keystone of left and republican politics. More precise language, however, underwrote popular pressure to crack down on prostitution. The report continued: "As it so happens, the police service receives numerous complaints that designate certain immigrant establishments [*établissements d'immmigrés*] that have not been the object of judicial investigation and ask to know what motivates this discrimination." The term "discrimination" had emerged in the 1950s as a key category for antiracist thinking and action.

From 1946 and into the 1970s, popular understandings linked Arab men to forms of criminality described as particularly exploitative, such as pimping, or to unsavory behavior that created newly miserable conditions for French people (prostitutes themselves, or the inhabitants of "immigrant" neighborhoods), such as frequenting prostitutes. Police statistics or analyses (and some subsequent historical research) might contest such claims. Yet French sex talk about prostitution made Arab men the enemy of equality and female agency, and even a noted source of discrimination.[50]

La Traite des Blanches and the Arab Man

It was in this context that anxieties about "the trade in white women" flourished. As one anti-*traite* association warned its members in 1978: "Have no fear about instructing your teen girls about the dangers of the *traite*. It can never be too early. Today, we encounter prostitutes as young as

49. June 1975; cited in *Le Monde*.
50. Heckenroth, le préfet délégué pour la Police, "À M. le minstre de l'Intérieur; OBJET: Lutte contre le proxénétisme 137/CAB" (Marseille, 18 February 1974), 3, in ADBdR 1650/W/1. On the antiracist category of discrimination, see Todd Shepard, "Algeria, France, Mexico," 273–297.

fourteen . . . Listen to the testimony of these eighteen- and twenty-year old girls, captured in Bordeaux by four North African individuals of the same age." While the young women were naive, their male peers were devious. The president of the association explained to members, "These guys had come up with an easy way to make money: drive these young girls out during the night to the large farms in Lot-et-Garonne, which hire numerous Moroccan workers." In the extensive publications that abolitionist groups produced—and which numerous media accounts drew from—Arab slave traders and Arab clients all took full advantage of French innocence.[51]

Existing histories of the *traite* in France—notably, of its political and cultural resonance—have focused almost exclusively either on the period before 1946 or on more recent debates around sexual trafficking, which reemerged in the late 1990s. In Mathieu's analysis, "Beginning in the 1960s [after France signed onto the international antitrafficking treaty], the 'model' of the *traite* disappeared from public discussions."[52] Yet my research reveals that during the 1960s and '70s, French journalists, politicians, and scholars had much to say about the topic, even if most subsequent scholars have ignored it. This was the very propitious context in which appeared Alain Corbin's magisterial study *Les filles de noce* (*Women for Hire*, 1978), a history of nineteenth-century France that investigated the intersection, as its French subtitle put it, of prostitution, supposedly the world's oldest profession, and "sexual misery," a concept first developed by the German Freudo-Marxist Wilhelm Reich in the 1930s, and which had flourished in post-'68 French discussions. From the late nineteenth century until the middle of the twentieth, as Corbin first demonstrated, those who warned of the *traite* often linked it to Jews, as well as "Eastern Europeans" and, in broad terms, "Mediterraneans." Since the early 1990s, French discussions have focused heavily on Eastern Europe and sub-Saharan Africa. Between the late 1940s and the late 1970s, however, Arabs, North Africa, and/or Islam were almost always close to the heart of such French discussions. As the historian Susan Cline argues, "Whereas narratives from earlier decades stereotyped traffickers as Jews, during the Algerian war and the years following, they were more often imagined as North Africans." Such racialized interpretations, as well as the parallel between antisemitism and anti-Arab racism that Cline identifies, went unrecognized at the time.

51. Odette Philipon, président, Oeuvre du Bel-accueil, "Chers Amis, chers associés" (Rennes, Lent [March], 1978). Consulted at Fondation Scelles/CRIDES.

52. Lilian Mathieu, *La fin du tapin, sociologie de la croisade pour l'abolition de la prostitution* (Paris: François Bourin, 2014), 53. Mathieu does note "not entirely," and references *La rumeur d'Orléans*, ed. Edgar Morin (Paris: Seuil, 1969), on which see below.

Social Christian abolitionists were the main source of such claims about the *traite*.[53]

Talk of the *Traite* and the Triumph of the Sexual Revolution

This is why the two-scene storyline that combines fears of Arab men and sex in the film *Diabolo menthe* (already sketched out in the introductory section of the previous chapter) is so telling. The two-scene story line is just a minor subplot in feminist filmmaker Diane Kurys' low-budget film, which garnered critical appreciation and also topped the French box office in 1977 (*Star Wars* came in second). *Diabolo menthe*, which was released in the United States in 1979 as *Peppermint Soda*, is known as the first French coming-of-age film from a girl's point of view.[54] It follows two young sisters as they grow from curious yet uninformed sexual subjects into young women who are sexually aware and who can experiment with their sexuality, often with consciousness that politics plays a crucial role in sex. It is a celebratory history of the first stirrings of the sexual revolution as a move from repression to knowledge. The film's chronology—it appeared in the late 1970s and is set in 1963, right after the Algerian war—maps nicely onto the era that this book explores. *Diabolo menthe* also offers clear descriptions of the political upheavals on the left and the far right that accompanied the end of the war, and of the arrival of pied noir repatriates: the mass exodus of close to one million French citizens from Algeria in the months surrounding the July 1962 transformation of French Algeria into the Algerian Republic.[55] Yet Anne's story of the *traite* is the only reference to Arabs in the film. What the film also celebrates is the history of a France that after 1962 had escaped Algeria. Like other recountings of France's sexual revolution, *Diabolo menthe* is a strikingly vanilla history unsettled by dark rumors of Arab men and the *traite*. The film's emphatic lesson, "There is no traffic in white women," was deeply political, a myth-busting dis-

---

53. Corbin, *Les Filles de noce*; Sharon Elise Cline, "Feminité à la Française: Femininity, Social Change and French National Identity, 1945–1970" (PhD dissertation, University of Wisconsin-Madison, 2008), 186–187.

54. John Berry, et al., "Diane Kurys," in *Fifty Contemporary Film Directors*, ed. Yvonne Tasker (London: Routledge, 2002), 219–227.

55. On the exodus and those who came, see Shepard, *The Invention of Decolonization*. Those people who came to France were mainly so-called Europeans, people of diverse origins who were not "Muslims" even if many had few if any family ties to the metropole where they resettled or "repatriated."

missal of the "Arab invasion" fantasy that deviant sex still linked the two peoples and threatened France (and especially young French girls).

As this chapter and the previous one detail, endless debates about prostitution in France between 1962 and 1979 continued to promote fabricated histories of dangerous ongoing French relationships with Algeria and Maghrebis. These fabricated histories almost always positioned both French men and women in relationship to male North Africans, and depicted the Maghreb as a wholly male-dominated space. In both cases, this maleness appeared as aberrant, like the threat of "Arabs" and "Africa" that frightens the young girls at the beginning of *Diabolo menthe*. These narratives thus worked insistently to discipline and chastise the failure of the French to reject such deviance, and detailed the ways in which weak French men and out-of-control French girls and women made it possible.

The presence of the *traite* in *Diabolo menthe*, although marginal, is particularly telling. For, as clearly indicated by its mockery of the comical warning naive young girls exchange about a penis that is "this long," this is a film that easily and proudly celebrates female sexuality and desire. Its candy-colored visual palette reinforces the idea that both those things have escaped from the economy of fear. To quote the preface Roland Barthes wrote for *Tricks*, it does so "as if that particular fight had already been won." In most of the usual domains—dating, petting, unwed pregnancy, shame— the film, in Barthes's terms, "overcomes the problems such a project poses: in all tranquility." This late 1970s recounting of a story that began in the early 1960s shares the position of sexual revolutionaries and popular opinion: erotic relations between men and women, even between teenage girls and boys, even if pre- or extramarital, were acceptable and normal. What Kurys draws attention to with these two scenes, I suggest, is how fears of the *traite* still seemingly required a direct rebuttal. This is because in these years, discussions about prostitution allowed sexually conservative arguments that otherwise had failed to stymie the sexual revolution to gain a hearing. They did so through incendiary references to Arab men.

Post-1962 Algeria as "Lobby" for the Worldwide Traffic in White Women

When Algeria won independence, the idea that Algeria and Algerians caused the *traite* in France almost immediately took on new life. A flurry of articles in the tabloid press in fall 1962 and early 1963 regularly "exposed" the scary phenomenon that threatened French women and French borders.[56] A six-part series in *Paris-jour* (titled "Women for Sale: The Traffic of Shame"), for example, stoked fear of the *traite* and tied it to Algeria.There was, author Eric de Goutel claimed, a spike in trafficking, a development "which saps an entire society and risks THE CONTAMINATION OF THE YOUTH [of France]."[57] To explain how this had happened, the series presented Algeria in multiple causal guises. The country itself "for a long time had been a big outlet for the *traite*," and "independence did not change much. In terms of 'clients,' the ALN [Army of National Liberation] took over the role of the French Army." The new country's leaders, who as a sign of their moral rigor "forbade Muslims to drink alcohol in cafés," nonetheless allowed its citizens "to frequent the 'bordellos.'" Moving quickly over the possibility that, in this choice at least, the leaders were merely leaving French regulations in place, the journalist Eric de Goutel reminded readers that now, "Algeria is only a link." No longer under French control, it had become "the lobby that opens onto Libya, Egypt, Saudi Arabia, etc." What happened there was foreign, Arab, necessarily un-French. The scandal sheet *Noir et blanc* disingenuously alerted readers in late 1962 that "in Algeria, the [French] brigade for the protection of minors is no longer able to intervene as it sees fit."[58] Yet, somewhat paradoxically, this "lobby" continued to be connected to France.

If Algeria was the destination most often given, in the *Paris-jour* series as well as elsewhere, it was Algerian men in France who managed to get French women to go there. Traffickers in France, in de Goutel's telling, were small time: "They have one girl, two girls, maybe three. Any more is rare. They run shops, not factories. Above all the Algerians."[59] One of de Goutel's key sources was a young woman who worked for the organization that Jean Scelles had founded, Les equipes d'action. All the traffickers she mentioned were Maghrebis. She told the story of a "young woman from Montpellier. She let herself be seduced by a North African who then forced her

---

56. E.g., "La naïve Arlette partait pour Alger avec 'M. Mohamed,'" *Paris-jour* (3 November 1962); "Encore une affaire de 'traite des Blanches' découverte à Orly," *Paris-jour* (6 November 1962); "Le gang de la traite a (peut-être) assassiné Rosa La Kabyle," *Paris-jour* (31 January 1963); "Malgré les lois de répression, prostitution toujours florissante," *Le Parisien* (1 February 1963); Gérard Bordeux, "La révolte de Peggy (20 ans) fait découvrir un 'réseau de vice,'" *France-soir* (23 November 1963).

57. Eric de Goutel, "Femmes à vendre: le trafic de la honte. La police répond à nos questions," *Paris-jour* 989 (28 Nov. 1962), 4.

58. Eric de Goutel, "Femmes à vendre: Le trafic de la honte. Des affaires d'import-export d'un genre un peu spécial," *Paris-jour* (27 November 1962), 12.

59. Eric de Goutel, "Femmes à vendre: Le trafic de la honte. Ces Monsieurs les proxénètes," *Paris-jour* 987 (26 November 1962), 9; "Même une innocente n'est pas à l'abri de la traite des Blanches," *Noir et blanc* (7 December 1962), 808–809.

into prostitution." Each time the young woman sought to escape from her pimp, "she got caught by one of those Algerians who, paid by pimps, hangs out in the bad end of town."[60] The final article in the series, "This Is Why Hope Springs Eternal," focused on the role of the young employee of Les equipes d'action and how her organization and others helped French prostitutes escape from the *traite*. It marked a clear shift from the first article, one week before, which told quite a different story: "Yet, it bears repeating, the trade in white women doesn't exist, as I was told recently by M. Sicot, secretary-general of Interpol." De Goutel took him seriously, noting that "in one sense, he is right. They do not kidnap little girls who are walking out of their first communion; high schoolers can safely walk about Paris." In large capital letters, the first article in the series led its readers to believe something that the final article, with its statement "Algerians who, paid by pimps, hang out in the bad end of town," aimed to make them forget: "ALL WOMEN INVOLVED IN PROSTITUTION HAVE—AS A MATTER OF *Um...* FACT—CONSENTED TO DO SO." Following in the footsteps of the British historian Judith Walkowitz, feminist historians have shown that this disconnect between public outrage about *la traite* and the reality of women's involvement in prostitution—which entailed forms of exploitation, misery, and sexual harassment that were not specific to venal sex but were endemic in public life under capitalism—has been a constant.[61]

Over the course of a week, the series thus shifted attention from police statistics and long-standing realities to recent developments provoked by Algerian independence. It acknowledged the enduring existence of prostitution and its various abuses. More specifically, it noted that French laws and political decisions—maintaining regulationism in Algeria after the Marthe Richard Law, along with the claim that Algeria was French—had encouraged the movement of women and men involved in prostitution across the Mediterreanean. The articles also drew attention to another tenacious actuality: "It doesn't matter where in the world you go; they are eager to welcome French women."[62]

Against this context, the investigative report announced a focus on what was new. It did not mention that until 1960 France had been one of the only Western countries that had refused to sign the 1946 International Convention on Trafficking. Instead it proclaimed, "FOR FOUR YEARS FRANCE HAS TAKEN THE LEAD IN THIS STRUGGLE" (a chronology that

60. Eric de Goutel, "Femmes à vendre: Le trafic de la honte. Voici pourquoi l'espoir n'est jamais perdu," *Paris-jour* (30 November 1962), 4.

61. Ibid., 14. See esp. Walkowitz, *Prostitution and Victorian Society*.

62. De Goutel, "Des affaires d'import-export," 12.

aligned with the birth of the Fifth Republic, if not with the more recent French signing of the treaty or any other substantive shifts).[63] More important, Algerian independence had clarified the foreign nature of the *traite des blanches* threat. Notably, the supposed importance of Algeria and Algerians in the *traite* revealed that country's reabsorption by the dangerous and immoral world of Islam and Arabs—where, according to de Goutel, "the harems are well guarded."[64]

Jean Scelles, the Marthe Richard Law, and the Algerianization of the *Traite*

The idea of North Africa as a site to which "slavers" sent white women had a long history. Notably, as Weiss shows, it was a key element in French debates that called for an invasion of Algiers in the late 1820s. Yet it had become deeply rooted in French discussions after French authorities decided not to extend the 1946 Marthe Richard Law to Algeria. Scelles evoked it in his 1957 *Le Monde* editorial, which ended with a lament for the "women who disappear toward Algeria and abroad." A 1951 Paris police internal report stated: "Several sources inform me that what has happened with the closure of houses of toleration in France and not in North Africa is: 1/ A veritable '*traite des blanches*' passageway has been organized toward Algeria and the whole of North Africa, where little by little a pimping network has emerged."[65] Who were these sources? They were social Catholics almost exclusively. In the wake of the Marthe Richard law, Scelles and other abolitionists had quickly fixated on the claim that, as he put it in a 1953 article,

63. French law concerning prostitution shifted substantially in the first years of the Fifth Republic, with the first new ordonnances in December 1958. The year 1960, however, marked a real shift. In Marseille, according to a very optimistic police report, "The application of Ordinance n. 60–1245 of 25 Nov. 1960, concerning the repression of proxenetism, has led directly to the progressive disappearance of prostitutes in the municipalites of the Bouches du Rhône Department." See Directeur départemental des Services de Police, "Objet: Activité de la Brigade spécial départementale des moeurs 101 DP/BD" (Marseille, 5 January 1962), 2, in ADBdR 1650/W/1. In Paris, "the number of hotels dedicated to prostitution [*hôtels de passe*] remained stable from 1946 to 1960, going from 400 to 350"; by 1968 there were only 180 that remained. See Amélie Maugère, *Les politiques de la prostitution du Moyen âge au XXIe siècle* (Paris: Dalloz, 195. Unfortunately, Maugère relies on the wholly unreliable Dallayrac for her statistics; see Dallayrac, *Dossier prostitution*, 127).

64. Eric de Goutel, "Femmes à vendre: Le trafic de la honte. La police répond à nos questions," *Paris-jour* 989 (28 November 1962), 4; Goutel, "Des affaires d'import-export," 12.

65. See Weiss, *Captives and Corsairs*; Raoul, dir. cab., "Objet: Prostitution Nord Africaine" (Paris 10 August 1951), in APP : H/A 19, 1.

"the girls of France feed the 'houses' in North Africa."[66] In 1956 the Christian Democrat (MRP) deputy Francine Lefebvre, a diehard abolitionist, denounced the disappearance of "thousands of women" (she affirmed that there were 122,762 cases) between 1945 and 1954. Lefebvre called on the government to end regulated prostitution in North Africa, in order to protect "the honor of the women and girls of France." The Orientalist implications were clear: these innocents must not be delivered up to "Muslims," a term that was deeply racialized in French conversations in those years.[67]

A dependence on racialized fears had long been central to abolitionist activism. A 1931 Paris police report on one abolitionist meeting described how Marc Sangnier, the much-celebrated forefather of French Christian Democracy, "got the audience behind him when he acerbically criticized 'those wholly legal establishments they set up for Niggers'"—a reference to bordellos in the colonies—"and in claiming that the French administration had reestablished 'white slave women so that Niggers can enjoy themselves.'" Yet this eagerness to deploy sexualized racism in order to condemn regulated prostitution became a more prominent aspect of social Catholic campaigns during and after the era of decolonization.[68]

From 1946 until his death in 1996, Jean Scelles, the leader of the most prominent social Catholic antiprostitution movement, castigated the French Republic's failure to ban bordellos in French Algeria. In a speech he gave to an abolitionist convention in 1959, he noted that "the illegal continuation of toleration for prostitution in Algeria contradicts announced projects to emancipate the Muslim woman," which were at the forefront of Fifth Republic propaganda efforts to prevent Algerian independence, and which went "against the traditions of Islam, of Judaism, of Christianity."[69] The policy, he argued, had stimulated the *traite*. In a 1951 proposal to the French Union Assembly, which would extend the ban overseas, Scelles affirmed that "the nonapplication [of the French law of 13 April 1946]

66. Jean Scelles, "Les filles de France alimentent les 'maisons'en Afrique du Nord," *Moissons nouvelles* 9 (October–December 1953), 3; North Africa was not the only suspect site. A 1970s tract that warned, "Young women and, above all, you teenage ladies . . . beware when an opportunity sounds too good to be true . . . especially trips abroad, especially to North Africa or Latin America." Mouvement du Nid, "Camps de concentration modernes" (undated, tract 2 pp), 1, in ADBdR 38 J 1–93.

67. *JORF* (16 March 1956), 1015.

68. Police judiciare, "Réunion organisée par l'union temporaire contre la prostitution réglementée et la traite des femmes" (7 February 1931), in APP : B/A 1689.

69. Scelles, "Congrès de Marseille, Contre le proxénétisme," *Le Commercial du Gard* (28 April 1959); consulted at the Fondation Scelles/CRIDES.

has . . . spawned an aerian traffic of metropolitan women to Algerian houses of prostitution." To convince the legislators to support a second proposal that he submitted only a few months later, Scelles wrote: "In April 1951 a young girl was 'drugged and sequestered in a hotel in Paris, forced into a taxi and taken to Orly' . . . [and] sold to Algerian houses of tolerance and then to hotel owners [tenanciers] of the red light district." If evidence was lacking, shocking narratives were in plentiful supply.[70]

In 1966, in response to a question from Dallayrac—"But does the white slave trade still exist?"—Scelles stated with clarity: "There's no reason to even ask that question, since every year several thousand women disappear so that they can be sent into prostitution." Scelles also systematically linked the traite to North Africans, in France and across the Mediterranean. Here, as so often in subsequent years, he cited a 1963 article that had appeared in the right-wing newspaper Aurore and reported that "80 percent of the total trade is the percentage of women sent to North Africa."[71] He failed to note, however, that he himself, as one of the experts whom the journalist had interviewed for the article, was the source of most of its "facts" and anecdotes. The anecdotes all recounted efforts by North Africans to take young French women forcibly to North Africa in order to make them prostitutes.

Why Did 1970s Abolitionists Target "Arab Men"?

Such inflammatory narratives played a foundational role in the antitrafficking campaign of the time, as they had in others. In this era's French versions, the bad guys were mainly North Africans or "Arabs." In her 1976 study Esclavage sexuel, torture, amour (Sexual Slavery, Torture, Love), Odette Philipon, one of Scelles's social Catholic allies in the abolitionist struggle, relied on Arab examples for her description of three of the four "methods" on which she claimed traffickers relied: false marriage proposals, drugs, and kidnapping. Several of the stories used in each example, for good measure, took place in Paris, Marseille, or Algiers. One took place on the

70. Jean Scelles et al., "Proposition tendant à inviter le Gouvernement à fermer en Algérie les maisons dites de tolérance en y appliquant effectivement la loi du 13 avril 1946 et à développer le dépistage et le traitement des maladies vénériens contagieux et la rééducation des prostituées," Annexe no. 164, Assemblée de l'Union Française, 1951 (Session of 22 May 1951), 2,465; Jean Scelles, et al.. "Proposition tendant à renforcer la lutte contre le proxénétisme en Algérie," Annexe no. 223, Assemblée de l'Union Française, 1951 (Session of 30 August 1951), 3. See Cline "Feminité a la Française."

71. Dallayrac, Dossier prostitution, 322.

"Israelo-Syrian frontier."[72] In another book, *Les "filles" victimes des hommes* (The "Girls" Whom Men Victimize), the first chapter, "Girls Like Any Others," opens with the simple question: "Do you read the back page [*faits divers*] of your newspaper?" It then procedes to explore recent reports of the *traite des blanches*, and gives the reader "at least a few excerpts." Four pages and multiple episodes follow, culminating in the question: "Do we really need to continue to list these upsetting stories? Tomorrow, your newspaper will inform you of new ones." Every single one of those stories involved sending the "girls" to Algeria.[73] In 1979, Philipon focused her claims on the trade in young children—"children handed over to beasts"—reminding members of her association that "in Muslim countries, the custom is to send a large number of minors of both sexes to serve in the harems." The source of this false claim is unclear, but not the message: What were French readers to do?[74]

To understand why Algerian, Arab, and North African men were so central to social Catholics' public efforts to fight prostitution, it is necessary to examine why the social Catholics fought it so vigorously. As the abolitionists' archives make clear, and as many of their leaders stated publicly, prostitution was merely the tip of the iceberg. The real problem was French society, secularism, ungodliness, "paganism," and immorality. "The Psychology of Prostitutes" was a seminar series taught by Abbé André-Marie Talvas, who founded le Mouvement du Nid, an important French abolitionist movement that ministered to and counseled current and former prostitutes. His initial lesson began with a reminder to his audience that it was first necessary to understand how, in today's France, "when the idea of God disappeared, so did the idea of Man, of the human person, of his dignity, of the the respect owed to women, of life, of the child." The exclusion of religion from the public sphere, he said, made humans devalue life and think that it had no value.[75]

In an era when such arguments were widely unconvincing, and in the midst of a dramatic decline in religious practice and belief, social Catholic

72. Odette Philipon, *Esclavage sexuel, torture, amour* (Paris: Téqui, 1976), esp. 62–71.

73. Bernard Coutaz, "Des filles parmi tant d'autres," in *Les "filles" victimes des hommes*, ed. Marie-Thérèse Boutin,et al., *Moissons nouvelles* 27 (1960), 17–20.

74. Odette Philipon, president, Oeuvre du Bel-accueil, "Chers Amis, chers associés" (Rennes, Sept.-Oct. 1979), 2, BnF: Oeuvre du Bel acceuil. Receuil: documents d'information (1979–1993).

75. Abbé André-Marie Talvas, "La psychologie des prostituées: Cours sur la prostitution donnée à l'Institut Catholique de Paris" (n.d. ca. 1969), 6, in ADBdR 38-J-1.

abolitionists targeted prostitution because people listened.[76] They seemed to have continually increased their focus on Arabs for the same reason. To talk about prostitution was to foreground a key metaphor of the erroneous path that their society was on. In their depictions, this group of pitiful yet exciting human beings and bodies seemingly reflected this tragedy. Because such formulations were sex talk, they drew the attention of far more French people than did the abolitionists' parallel efforts. To blame prostitution on Maghrebis grabbed the attention of even more French people, and encouraged them to focus on what these Catholics saw as the emptiness and moral bankruptcy of post-decolonization French society. Talk of *la traite* made this visible. If it failed to stimulate new conversions or increase religious practice, it did spread assertions that Arab men were sexual beasts quite widely.[77]

Rumors of Arab Slavers

Superficially, the era's most influential discussion of the *traite* appears disconnected from these developments. The 1969 study *The Rumor of Orléans*, with the French thinker and sociologist Edgar Morin listed as primary author, analyzed the wildfire spread of rumors of the *traite* in a midsized French city.[78] In the early summer of 1969, Morin assembled a team to rush to the city of Joan of Arc just weeks after a rumor about trafficking in young women swept through large sections of the town's population. The focus of popular suspicion was a cluster of six clothing stores, all owned by (or, more important, widely described as owned by) what Morin describes as "assimilated" Jews ("It's the Jew who does not seem Jewish who is under suspicion").[79] Just as in *Diabolo menthe*, what supposedly happened here was that young women went into these stores, were stuck with needles and knocked out, and were then sold into white slavery. The key difference with the film was that in Orléan the "slavers" were identified as Jews, whereas *Diabolo menthe* named Arabs. *The Rumor of Orléans* incisively links such fantastic claims to fears of sexual liberation, with a particular attention to female sociality, women's sexuality, the role of consumerism, and fears about

76. On this decline, see Todd Shepard, "Algerian Nationalism, Zionism, and French Laïcité: A History of Ethno-Religious Nationalisms and Decolonization," *International Journal of Middle Eastern Studies* 45 (August 2013), 445–467.

77. Robcis, "Liberté, Egalité, Hétérosexualité."

78. Alfonso Montuori, "Edgar Morin: A Partial Introduction," *World Futures* 60, no. 5-6 (2004), 52, 349–355. See Mathieu, *La fin du tapin*.

79. *La Rumeur*, 132.

feminism. Yet the book's explicit payoff is a deep sounding of how a rumor is fabricated in a particular locale and comes to saturate it. The book drew much attention, however, to the phenomenon around which this particular rumor was organized: the *traite*.

In 1970, one of the most important organizations that sought to fight prostitution in France, le Mouvement du Nid, published an article in its flagship magazine, *Femmes et mondes*, titled "A Myth: The Slave Trade in White Women." The article drew from Morin's 1969 book for its frame, and sought to make the important point that while "there is undeniably a 'trade' in women who are already prostitutes and also a 'trade' in teen girls and young women who, freely and voluntarily, go abroad tempted by beautiful promises and mind-boggling contracts," all the rest was a myth. Internal police reports from Marseille and Paris, along with other investigations, agreed.[80]

The Rumor of Orléans itself does not make such emphatic claims. In his chapter "The Structure of a Myth," Morin stipulates that the *traite* is "a very real phenomenon, which has been signaled, described, made visible, and authenticated in human interest stories [*faits-divers*] and news reports." For Morin, this reality is one of the "foundations of the mythological scaffolding of Orléans." As Morin and his associates explain it, the myth has two parts: that the *traite* was taking place around six shops in Orléans in spring 1969 and that Jews controlled the *traite*. The book's 1970 "newly revised edition, with the addition of 'The Rumor of Amiens'" (conducted in early 1970), asserted that the *traite* itself did not exist. In that 1970 edition, Morin's associate, the sociologist Claude Fischler, stated unambiguously that the "*traite*" itself was a myth: "mythic, in reality, if one is to believe the police detectives, lawyers, specialized judges: the *traite* in the form of a sudden disappearance by kidnapping and violence, as a split-second shift from an honorable life to one of servitude, does not exist." The difference in sources cited is telling: whereas Fischler invoked judicial authorities, Morin invoked articles in the mass media. Morin also relied on those articles to identify the real actors behind the *traite* (Fischler, of course, identified no actors because he presented the *traite* itself as mythic), with the claim that "the traffic in white women is criminal activity, tough guys. . . . Corsicans, North Africans, or '*métèques*' [outsiders] play the main roles." What Morin sought to establish, however, is that "in France, the Jewish theme is rarely evoked." The claims that there were other actors discredited arguments that Jews participated, and emphasized the novelty of an association between

---

80. "Un mythe: La traite des blanches," *Femmes et mondes* 10 (Summer 1970), 5.

"*traite*" and "Jews." The centrality of this theme to the rumor of Orléans and Amiens is what was explicitly at stake in the studies of Morin and Fischler. Of course, Morin's claim about the rarity of the "theme of the Jew" in French discussions about the *traite* was wholly wrong, as Corbin soon demonstrated in his 1978 book; this is a point that other scholars subsequently have detailed.[81]

The Erasure of Arabs in *The Rumor of Orléans* and the Traces that Remained

Although the just-mentioned list of suspect groups does appear elsewhere in *The Rumor of Orléans*, only the references to North Africans have historical purchase. Morin repeatedly asserted that the basic story of the *traite* that surfaced in Orléans in 1969 had coalesced in 1958 or 1959 alongside the emergence of the Fifth Republic, in the heat of the Algerian revolution. What anchored his certainty was a story that a friend of his, Annette Roger, had heard while she was "incarcerated in the women's prison at Marseille for aiding and abetting the Algerian FLN. While there she made the acquaintance of another detainee who had been jailed for complicity in a white slaving affair." Morin, who established that rumors of this event had become widely discussed in 1959, suggested that this 1958 incident of self-confessed white slavery birthed '60s French discussions of the phenomenon ("Serait-ce là l'événement originaire de toute une prolifération mythologico-informative?").[82] The book's focus on the supposed slave traders and their imagined potential victims sets aside the question of destination: For whom and where were the enslaved women to be sent? Evidence collected in its appendixes, however, detail that here, too, "Arab" references were at play. In a June declaration condemning the rumor before Morin's study began, the local chapter of the International League to Fight Racism and Antisemitism (LICRA) indentified the place as "the Middle East." The anonymous phone calls that tormented the victimized store owners tauntingly made reference to Tangiers or Beirut (though the book asserts that allusions to the Lebanese capital should actually be understood as the unmentioned Jerusalem).[83]

81. *La rumeur d'Orléans: Edition complétée avec la rumeur d'Amiens (de Claude Fischler)*, ed. Edgar Morin (Paris: Seuil, 1970), 39, 232. See Watson, "The Trade in Women"; on the British case, see also Edward Bristow, *Prostitution and Prejudice: The Jewish Fight against White Slavery, 1870–1939* (Oxford, UK: Clarendon Press, 1982).

82. *La rumeur d'Orléans: Edition complétée*, 18.

83. *La rumeur d'Orléans: Edition complétée*, 28, 134, 203.

However, the "Arab" resonance the book does explore is wholly causal, and is relegated to the appendices. The man who suggested that Morin rush to study the Orléans rumor and who organized funding for the team, Léon Poliakov, historian of the Shoah and of European antisemitism, also proposed a hypothesis: "The pro-Arab line of left-wing students had disabled the usual mechanisms that allow antisemitism to be rejected out of hand." (With Israel's 1967 invasion and occupation of East Jerusalem, the Gaza Strip, and the West Bank, small elements of the French far left had begun to support Palestinian nationalists, whom they saw as a radical inspiration; in 1968 and 1969 the Palestine Liberation Organization committed itself to "revolutionary" action and then elected Yassir Arafat as leader.) Morin did investigate what if any role anti-Zionism may have played in altering late-1960s discussions of Jews. His team found no evidence to support the accusation that anti-Zionism had caused the rumor. It determined that the student left, which Poliakov blamed, instead "was exceedingly virulent in its rejection of the rumor."[84] Yet the researchers do record multiple accusations that the rumor resulted from a conspiracy guided by "Arab antisemitism" or "the revenge of the Arabs."[85] In his investigation in Amiens, Fischler cites "the primary leader of an antiracist organization [who] confided, with a large smile, that this all resulted from a Palestinian plot aimed at ruining the Jews of France so that their financial support of Israel would cease." Fischler too, found no evidence of "Arab" involvement in the emergence of the rumor. What all the people involved in the project failed to understand—and this was particularly troubling in the case of Poliakov, given his historical knowledge of how antisemitism functioned—was why, after 1962, they felt obliged to look for Arabs. The long, dense Western history of obsessive anti-Jew hatred and the very recent Shoah seemingly blinded them to the post-decolonization intensity of anti-Arab racism in France.[86]

Conclusion

After World War II and during the Algerian war, stories about prostitution reemerged with new intensity. The "French system" supposedly was no more, which encouraged uncertainty about how prostitution operated and what involvement in it meant. Parallels to the story can be told about

84. *La rumeur d'Orléans: Edition complétée*, 86, 110.
85. *La rumeur d'Orléans: Edition complétée*, 143, 185.
86. *La rumeur d'Orléans: Edition complétée*, 227.

France and Algeria, but also about France and the Jews—as the fever of collaboration and the Shoah was followed by less friction around "the Jewish question"—or about the French Republic and Catholics, as Catholics gained new recognition from the republic in the very years that a steep decline in their practice and faith began.[87] Claims about the *traite* brought all of these unsettled questions into the same picture. As the sexual revolution and other dramatic social changes, notably consumerism and feminism, celebrated the individual, narratives of the traffic in white women, and of prostitution more generally, allowed anxieties and fears to be spoken. These narratives revealed or insisted that questions of individual desires and erotic connections resulted from power, which was organized around identities.

Thinking Identities, Ignoring Acts

Far more than identities were at stake in post-1962 sex talk, despite the steady drumbeat of references to "Arabs," "Jews of France," "immigrant workers," and "homosexuals," as well as to pimps, prostitutes, and clients. Yet the context made questions of identity particularly pressing, for it was over the course of the 1970s that the relationship between sexual acts and identities emerged as a crucial site for political activism and scholarly reflection. A number of feminist activists and theorists vigorously explored this connection, notably in discussions about what rape meant in terms of heterosexual, homosexual, female, and male identities (this was often connected to a less intense but also controversial effort to think male-female coïtus).[88] Perhaps the most well-known evocation of the acts/identities nexus was Michel Foucault's 1976 *History of Sexuality*, vol. 1. Foucault offered a history of how condemnation of the act of sodomy became channeled into a diagnosis of a homosexual identity, or identity problems. "Homosexuality appeared as one of the forms of sexuality when it was transposed from the practice of sodomy onto a kind of interior androgyny, a hermaphroditism of the soul," he wrote. As Foucault influentially

87. On the post-1945 relationship between the French Republic, Catholics, and French Jews, see Shepard, "Algerian Nationalism." See also Vinen, "The End of an Ideology?"

88. These were key questions for two major schools of feminist philosophy. The first school defines rape as "violence, not sex," and is characterized by the work of Susan Brownmiller, while the school associated with Catharine McKinnon and Andrea Dworkin represents rape as an extension of compulsory heterosexuality. Press coverage of rape and sexual abuse grew exponentially over the 1970s. See Jenny Kitzinger, "Media Coverage of Sexual Violence against Women and Children," in *Media and Women: International Perspectives*, ed. Karen Ross and Carolyn M. Byerly (Oxford, UK: Blackwell, 2004), 13–38.

explained, modern society gave a new importance to densely structured sexual identities, with homosexuality an especially telling example: "The sodomite had been a temporary aberration; the homosexual was now a species." Although it is explicitly about sexual identity, Foucault's history was also one of many post-1962 French efforts that turned to the act of sodomy so as to rethink how power works. The next chapter explores why what I call the "sodomy vogue" of the 1970s had Algerian contours, and why efforts to think about power through sodomy in reference to histories of colonial violence and post-decolonization racism collapsed.[89]

89. Foucault, *The History of Sexuality*, 43.

SEVEN

Power, Resistance, and Sodomy in Post-Algerian France

Do you know that France already has cities that have a foreign majority? Maghrebi immigrants make up 60 percent of Roubaix! If you wait until things start to burn before waking up. . . . Have you seen the crowds in Egypt, in Tunisia, in Syria? The day that you have a crowd like that marching down the Champs-Elysées! . . . Who will stop them? And if they march down the Champs-Elysées, it's not to fool around. One of their goals, for example, is to sodomize the president. They want to make it to the rooster-adorned gates [of the Presidential Palace], break through them, and then to "spike" him [*LE "SABRER"*]. I repeat: who will stop them?

—Jean-Marie Le Pen, 2011[1]

In May 1977, *Libération* published a long letter, which began with a strong thesis: "The reputation that the Arab suffers, of a man whose sexual organ cuts like a knife, is nothing less than a systematic aggression against him." There were six signatures attached, five male names and that of one woman; their names also indicated other differences, as half of them read as Maghrebi: Mostefa Djajam, Ali Ghalem, and Mahmoud Zemmouri, alongside Jean Duflot, Pierre Boiron, and Jacqueline Narcy.[2] Their striking image—"*l'Arabe au sexe-couteau*"—foregrounds well-burnished linkages. "Between the Algerians and the French, there's a knife," was how the philos-

---

1. "Jean-Marie Le Pen: 'Je ne ménage pas Marine, je la respecte,'" *France-soir* (18 April 2011).
2. Djajam, et al., "Courrier." All authors ot the letter, it turns out, had some connection to filmmaking; the most well-known at the time, Ghalem, had released his first feature film, *Mektoub*, in 1970, with *L'autre France* distributed in 1977. Zemmouri had acted in the latter film, and his own first film, *Prends 10000 balles et casse toi*, came out in 1981. On the 1977 debates that this letter engaged, see Bourg, *From Revolution to Ethics*.

opher Cornelius Castoriadis put it. "And this knife, it sums up the French imaginary as it concerns Maghrebis, particularly Algerians, at once in terms of murder and in sexual terms." The beachside encounter in *The Stranger* (1942) by Albert Camus, which depicts Meursault taking out his (phallic) pistol to murder "the Arab," whose (phallic) knife blade glints in the sun, is one particularly vivid example of this association.[3] The correspondents went on to critique how an earlier letter to the editor, to which they were responding, had relied on a depiction of "the supposed venality of the Arab homosexual." Their analysis emphasized how this was "described as a dangerous and powerful institution, in the proper sense of the term, a cruel buggerer [*enculeur*]." It was a rare moment in 1970s French discussions; the terms located the identities "Arab" and "homosexual" in the same person, and fixated on a particular relation to a particular sexual act—"cruel *enculeur*"—as synonymous with this dual identity. Here, Djajam, Ghalem, Zemmouri, and their coauthors extended the importance of the claim: "Yet we know what this stereotype obscures." They explained that in the text to which they were responding, given the ways in which it deployed sexualized descriptions of "Arab men," "if it weren't [the emphatically leftist] *Libé[ration]* that published it, the tone of racist recrimination would seem like another piece of garbage from [the far-right weekly] *Minute*, from the rubric: The coon [*le raton*; a pejorative term that targeted Maghrebis] is a knife-wielding animal." The astute missive, dense with references, drew attention to the potent force of this particular stereotype. Even as the letter-writers distinguished between homosexual and nonhomosexual Arab men, they critiqued how the act of sodomy haunted French discussions of both groups, with the specter of venality—prostitution—being one aspect of this haunting. Such an invocation of a specific sexual act, a usually taboo act tightly associated here and elsewhere with violence, domination, filth, and shame, merits special analysis. As the letter to *Libération* made clear—and as this chapter scrutinizes—links to anal sex played a central role in French depictions of Arab males as sexual deviants over the 1960s and 1970s. These links drew on long-standing Orientalist stereotypes but also intersected with an agitated debate, which the sexual revolution made possible, about the act of sodomy itself. By the time this letter appeared, let us note,

---

3. Cornélius Castoriadis in the documentary *Les Années algériennes*, cited in Benjamin Stora, *Le Transfert d'une mémoire: De "l'Algérie française" au racisme anti-arabe* (Paris: La Découverte, 1999), 90. In 1998, the British critic David Macey wrote that "the spontaneous association between 'Algerian' and 'knife' is so strong that we almost fail to notice just what happens in that famous scene on the beach near Algiers in Camus' *L'Etranger.*" See "The Algerian with the Knife," *Parallax* 7 (1998), 159–168.

the most fruitful discussions, which this chapter analyzes, had already bloomed and then faded from view.

How to Do the History of a Sexual Act

In the early 1970s there blossomed a vigorous political and theoretical discussion that subsequent commentators largely ignore, and which invested anal sex with much meaning. Most French discussions turned around variations of the words "sodomy" or the more graphic "*enculer*" (to bugger). The first word, with its Biblical implications and long list of historical resonances, is linked to a long-gone city and to the deep past of monotheistic civilization. The second word could be either intensely specific or vaguely (if insultingly) offhand, and one that, when conjugated (*se faire enculer* makes one an *enculé*; *enculer* makes one an *enculeur*), clearly signaled the relationship of a given subject to the act and to the other persons involved.[4] In broader discussions in the 1970s—despite Foucault's oft-cited insistence that, historically, the category itself was "utterly confused"—sodomy almost always meant anal sex, even if it increasingly was described as something that happened between men and women as well as between men and men. The possibility that it could also describe something between women and women actually seemed to fade over the course of these years.

Particular sex acts have a history. A few scholars have used compelling evidence drawn from discourses about what counts as "sex" and what such acts, encounters, and experiences mean in particular contexts to historicize sex acts. Yet most historians, including students of the sexual revolution and sexuality, have hesitated to map such developments.[5] There have been endless discussions of Foucault's invocation of "the sodomite" in *The History of Sexuality*, vol. 1 (1978), which anchored his larger challenge to presumptions that sex was repressed in the nineteenth-century historical shift

4. These possibilities, although available in other Romance languages, have no exact English-language equivalent. All English-language slang I have identified that references the engagement of one person in a sodomitical coupling speaks only of the "active" partner, with the exception of the very infrequently used term "buggered." "To bugger," notably, allows for "buggerer," but "to be buggered" has no subject position equivalent to *enculé*.

5. One model for such histories is Henry Abelove, "Some Speculations on the History of Sexual Intercourse during the Long Eighteenth Century in England," *Genders* 6 (1989), 125–130; see also Valerie Traub, *Thinking Sex with the Early Moderns* (Philadelphia: University of Pennsylvania Press, 2015); Thomas W. Laqueur, *Solitary Sex: A Cultural History of mMsturbation* (New York: Zone Books, 2003).

from a discourse of sexual acts to one of identities: the birth of "sexuality." All these commentators have failed to contextualize his mid-1970s choice to historicize the act of sodomy in order to make his argument. Foucault's choice was exemplary, not exceptional. In the midst of that era, a wide range of activists, artists, and theorists turned to sodomy in order to re-think how power, domination, repression, and resistance functioned. Their claims drew from long-standing certainties about anal sex, yet all suggested that the act itself was becoming more common and that, because of this, it was ripe for political interpretations. Rather than a variable of homosexual identity, this act appeared mutable and potent, with wide implications.[6] While what I term the "sodomy vogue of the Seventies" crossed national boundaries, it was in French discussions that the need to link sodomy, vio-lence, and the aftermath of empire to new conceptions of how power func-tioned was most visible, because invocations of "the Arab man" rung so clearly. This chapter explores why that was so. What emerged was a deeply ambiguous yet densely productive site of meaning, where it seemed possi-ble to analyze post-decolonization (and postcolonial) specters of violence, shame, and sex both together and to political ends. Like so many other ef-forts in these years to think of sex, empire, race, and violence together, this space of possibilities exhausted itself rather quickly. Its complications and contradictions facilitated its dissipation.

When Sodomy Became a Site for Rethinking Power

The basic elements of this debate, notably the image of "*l'arabe au sexe-couteau*," have remained pregnant with implication in French popular dis-cussions. Since the late 1980s, as well, many of the analytic claims about the act of sodomy have reemerged in anglophone scholarship that theo-rizes AIDS, anal sex, and the "queer." Yet these authors ignore the imperial and racialized foundations of the claims they deploy. What disappeared over the course of the1970s was why, together, the intersections of post-decolonization masculinity and sodomy had seemed meaningful, propi-tious for thinking differently about politics and power.[7]

6. For an extended analysis of how philosophers and thinkers such as Foucault, Gilles De-leuze, Félix Guattari, and Guy Hocquenghem deployed "sodomy," see Todd Shepard, "What Drew Foucault to Sodomy," at the online journal *Foucaultblog*; consulted on 10 March 2016: http://www.fsw.uzh.ch/foucaultblog/issue/131/what-drew-foucault-to-sodomy.

7. See Robert L. Caserio et al., "The Antisocial Thesis in Queer Theory," *PMLA* 121 (2006), 819–828.

The '70s sodomy vogue, like other aspects of the sexual revolution, stretched well beyond France. The international popularity of the Bernardo Bertolucci film *Last Tango in Paris* (1972)—and the excited commentary on "the butter scene" (in which the character played by Marlon Brando sodomizes the character played by Maria Schneider) that accompanied its travels—is the most obvious reminder of this forgotten phenomenon. It took on a particular role in France, however, notably in how it shaped political and theoretical efforts to think about power. The modern history of sodomy in France—the fact that the concept disappeared from French legislation under Napoleon, and the particularly important place of *"enculé"* in French invectives—surely affected this 1970s history.[8] Yet the way that Arab resonances played out mattered more. They rang with revolution.

After decolonization, the metaphor of sodomy was weighted with the somewhat dirty implications of imperial invasion and expulsion, of shame, of pain, and of revenge, but also of unexpected possibilities of pleasure, of intense connections. This resulted from the unexpected shock of post-1945 anticolonial uprisings, the violence that ensued, and anticolonial victories, the revolt of "the wretched of the earth"—especially the Algerian revolution. Most French leftists had seen little of political interest in this nationalist "bourgeois" struggle, and vigorously rejected its supposedly ignoble weapons, most especially terrorism. In response, "Third-Worldism," which Frantz Fanon's analyses of the Algerian situation inspired, privileged the radical potential of the dialectic "colonized-colonizer" over that of the coupling "proletariat-bourgeoisie." Algeria's unexpected triumph encouraged radical observers to turn to such novel interpretive schemas as they sought to reproduce similar victories in the name of the oppressed. Far-right actors, too, worked to reposition their movement in response to what they viewed as a shocking humiliation, something outside the natural order of things. Actors in both these post-1962 discussions, the evidence reveals, seized on sodomy to conceptualize what this unanticipated situation meant about power and human relations. This made it newly ripe to reenvision the workings of history and power.

8. On sodomy laws, see Scott Gunther, "Introduction: Republican Values and the Depenalization of Sodomy in France," in *The Elastic Closet: A History of Homosexuality in France, 1942–Present* (Basingstoke, UK: Palgrave Macmillan, 2009), 1–24. On French use of *"enculer,"* see, e.g., Muriel Walker, "Pour une lecture narratologique d'Histoire d'O." *Études littéraires* 33, no.1 (2001), 149–168. In his 1968 ethnology of French gangs ("les blousons noirs"), Jean Monod wrote, "Un mot revenait de façon obsédante: le mot 'enculé'" ["One word recurred obsessively: the word *'enculé'*"]; see J. Monod, *Les Barjots: Essai d'ethnologie des bandes de jeunes* (Paris: Juilliard, 1968), 62; cited in Revenin, *Une histoire de garçons*, 115.

"The Evian Accords Have Spread Sodom's Version of Man against Man"

In the months following Algeria's independence on 5 July 1962, the far right, which had thrown itself wholeheartedly into sometimes extremely violent last-ditch efforts to defend French Algeria, embraced references to sodomitical rape and sodomy in order to explain what had happened. These references worked to describe France after empire and to analyze questions of domination, power, and humiliation, even as they also provoked shock, a disdainful smirk, or both. As France gave up control of Algeria, various organs of the far-right press published reports that soldiers of the nationalist movement, the Algerian National Liberation Front, had raped French soldiers. These sodomitical rapes, they proclaimed, occurred as French forces retreated from their positions to allow FLN troops to enter Algeria. The government, according to these exposés, helped by "the press, which follows its every order, have carefully hushed up the new gangrene." Leftist critics had popularized the term "gangrene" to castigate French forces' wartime embrace of torture. The diagnosis resonated with their description of torture as a dangerous attack on French democracy and principles as well as on human values and bodies; it warned that French people would suffer as a result. As the war ended, far-right writers used "gangrene" to target another form of bodily invasion: sodomitical rape. Leftists during the Algerian war had emphasized that torture was not merely an abuse, a regrettable if inevitable side effect of war, but something systematic and thus revelatory of something larger and wrong. In the same way, this anonymous far-right writer insisted that these rapes, "which in any other era, if the powers that be had any dignity whatsoever, would have been a minor incident," meant something more. The version that *Europe-action* gave focused on "the 'misfortune' that recently befell several airmen in the Algiers suburbs," and said that the lesson to be learned was straightforward: "The Evian Accords have spread Sodom's version of man against man." Unlike left-wing critiques of torture, these articles and their claims about the systematic rape of French men by Algerians were based on no verifiable evidence, neither from documents nor individual testimonials.[9] Their incendiary accusations instead epitomized the rage and the

9. The term "gangrene" evokes one of the most important antitorture testimonials published during the Algerian war, the collectively authored (Béchir Boumaza, Mustapha Francis, Benaïssa Souami et Moussa Khebaïli) *La gangrène* (Paris: Minuit, 1959). Archivally anchored historians, notably Raphaëlle Branche, have shown that French authorities' use of torture was systematic; no subsequent analysis confirms these accusations of widespread male-on-male

analysis shared by many who had defended French Algeria until the bitter end, and after. In January 1962 a journalist quoted a police officer who insisted that "when the OAS first seized control, Arabs would run to us to inform on the FLN." With reports announcing Algerian independence, "that is finished. We have our legs spread like faggots. We are dropping our pants, spreading our legs." In turning a war between men into one over which male is really the man, such images raised the question of whether sodomitical possession, presented as the tribute the conquered male rendered to his superior, was desired because of deviance or imposed because of weakness.[10]

A November 1961 tract that circulated in Algiers dramatized the metaphorical importance that sodomy qua act, even when not linked to rape, held in such discussions (figure 17). Tagged with the oft-used title "La raie-publique" (with "raie," short for raie des fesses or "butt crack," qualifying "republic"), it depicted a bent-over and smiling Charles de Gaulle with his pants dropped to his knees, and a large number of be-fezzed and erect penises. Most of the penises were lined up in the closed ranks of a military parade, led by one carrying a star-and-crescent flag, but two others stood ahead, identified as "Ben Bella" (i.e., Ahmed Ben Bella, a then imprisoned leader of the FLN, who would soon become president of the Algerian Republic) and "Hassan" (Hassan II, King of Morocco), while yet another, "Bourguiba" (i.e., Habib Bourguiba, president of the Tunisian Republic), sodomized the French leader.[11] Like other pro-French Algeria arguments that there was no larger reason that could explain France's retreat, no "tide of history" nor national interest, these accusations targeted moral weakness and failed masculinity, and emphasized the humiliation and subjugation of Frenchmen that resulted.[12] One amateur historian, in a self-published 1971 text that targeted former Prime Minister Michel Debré as "France's shame," explained that "through the demonic will of one individual [Charles de Gaulle], France has lost face vis-à-vis the Algerians. This is why they allow themselves to insist, widely and loudly: 'France is a coun-

---

rape by FLN forces. See La torture et l'armée pendant la guerre d'Algérie, 1954–1962 (Paris: Gallimard, 2001).

10. Philippe Hernandez, "En Algérie, j'ai vu la France assiégée par l'OAS," in France-observateur 610 (11 January 1962), 8–10.

11. Service départemental des renseignements généraux, "Photocopie d'un tract qui circule actuellement à Alger: n. 11067 RG.I" (Algiers, 28 November 1961), 1+tract, in Archives nationales d'outre-mer, Aix-en-Provence, France: 91/3F/59.

12. On "the tide of history," see Shepard, The Invention of Decolonization, ch. 2.

"LA RAIE PUBLIQUE"

Figure 17. "La raie-publique"—a punning term that translates roughly as "the butt-crack republic"—is a photocopy of a tract found in the streets of Algiers in 1961. The name of the king of Morocco identifies the be-fezzed flying male organ, and that of the leader of the FLN is on the second in-flight organ. The name of the president of Tunisia is on the flying organ that penetrates the cartoon figure of French President Charles de Gaulle. The flag carried by the be-fezzed male organ leading the column on the right is that of the FLN. At the top, the "K" on the phallic missile heading down toward de Gaulle might refer to Soviet Premier Nikita Khrushchev. Permission to reproduce graciously provided by the Archives nationales d'Outre-Mer, Aix-en-Provence, France.

try full of *enculés* [people who get buggered]!"[13] By 1972, a supposedly "ethnographic" study of "sexuality and magic in Black Africa" presented as fact the most durable story of a Frenchman in uniform sodomized by FLN men at the moment of independence. The author, Jacques Lantier ("pseudonym of a senior civil servant, former secret agent"), informed his readers that "at the time of the events in Algeria, the Arabs had a French diplomat publicly sodomized in the belief that our country would be henceforth dishonored." (It was this story that, in accounts given by his daughter as well as his lawyer, underwrote the odd claim made by Jean-Marie Le Pen in this chapter's epigraph: "One of their [i.e., Maghrebi immigrants'] goals,

13. Pierre Porthault, *Être ou ne plus être* (Paris: Chez l'auteur, 1971), 49–50.

204 / Chapter Seven

for example, is to sodomize the president." In a televised debate, National Front presidential candidate Marine Le Pen insisted that her father referred to "a historical event"; in a newspaper interview, Wallerand de Saint-Juste noted that "Jean-Marie Le Pen made reference to an episode that he cannot forget, which is what happened on 17 July 1962 to the French consul-general in Algiers, who was publicly sodomized on the beach at Sidi Ferruch.")[14] Lantier used the anecdote to demonstrate his claim that "in this way the human male believes that, if he plunges his rod into the body of another (masculine or feminine), he profoundly humiliates the other."[15] The book was roundly criticized by actual anthropologists, who dismissed it as merely anecdotal and scandal-mongering. Still, Lantier's interpretation of the social importance of the act of sodomy rehearsed widely accepted social scientific certainties. In a 1955 medical journal article, the psychologists H. Collomb and P. Robert claimed that, among "North African Muslims . . . the chiefs of conquering tribes forced anal coitus on their vanquished adversaries. This act did not have a libidinal value but a social value; it consecrated the victory, demonstrating the supremacy of the victor

14. For de Saint-Juste, see http://www.lexpress.fr/actualite/politique/jean-marie-le-pen-derape-encore_984298.html, accessed 6 June 2015. Marine Le Pen made her statement on the television show *Les paroles et les actes* on France 2, 23 June 2011. Jean-Noël Jeanneney discusses this claim and how his father, Jean-Marcel Jeanneney, investigated and disproved it at the time. (See Jean-Noël Jeanneney, "Préface: Commentaire, Témoignage," in Anne Liskenne, *L'Algérie indépendante: L'ambassade de Jean-Marcel Jeanneney (juillet 1962-janvier 1963)* (Paris: Armand Colin, 2015), 22–23. In online and published discussions, far-right sources referenced a web page on the site of the French Institut national de l'audiovisuel (INA) as proof of this claim. It presented an excerpt from the television nightly news of 16 July 1962. The excerpt is mute. (See http://www.ina.fr/video/CAF94059610/m-video.html , accessed 6 June 2015.) Its title is "M. Jeanneney at the Elysée Palace"; Jean-Marcel Jeanneney had been named the French ambassador and high representative of France to the Algerian Republic on 17 July 1962. Until mid-2013, the INA summary of the clip asserted that he was there to discuss the incident on the beach at Sidi-Ferruch (the actual Sidi-Fredj). When I wrote the site to ask what sources they relied on to make this assertion—about an event that supposedly happened the day *after* this news report—the description disappeared.

15. *La Cité magique: Sexualité et magie en Afrique noire* (Paris: Fayard, 1972), 102. For author description, see verso. French anthropologists dismissed the book as embarrassing, a collection of anecdotes meant to shock Western readers. Yet, as historian of Germany Lora Wildenthal recounts, it played a key role in the embrace by many European feminists of anti–female circumcision activism. The French feminist writer Benoîte Groult relied on Lantier's book for the account she gave in her influential *Ainsi soit-elle* (Paris: Grasset, 1975); a 1977 press conference at which she spoke about the practice alerted other Swiss and West German feminists about the phenomenon, and this led to a transnational movement. Wildenthal notes that Alain de Benoist and another French ultra-right thinker, the sexologist Gérard Zwang, both participated in the press conference. See Lora Wildenthal, *The Language of Human Rights in West Germany* (Philadelphia: University of Pennsylvania Press, 2012), 146–150, 252fn86.

and the pitiful condition of the defeated."[16] In 1961, Jacques Berque, an esteemed scholar of Islam and North Africa, noted that in the Maghreb, "active homosexuality appears, in certain cases, to act as a form of compensation for inferior status." But in 1970 he wrote that "active pederasty itself was understood as resulting from super-masculinity [*sur-masculinité*]." There is no indication that he changed his mind due to new evidence. Berque's affirmation of such clearly distinct explanations reveals at once how useful sodomy was to anchor arguments about power and a shift in its valence over time, after Algerian independence.[17]

The "Arab Invention" of Sodomy in Post-1962 France

After 1962, talk of sodomy in far-right writing and the popular press often suggested that the end of French Algeria had brought "Arab" sodomy to France. The presence of large numbers of Arab men in France was supposedly a key reason acts of sodomy had become widespread. This could be a source of amusement as well as worry. In a study titled *The Psychology of Prostitutes*, published in 1969, a long analysis of the growing role supposedly played by Algerian pimps in French prostitution ended with the claim, "This is the vision that emerges from the joke about the Arab who is visiting his native Algeria (but is it just a joke?): In France, I b—— [*baise*, or fuck] the women and I e—— [*encule*, or bugger] the men."[18] Such stories typically presented the Arabs as the active sodomizers, the *enculeurs*. This positioning emphasized the play of power, in that sexual "dominance" was assigned to men who were on the bottom of French society (whether because of natural or cultural incapacity to succeed, because of sociology, or because of racism; interpretations varied). Social scientists and popular wisdom agreed that a sodomitical economy typified North Africa. After decolonization, such talk asserted, it now also functioned in the metropole.

---

16. Henri Collomb and P. Robert, "Le thème de l'homosexualité chez le Nord-Africain musulman" *Annales médico-psychologiques* (1958), 531–534; 533.

17. Jacques Berque, "Recent Research on Racial Relations: The North of Africa," *International Social Science Journal* 13, no. 2 (1961), 177–96; 182–183; Berque, *Le Maghreb entre deux guerres* (Paris: Seuil, 1970), 357n2. Berque notes also that "the trivial term meaning 'to copulate with,' *niquer*, also means 'to prevail over, to humiliate.'" English and French equivalents of the word have the exact same polysemic implications. For a historical and theoretical overview of Western understandings of the male "active sodomite" and the roles of power and domination in these understandings, see David M. Halperin, "How to Do the History of Male Homosexuality," in Halperin, *How to*, 104–137.

18. Durban, *La psychologie*, 155.

While many statements left unclear whether sodomy was imposed by violence or was mutually desired, others pointed to the responsibility of leftists and French homosexuals. The law identified the latter as a "social plague"; extreme-right analysts linked these groups and warned that both were spreading. For the far-right chronicler André Figueras, what Arab immigrants had brought to France was the normalization of sodomy between men: "An Arab proverb tells us more or less that one must turn to women to fulfill needs, and to boys for pleasure. Sodomy is such a natural thing in North Africa, even vaunted, that pederasts who in Paris could never get over their discomfort and often their fear, flourished when surrounded by Arabs." For Figueras, this explained the key role that homosexuals (along with sexually frustrated French women) had played in losing French North Africa: "How then, given that, would one not find such understanding people understandable?" Figueras made explicit what so many others merely implied: "If I had the time, I would be eager to complete a dissertation on the sexual causes of decolonization." Instead, like many of his ideological comrades, he made such claims to deflect discussions of why colonial oppression had led to the Algerian revolution as well as to reject "sexual liberation" in France.[19] In *Minute*, a late 1972 warning about leftist efforts to stir up "a revolt among the North Africans of France" warned that "at Nanterre, every day, [male] students are molested by North Africans, with the encouragement of leftists. [The North Africans] steal, molest, even sodomize on occasion, in that gaping silence that fear produces."[20] French defeat at the hands of Algerians had opened up French men to new forms of humiliation, which leftists worked to encourage.

A crescendo of far-right references to sodomy had crystallized around the 1966 performance of Jean Genet's play *Les paravents* (The Screens) at the state-run Odéon Theater. Both the play and its staging exaggerated Genet's long-standing interest in writing about anal sex as a means to address questions of desire, power, and evil. Indeed, although the setting was Algeria during an unnamed war, one British critic argued that the play's "profuse depictions of anal eroticism displaced any anti-colonial implications."[21] That was not, however, the interpretation of many on the extreme right, who insisted that both things were connected. In the anti-Gaullist right-wing weekly *Aux écoutes du monde*, the journalist Simon Glady (with a title that summarized one strongly held view of the moral implications of de-

19. Andre Figueras, "Sexualité et politique," *Pan!* 6 (1972), 58–62.

20. "Intolérable! Sartre veut soulever les arabes: Sous un faux prétexte, un appel à la révolte des Nord-Africains en France," *Minute* 558 (20 December 1972), 9.

21. Martin Esslin, *The Theatre of the Absurd* (London: Taylor & Francis, 1968), 224.

colonization, "Tide of History and the Inversion of Values") warned that the play "systematically inverts every value after injecting each with fecal eroticism."[22] It was in response to such reports of sodomitical menace that far-right protests began in late spring. By autumn, when the play reopened after a summer hiatus, increasingly violent efforts to impede any further performances became a nightly event, with infiltrators using catcalls and smokebombs, and rushing the stage as other protestors massed outside. Although the protests failed to stop the theatrical run, they drew national attention and provided new resonance to a far-right vocabulary, renovated by the fight against Genet, of rats and a rich vein of allusions to anal sex, such as "ass-*haute* culture" [*trouduculturel*]," and "scatologists of thought [*scatalogues de la pensée*]."[23]

In 1968, Pierre-Jean Vaillard, gossip columnist of *Minute*, warned his readers that "the capital's small number of scatologs and scatologists will be in heaven." *Les paravents* was to be restaged, a fact that he held up as clear proof that the French Army had been "umanned by the effort of the All-Powerful of the moment [de Gaulle]," who had chosen defeat in Algeria. Only this could explain how "a public theater is free to flaunt 'ass-*haute* culture' with nary a worry." Vaillard was quite insightful in his presentation of anticolonial revolt as the matrix of the mass movements that sought to change France in 1968 and after. His insistence that sodomy could only be a source of suffering and filth, however, merely repeated old claims. Others, not just Genet, saw new possibilities for political insights and action, which Algerian lessons had helped to reveal.[24]

The Sodomy Vogue

The cutting title of a late 1971 article in the gauchiste *Politique hebdo* posed a rather straightforward question: "Is Being Sodomized by an Arab All It Takes to Be a Marxist-Leninist?"[25] But the article's rather sympathetic exam-

---

22. Glady, "Les paravents de Genet: Vent d'histoire et inversion des valeurs," *Aux écoutes du monde* (14 April 1966), 31. "Inversion" was a term widely used in the late nineteenth century to describe those whom more recent commenters would call homosexuals, although its referent differed. See, e.g., Richard Krafft-Ebing, *Psychopathia sexualis, avec recherches spéciales sur l'inversion sexuelle: Tr. sur la 8ᶜ éd. allemande* (Paris: Carré, 1895).

23. Charpier, *Génération Occident*.

24. Pierre-Jean Vaillard, "Minute . . . Babillons," 31.

25. Duburg, "*Tout!* Ou rien?" 13. In response to Glazounov, "Révolutionnaires par la bande?" 26, a letter from Françoise d'Eaubonne in a subsequent issue insisted that FHAR rejected exactly this proposition. See "Deux lettres à propos de l'homosexualité," in *Politique hebdo* 8 (nouvelle formule; 1971), 3.

ination of the question was emblematic of a novel context in France, where it had become increasingly accepted that the political implications of sodomy were worth thinking about. It also indicated how Arab men shadowed this discussion. The term "sodomy" was the same as before, but what it meant supposedly had changed. Indeed, the very fact that sodomy was a topic of political discussion appeared to signal new possibilities. An article title in the *Nouvel accord* was rather typical of the media echo: "Sodomy: All the men want it. Nearly all women are afraid of it; is it dangerous?" To explain the gendered responses, the magazine argued that, "sodomized, [women] have the impression of being treated like an object, 'possessed' by a partner whom they can't even see in the midst of coitus." For men it was "quite the opposite; the dominating instinct . . . his 'phallocratism,' often finds what it needs through sodomy." Yet, despite such static interpretations, the article made it clear that change was afoot. In response to the question "In what countries is sodomy practiced and why?" it cited "several authors" to affirm that "several Muslim countries are those that come out on top"; and it cited Koranic restrictions on postnatal sex to explain why. Sodomy in those countries, that is, was traditional, backwards sodomy, which such men turned to because of age-old limits on male access to females. In the age of the pill and sexual experimentation, however, modern people turned to sodomy for different reasons. "But the United States," the article emphasized, "and in a more general sense all Western countries are right on the heels of these presumed champions, if they haven't already passed them by!"[26] These invocations of modernity and pleasure were in constant tension with popular understandings of the act—understandings that the article's invocations of "Muslim countries" encapsulated, and which linked it to more threatening sensations.

It was because references to sodomy continued to shock and to imply the use of force that its novel popularity as a topic of public discussion came to seem so politically meaningful, even revolutionary. This trend traversed borders. A 1975 American academic study of pornographic films in the United States suggested, "That a preference for the latter act [anal intercourse] is swelling rapidly has been evident in the arcades for the last eighteen months. The largest number of quarters go into machines showing 'fanny films,' in which males copulate anally with females." The article continued to make claims that were quite typical of the era, though in the name of analysis: "The new emphasis on anality raises questions. Hetero-

26. "La sodomie: Tous les hommes en ont envie. Presque toutes les femmes en ont peur; est elle dangereuse?" *Nouvel accord* 5 (April 1974), 4–11.

sexual audiences [for porn] by and large seem to be turned off by extreme violence, by overt male homosexuality and by blatant scatology, but are stimulated by an activity which is associated with all three." The author's argument, after touching on the writings of Sigmund Freud, Max Weber, and the American Freudian philosopher Norman O. Brown (with a particular focus on the symbolics of excrement), was that "anality loosed from repression can be powerful to the point of political statement"—more so, the article suggested, than was sexuality alone or, for that matter, other sex acts.[27]

French discussions in the early 1970s held up brutality and filth as signs of sodomy's political potential, which explained "bourgeois" disdain. In 1972, an important article by Pierre Baudry in the *Cahiers du cinéma* on shit (*la merde*) in contemporary film concluded with the claim that there now existed "a type of film (we could call it heterological or, following [Georges] Bataille, scatological) that redefines what is in opposition by placing the bottom against what's on top. . . . A way, that is, of metaphorizing the class struggle. . . ." Baudry cited the 1971 Sergio Leone Western *Giù la testa, coglione* [*Duck, You Sucker!*], in which several rich onlookers, confronted with the crudeness of a poor peon, comment on the peons' "promiscuity . . . bestial instincts . . . beasts, that's what they are, just like blacks are animals for North Americans." For Baudry, "What is in play then is a critical reprise of a nineteenth-century bourgeois thesis," but one that, rather than simply being "reversed," is, in Baudry's terms (which he attributes to Mao Zedong), "displaced." Racialized and colonized subjects were crucial in such efforts to identify how conflicts over domination could be recognized and made into sites of political action.[28]

A number of authors deployed sodomy to introduce novel ways of thinking about power and human relations. The climatic episode of the Algerian author Rachid Boudjedra's best-selling (Francophone) first novel, *Repudiation* (1969), is among the most interesting examples. The episode begins as the narrator, Rachid, flees a hammam after his seeming acquiescence to grasping male hands leads to an attempt to penetrate him. It ends with a flashback to a scene where his mother tells her children, "It's nothing but a rough game," as they stare bewildered at Rachid's oldest brother, Zahir, lost in passion inside another boy. As Rachid recalls this moment

27. Joseph W. Slade, "Recent Trends in Pornographic Films," *Society* 12, no. 6 (September/ October 1975), 77–84; On popularity, see also Scott MacDonald, "Confessions of a Feminist Porn Watcher," *Film Quarterly* 36, no. 3 (Spring 1983), 10–17.

28. Pierre Baudry, "Figuratif, matériel, excrémentiel," *Cahiers du cinéma* 238-239 (May-June 1972), 75–82.

while in flight from the hammam, he knows that "only Zahir would be able to explain."[29] The contrast between the threat of sodomy, which Rachid flees and his mother describes, and the access to understanding that Rachid assigns to his sexually active brother speaks to the potent implications of the act.

A surprising number of contemporary observers presumed that talk of sodomy could convey important political messages. This was visible in certain literary discussions in the Arab world. A 1970 Arabic-language novel, *Hammam al-Malatili* (The Malatili Bathhouse), by Isma'il Waliy al-Din, depicted a poor young man raping a rich older man as an act of revenge. The literary critic Joseph Massad claims this was the first novel to reverse the long-standing trope in Arabic-language literature of the subaltern man or boy anally raped by an elite man. This reversal, which proposed active anal sex as a weapon of the oppressed, was emblematic of the possibilities and the limits of most writers' engagement with this discussion in the 1970s in France and elsewhere; when the politicization of *enculage* was about the battle over which male was the "man," the victim of rape disappeared—as did the possibility that anal sex could be mutually desired.[30] In these debates about films and fiction, active sodomy appeared as a political weapon particularly suited for a radical left that had moved beyond a celebration of proletarian nobility, the limited analyses of the nineteenth century. It was an arm for the lumpen, those at the bottom, whom Marxists had always disdained, but whom "Third World" struggles had revealed as powerful. As the philosopher Guy Hocquenghem put it, in a description of the revelatory impact of the FHAR and others on left-wing discussions, groups that challenged sex and gender norms had played "the role of the crevasse which brutally revealed the reactionary implication of the expectation that a manly proletariat would bring radical change."[31] The new leftists looked to the peasants (of China, Mexico, and Algeria), and to the "blacks" of the United States—to those "at the bottom," rather than only those situated correctly vis-à-vis the means of production. As Baudry wrote in an open letter meant to explain why he quit *Cahiers du cinéma*, "The proletariat, as it currently exists, is largely under the sway of revisionism." His use of the

29. Rachid Boudjedra, *La Répudiation* (Paris: Denoël, 1969); quotes from *The Repudiation*, trans. Golda Lambrova (Colorado Springs, CO: Three Continents Press, 1995), 163–166.

30. Isma'il Waliy al-Din, *Hammam al-Malatili* (Cairo: Kitabat Mu'asirah, 1970), as analyzed in Massad, *Desiring Arabs*, 310–314.

31. Guy Hocquenghem, *Le désir homosexuel* (Paris: Fayard, 1972), 104.

term "revisionism" gave a post-'68 French Maoist spin to the Marcusian claim of "quietism."[32]

Last Tango in Paris, Anality, and the Algerian Revolution

The immediate and intense international reaction to Bernardo Bertolucci's film *Last Tango in Paris* upon its release in 1972 made strikingly visible how closely the increase in public invocations of anal sex was enmeshed with its political revalorization. For Bertolucci, as for a number of his contemporaries, references to sodomy seemed uniquely efficient, able to subvert established authority rather than merely offend standards of good taste or prudery. The film was also revelatory of how crucial "Algerian" references were to this discussion, although this was little noticed at the time.[33] It follows a series of encounters between an American man in his mid-forties and a twenty-year old French woman in an unoccupied Paris apartment, where they first meet by accident and then return over the next three days to talk and have all kinds of sex. The film tracks each character outside the apartment as well: first the young woman, as she performs in a film her young fiancé is making; then the man, as he deals with the aftermath of his wife's suicide; and finally both characters, as they venture out together. In a crucial scene Paul, played by Marlon Brando, sodomizes Jeanne, played by Maria Schneider, and uses butter as a lubricant. The film contained multiple other scenes rife with "anality" as well as other nonnormative sex acts, but this was the scene that provoked cries of scandal and made the film an international phenomenon known far beyond the circle of cinephiles.

When *Last Tango* was released in Paris, two months after its first screening in New York was reputed to have sparked outrage, a large majority of French critics invoked the scandal the film had caused but did not mention that its representations of anal sex were the proximate cause. (The review in *Minute* did winkingly make the argument that, like sex, "going to the can [was] also a function of nature" that did not need to be shown on film).[34] Claude Mauriac, in *L'express*, mastered the genre, with a review that

32. Pierre Baudry, "Chers amis" (9 February 1973), published in "À propos de la démission de Pierre Baudry," *Cahiers du cinéma* 245-246 (1973), 88–90.

33. See Esther Rashkin, "Sex, Sadism, Encrypted Loss and Encrypted History in 'Last Tango in Paris,'" *Parallax* 15, no. 1 (2009), 55–66.

34. Jan Mara, "Le 'dernier tango à Paris': Arrêtez la musique," *Minute* 558 (20 December 1972), 36. In press coverage of the film's French opening, only four critics—Duron, Chapier, de Gasperi, and Tallenay—mentioned anal sex; the term of choice was "sodomization."

both hailed and condemned the film while remaining loudly silent on the source of the scandal. He cited "Pauline Kael, film critic at *The New Yorker*, on whom 'Last Tango in Paris' had 'the greatest impact that (she had) ever experienced in twenty years of cinema.'" Mauriac's next line spoke volumes: "I said nothing. It's because it's unspeakable. Try and imagine the worst possible thing. No, not that. . . . How could you even think that! Well, Bertolucci thought exactly that, and Marlon Brando makes Maria do it." With either a wink or a huff, he added: "Absolute ignominy."[35] In one of the first French gay male / bisexual illustrated porn magazines, *Olympe*, the editor Pierre Guénin coyly asked, "And another thing, for those who have yet to see it: What is the deal with this *Last Tango in Paris*? Why does it so often come up in conversation? Why does everyone go on (while layering on a bit of hypocritical discomfort) about the providential 'pound of butter' thanks to which Marlon Brando is able to sodomize his young partner?" (See figure 18.)[36] An American critic made a similar point about the unspeakable, invoking the banter of the country's so-called king of late-night television—"smarmy witties on the Johnny Carson show (where sodomy is still one of the taboo topics—at the moment)"—to explain how *Last Tango* had become the topic of popular double entendres. Such public ribaldry might, she suggested, help make the act something that could be openly discussed. Explicit talk of an act such as anal sex mattered, in her view, because it could allow a franker reckoning with how misogynist domination functioned in sex.[37]

What almost every French critic at the time also avoided was an examination of the quite visible, indeed crucial, role of the Algerian war and Arabs in *Last Tango*. Among the many articles that appeared in the Parisian press in the weeks after the film opened, only one, in the Communist daily *L'Humanité*, noted that the film had anything to do with Algeria.[38] François

35. Claude Mauriac, "Brando comme on ne l'avait jamais vu," *L'express* 1118 (11–17 December 1972), 103.

36. Pierre Guénin, "Élections et tango à Paris," *Olympe* 58 (March 1973), 18.

37. Judith Crist, "'Last Tango,' but Not the Last Word," *New York Magazine* (5 February 1973), 34–35.

38. Louis Chauvet, "'Le dernier tango à Paris,'" *Le Figaro* (16 December 1972), 29; François Maurin, "Au seuil de l'abîme: 'Le dernier tango à Paris,'" *L'Humanité* (16 December 1972), 6; Jean-Louis Tallenay, "'Le dernier tango à Paris': Triste voyeurism," *Télérama* (20 December 1972), 73; Pierre Billard, "Un enfer nommé désir," *Le journal de dimanche* (17 December 1972), 17; Jean-Claude Mazeran, "Non, mon film n'est pas pornographique," affirme le metteur en scène," *Le journal de dimanche* (17 December 1972), 17; Anne de Gasperi, "Bertolucci: 'Un poème sur la sexualité,'" *Le Figaro* (16 December 1972), 29; Jean-Louis Bory, "Huis clos sur un matelas: Quand l'amour physique retrouve l'innocente sauvagerie des jeux enfantins," *Nouvel observateur* 424 (23–29 December 1972), 59; Henri Chapier, " 'Le dernier tango à Paris.': Pour

Figure 18. This collage appeared in the March 1973 issue of *Olympe*. Despite increasingly explicit references to male homosexual identity and desire, the magazine continued to define itself as a publication for nudists. The text and image fragments in this collage linked the scandal over the (sodomitical) "butter scene" in the film *Last Tango in Paris* to the March 1973 elections for the French National Assembly and other explicitly political French controversies. The images are of actors Maria Schneider and Marlon Brando, who star in the film.

Maurin described Jeanne as "the daughter of a colonel killed in Algeria" who had "fallen out with her mother, whose sole preoccupation is the cult of the lost father." In his review of *Last Tango* in the *New York Review of Books*, which came out several months after the film opened, the American novelist Norman Mailer summarized how Jeanne presented herself to the camera of her fiancé, played by Jean-Pierre Léaud: "She is the daughter of a dead Army officer who was sufficiently racist to teach his dog to detect Arabs by smell." For Mailer, she embodies the French bourgeoisie: "She is well brought up—there are glimpses of a suburban villa on a small walled estate." And this is why what he terms the film's "historic buggeries and reamings" are "historic": "It is nothing less than the concentrated family honor of the French army she will surrender when Brando proceeds a little later to bugger her."[39] Mailer was one of many to analyze the film's exploration of the history of the bourgeoisie and its rule: his discussions, like those of others, grappled with the ways in which "sodomy and anal stimulation" in the film represented power and domination. Yet Mailer was one of the few to draw attention to the film's exploration of the history of French imperialism, notably in Algeria, and of present day anti-Arab racism in France, as well as their intersections. And such references in the film were far more extensive than he or others noted at the time.[40]

"A Precise Depiction of Race Relations in the Paris Suburbs"

The first explicitly "anal" scene in the movie follows directly after Jeanne's recounting, to her fiancé (and his camera crew), of her father's death; she says the French army colonel was killed in May 1958, in Algiers. (The film fails to explain that this was during the attempted military coup d'état meant to keep Algeria French, which led to the collapse of the Fourth Republic and the return to power of Charles de Gaulle.) As the onscreen cam-

une révolution des sentiments," *Combat* (14 December 1972), 6; Pascal Bonitzer, "L'expérience en intérieur ('Le Dernier tango à Paris,' 'La Grande Bouffe,' 'La Maman et la Putain')," *Cahiers du cinéma* 247 (July-August 1973), 33–35; Michel Duron, "'Le dernier tango à Paris' (une débauche de talent)," *Canard enchaîné* (20 December 1972); Robert Benayoun, "Le tango par qui le scandale arrive," *Le point* 12 (11 December 1972), 8. There are no mentions of Algeria in any of the reviews cited and excerpted in "'Le dernier tango à Paris': La critique," *L'avant-scène cinéma* 133 (February 1973), 57–58.

39. Norman Mailer, "A Transit to Narcissus," *New York Review of Books* (17 May 1973), 3–9. While Mailer attributes the information about the dog (named Mustapha) to Jeanne, it is the maid, Olympia, who laughingly recounts this to the fiancé; Jeanne immediately tells him that her maid is "racist."

40. Pauline Kael, "The Current Cinema: Tango," *New Yorker* 48, no. 36 (28 October 1972), 130–138; Crist, "'Last Tango.'"

era keeps running, and the whole group, led by the family maid, enters the garden within the "small walled estate," the film switches perspectives so that we see them all walking towards the viewer, who can also discern six little kids squatting, hidden with their backs to the camera, amid the budding branches of the bushes. "What are you doing?" asks Jeanne when she sees them. "We are going poopoo," says one. "We're pooping," says another. "Let's go!" a third joyously yells. As they begin to run off, Olympia, the maid, yells after them, "Go! Go take a dump in your own country, dirty Arabs!" In the background we hear her continue to complain about the "dirty Arabs"; in the foreground, Jeanne approvingly comments on her fiancé's excitement that they got the incident all on film. "Olympia was sublime," she tells him, applauding the frankness of a woman whom she had described minutes earlier as racist. "This way we have a precise depiction of race relations in the Paris suburbs [*banlieue*]," she says.

While Mailer's description suggests that Paul is a metaphor for Algeria and that Jeanne signifies France, a recent study by the literary critic Esther Rashkin argues that in the film both Paul and Jeanne alternately represent (colonized) Algeria and (colonizing) France. Such an interpretation resonates with their final scene together, when, before asking that they break their pact and reveal their names to each other, Paul puts on the képi her father was wearing when he died in Algiers. Jeanne takes her dead father's pistol and shoots Paul dead. When the police come, she tells them that he—an immigrant in France, and perhaps a metaphor for Algeria, it should be emphasized—came out of nowhere and tried to rape her.[41]

There are good reasons why the film has been primarily remembered as "the butter film." That scene was, according to Bertolucci and others, clearly political in importance. In an interview that accompanied the film's French opening, the director explained that "the most magisterial of lessons" is "in the sodomization scene, a moment when 'ties' are demystified because, at the same moment, [Paul] presents [to Jeanne] insolent propositions about the very idea of sentiments, about the family." In the film, as he violates her, Paul mutters "about the family. A holy institution, meant to breed virtue in savages. . . ."; the term "savages," of course, resonates

---

41. Rashkin, "Sex, Sadism." There are several other clear references to these contexts, as Maria lodges in a hotel where the concierge, who insistently grabs her and tries to speak to her, is a black woman from the Antilles, and the maid who worked for Paul's now dead wife recounts how Paul suddenly "one day, landed in Tahiti," part of the French colony of Polynesia. Besides Rashkin, other Anglophone film critics recently have begun to foreground the Algerian context of the film. See, e.g., Stephanie H. Donald, "Tang Wei Sex, the City and the Scapegoat in Lust, Caution," *Theory, Culture & Society* 27, no. 4 (July 2010), 46–68.

directly with long-standing European depictions of non-Europeans, notably in colonial situations. Paul continues, talking about the "holy family,
church of good citizens," and then details the lie of "freedom" as he (in
Mauriac's phrasing) "makes Maria do it."[42] Yet, while much has been said
about the politics of the film's representation of sodomy, it is the density of
explicit references to the Algerian war, to Algerian immigration in France,
and to violence as well as racism that is both striking and emblematic of
the larger French context. This is why French critics at the time took the
references for granted, whereas a number of Anglophone critics noted their
presence. It is the intersection of "Algeria" and sodomy that now requires
explanation.[43]

"We Have Been *Enculer* by Arabs": Gay Liberation and the Anticolonial Politics of Anal Sex

These early 1970s artistic and theoretical efforts to grapple with the politics of sodomy foregrounded cross-gender sexual relations. Yet the most
explicit—and explicitly political—contemporary discussions fixated on
sodomy between men, and placed the role of Arabs at the center (and on
top). In 1971, the first "manifesto" of the FHAR placed the coupling in its
first line: "We have been *enculer* by Arabs" (figure 12).[44] It parodied a manifesto that had appeared one month before, which 343 women had signed
and which satirists immediately had nicknamed "the Manifesto of the 343
Sluts." Like the feminist statement by women who announced that they
had had abortions, the FHARist provocation thrust into public view something shameful and, many imagined, somewhat violent and dirty—an act
intimately related to sex, but of the wholly nonreproductive kind. Both
texts broke with previous strategies. Abortion laws in the secular French
Republic had been justified as part of the national crusade against demographic decline and reformers faced accusations that allowing abortions
would sap national strength.[45] The women who signed it dramatically
challenged such arguments; they also risked criminal charges, since abortion was illegal. The 1960 law that stigmatized homosexuality as a "social
plague" referenced similar claims. Yet, in France, sodomy was not a crime.

42. De Gasperi, "Bertolucci," 29.
43. E.g.., Joan Mellen, "Sexual Politics and 'Last Tango in Paris,'" *Film Quarterly* 26, no. 3 (1973), 9–19.
44. From centerfold of *Tout!* 12 (1971).
45. Jean E. Pedersen, "Regulating Abortion and Birth Control: Gender, Medicine, and Republican politics in France, 1870–1920," *French Historical Studies* 19, no. 3 (1996), 673–698.

Even so, there were no names attached to the FHAR's original "manifesto." Through parody, however, it embraced the betrayal of the nation—a subsequent FHAR newsletter took *Social Plague* as its title—and used the most shocking variant of transnational sodomy—Arab on French—to jettison "reform," legal or otherwise. Every aspect of the text emphatically rejected all previous efforts to ameliorate French discussions about homosexuals. Since 1953, France's only substantive organization that spoke to and for homosexuals, Arcadie, had curried favor with authorities, seeking to inflect legal, religious, medical and educational measures. Arcadians had insistently worked to impose the term "homophile," so as to hold any reference to sexuality, much less talk of sex acts, at a distance—especially talk linked to anal sex or, for that matter, sex with Arabs.[46] The "revolutionary homosexuals" thrust references to both those things together, and did so to insist that individual desires, precisely because colonial history had shaped them, created connections that were political, indeed potentially revolutionary. Just like arguments that appeared in contemporaneous publications such as the *Nouvel accord*, the FHAR maneuvered constantly between ahistorical statements about the act and how others understood it, and explicitly historicized claims about what sodomy could mean given current circumstances. The FHAR sought to address this tension through political analysis.

In France, the FHAR asserted, the act of sodomy transformed polymorphous desire into reality and produced a connection between "homo" and "Arab" (two distinct categories) that was deeply political: "Do you believe we could have the same relationships with Arabs as everyone else or as the average Frenchman when we commit with them the act that bourgeois morality most denigrates?" The shared experience of sodomy made possible a different form of connection, one that could not be reduced to the merely sexual. In placing such arguments at the center of their publications, they did more than shock *la bourgeoisie*: they drew explicit attention to Orientalist certainties about "Arab" deviance and to homophobic beliefs. The former presented active sodomy as emblematic of the excessive virility of Arab and Muslim societies—an uncontrolled, uncivilized, and crude exercise of male power that used sexual penetration to dominate women and boys,

46. Sébastien Chauvin, "Les aventures d'une 'alliance objective': Quelques moments de la relation entre mouvements homosexuels et mouvements féministes au XXe siècle," *L'homme et la société* 4 (2005), 111–130. As Julian Jackson shows, depictions of Arcadie as "asexual" were exaggerated and, by the mid-1970s at least, explicit talk of anal sex did appear in the regular journal. Letters to the editor, Jackson notes, had long contained quite explicit references. See Jackson, *Living in Arcadia*, 164–165.

and even to degrade other men. The latter proposed that male same-sex sexual desire resulted from failed masculinity and fixated on male effeminacy and sexual passivity as emblematic of how homosexual desire and identity resulted from moral weakness, neuroses, and/or organic sickness. In a preemptive response to potential critics of their multiple depictions of Arabs sodomizing "French" men and boys, the editors of the special issue of *Tout!* explained that what they were referring to was different from the sodomitical pursuits of "great men" such as André Gide, Henry de Montherlant, Pierre Loti, or the many others who had taken advantage of French imperialism to satisfy desires judged harshly in the metropole. Because of anticolonialist victories, they insisted, things were now different.[47]

The shift from North Africa to France and, most important, the victory of the colonized over the colonizer in Algeria created a new context and new political possibilities. An article in *Tout!* no. 12 insisted that the sex act revolutionary homosexuals celebrated was a form of anticolonial critique: "Let us note that, in France, it's our Arab friends who bugger us and never the reverse." In the metropole, after Algerian independence yet in a context of continued "colonial" racism, the authors proposed something weightier than the confirmation of a stereotype: "Isn't it obvious that this is a form of revenge, offered to them by us, against the Western colonizer?" While multiple other readings seem possible, the text's striking deployment of political concepts such as "consent" and "revenge" alongside sodomy was explicitly tethered to an anticolonial and antiracist analysis of the Western past and the French present. That is, invocations of sodomy were key to these sex radicals' claims to decolonize eroticized Arab references.

The argument that, in the current moment, a relation of sodomized to sodomizer, of "French homo" to "Arab man," allowed each to benefit politically—as well as erotically—appeared repeatedly in the early 1970s. The author of a piece in "Three Billion Perverts" (sarcastically presented as an excerpt of the unpublished writings of Stéphane Mallarmé) claimed, "In buggering me [*m'enkulant* (sic)] the way he did, Hassan had wanted to wipe away the French presence from Morocco. . . ." The image that accompanied the text (figure 19) made the imperial play of power explicit, with a French naval officer carrying a heavy cannon between his hands and legs as he approaches a distressed Arab sheik from behind.

In a 1976 play, the well-known gay writer Yves Navarre made a similar claim, but to rather different ends. The only transvestite client of a gay sauna, Vicky, speaks of her relations with the North African men she sleeps

47. On these authors, sex, and imperialism, see Aldrich, *Colonialism and homosexuality.*

En m'enkulant comme il l'avait fait, Hassan avait voulu me faire expier la présence française au Maroc, expier la reconquête de l'Espagne, expier Poitiers. Le chef des envahisseurs sarrazins repoussé par Charles Martel s'appelait déjà Abderamane.

L'idée de le revoir le lendemain matin me semblait tout à coup impossible. Jamais je ne pourrais soutenir son regard. J'avais envie de fuir, de quitter à l'instant cette maison, cette oasis, ce désert, ce pays, ces gens chez qui je n'avais rien à faire, ces gens pour qui je ne serai jamais que l'oppresseur ou la proie en puissance, l'intrus . . .

La petite crise de parano a continué un bon moment dans ma tête et puis, peu à peu, ça s'est calmé. J'avais moins mal au cul, je n'avais plus la vérole. J'ai éclaté de rire en pensant à l'histoire de l'arroseur arrosé et le sommeil m'a pris « le lourd sommeil sans rêve ».

Figure 19. This image, which looks as if it were cut out of a textbook, offers a classic example of the embrace by FHAR militants both of Debordian *détournement* and of talk of sodomy to analyze power. It appeared in the short story "Kouché!" (*sic*)—which might be translated as "Zpread Your Legz!"—one of the pieces that made up the "The Arabs and Us" section of "Three Billion Perverts" (1973). The editors of "Three Billion Perverts" farcically attributed the short story to Stéphane Mallarmé, the renowned nineteenth-century French symbolist poet. The image proposes that French invasions of the Maghreb aimed to dominate through sodomitical possession. Note that the "French" man and the "Arab" man are each depicted as elite; in the accompanying short story, the son of a sheikh rapes his father's guest, the narrator. In the story, as in the image, the struggle to bugger (*enculer*) is presented as an effective way to dominate another elite male. The fragment of "Kouché!" just below the image, which works as epigraph, interprets the act in terms of anticolonial revenge: "In buggering me as he had, Hassan had wanted to make me pay for the French presence in Morocco," etc.

with: "Me, when I ask them their name, they just smile and give me the signal to turn around; clap, clap. I work toward Franco-Algerian reconciliation." The refusal to exchange names echoes with both "the war without a name" (as many termed the Algerian war) and, contemporaneously, *Last Tango*.[48] Through the pleasures and the play of power particular to anal sex between "Arab men" and "French homosexuals," colonized realities could be confronted. Note how different Navarre's promise of "reconciliation"

48. Yves Navarre, "Les dernières clientes: Pièce en deux actes et 21 scènes," in Navarre, *Theatre 2* (Paris: Flammarion, 1976), 139–224.

was from the "revenge" that the FHAR pretended to offer, and note also that the play appeared after the FHAR had already disappeared.

The Politics of Sodomy, Exhausted (1973–1979)

The hugely controversial "Three Billion Perverts: The Big Encyclopedia of Homosexualities" (1973) announced the exhaustion of the early 1970s French vogue for thinking about how power works through sodomitical references, as well as the end of revolutionary homosexuality. A collective made up of men and women who had been involved with the FHAR had put together the issue over the course of some six months. The government, however, waited only a few weeks after the issue's release in March 1973 to ban it. The authorities condemned it as the "libidinous exhibition of a perverted minority," and ordered all copies seized. In May 1974, the resulting trial of Félix Guattari, director of publication for *Recherches*, for "offence against public decency" ended in his conviction. ("Three Billion Perverts" was one of only two political publications that the French government banned over the course of the 1970s. The other was the FHAR-produced *Tout!* no. 12 [1971]; the publisher, philosopher Jean-Paul Sartre, faced charges but was cleared.) The judge ordered all copies of the journal issue destroyed and imposed a fine of six hundred francs on Guattari. This was a very public scandal. Among militants themselves, controversies around how the publication came to be and, specifically, its "Arab" content helped provoke the collapse of the FHAR, a demise that coincided with the completion of the special issue.[49]

Many of the articles, drawings, and excerpts that made up the longest section of "Three Billion Perverts," "Arabs and Us," insistently presented sodomy as the connecting force between "homos" ("us") and "Arabs," with a set of claims that catalyzed ongoing tensions among homosexual revolutionaries and their allies. For the philosopher Guy Hocquenghem, who had coordinated the whole publication, the transgressive force of evocations linking "homos" and "Arabs" created reactionary resistance. Many others at the time, however, instead argued that the racist exoticism on which claims about Arabs and sodomy depended made them untenable. This was visible in the two very critical pieces that were published in the pages right after "The Arabs and Us": "Sex_pol in Action (concerning the text 'The Arabs and Us')" and "The Arabs and the 'WHITES [/WHITE SPACES].'" Both pieces were unsigned.

49. See Genosko, "The Figure of the Arab," 60–78.

Gilles Deleuze, the philosopher Gary Genosoko argues, authored the first piece, which began with the accusation that "some men from FHAR who do not represent the FHAR came together. . . . What they have in common is their quest for Arab men, to be buggered [*se faire enculer*] by them." In Deleuze's summary of "The Arabs and Us," these "men from FHAR" had sought to explore "this machine of desire that only functions through the ass, with Arab men. . . ." Among the questions they raised, Deleuze noted, was "Should Vaseline be part of this machine" or "should it not be?" Such attention, it is worth noting, reflects the important place that anal sex played in the recently published *Anti-Oedipus* (1972), which Deleuze had coauthored with Guattari (the term they preferred was *enculage*; the English translation misleadingly mistranslates the book's multiple uses of *enculer* as "fucked"). Deleuze offered an incisive critique, which targeted how "Arabs and Us" "shoves together all sorts of confused elements . . . politically revolutionary elements mixed in with perfectly fascist and racist elements." To analyze this mix, the philosopher homed in on one line in the midst of a transcribed discussion among FHAR activists about their relationships with their Arab sexual partners:" "I want there to be no more people, no more egos." On the one hand, Deleuze argued, "here, again, racism peeks out, if it's the Arab who is supposed to represent the nonhuman." On the other, he suggested that "everything's different if the nonhuman designates in each one of us this node where what defines each sex as well as the very difference between sexes is abolished." To map out the *va-et-vient* between racist/fascist and revolutionary elements in the texts, Deleuze quite strikingly fixates on identities (male and female; homo- and heterosexual) and also organs: "to become the sexual organ, the asshole of the other, to turn oneself into the other sex." Yet, tellingly, he ignores the act his opening summary has so notably highlighted: anal sex.

The political implications that FHAR writers, most notably Hocquenghem, had sought to assign to their joined invocations of sodomy and Arabs depended on two frames Deleuze dismissed: the potent politics of being sodomized (*enculés*) on the one hand, and the particular historical context of post-decolonization France on the other. Amid the convincing charges of racism, the connections between the two frames would fade from discussions among gay liberationists alongside the disappearance of the FHAR.

The Whitening of Sodomy

In 1977, the "new philosophers" Pascal Bruckner and Alain Finkielkraut published a sharp critique of the sexual revolution to wide acclaim. The

Figure 20. Cover of the 1979 paperback edition of *Le
Nouveau désordre amoureux* (The New Chaos of Love, 1977)
by Pascal Bruckner and Alain Finkielkraut. © Éditions du
Seuil, "Fiction & Cie," 1977, "Points documents," 1997.

front cover of their book *Le nouveau désordre amoureux* (The New Chaos
of Love; figure 20) depicted an odd scene of sodomy in which a cartoon
snowman takes a cartoon snow-woman from behind. Against calls by De-
lueze, Guattari, and others for multiplying differences and connections, the
text summoned a renewed heterosexuality: for the new pleasures the sexual
revolution had enabled to flourish rather than wither, it was necessary to
embrace the difference between the sexes as foundational.[50] Rather than

50. Pascal Bruckner and Alain Finkielkraut, *Le nouveau désordre amoureux: Essai* (Paris:
Seuil, 1977); see also their interview in Andrée Fortin, "Amour et utopie," in *Nuit blanche* 12
(1984), 46–49.

being disruptive or historical, the sodomy the book celebrates reaffirms long-standing conventions. Bruckner and Finkielkraut trumpet that the different responses of women and men to the act, as well as their different positions in it, reveal crucial truths and do not require radical reevaluations. The cover's depiction of the act as snowy white—so clean, no dirt, and certainly not "Arab"—speaks volumes.

Arab references, it must be emphasized, did remain widespread in French public invocations of sodomy in the late 1970s and after. What largely disappeared were the political reflections that had accompanied such links just a few years earlier. Critique was left to those whose identities were targeted, such as the authors of the 1977 letter from film professionals to *Libération*, which opened this chapter. (Their letter, it is important to note, is one of the few instances when Maghrebi perspectives appear in this chapter.) The authors' effort to expose the overdetermined history of the idea of the "Arab . . . man whose sexual organ cuts like a knife," of *le sexe-couteau*, came after the larger echo chamber had disappeared. The intersections between talk of sodomy and French certainties about Arab men had briefly rendered visible specific histories of domination and emotional intensity, or what might fruitfully be thought of as the political mystery of imperial power and its aftermath. That connection was then, yet again, obscured. From 1962 through the mid-1970s, the discourse around sodomy had summoned the ideologies and the violence that had first forced French and Algerians together and then ripped them apart. Afterwards, philosophical and other deployments of the metaphor of sodomy became decontextualized, as authors relied on its abstraction as a political symbol to reveal "universal" truths.

Discomfiting attention to sexual acts clearly mattered in the 1970s, as this chapter and book show. Yet too many commentators reduced such sex talk to signs only of identities. Writing in those years, Foucault described how late-nineteenth-century France witnessed a shift from condemnations of sodomy to analyses of homosexuality. The first volume of his *History of Sexuality* (1976) ironically led some observers to conclude that the tension between acts and sexuality was a thing of the past. The Algerian history of France's early 1970s sodomy vogue reveals, to the contrary, how talk of acts had reemerged as a dense site for thinking of power. This postdecolonization context provided the terms and made it possible for Foucault to unpack how sexuality had become a key explanation for identities: of discursive efforts to pin down meaningful distinctions between people in order to facilitate the work of power, and of individual self-discipline which anchored modern forms of governmentality. Foucault historicized efforts to regulate sexual heterodoxy and define normalcy. His approach attends to sharp changes over time; it insists that this instability mattered, and that it demands analysis. Too many scholars and, notably, historians prefer to debate comforting versions of some of his conclusions about what happened in the past. The historical approach this book relies on seeks to take up and extend some of the ways in which Foucault asked questions in dialogue with archival material.

Sodomy and Rape: Acts and Identities in Question

The next two chapters center on French debates about rape in the 1970s. Talk of rape opens up a very different perspective from that of sodomy on the ways that sex, identities, bodies, and violence were enmeshed in histories of empire, racism, and decolonization that tacked constantly between Algeria and France. The question of rape, of course, hovered over many of the early 1970s texts that grappled with how sodomy offered new ways to think about power and domination, as well as sex, whether in Bertolucci's film or in the testimonials in *Tout* no. 12.[51] In early 1970s France, however, sodomitical acts did not legally qualify as rape. "What does the law tell us about it?" the adult magazine *Union* asked its readers in 1973. "The victim by definition is a woman. The situation in which a male rapes another man does not constitute a rape. It is punished by the law, of course, but less severely ([it is considered] indecent assault). . . . Finally, rape necessarily involves the rod penetrating the vulva. This excludes, for example, a situation where the victim has been sodomized against her will."[52] At the end of 1980, the French parliament changed the law defining rape on the basis of a bill that the feminist and center-right senator Brigitte Gros had first proposed in 1978. The 1980 law established the first-ever French juridical definition of rape: "any act of sexual penetration, of whatever kind, imposed on another person through violence, obligation, threat, or surprise." The legislation broke sharply with court precedent, which targeted "illicit coitus," for this new law clearly defined rape as the "sexual penetration" of the victim's body without consent, and included both sexes as potential victims and perpetrators. This reform also defined rape as a crime against the victim's dignity, which broke with previous legal arguments that it was "a crime against the owner of the woman [*le propriétaire de la femme*]," i.e., the husband or father, her "head of family." Feminist-driven debates and

51. Mailer, "A Transit."
52. Christian Demay, "Le Viol," *Union* 15 (September 1973), 6–15.

developments that produced this reform have been the overriding focus of much scholarship, and with good reason. Yet attention to the place of Arab men in this history opens up new perspectives. Post-1962 questions undergirded the concerted 1970s deployment of rape as metaphor—the focus of the next chapter—which became crucial to leftist efforts to contest racism early in the decade. The "Arab man," as chapter 9 will show, raised questions that contoured the post-'68 struggle of a new generation of radical feminist activists to combat rape by forcing French society to take it seriously. These two phenomena intersected in complex ways across the decade.

EIGHT

Rape as Metaphor in the 1970s

What does Pougatchev [the new owner of the daily *FRANCE-SOIR*] want? If we look at what the evidence suggests, it's to take a sharp right turn, so as to go after new readers and, if possible, more everyday folks. . . . One of his preferred headlines needs no commentary: "Arabs Are All Rapists!"

—Renaud Revel (2010).[1]

References to Arab men, Algeria, colonial violence, and anti-Maghrebi racism played a substantial role in 1970s French discussions about rape, as did actual anti-Arab racism. The decade marked a turning point in how French society grappled with sexual violence, because a new generation of feminist activists, a "second wave" that moved beyond their predecessors' fight for the vote and legal equality to address other factors that produced inequality and misogyny, finally forced the issue of sexual violence into public debate.[2] That led to changes in the law, in the treatment of perpetrators and victims, and in how rape was prosecuted. This history cannot be reduced to "Algerian questions." Fundamentally, what was at stake were the dramatic effects of sexual violence, how it shaped lives and possibilities—especially

---

1. Renaud Revel, "Nouvelle crise à *France-soir*: Pougatchev, qui veut du trash, menace de virer le patron de la rédaction." Immédias, blog de Renaud Revel, 11 August 2010; accessed 15 September 2014 at http://blogs.lexpress.fr/media/2010/08/11/nouvelle_crise_a_france_soir_p/.

2. See esp. Françoise Picq, *Libération des femmes: Les années-mouvement* (Paris: Seuil, 1993) and Françoise Thébaud, "Le privé est politique: Féminismes des années 1970," in *Histoire des mouvements sociaux en France: De 1814 à nos jours*, ed. Michel Pigenet and Danielle Tartakowsky (Paris, La Découverte, 2014), 509–520. On the antisexual violence campaigns, see, e.g., Delage, "Après l'année zéro"; and Kathryn Robson, "The Subject of Rape: Feminist Discourses on Rape and Violability in Contemporary France," *French Cultural Studies* 26, no. 1 (2015), 45–55.

those of women and girls—as well as the direct damage it did to the over-whelmingly female victims, who were attacked by overwhelmingly male perpetrators. Yet the "Arab man" did shape the French discourse of rape in striking ways that have been ignored, and which this chapter and the next bring to light.[3]

In the late 1970s, rape would become a giant public issue in France, as it had become in numerous other countries. The new post-'68 genera-tion of French feminists, however, had been vigorously raising it since at least 1970, when the seminal special issue of the new-left quarterly *Parti-sans*, "Women's Liberation, Year Zero," first emphasized the importance of sexual violence.[4] In May 1972, for example, Movement for the Liberation of Women (MLF) activists organized "Days to Denounce Crimes Commit-ted against Women" in order to publicize some of the urgent problems that drove their struggle: they put rape and other forms of sexual violence front and center.[5] There were also many other issues, for the post-'68 femi-nist movement challenged sexist and misogynist social attitudes, and the lack of political interest in such concerns, notably on the radical left, in addition to laws and regulations. The pages that follow will only touch on some of these combats, and will do so primarily in chapter 9. And indeed, the "Arab lens" that organizes this book brings into focus only aspects (or, in some cases, outlines) of the diverse forms that the feminist fight to end sexual violence took across the decade. This approach, however, also situates this feminist history in the larger context of post-decolonization France. Existing accounts of 1970s French feminism and struggles against sexual violence narrate a history of progress for anti-rape campaigns, which subsumes the stumbles of the early 1970s into the post-1975 success story: feminist activists, in this teleology, applied lessons that their mid-1970s victories in challenging the ban on abortion had revealed. Yet these were two distinct moments, both important to multiple discussions, and Arab

3. Several historians implicitly analyze how problems around those whom I name "Arab men" shaped late-1970s feminist anti-rape campaigns. The French historian of feminism Fran-çoise Picq defines the challenge that leftist critics posed to feminists as centering around the "immigrant worker" question. The American historian of post-1968 French intellectuals Julian Bourg identifies the issue as that of "racism." Both Picq and Bourg accurately encompass the issues raised, yet scholars' avoidance of the category of "Arab men" erases crucial aspects of what was at stake. See Picq, *Libération des femmes*, 235–243; Bourg, *From Revolution to Ethics*, 179–226. Other historians, such as Georges Vigarello, *Histoire du Viol, XVIe–XXe* (Paris: Seuil, 1998), simply ignore these questions.

4. Emmanuelle Durand, "Le viol," *Partisans* 54–55 (July-October 1970), 91–96.

5. Cf. Picq, *Libération des femmes*, 137; and Colette Pipon, *Et on tuera tous les affreux: Le féminisme au risque de la misandrie, 1970–1980* (Rennes: Presses universitaires de Rennes, 2013), 22.

men and Algerian references were central to both. In the early 1970s, and specifically in late 1973, feminist efforts to confront rape and the conditions that encouraged sexual violence broke into post-'68 leftist discussions. This drew intense reactions which closed down that discussion, even though feminists kept up the fight. In the late 1970s, particularly in 1977 and 1978, prominent feminist militants targeted the justice system to advance the anti-rape cause with real success. This effort, too, inspired debate on the far left, but the echo chamber was national and the discussion durable. The end-of-decade fight led to changes in legal procedures and laws as well as in the ways in which sexual violence was discussed, and that fight is at the heart of the next chapter. This chapter explores the little-known first moment, which was framed by a wide-ranging discourse around rape that stymied feminist efforts to confront the reality of sexual violence.

In the early 1970s, French evocations of rape were widespread, but they ironically left little space to engage feminist arguments or the reality of widespread male sexual violence against women and girls. This was because rape emerged in the early 1970s as the central metaphor for French efforts to identify and combat anti-Arab racism, particularly among leftists, in direct response to the sexualized frame of contemporary anti-Arab racism. The importance of this metaphor both informed and hindered new-left thinking about the reality of rape and new-left responses to feminist anti-rape activism. Historically, rape-as-metaphor usually proposed that the problem was between men, and this problem obfuscated how most actual rapes affected women: men protecting "their" women and girls, men humiliating other men. This was just as true, this chapter shows, of claims that "Frenchmen" were unjustly accusing "Arab men" of rape as it was in other situations, diverting attention from the ways that instances of sexual violence shaped lived reality and damaged specific individuals. The immersion of feminist activists and theorists in France's antiracist milieu, then, profoundly complicated their efforts to focus attention on rapes themselves. This dynamic set the stage for a late-1970s crisis that in key ways sundered feminist concerns and antiracist sexual liberationist struggles one from the other, as will be analyzed in chapter 9. Certain commentators on the period continue to argue that French feminists ignored questions of racism. This is inaccurate. These commentators have failed to appreciate how profoundly empire, colonial violence, and their aftermath shaped questions of rape in France, and thus the ways in which feminists confronted these issues.[6]

6. See, e.g., Delage, "Après l'année zéro," 21–35.

Statistics, Arab Men, and Sexual Violence

There was a larger post-decolonization French discussion about sexual violence, beyond what feminists proposed, and it turned around Arab men. Seen retrospectively, both the sheer accumulation and the specificity of claims throughout the late 1960s and 1970s that insisted that North African men were a danger to French women and girls are quite impressive. A constant on the post-1962 far right (a focus of chapters 1 and 2 in this book), such accusations found their way into multiple other published forums as well. In 1968, a cheeky guide titled *The Naughty Sites of Paris* alerted those "*mesdames, mesdemoiselles*" who felt "within themselves any inclination to experience some intense emotions" that they could "go get [themselves] raped" in the Goutte d'Or. "Each night, you will find there a sufficient number of Mediterraneans, always ready to subject you to the worst degradations."[7] A 1981 dissertation that studied the coverage of "immigrants" in the regional press in 1978 made a convincing case that unfounded accusations of sexual violence were used to inflame press and political debates about the presence of Algerian immigrants in France. In this work, the sociologist Pierre Seguret rejected claims by 1970s leftists (discussed below) who blamed the press for exaggerating "immigrant" criminality. Seguret argued that a statistical examination of the five largest regional newspapers showed that coverage of "immigrant" criminality was actually underreported: he compared the percentage of crime-related articles mentioning immigrants to the percentage of immigrants among prisoners, as well as to the percentage of immigrants in the metropolitan population. In almost all categories of crime, he calculated, statistics showed that the press minimized the involvement of immigrants. One category of crime, however, looked radically different: immigrants—overwhelmingly North Africans—were blamed in 38 percent of stories about sexual violence and rape. This was more than two times the percentage of immigrants among prisoners, and even more than that compared to the percentages of immigrants among men in prison for sexual crimes, or in the general population. Seguret's statistics dramatize an analysis that virtually every government inquest into the question rehearsed: public depictions of Arab sexual criminality far outweighed any verifiable incidence.[8]

    7. Ange Bastiani, *Les mauvais lieux de Paris* (Paris: André Balland, 1968), 165.
    8. Pierre Seguret, "Images des immigrés et de l'immigration dans la presse française: Étude de cinq grands quotidiens d'information" (Thèse [3e cycle] Université Paul Valéry à Montpellier Sociologie, July 1981); dir. de la Population et des Migrations; sous-dir. des programmes sociaux en faveur des migrants, "Note relative à la création d'une 'banque de données' sur les

Internal police statistics and evidence contrasted sharply with public impressions. Over the course of the late 1960s and 1970s, police and other French officials repeatedly investigated various complaints from the public about excessive Arab criminality or "social or sexual deviance."[9] In terms of criminality, a 1973 police report was typical of their findings. It stated that delinquency "among foreigners is more elevated than in the French population. In 1972 . . . while foreigners make up 7% of the population, they make up 10% of the persons implicated in crimes and misdemeanors." The qualifiers, however, were crucial: "It is however necessary to underline that the composition of the immigrant population is quite different from the French population; there are far less women and children." Young men committed almost all the criminality imputed to the "immigrant" population (which the document quickly made clear meant, first and foremost, the Algerian population). Their rate of delinquency was similar or "sometimes even inferior to that of nationals": this was especially the case with violent crimes, and even more so with sexual crimes.[10] "It is really quite difficult to reach firm conclusions based on these figures," another police report cautioned, "because among the immigrants the proportion of women and children is less than for the general population."[11] Throughout this period, there were similar debates about statistical claims. In 1974, for example, a medical researcher submitted a project to use the "Rosenzweig test" to assess "Maghrebi subjects who have applied to stay in France," because "the rates of morbidity, physical or mental, or of delinquency, sexual or social, are more elevated among these immigrants." A Ministry of Health official responded that he "regrets that the document under assessment con-

problèmes de l'immigration; JHR/PJ-PSM 2/n. 655" (Paris, 10 September 1974), 2, in CAC: 19860269/11; J. Hainzelin, sous-dir. des programmes sociaux en faveur des migrants, "Opinion publique" (April 1971: PSD 2/n. 204), 1, in CAC: 19930317/16.

9. In Paris, police efforts to measure "North African" criminality had begun quickly after World War II. By the end of 1946 the Paris police had collected information that allowed them to calculate statistics on crimes and misdemeanors committed by North Africans, which gave separate details for the number of French citizens ("Algerians") and Tunisian and Moroccan nationals even as they also were lumped together. The racialization of these statistics emerged blatantly by 1951, when vaguer statistical comparisons between overall crimes and misdemeanors and those committed by "North Africans" were joined by charts that compared North-African and European criminality. By 1956, only Muslim French citizens from Algeria, or FMA, were included in the statistics. During this period, debates about how to interpret the statistical evidence emerged that mapped closely onto similar intrapolice debates in the 1970s. See APP: H/A 19.

10. Dir. de la Règlementation; dir. gén. de la police nat.; Min de l'intérieur, note objet: Problèmes posés par l'immigration étrangère—Projets de solutions" (Paris 29 August 1973), 3, in CAC 19960134/6.

11. Anonymous, "L'immigration étrangère en France" (Paris, April 1970), 8.

tains no statistical evidence that would allow us to evaluate the author's assertion."[12] To the contrary, the official wrote, "there is as far as I know no such evidence that these rates are more elevated among foreign workers than among autochtone workers."[13] Archival evidence suggests that such statistical critiques of racist claims were distributed to elected officials and, on occasion, invoked by some political activists.[14] In 1973, in response to racist attacks against Algerians around Marseille, a departmental federation of the recently formed Socialist Party (PS) declared, "We know that *it's a lie* to claim that delinquency is greater among immigrants. Police statistics disprove it."[15] Evidence-based claims, however, barely registered in public debate, though on occasion they did affect official policy and police responses.

"Common Sense," Statistics, and Official Policies: Fabricating the "Threshold of Tolerance"

Most officials, both elected and appointed, relied on common sense and unfounded estimations about Arabs or "immigrants" when proposing policy. In the Rhône, the prefect cited "the insecurity that women and girls feel as a result of this concentration of men living as bachelors" as the primary reason that mayors gave for blocking construction of "hostels, hotels, or transit dorms" for immigrant workers, "even though the existence of a transit dormitory has never, in this department, led to any problems that trouble the local neighborhood." There is, let me be clear, every reason to think that large concentrations of young men in one place produced unease in at least some women and girls. There is also no reason to think that Prefect Moulins took seriously such concerns. As feminist activists at the time pointed out repeatedly, however (see chapter 9), arguments for anti-immigrant measures were virtually the only venue in which these anxieties found an official echo.[16] Statistics showed that immigrants were not dis-

12. M. R. Mamelet, sous directeur de la protection sanitaire, Min. de la Santé, "Note pour M. le sous-dir. de l'hygiène publique; Objet: sélection des sujets maghrébins, candidats à un séjour en France, par le test de Rosenzweig; DGS/45/MS.1" (9 January 1975), 1–2, in CAC: 19810568/18.

13. André Roussel, "Les problèmes de santé publique posés par la migration des travailleurs," *Bulletin de l'INSERM* 21, no. 5 (1966), 1121–1138.

14. Dir. de la population et des migrations; sous-dir. des mouvements de population, "Information et sensibilisation des élus" (Paris, 7 December 1976), 3, in CAC: 19960405/11.

15. Parti Socialiste Fédération de l'Essonne, "La gangrène" (1973), 2, in CAC: 19950493/8; underlined in original.

16. Max Moulins, prefect of Rhône Department, "Note sur l'immigration étrangère dans le Rhône" (Lyon, 15 August 1971), 25, in CAC: 19860269/11.

proportionately responsible for these crimes, even as unfounded accusations that they were responsible increasingly shaped policy.

Police statistics contested public impressions. Yet explicitly sexualized fears of Arab men played a foundational role in the emergence of the decade's most discussed "social scientific" tool to fight racism, which demographers elaborated and bureaucrats embraced. The new analytic category of "the threshold of tolerance [le seuil de tolérance] proposed that statistics could wholly explain the emergence of xenophobic public reactions."[17] A 1971 report summarized this idea: "No possibilities for adaptation exist when there is an overly large concentration of immigrants in a given site." The "possibilities for adaptation" in question were envisaged as both immigrant and French. As numerous left-wing critics noted at the time, the concept of the "threshold" meant that there was no need to take seriously racist statements, acts, or organizations, which the theory presumed carried little weight in comparison with the force of percentages. One form of empirical reality trumped the force of ideas as well as the actual behavior of "immigrants," or at least this was the claim.[18] Seen from this perspective, racism resulted primarily from public reaction to transgressions of "thresholds of tolerance" (the supposed "tipping point" percentage was different in housing than in education or public services) that for the category's proponents were objective and measurable. These "mechanisms," as one 1969 analysis put it, supposedly functioned in any situation when a given "nonindigenous" population became visible amid an "autochtone" community.[19] When scholars and government officials tried to define the "threshold of tolerance," however, the historically specific problem posed by one "nonindigenous" group—"Maghrebis," which almost always meant Algerians—emerged clearly. Proponents of the "threshold" thesis asserted publicly that "once the foreign population, no matter what their ethnicity, surpasses a given percentage . . . unfavorable reactions come to light." In practice—as internal discussions that produced the just-cited 1969 report averred—the purportedly universal social effects of violating the "thresh-

17. See Todd Shepard, "Comment et pourquoi éviter le racisme: Causes, effets, culture, 'seuils de tolérance' ou résistances? Le débat français entre 1954 et 1976," Arts & Sociétés: Lettre du séminaire 51 (March 2013), http://www.artsetsocietes.org/f/f-index51.html, accessed 12 May 2014.

18. Pierre Sommeville, dir. de la réglementation, "Enquête sur la situation de l'immigration" (Paris, 14 September 1971), CAC: 19960134/12, 32.

19. H. Vidal, "Eléments pour une intervention . . ." (12 November 1969), 3, CAC: 19950493/6.

old" applied exclusively to "a mainly Maghrebi population."[20] Further, despite experts' public claims about abstract "reactions," internal discussions made clear that sexual tensions were crucial.

Key texts and key proponents of the "threshold" hypothesis explicitly discussed the particular role of sexualized fear in the rejection of Maghrebi immigrants. One crucial figure who worked to establish the "threshold" as a causal explanation for problems of racism was Michel Massenet, a senior civil servant who had long overseen Algerian immigration in the metropole. In June 1970, in a speech to the Academy of Moral and Political Sciences, he sought to explain the supposedly automatic emergence of fear of the foreigner by noting that large numbers of Arab men in certain towns had made it so that "women and young girls dare not leave the house because they fear they will be attacked and raped." His proposed solution was not to combat sexual violence, nor to empower potential victims, but to disperse immigrants and end immigration.[21] A study group set up in the late 1960s by the French Ministry of Housing focused on two housing developments in the Parisian region. Its report "The Cohabitation of French and Foreign Families" became the go-to reference for early proponents of relying on the "threshold" to make public policy. Its argument depended on the explanation it offered of the failure of policies meant to build links between different groups—that is, to combat racism. To this end, researchers had examined factors that stymied projects to encourage extracurricular activities for teenagers. The central problem, in their diagnosis, was that "girls desert clubs as soon as the number of Arabs increases"; this was the proof that authorities relied on to call for a change in percentages rather than in context or attitudes.[22]

There does not seem to have been a concerted campaign by either media sources or public officials to stoke such fears. Both groups did so, however. In their effort to deny that preexisting racism or racist ideas caused negative reactions, French officials proposed abstract categories ("thresholds") and policy measures to counter growing public concern about "foreigners" (i.e., to reduce "concentrations" of "the nonindigenous"). These measures obfuscated what their evidence and analyses revealed. As we can see, however,

20. Service de liaison et de promotion des migrants, "La population étrangère dans la région Rhône-Alpes" (May 1973), in CAC: 19930317/16.

21. Massenet, "Les problèmes posés," 239–260.

22. Groupe de recherches et d'études sur la construction et l'habitation (GRECOH); Service de l'habitation; dir. de la construction min. de l'équipement et du logement, "La cohabitation des familles françaises et étrangères" (August 1970), 22, in CAC 19771141/17.

the stigmatized population was not abstract; only "Maghrebis," and more specifically Algerians, posed a problem. The fears were also not abstract; they were strikingly sexualized.

Talking about Sexual Violence While Ignoring Feminist Arguments, 1962–1975

In the early 1970s, public discussions of rape or even accusations of rape remained infrequent. Men who raped women or men were almost never judged newsworthy by mainstream journalists. Politicians and public officials, too, avoided the topic. Media coverage of rape was limited to individual crimes that the press deemed particularly spectacular—that is, likely to draw readers. The new post-'68 feminist movement sought to counter this silence; feminist publications addressed it frequently but had little echo. There was, however, a smattering of more serious articles in various media outlets, in some leftist periodicals, and, of particular note, in the new pornographic and semipornographic press. Prodded by feminist claims, this stunted discussion often presumed that rapes were happening more frequently now, rather than analyzing why there had been so little discussion of rapes previously. Frequently, these rare early-1970s (nonfeminist) reports invoked the Algerian war to explain this nonexistent increase and to explain rape more generally. "Among the crimes that took place during the Algerian War," one journalist wrote in the pornographic magazine *Union*, "we learned of many victims who were first raped then butchered by their aggressors. This demonstrates clearly that rape is just one sign among others of an aggressivity that gives free rein to the instincts, which education and the fear of repression normally hold back." This and similar efforts to analyze the phenomenon of rape appeared in a moment when feminists summoned French people to address the massive problem of male sexual violence. But they ignored contemporary feminist analyses.[23]

Many early-1970s leftist evocations of sexual violence instead developed claims made by left-wing critics of France's violent campaign to crush the Algerian revolution, who had warned that the security forces' systematic use of torture and extreme violence, notably rape, would "gangrenize" the French. *The Question* (1958), Henri Alleg's well-known account of how he was tormented by French paratroopers for pro-FLN activity, had

23. Demay, "Le Viol."

described torture as "a school in perversion for young French men."[24] The leftist journalist Gilles Perrault's *Les Parachutistes* (1961) had focused attention on how French violence against Algerians—especially the systematic rape of Algerian women—destroyed the morality and integrity of French conscripts. Perrault wrote that a young man "arrives among the paratroopers intact without complexes, virginal with regard to any resentments." He has "a pink past and a white future." Yet, as historian Emma Kuby astutely reads Perrault's argument, when the young conscript joins in the violence of his peers, he is "sullied (in essence, raped) by 'the bitch [*la garce*]' of colonial warfare," a metaphor "seemingly figured as female but, because of the derivation of *garce* from *garçon* [boy], also possessing clear homoerotic connotations." It was this experience of victimization by war itself that gradually transformed the French soldier into a sadist—and often, Perrault suggested, into an outright rapist. Such accounts focused on how French atrocities victimized their French perpetrators, and warned French readers that these men could well return to the metropole and rape and terrify French women, French children, French people. Taken to their logical conclusion, such fears suggested that the main reason it was necessary to stop the rape, torture, and mass killing of Algerians, was first and foremost that France had to be protected from this gangrene.[25] After 1962, numerous new left commentators drew from this critique when they evoked sexual violence in France.

Against the Stereotype of the "Arab Rapist"

A far more substantive early-1970s discussion of rape on the left had even less to say about rape victims or gender relations: it fixated on the harm that unjust accusations of rape inflicted on Arab men in France. As the need for antiracist activism became increasingly evident to many militants, so too did concerns that the most emblematic form of contemporary French racism was the charge that "North African men," notably Algerians, were rapists or sexual criminals. In her 1973 study of "foreign workers,"

24. Henri Alleg, *La question* (Paris: Minuit, 1958), 78. On "gangrene," see *La gangrène* (Paris: Minuit, 1959). The government banned both books as soon as they were released.

25. Emma Kuby, "From the Torture Chamber to the Bedchamber: French Soldiers, Anti-war Activists, and the Discourse of Sexual Deviancy in the Algerian War (1954–1962)," *Contemporary French Civilization* 38, no. 2 (2013), 131–153; Gilles Perrault, *Les parachutistes* (Paris: Seuil, 1961), 83, 180. For a historical analysis of the widespread reality of rapes committed by French forces in Algeria, see Raphaëlle Branche, "Des viols pendant la guerre d'Algérie," *Vingtième Siècle: Revue d'histoire* 75 (July-September 2002), 123–132.

scholar Juliette Minces argued that there was "a certain hierarchy within the racism" that French people expressed. "When it comes to Maghrebis, and above all Algerians, people fixate on problems with sexual origins."[26] According to some leftists, the media and the authorities actively sought to convince the public that French women and girls lived under constant threat from these men. In 1975, for example, a one-off satirical newspaper, *Le Parichien déchaîné* (a title that parodied the newspaper titles *Le canard enchaîné* and *Le Parisien libéré*, and which can be roughly translated as "The Unleashed Parisian Dog"), aimed to expose the demagoguery and racism of the mainstream press. To illustrate its critique, the canard sarcastically placed "Yet Another Young Woman Raped by an Arab" in giant letters on its masthead (there was no accompanying article).[27]

Over the course of the decade, numerous men of Maghrebi descent evoked the frequency of the accusation and told of how the stereotype of the "Arab rapist" affected them. Naceur Ktari, in his 1975 film, had an apparently racist old man assert, "They rape our women." Many drew direct links to colonial domination. In *Belka*, the 1974 book-length "first-person account" of an Algerian man who had immigrated to France, the narrator recounted how, as an eight-year-old boy in Algiers, he had been hired to work in the house of a pied noir widower and his daughter. A new wife arrived. "One day I was playing with the little girl, and she [the new wife] took the opportunity to ask [her husband]: 'Don't you think you should keep an eye on your little Arab when he's alone with Lucette? You know me, I would never leave my daughter around them.'"[28] In the first of a series of pseudonymous letters that would make him a loud voice in such discussions, a man who went by the name "Mohamed" wrote to the leftist *Tout!* magazine. In his missive, he decried the attitude of the typical "white" leftist woman toward a North African man such as himself. He described how such a woman "sees me in the shape of a famished animal, with her white woman's body in the shape of bait."[29] Others turned to contemporary life to understand these stereotypes. As if responding to "Mohamed," one of the Algerian interviewees in Minces's study stated, "You know, me, I think that they're right, the girls." It did not matter how he and his fellow immigrants behaved. "Because, you know, there's all these articles in the classifieds or the newspapers, which warn: 'Watch out!'" He addressed his

26. Minces, *Les travailleurs étrangers*, 409.

27. *Le Parichien déchaîné*, 19 April 1975, in BDIC (fonds Immigration en France) F delta rés. 705/1/2.

28. Belkacemi, *Belka*, 42.

29. "Lettre de Mohammed," *Tout!* 14 (7 June 1971), 5.

fellow interviewees: "You see, that's the reason the girls won't go out with you, or with me, or with him."[30] In 1973, an Algerian interviewed for a TV news program called *Le racisme et les migrants* (Racism and the Migrants) recounted, "One time, I got on a bus, and me, because I am Arab, a woman said to me that I must not sit next to her." Onscreen, the image cut to a white woman placing her bag on a seat to prevent a young man from sitting down. The camera cut back to the interviewee, and when the interviewee continued, with a brief wry smile on his face, he stated ironically, "I don't know; perhaps I might rape her in the bus, I don't know."[31] Whether in anger, frustration, or befuddlement, men associated with the Maghreb had no choice but to negotiate such stereotypes.

The metaphor of rape plays a particularly important role in Algerian novelist Rachid Boudjedra's third novel, *Topographie idéale pour une agression caractérisée* (An Ideal Topography for a Stereotypical Murder, 1974), his first work in which part of the action takes place in France. At the climax of the novel, the Algerian protagonist is attacked when he exits the Parisian underground into a city in darkness. The deadly incident is described as a violent penetration of his body by a band of vicious French (white) men. Boudjedra depicts them as little more than animals, driven by lust and rage. What makes this metaphorical rape (of a man by other men) particularly easy to read as rape—and as a commentary on contemporary French discussions—is that the police who investigate the murder try to find evidence that the Algerian has been killed because he tried to rape a French woman.[32]

Mainstream journalists, too, increasingly raised red flags about what they defined as a particularly vicious and hurtful form of sexualized racism, which fabricated fear and hatred of North Africans. This phenomenon, reports claimed, further isolated immigrant workers from the general population, and contributed directly to the intense form of "sexual misery" from which, it was said, so many suffered. The 1973 television news broadcast *Racism and the Migrants* was just one of many forms of media coverage that linked stereotypes of violent sexual deviance to the larger phenomenon of racism. For example, a 1977 report titled "Our Daily Racism" in the newly launched pro-Socialist Party daily *Le matin de Paris* reported that Maurice Arreckx, mayor of Toulon, had told the "Swedish newspaper *Dagens Nyheter*" that in his city, around the Place du Théâtre, "A French woman

---

30. B., 39 ans, construction worker, cited in Minces, *Les travailleurs étrangers*, 450.
31. *Mise au point: Le racisme et les migrants* (1ère partie), (1973), 3rd Channel.
32. Boudjedra, *Topographie idéale*, 125, 184, 186.

can't sit down for two minutes without three Arabs coming up to her and brandishing what they have in their pants." Such racialized descriptions of sexual harassment, in this reading, produced problems between "French" and "Arabs," rather than reflecting them. Such racialized stereotypes displaced a feminist focus on how men treated women onto the vilification of Arab men. More generally, journalistic critiques of racialization largely ignored female perspectives.[33]

Dupont Lajoie (1975): Rape as Metaphor of Anti-Arab Racism

The most widely discussed effort to expose this form of xenophobia was Yves Boisset's 1975 film *Dupont Lajoie*. In the film, Isabelle Huppert plays Brigitte, the sixteen-year-old daughter of one of a group of families who meet up each summer when they vacation in the same campground. As Brigitte is sunbathing by a river, Georges Lajoie, a Parisian café owner and friend of the family, approaches her, begins to come on to her, and soon attempts to rape her, a violent attack that ends with her murder. When the police seem slow to investigate the crime, a crowd of campers storms the nearby shack that houses a number of Algerian men, who are there to build a hotel. The avenging mob murders Saïd, the presumed rapist, an innocent man who is one of the immigrant workers. The film was an enormous box-office success, with more than 1.5 million tickets sold in France, and it has drawn much analytic attention. In one critic's read, *Dupont Lajoie* "seems to have sparked an ever-increasing attention to the theme [of France as racist] on television." More recent critics have been particularly interested in its supposed role as catalyst. The philosopher Jean-Claude Michea mocks the film as "giving birth to a new Left, in which the disdain for the popular [lower-middle and working] classes that had, until then, been held in check could now be affirmed without the least concern." In his reading, the film helped set the stage so that "'antiracism' . . . could be methodically substituted for the old *class struggle*" as the explanation for left-wing politics.[34] A parallel critique appears in *Le suicide français*, the 2014 best seller by the anti-Arab, anti-Muslim polemicist Eric Zemmour, who defines his view of how "political correctness" impedes "truth telling" about "Muslim," "Arab," and "black" violence with the rallying cry: "We are all Dupont

33. Hervé Chabalier, "1. Notre racisme quotidien,"*Le matin de Paris* (10 May 1977), 16–18.

34. Édouard Mills-Affif, *Filmer les immigrés: Les représentations audiovisuelles de l'immigration à la télévision française, 1960–1986* (Brussels: Ed. de Boeck, 2004), 19; Jean-Claude Michéa, *L'empire du moindre mal: Essai sur la civilisation libérale* (Paris: éd. Climats, 2007).

Lajoie!" Zemmour's claim is that false accusations of racism against French people, with the film as a key example, made it difficult for them to defend themselves. (In France, the name Dupont evokes "everyman," the French equivalent of "Jones.") As he told the *New York Times* earlier that year, France's "white proletariat" is thus left "helpless before the 'ostentatious' virility of black and Arab competitors seducing numerous young white women."[35] What these scholarly reactions miss, and what Zemmour's bile gets right, is that it was the larger post-1962 discussion that produced the film and its message, which were thus symptomatic rather than causal.

The film *Dupont Lajoie* repeatedly linked French racism to Algeria. The character who inspires the film's lynch mob, Camille, dresses in camouflage and a paratrooper cap, and quickly identifies himself as a veteran of the Algerian war. He loudly links Brigitte's murder to an earlier scene, one he has not witnessed—"I wasn't at the dance"—but which clearly has been the subject of campground gossip: "But everyone told me that el-Prick came and pestered" her. Saïd and Brigitte have exchanged chitchat at the dance. (This same sexualized insult—"el-Prick"—had appeared in a racist far-right poster distributed by *Europe-action magazine* in 1966; see Figure 6.) A newcomer to the campground, a pied noir of Italian origin, holds back one of the friends, who tries in vain to restrain the mob. "Don't go," he warns them. "Once they begin to 'coon hunt' [*à ratonner*], you can't do anything. I know from Algeria." Camille spurs on the action in the scene that follows, with constant references to the Algerian war: "What are we going to do? Just like in Algeria, guys!" The day after the brutal murder of Saïd, the local police inspector pushes an official from the Ministry of Justice to investigate the crowd's action, insisting, "It was a lynching," before launching into a speech meant to challenge the silence around racism. "OK, I see. . . . It's the word [*lynchage*] that bothers you. It's good for the Americans and their blacks, but not here in France. This man was the victim of a hunt for Arabs. In French, that's called a 'coon hunt' [*une ratonnade*, a term tied to anti-Algerian violence]." The mixture of ongoing racism (which, for most in France, happened only in places like the United States or South Africa) and very French colonial histories (which still resonated) was particularly clear.

Dupont Lajoie explicitly relied on rape-as-metaphor to explain how the racialization of extreme sexual tensions led to anti-Algerian racism, allow-

35. Eric Zemmour, *Le suicide français* (Paris: Albin Michel, 2014); the central chapter bears the title "Nous sommes tous des Dupont Lajoie!" Sylvain Cypel, "A French Clown's Hateful Gesture," *New York Times* (23 January 2014), 27.

ing this process to become visible to viewers. In doing so, it left rape itself
as a screen that deserved no particular analysis. The film critic Jean-Pierre
Oudart argued in *Cahiers du cinéma* at the time that *Dupont Lajoie* captured
the way that racist reactions could be fabricated "in the heat of the moment." His analysis responds directly to assertions such as those the mayor
of Toulon made to a Swedish newspaper. As Oudart put it, "Bourgeois racism spins out of control when it comes to sexuality, the couple, the family. These unleash fantasies that women will leave the conjugal institution,
will subvert the rules." In this economy, rape was a defensive maneuver,
caused by racism. Oudart continued: "You are obsessed with the idea that
the Arabs are going to take your women from *you*—so you"—like George
Lajoie—"go off and rape the daughter of your neighbor."[36] Oudart's address to (presumed male) readers had nothing to say about the rape victim,
although Serge Daney, writing in the same issue, did note that the film
offers no shots of the rape scene from Brigitte's point of view.[37] The film
ends with Saïd's brother killing Lajoie to avenge Saïd's death, which also
ends any chance that the truth of how the girl was murdered will emerge.
In Boisset's film, as in Boudjedra's novel and many leftist critiques, sexual
repression offers the primary explanation for sexual violence, and what
is silenced is not rape. In each case, rather, supporting characters repeatedly raise the possibility of rape and insist that it must be punished. These
works force their public to see the ways in which Algerian men are sexualized, and the suffering that results.

Rape-as-Metaphor and Government Policy

Remarkably, this argument—that the primary reason why it was necessary
to attend to talk of sexual violence was to understand how French anti-
Arab racism worked—was at the center of a classified 1976 study that the
office of Prime Minister Jacques Chirac commissioned on French attitudes
towards immigrants. Following the affirmation that "the immigrant plays
the role of a screen on which fear is projected but also desired," the report
explains that "the male foreigner who accosts a European woman incites
sexual desire in her; she rejects the image of a desirable woman that he of-

36. Jean-Pierre Oudart, "Une certaine tendance du cinéma français: Imaginaire et racisme," *Cahiers du Cinéma* 257 (1975), 20.

37. Serge Daney, "Une certaine tendance du cinéma français," *Cahiers du Cinéma* 257 (1975), 19. Daney fails to note that the film in fact contains no scenes at all from the point of view of any female character. On the male gaze, see the contemporaneous and seminal article by Laura Mulvey, "Visual Pleasure and Narrative Cinema," *Screen* 16, no. 3 (1975), 6–18.

fers her, [a rejection] that she then expresses as disgust for him."[38] Because these "truths" were unspeakable, such analyses suggested, false accusations against Arab men were able to obfuscate the insidious melding of French racism and French sexual violence—including the sexual violence French soldiers and colonists had inflicted on women and girls in Algeria.

The intentions, desires, and challenges faced by women were absent from these warnings about the dangerous effects of the French sexual objectification of Arab men. This was quite similar to how other histories in which rape-as-metaphor had played an important role played out. The metaphor's important place in the 1970s efforts to fight anti-Arab racism, of course, is hardly surprising, given the long history of the deployment of rape to describe imperialism as well as other forms of domination. In 1974, for example, a woman doing sex education work among female North African women in Paris worried, "Wasn't I about to commit the well-known rape of personality for which colonialism so often had been criticized?"[39] Still, the antiracist French left's attention to the metaphor of rape resembles developments after 1945, when German women were raped on a mass scale during the overthrow of Hitler's regime by invading troops. As the historian Elizabeth Heinemann recounts, "Discussion of women's rapes became taboo a few years after the end of the war." This silencing, she notes, happened even as "references to rapes. . . . permeated the culture." Heinemann analyzes how such "references to rapes of women" ceased, to be replaced by allusions to "the rape of Germany," whether by Soviet-inspired Communists or by US-inspired consumer culture.[40] Rape-as-metaphor silenced questions of female sexuality and subjectivity.

Feminists and the End of Silence

At several points during the early 1970s, the insistent use of rape-as-metaphor to describe anti-Maghrebi racism collided with French feminist arguments about rape-as-sexual-violence. Although absent from scholarly

38. "'Motivation des Français a l'égard des travailleurs immigrés': Rapport préparé par l'Institut Pierre Bessis à la demande du service d'information et de diffusion [du Premier Ministre]" (Paris 16 February 1976), 32, 34, in CAC: 19960405/11. As discussed in the introduction to this book, the report made clear that the real reference for "immigrants" was "Algerians."

39. NSSFNA, Service sociale familial nord africain, "Guide pour les cours de planification familiale à l'usage des cours des femmes et en particulier des femmes maghrébines" (July 1974), in Papiers Nelly Rouget (private collection).

40. Elizabeth Heineman, "The Hour of the Woman: Memories of Germany's 'Crisis Years' and West German National Identity," in The Miracle Years: A Cultural History of West Germany, 1949–1968, ed. Hanna Schissler (Princeton, NJ: Princeton University Press, 2001), 21–56.

discussions, these post-decolonization tensions set the stage for the quite bitter conflicts between various leftists and antirape feminists that became very visible in the late 1970s. The story we know emphasizes how the trans-Atlantic exchange between feminists reinvigorated the French antirape campaign, notably the French translations of key texts by American feminists Kate Millett (*Sexual Politics* [1970], translated as *La politique du mâle* [1971]) and especially Susan Brownmiller (*Against Our Will: Men, Women, and Rape* [1975], translated as *Le viol* [1976]).[41] US-born tactics, too, helped publicize antirape campaigns. French feminist activists adopted the idea of "Take back the night" marches, which began in France on 8 June 1974, when women-only groups marched through the streets of Paris after dark. Protesters called for an end to the male violence that regularly rendered the public sphere dangerous for women, especially after dark. Speakouts (meetings where women were encouraged to share their own histories of rape in whatever way each speaker chose) were also American imports. Feminists embraced what could be learned from this trans-Atlantic cooperation.

French feminists paid particular attention to how American antirape activism connected with American histories of imperialism and racism. In 1976, the journalist Martine Storti wrote a review of Brownmiller's newly translated *Le viol* in *Libération*. Storti both celebrated what she termed "the end of the silence" around the topic and explained to readers the important role that debates about rape had played on the left in the United States. "It was around the question of rape that American feminists broke off from the peace movement," she argued. This happened in two stages, both of which had to do with racism. "For these women, the slogan 'Stop the rape of Vietnam' did more than invoke the destruction of the insurgents; it also spoke of the rape of Vietnamese women [by American soldiers. The feminists] were ignored." Brownmiller had revealed that alongside its racist imperialist violence, the United States also had a more complicated domestic history of racism. Storti continued: "Nor were [feminists] listened to when they spoke of interracial rape." It was "undeniable," Storti insisted, that in the United States, "Black rapists have always faced harsher treatment than white rapists." The rhetorical question she asked next moved beyond the

---

41. E.g., Delage, "Après l'année zéro"; Manus McGrogan, "Militants sans Frontières? Fusions and Frictions of US Movements in Paris, 1970," *Contemporary French Civilization* 39, no. 2 (2014), 197–222; Kate Millett, *Sexual Politics* (New York: Doubleday, 1970) and *La politique du mâle*, trans. Elisabth Gile (Paris: Stock, 1971); Susan Brownmiller, *Against Our Will: Men, Women, and Rape* (New York: Simon and Schuster, 1975), translated as *Le viol* (Paris: Stock, 1976).

usual self-satisfied French invocation of American racial problems. "Does that justify, however, that the liberal left, in the name of the fight against racism, must endorse the rape of white women by Black men?"[42] As so often in French invocations of the United States, Storti deployed these examples to intervene in French debates. She strongly suggested that the same thing was happening on the "liberal left" in France. The mid-1970s, American-inflected renewal of French antirape activism set the stage for the new prominence of this struggle in the years ahead.[43]

Libération and One Story of Rape (1973)

Earlier feminist efforts, however, had crashed into the wall of post-decolonization antiracism. In late 1973, the relationship of the French left to feminists and the problem of rape surged into public view thanks to an article in Libération. The new leftist daily had begun publishing only a few months before, with the name of the philosopher Jean-Paul Sartre on its masthead. The geographer, feminist activist, and future novelist Annie Cohen drew readers' attention to an affair that already had troubled the "inhabitants of a hostel for immigrant workers who are faced with an expulsion order . . . the committee that supports their struggle and . . . the committee that oversees their struggle." In Cohen's telling, "A young woman member of the Movement for the Liberation of Women, of Vietnamese origins, was raped IN HER HOME, by a militant of the immigrant workers' struggle." The female victim had been uncertain about what to do. "Given that the rapist was black," she had worried that "*Minute* and its allies would appropriate the affair and use it for racist ends." Cohen criticized the double bind imposed on the woman by Cohen's own allies on the far left: "In the name of the Revolution, we demand that women keep quiet about the humiliations to which they are constantly subjected. It is a fact that immigrant workers live in conditions of great sexual misery. Must we [women] pay the price?" Cohen moved quickly from rape to broader issues of cross-sex sexual interaction ("Must we be guilt-tripped if we reject the advances of an Algerian or a Black; must we immediately have to face accusations that we are racists?") even as she also sought to enlarge the circle of those at fault beyond "immigrant workers," Algerians, or blacks:

42. Martine Storti, "Viol: La fin du silence," *Libération* (25 November 1976), 14.
43. See Éric Fassin, "Good cop, bad cop: Modèle et contre-modèle américains dans le discours libéral français depuis les années 1980," *Raisons politiques* 1 (2001), 77–87.

"The struggle against racism is a struggle that all revolutionaries accept as valid. Sexism, which is to say the power that men exercise over women, has no such recognition." This trenchant assessment resonated in subsequent public and intrafeminist discussions.[44]

Cohen's accusations provoked strong reactions among antiracist leftists. As Sartre put it one week later (and as published readers' letters made clear): "To use this story to open up a debate about sexuality appeared inopportune, even shocking, in the eyes of some." Sartre's introduction to the initial article had already raised this concern, and Cohen had attributed to the raped woman the same worry that racists might appropriate her story. Sartre also emphasized the very contemporary context Cohen had invoked, and pointed out that the right-wing press had "launched a racist campaign" in which Algerians were the target. Note that the three main actors who had brought this affair into public view thought it worthwhile to think about women's liberation—or a complicated question of "sexuality," as Sartre saw it—in conjunction with antiracist activism.[45]

Sartre and Cohen went further, reframing an affair that involved "a Black man" and "a Vietnamese woman" (i.e., no Algerians or Arabs) in terms of (anti-Algerian) racism. Cohen's addition of the fairly specific term "an Algerian" alongside the broader category of "a Black man" was in fact typical of most published responses to the affair. One woman wrote in the name of "we, the girls who sleep with Blacks and Arabs," whom she shorthanded as "we 'bougnoules'-girls [an anti-Arab slur]," in order to remind readers that such women knew full well what was said "about the sexuality of Black and Arab men." She did not elaborate on this intimation of hypersexuality or deviant masculinity, which other letters also invoked.[46] Another woman wrote in to analyze her own realization that "I am only racist against the male (North African, Black, etc.)." Another letter brought in Islam, and moved between "Arab" and "North African."[47] Once the Arab man entered the frame, even this seemingly specific discussion about "sexuality"—or, more accurately, male sexual violence against women—became absorbed into Algerian histories.

---

44. Annie Cohen, "Tribune libre: Au nom de la révolution," *Libération* (8 November 1973), 8.

45. Sartre, "L'article: Au nom de la révolution,'" *Libération* (15 November 1973), 4.

46. Fr. P., ". . . et le courrier à propos de l'article 'Au nom de la révolution,'" *Libération* (15 November 1973), 4.

47. EA, "Une lectrice écrit: Je me suis aperçue que j'étais raciste," *Libération* (22 November 1973), 8; AK, "Les femmes et le racisme: N'est pas de cet avis,"*Libération* (13 December 1973), 9.

Two Maghrebi Perspectives

Letters from two self-identified Maghrebis unsettled this epistolary and journalistic discussion in which, despite the identification of the accused as "a Black man" and the accuser as "a Vietnamese woman," all the speakers had identified as simply French, which everyone understood to signal "white European." Five weeks after the first article, among other letters on the subject, the editors printed and (exceptionally) responded at length to one from "Yamina" and another from "Mohamed" (the same pseudonymous author evoked earlier in this chapter). Yamina sought to highlight what she termed "the problem of relationships between emigrants . . . which has never been discussed in Libé[ration]." The details she gave, of "sixteen-year old girls in forced marriages who have been dragged back [to France from their homeland] by emigrants at the end of a month of vacation," for example, relied on widespread conceptions of North Africans. She suggested that the reason for this silence around how male emigrants treated female emigrants was "complicity toward a social category that there is an effort to win over" on the part of "the French far left." Mohamed described the repression he experienced in all sort of domains, notably sexual, and lashed out by saying that the only response the far left offered to men like him was a warning: "Most important, I must commit no 'crime.' Don't, for example, rape a revolutionary activist woman. Above all, not an activist. . . ." Both Yamina and Mohamed, that is, defined the connection between "the French far left" and "Arab men" as one of subject to object. These two Maghrebi perspectives played a crucial role in this "affair" of intramilitant rape in part because the editors of Libération drew attention to the status of Yamina and Mohamed as "first-person witnesses" and, in responding to their letters, sought to shape how their arguments should be understood.

The weighty role that rape-as-metaphor played in contemporary discussions of anti-Arab racism was particularly visible in the editors' responses to these two letters. Answering Yamina, the editors both specfied that "the woman in question is Vietnamese" and insisted, given the shared condition of all women, "that, in any case, whatever race she might be, the problem of rape must be posed." Interestingly, however, the editors' response on the same page to the Algerian man was strikingly different. "It is true that alongside the question of rape, [Cohen's] article raises another problem, which is that of the queasiness many women feel vis-à-vis immigrant workers." (Note that the category "women" was unmarked by questions of origin, religion, or "color.") In this response to Mohamed, the editors seemed to suggest that the initial framing by Cohen and Sartre of this incident of rape had ignored this "queasiness," which subsequent letters to the editor had revealed. The editors claimed credit for publishing these women's letters that "broke the silence," as they phrased it, around racism. What justified their decision to evoke this particular rape, that is, was how the subsequent debate allowed leftist women's racism to become visible. The editors did not take up Yamina's effort to raise a different question, of heterosociality among "immigrants."[48]

By late 1973, even as numerous feminists continued to denounce rape, the struggle faded from *Libération* and other left-wing forums. Against a backdrop of racist violence and racist press campaigns, the immigrant or Arab frame had quickly encompassed this first "antirape affair." In new-left discussions, metaphor still mattered more than act, at the same time that efforts to speak from situated positions, as feminists, women, or Maghrebis, remained marginal.

French Feminists' Algerian Lessons

The MLF's own reliance on Algerian references, both to make public claims on behalf of women's rights and to speak to each other, also stymied feminist efforts to negotiate the post-decolonization context, and especially the ways in which antiracist use of rape-as-metaphor affected antirape campaigns. Perhaps nothing captures this Algerian heritage of French '70s feminism better than the resounding ululations—"*youyous*"—that encompassed any number of their demonstrations. In one of her earliest films, the radical activist and innovative Swiss documentary filmmaker Carole Roussopoulos offers a sweeping shot of a Paris demonstration for abortion rights, with the rhythmic sound of *youyous* audible in the foreground. It is a vibrating cry that, in France since at least the 1830s, has summoned images of Algeria and of Algerian women—Berber and Arab, Muslim or Jewish—defiant, happy, or in mourning. The final scene in Pontecorvo's *Battle of Algiers* (1965)—a film in which the sonic texture, most famously the Ennio Morricone soundtrack, conveys potent political as well as artistic signals— depicts a defiant woman stomping the beat of Algeria's now certain triumph in such *youyous*. One participant in an 8 March 1978 march to celebrate International Women's Day gave a quite specific description of how and

---

48. Yamina, "Des lettres 'Les femmes et le racisme': L'oppression des femmes immigrées," *Libération* (13 December 1973), 9; Mohamed, "Des lettres 'Les femmes et le racisme': Je suis jeune, reprimé," *Libération* (13 December 1973), 9.

why feminists used this call to fight male supremacy: "We sing, we scream, we shower the cops who blocked us with our hysterical 'youyous,' which most certainly raise for some of them painful memories of Algeria."[49] This cry became so associated with feminist activism on the far left that, by the late 1970s, *Libération* regularly used "Youyous" as the general rubric for its articles about French feminists.[50] The inspiration the MLF drew from Algerian models made the feminists typical of the new left from which it had sprung. As the sociologist Dominique Fougeyrollas-Schwebel describes, MLF members came *together* around the fight for abortion rights, but they came largely *from* various radical, often Marxist- or anarchist-inspired groups, rather than from preexisting "reformist" feminist organizations.[51] They shared the fascination of this red-and-black constellation with Algeria's victorious struggle, as well as with the revolutionary potential of Algerian workers in France. Indeed, this two-layered "Algerian reference" was in many ways the shared horizon of the French new left, its promises linking diverse groups despite their mutual disagreements and growing divisions.

Algerian references were hardly limited to symbolic or verbal appeals. In her 1976 film *Lip V: Monique et Christiane*, Roussopoulos focuses her camera on a woman who was a key figure in the six documentaries Roussopoulos made about the striking workers of the Lip watch company in Besançon. The series follows the story of the Lip workers who take over and run their factory after a conflict with management. Their struggle has rallied many on the new left.[52] The fifth episode in the series follows the transformation of Monique Piton into an avowed feminist. Earlier films in the series documented Monique's growing recognition that she and other women were being treated unfairly in the workplace. Now, she seeks to explain to others the importance of this insight. Addressing the camera directly, she says, "I will replace the word 'man' with the word 'white' and the word 'woman' with the word 'Arab.'" This magic formula, she implies, will make her feminist argument convincingly clear.[53] It is a gesture similar to one that Roussopoulos and her fellow filmmakers (known as "Les

49. Carole Roussopoulos, "Y a qu'à pas baiser" (1973); Collectif de rédaction, "Viol de nuits, terre des hommes . . . Mercredi 8 mars à Paris," *Le temps des femmes* 2 (April-May 1978), 26. I thank Tamara Chaplin for drawing my attention to the *Battle of Algiers* connection.

50. Martine Storti, "YOUYOUS: Petite manifestation des femmes à Paris," *Libération* (9-10 May 1979).

51. Dominique Fougeyrollas-Schwebel, "Controverses et anathèmes au sein du féminisme français des années 1970," *Cahiers du genre* 2 (2005), 13-26.

52. See, e.g., Frank Georgi, "Le moment Lip dans l'histoire de l'autogestion en France," *Semaine sociale Lamy* 1631 (19 May 2014), 65-72.

53. *Lip V: Monique et Christiane*, dir. Carole Roussopoulos (Paris: Vidéo Out, 1976).

Insoumuses," a moniker that transformed the passive feminine figure of the muse into a rebellious resister) deployed in the film *Maso et miso vont en bateau* (Maso and Miso Go Boating), their powerful 1975 critique of the incapacity of "governmental feminism" and the "International Year of the Woman" to address French sexism and misogyny. The film includes a clip of the journalist Anne Sinclair interviewing Pierre Bellemare, a television journalist and writer who tells her that "there are a few female [radio and TV] presenters . . . to me it seems like this is a profession not really made for women." A title card appears on the screen, with the phrase "A profession not really made for:" and three arrows each point to a term: "a Jew"; "a black"; "an Arab." As in the United States, multiple antiracist struggles offered key reference points for feminist activism. In France, however, Arab struggles proved the most frutiful.[54]

For Roussopoulos, whose own work included radical depictions of the Palestinian struggle and a recurrent interest in Maghrebi workers in France, the parallel between "Arab" and "woman" worked pedagogically. Other feminists invoked it more critically. In 1970, an important Marxist feminist manifesto coauthored by, among others, Monique Wittig, a noted novelist who helped found the MLF in that year (and whose later theoretical work has been foundational for efforts to think in new ways about gender and sexuality), deployed this comparison to critique radical leaders. The collective of feminists asserted that "there are only very few [on the left] who give as much importance" to the oppression of women "as they do to that of Blacks in the USA or for that matter to that of emigrant workers here." It is noteworthy that, unlike in most subsequent feminist analyses, the authors did not use references to either racism or imperialism to explain patriarchal oppression (the text relied wholly on a class analysis). They merely examined the failure of existing class-focused organizations to take the specificity of women's oppression as seriously as the same organizations did racism and imperialism.[55] Their goal, like that of other key feminist voices in the early 1970s, was to establish the fight against sexism as a political priority. As Emmanuèle Durant argued in her article on rape in the special issue, "Women's Liberation, Year Zero," "The worst form of racism

54. *Maso et miso vont en bateau*, dir. Nadja Ringart, Carole Roussopoulos, Delphine Seyrig, and Ioana Wieder (Paris: Les Insoumuses,1975). On Rousopoulos and the Insoumuses, see Ros Murray, "Raised Fists: Politics, Technology, and Embodiment in 1970s French Feminist Video Collectives," *Camera Obscura: Feminism, Culture, and Media Studies* 31, no. 1 (2016), 93–121.

55. Marcia Rothenbourg, Margaret Stephenson, Gille Wittig, Monique Wittig, "Combat pour la libération de la femme: Par delà la libération-gadget, elles découvrent la lutte des classes," *L'Idiot International* 6 (May 1970), 16. For a contemporary analysis that relies wholly on class-based terms, see "Qui est petit bourgeois?" *Tout!* 14 (7 June 1971), 8.

is sexism." For many feminists, however, both struggles mattered, and people involved in both had much to learn from the Algerian revolution and the ongoing fight against French racism. But if these convergences, as the next chapter will detail, mattered to many feminists, the overriding intensity of the struggle against rape and sexual violence—and the ways in which Arab men repeatedly entered the discussion—made their desire to continue learning from France's Algerian history difficult indeed to fulfill.[56]

56. Emmanuèle Durant, "Le viol," *Partisans* 54–55 (July-October 1970), 91–96.

NINE

Rape as Act in the 1970s

Throughout the 1970s, many French feminists made intense and creative efforts to pursue their own concerns and political demands while taking account of post-decolonization questions. In early 1974 the French-Vietnamese writer and activist Maï analyzed the relationship between French imperialism and misogynist violence. Her essay "Such an Ordinary Rape, Such Daily Imperialism" appeared in the groundbreaking special issue that philosopher Simone de Beauvoir had assembled for *Les Temps modernes*, "Les femmes s'entêtent" (Women Speak Out). Maï's analysis turned around one event: the 1973 rape "of a militant of the immigrant workers' struggle" that *Libération* had made a cause célèbre (briefly, as discussed in the previous chapter), before Algeria had engulfed the story. That rape, she explained, was her rape. She quickly established that the man she accused of raping her was not an "immigrant worker," even if this was how most of the 1973 letters-to-the-editors defined him (and indeed what the *Libération* articles seemed to suggest): "'He' was part of the committee of supporters, so outside of the hostel, just like me." She and he both, however, were people of color. "He comes from a country that is a French colony, [he is] Martinician, or Guadeloupian? and I am of Vietnamese origin living in France." What Maï's article emphasized was how French imperialism had affected both her and her assailant. Maï described her assailant's repeated verbal efforts to overcome her rejection, which she linked to the rhetoric of the typical Marxist "revolutionary." She argued back. As she saw it, "He pushed me to belong to him even though I didn't want to, just as an imperialist aggressor does with a foreign country he wants to possess." When he would not listen, "I laid out the parallels between the oppression that women suffered and that to which colonized peoples were subjected," Maï explained. He still raped her, although Maï gives no description of the violence. With its forceful deployment of anti-imperalism, its careful cri- tique of class analysis, and the ways in which it both raised and sidelined questions of race and racism, the piece spoke directly to ongoing discus- sions about rape among feminists and between feminists and others on the left.[1] While striking on many levels, this article seems to have inspired little commentary, in 1974 or since. And yet it nevertheless bears noting that Maï relies wholly on anticolonial analyses to unpack how and why she was raped.

This chapter demonstrates that attention to how the post-decolonization nexus of imperialism and race shaped the late-1970s antirape campaign opens up new perspectives on the era. True, many key factors of the femi- nist battle to analyze and stop rape that have drawn scholarly attention re- main crucial: notably the importance of agency and victimization, of male leftist misogyny, of concerns about ethics and morality, and of growing un- certainties among feminists about how to navigate institutional and legal terrain from a position of social critique. Yet a post-Algerian lens empha- sizes why the antirape campaigns and feminism were so central to French history writ large in these years.

Indeed, while this chapter aims to contribute to scholarship on feminist activism, it follows the trajectory of antirape feminism—how Arab ques- tions and Algerian lessons inspired, buffeted, and shaped this activism be- fore they came to seem too complicated to hold onto—primarily in order to map larger dynamics in 1970s France, especially on the left.[2] Maï navi- gated the difficult intersection between a number of concerns: the need for assertive feminist action; the durable reality of misogyny and male sexual violence; a contemporary context of surging racism and racist violence; a commitment to radical leftist politics, notably to building coalitions across struggles; and a profound attachment to the lessons of anti-imperialist struggles and theory. A post-decolonization perspective brings into stark relief how the very tensions that made these distinct but still linked issues so difficult to navigate undid efforts to think them together. These tensions were nonetheless emblematic of the multiple horizons that inspired post- '68 feminists as well as the new left discussions from which those same feminists emerged.

1. Maï, "Un viol si ordinaire, un impérialisme si quotidien," *Les Temps modernes* 333– 334 (1974), 1872–1889. One of the few scholars who discusses the text also mistakenly identi- fies the accused rapist as an "immigrant worker"; see Delage, "Après l'année zéro."

2. See esp. Robson, "The Subject of Rape"; Picq, *Libération des femmes*, 235–243; Bourg, *From Revolution to Ethics*, 179–226; Fabrice Virgili, "Viol (Histoire du)," in *Dictionnaire de la vio- lence*, ed. Michela Marzano (Paris: PUF, 2011), 1423–1429; Vigarello, *Histoire*, 241–282.

Maï's article aptly reflects the coalitional politics evident in the movements she describes, as well as the complexity of the intersecting issues they sought to address. These coalitions, however, did not survive the tensions that Maï so easily navigated in print. One reason, perhaps, is that her willingness to parse the metaphorical implications of rape in reference to her own rape involved—required?—silence about the actual attack. This approach proved atypical, perhaps untenable, particularly in an era where bearing witness and testimonial—about the "immigrant condition," about "coming out," and about sexual violence—provided powerful tools for explaining political activism that abstract analysis seemed to lack. The very title of the special issue, "Les femmes s'entêtent," evokes something quite different from what she offered, or so it seems (it has been the subject of diverse intepretations). But her decision to rely wholly on anticolonial feminist theory to describe her experience, in the absence of any painful, psychological, or bodily details, did not seem out of place to de Beauvoir or others at the time. This moment in the history of French feminism was more complicated than subsequent depictions have revealed, perhaps because of its embrace of the idea that the personal was political.

Feminist analyses and tactics drew from the repertoires of antiracist and anticolonial struggles, synthesizing elements of the two. This synthesis was particularly fraught because of the sharp distinctions that French political analysts saw between anticolonial struggles and efforts to overcome racism. In their eyes, anticolonial struggles established new boundaries and allowed the people that colonialism had previously excluded to reenter history, while antiracist efforts within France (or in French discussions of racist societies such as the United States) maneuvered between reassertions of republican universalism and fraternity, and newly pressing leftist summons to recognize "the right to be different" ("le droit à la différence"). Feminists, like others on the post-'68 left, struggled to negotiate such complicated terrain. Given their understanding of how political struggle worked, they had no choice. But as feminists sought to fight rape, to target men who committed rape, and to fight against existing social structures that, in refusing to take rape seriously, put all women at risk, they encountered—at every step of the way—the specter of the Arab man.

The Political Trials of Antirape Feminism

Over the course of the late 1970s, numerous feminists insistently reflected on how racism and the aftermath of empire complicated their fight against sexual violence.[3] The success of the renewed antirape campaign, which overshadowed other ongoing discussions, made this reflection particularly necessary. By 1976, feminist publications such as *Les pétroleuses* (Women Incendiaries) revealed concerted thinking about the contexts and challenges that had forced the discussion of rape from nonfeminist left-wing circles. The larger goal, as a 1976 tract from a group called Commission Rape-Violence-Self-Defense put it, was to "refuse to allow ourselves to be trapped into a debate about the justice system and rapists," as had happened in 1973.[4] If others on the left tried again to force feminists to abandon the fight against rape in the name of boycotting "bourgeois justice," Martine Storti warned readers of *Libération* in May 1976, then "no one, whatever the reason, must ever call the police or appeal to the courts." Storti's examples seemed chosen to head off a repeat of the previous aborted discussion in the newspaper she worked for: "Even if an Arab gets beaten up in the street . . . or *Libé*[*ration*] suffers a bombing," she wrote, neither courts nor police must be called upon.[5] If the bourgeois and racist nature of French society meant that feminists had to abandon their fight to end rape because it might hurt some "oppressed" men, then all leftist movements should reevaluate their tactics. In reality, Storti made clear, such calls were simply hypocritical. In June 1976 the "Manifesto against Rape," a text published in *Libération*, catalyzed renewed discussion on the left. The manifesto rejected "the imperialism of [male] sexuality" to help readers make sense of its argument that "rape is not something women desire or take pleasure in." The tract also helped publicize a large meeting on 26 June 1976 in Paris for "Ten Hours against Rape," which brought together some three thousand women.[6] In her report on the meeting, Christiane Chombeau from *Le Monde* emphasized the disagreement between women "who speak of rape as a 'product of capitalist imperialism'" and those who see

3. Picq, *Libération des femmes*, 235.

4. Commission Viol, "Violence autodéfénse," (tract 1 p., 1976), in Bibliothéque Marguerite Durand: Dossier "Viol" 1976.

5. Martine Storti, "Demain, il sera trop tard," *Libération* (17–19 May 1976). Some on the far left argued for such coherence. After the murder of fifteen-year-old Djillali Ben-Ali by a man who suspected the boy was sleeping with his wife, for example, Maoist activists declared, "We do not, nor do the Arab workers of the Goutte d'Or, ask for the head of the concierge and his companion"; "Mercredi 27 octobre, le jeune Djallali Benali, 15 ans et demi," *Agence Presse Liberation* [APL] *informations* n. 68bis (4 November 1971), 5 in BDIC (fonds Assia Melamed) F Delta rés. 696/22/1–3.

6. For attendance, see Martine Storti, *Je suis une femme, pourquoi pas vous?* (Paris: Michel de Maule, 2010), 103–107. Other authors cite Christiane Chombeau, "A Paris: Un millier de femmes ont participé aux 'dix heures contre le viol,'" *Le Monde* (29 June 1976), 10.

it "as 'a result of the patriarchal system.'" To clarify, she explained that whereas some foregrounded "a class analysis . . . evoking the sexual misery of certain men, immigrant workers for example," others defined all men as a category of oppressors. While this conflict between feminists has larger causes and implications, the "immigrant worker" question proved central in large part because it shaped feminist thinking about political action more broadly in these years.[7]

By the mid-1970s, feminist analyses of "class" systematically used references to "immigrant workers" and "Arab men" to signal working-class identity in men. In the Trotskyist weekly *Rouge*, a writer named Nelly Vandale, who identified herself as a feminist and quoted other feminists, mapped what she qualified as the racist criteria that determined convictions for rape. Vandale cited a tract from "the militants of the women's center of Lyon," which claimed that the powers that be "want to make us believe that rapists are all immigrants." Although the cases she criticized all involved men with Maghrebi names who were "immigrant workers," the title and the conclusion proclaimed, "We reject this class justice!" When feminists announced class analysis, it was anti-Arab racism that focused their critique.[8]

Questions about the justice system remained central to debates around rape because this was precisely the arena in which many feminists pursued the fight against sexual violence. In 1976, the famed leftist feminist lawyer Gisèle Halimi and her allies decided to deploy a tool they termed the "political trial" in the fight against rape.[9] The group Halimi led, Choisir la cause des femmes (Choose the Cause of Women), had pioneered the tactic during the struggle to decriminalize abortion in 1971. Published in the left-leaning weekly *Nouvel observateur*, their "Manifesto of the 343," in which a bevy of celebrated women including de Beauvoir, actress Jeanne Moreau, and novelist Marguerite Duras affirmed, "I had an abortion"—at

7. Chombeau, "A Paris."

8. Nelly Vandale, "Assises du Rhône: Oui à la reconnaissance du viol. Non à la justice de classe," *Rouge* (27–28 November 1976), in Bibliothèque Marguerite Durand: Dossier "Viol" 1976. For other examples, see "Viol," *Front libertaire des luttes de classe* 25 (December 1976), 4, in Bibliothèque Marguerite Durand: Dossier "Viol" 1976; "Il est commandant des pompiers; il viole une femme: 15 jours de prison," *Rouge* (9 February 1977). A 1973 study by Henri Michard used empirical evidence to show that gang-rape aggressors were more likely to come from more privileged social groups; see Henri Michard, "La délinquance des jeunes en France," *Notes et études documentaires* 3987–3988 (1973), 24–25.

9. On the "political trial," see, e.g., Gisèle Halimi, "Le crime," in *Viol, le procès d'Aix-en-provence: Préface de Gisèle Halimi* (Paris: Gallimard, 1978), 26; Julian Bourg, "Les contributions accidentelles du marxisme au renouveau des droits de l'homme en France dans l'après-68," *Actuel Marx* 32, no. 2 (2002), 125–138.

the time, a criminal act—had exposed the signatories to the full force of the law. Halimi, who had also signed the manifesto, helped found Choisir in order to respond to any legal action against the signatories. Soon after, she took over the defense of a young girl, "Marie-Claire" (who had become pregnant after being raped), and her "accomplices" (including the girl's working-class single mother), all on trial in the Parisian suburb of Bobigny for the crime of abortion. Halimi's goal, pursued with great success, was to use the trial to draw public attention to the need to legalize abortion.[10]

Gisèle Halimi and the Political Trial Tactic

Halimi had also been deeply involved with the struggle for Algerian independence, as had many of the feminist lawyers who were on the defense team for the Bobigny Trial.[11] Halimi herself had become a public figure in large part because "over the course of her career she has always worked to defend activists fighting for national liberation," as the opening lines of a 1978 article in *Libération* describing her involvement in the Manifesto of the 343 put it. Readers learned that "beginning in 1958, she was the lawyer for Tunisian union militants: she won a stay of execution for thirty-five Algerians condemned to die in the El Alia trial." Interestingly, her most well known case was only evoked briefly: "She defended Djamila Boupacha, FLN militant"—who, the paper declined to note, had been tortured and raped by French soldiers. For the far-right weekly *Minute*, "from the FLN to the 'fight for women,' Halimi always has her left-turn signal on." Born in Tunis, Halimi publicly linked her Jewish and Tunisian identities to her politics.[12]

The renewed feminist campaign against rape targeted the courts. What drew the attention of leftist commentators were feminists' efforts to have rape cases judged as felonies, in the Assizes Courts, rather than as misdemeanors, in criminal courts. A shift to the Assizes opened up the possibility of jury trials rather than wholly judge-run trials, and opened the way to harsher sentences. Activists who pushed for this shift wanted acknowledgment that rape was serious.[13] Public trials also would expose the public

10. See esp. Bibia Pavard, *Si je veux, quand je veux: Contraception et avortement dans la société française (1956–1979)* (Rennes: Presses universitaires de Rennes, 2012).

11. See the important article by sociologist Sandrine Garcia, "Expertise scientifique et capital militant," *Actes de la recherche en sciences sociales* 158 (2005), 96–115.

12. Cited in Garcia. *Minute* 838 (10 May 1978), 5.

13. Historians of the French justice system have shown that, in the late nineteenth century, the French justice system shifted prosecution of a large majority of cases that could have been tried at Assizes Courts (*Assises*) to criminal courts (*Tribunaux correctionnels*). One reason was

to the widespread and devastating effects of rape on all women and girls, something activists hoped would facilitate political action and help change both public attitudes and male behavior.

Beginning in 1974, feminist groups in places such as Marseille and Pau adopted the *procès politique* (political trial) method in the battle against rape. They insisted that their goals were fundamentally political, aimed less at punishing individual rapists than at condemning and changing the society that produced such acts. What they wanted, a journalist in the *Nouvel observateur* explained in fall 1975, was explicitly not "to behead the aggressor, to lock them up, to have them castrated, lynched, or to expose them, nude and daubed with paint, to public opprobrium. . . ." Indeed, in their struggle to bring "a case of rape before the courts . . . they [sought] no vengeance whatsoever."[14] Note the importance assigned to intentions, which resonated with the very types of questions that rape cases tended to bring to the fore, whether in cross-examination or in public discussions. In February 1976, a judge agreed to a request to transfer a case involving the rape of two Belgian women from the criminal court to the Assize Court of Aix-en-Provence. Gisèle Halimi would lead the legal team when the trial took place in May 1978. This victory and the subsequent trial have been the focus of most scholarly analyses of 1970s antirape feminism in France. Yet over the course of 1976 and 1977, the lawyers of Choisir had worked to transform a series of trials into public events, which would make visible both male violence against women and the failure of the state or society to respond to it. The May 1978 trial, that is, came *after* most of the debates that wracked the far left and feminists had been settled, a crystallization that the turn to the courts had precipitated.[15]

In what quickly became known as the "Aix Trial," there were no Arab men involved. Yet the Arab question had already reemerged in 1976 and 1977 as the crux around which left-wing debates about the feminist campaign turned. By no means was it the only issue that far left-wing groups raised as they targeted feminist attempts to use the justice system to fight rape. As in 1973, the explicit issues were, on the one hand, classism, which critics presented as inherent to any reliance on "bourgeois" justice, and, on

---

that the authorities privileged the symbolic importance of extremely harsh penalties for crimes, which juries were hesitant to apply. The shift thus preserved the harsh penalties, while accused criminals were tried on lesser charges in judge-run trials, which did not involve jurors. See, e.g., James Michael Donovan, *Juries and the Transformation of Criminal Justice in France in the Nineteenth and Twentieth Centuries* (Chapel Hill, NC: Univ of North Carolina Press, 2010).

14. Marielle Righini, "Des petits viols sans importance," *Nouvel observateur* (29 September. 1975), 51.

15. See Bourg, *From Revolution to Ethics*, 194–195.

the other, antisex puritanism. Both these issues, critics claimed, meant that increased repression against "immigrant men," rather than greater justice for women, would result. In early 1977, Alice Soledad, writing in *Rouge*, explicitly acknowledged that in rape trials in which MLF activists had taken part, they had "denounced class justice when they went before the bench." Yet, she argued, while punishment for certain rapists and publicity about the crime had increased, the feminist effort to challenge class justice had failed.[16]

Both left-wing critics and those feminists who defended the turn to the courts repeatedly offered Arab references to explain their position. In early 1977, feminist members of an anarchist group proposed an alternative to the political trial tactic. "To fight rape, we have formulated two propositions," they announced, both of which broke completely with efforts to involve the courts (as well as with feminist critiques of violence.)[17] "The first is to set up 'anti-rape brigades,'" they declared. The model these anarchist feminists proposed was activism against anti-Arab violence, anchored in Algerian precedents. "Just like what happens after a coon hunt [*ratonnade*], when immigrants join together to punish those responsible, women must give ourselves the means to physically respond to rapists." What made this suggestion particularly interesting was that it followed a critique of anarchist comrades who resisted feminist efforts to fight rape. "Why try and make us feel guilty by playing the rejected-immigrant card: 'Why don't you want to go with an Arab, a Turk?'" These feminist anarchists declared, "The far left has been using this effort to summon pity since [May 19]68. We are done with being understanding, because guys have been telling us to understand them for millennia." They spoke of antiracist and antiimperialist militancy as a model for action and to warn of the ways men had used such political commitments to demand that women make themselves sexually available. They connected this trap to the dangers that male leftist celebrations of sexual liberty posed to women.[18]

The "Brigitte" Rape Trial: "Your Struggle Is Reactionary"

Several weeks later, in March 1977, the "Brigitte" rape trial brought these debates and their Arab resonances into a far more public domain. Several

16. Alice Soledad, "Viol: Le silence rompu," *Rouge* (3 January 1977), 3.

17. On nonviolence, see esp. Pipon, *Et on tuera*.

18. Fédération locale Paris Nord-Est Organisation communiste libertaire (OCL), "Le viol, produit du capitalisme?" *Front libertaire des luttes de classes* (10 February 1977), in Bibliothèque Marguerite Durand: Dossier "Viol" 1977.

feminist lawyers had volunteered to represent the interests of Brigitte in the courtroom, and all had agreed that the case of this young feminist activist deserved public discussion. Eleven months earlier, the woman had gone to the police to report that she had been raped. Only days before the accused was to stand trial, Brigitte told a journalist at *Libération*, "I had to go through different stages. At first, the fact that he was a foreigner, for example, raised a lot of issues for me." Brigitte complained that the police had "tried to make me say that I was very happy that it was an Arab." What Brigitte described next encapsulated much of the controversy that the case engendered in leftist circles: "But there's so many different things in this attack: death, sex, this guy who is Arab and me who is French, this guy who is a man and me, a woman—everything is in there, it's a crucible." Brigitte's rapist, Youri Eshak, was a twenty-seven-year old Egyptian student at the Université de Vincennes, and his status as Arab quickly engulfed the public debate. Several commentators went so far as to transform him into an "immigrant worker."[19]

On the very same page of *Libération*, Eshak's lawyer, Roger Koskas, mustered an aggressive defense of his client, which he anchored in explicitly left-wing analyses, including some that had come to prominence during the sexual revolution: "We readily talk of economic misery, of how the underbelly of the proletariat encourages delinquency. Why then, when it comes to sex, not state that there's sexual misery?" He also insisted that the debate about rape should take place "within the Left" rather than in a courtroom. "Because in this battle, it's the right that will benefit on every single level." Conservative politicians and reactionary policies, in his read, would gain support if rape cases were tried more frequently or gained more publicity.[20] Days later, in the courtroom, Koskas struck harder. He addressed Brigitte and her lawyers. Their pursuit of this case, he affirmed, was "a summons to the lynch mob, a call for murder. Your struggle is reactionary." The journalist from *Nouvel observateur* saw something different, emphasizing "how difficult it is to plead against a foreigner, who is in some ways himself oppressed by his culture and our racism." However, she then quickly castigated the defense lawyer for his argument: "Women are forced to justify their decision to turn to the courts against rapists, whereas"—here her arguments echoed with key terms from French discussions since 1973— "in all the struggle against racist Dupont-la-Joies, against businessmen who

19. Martine Storti, "Histoire d'un viol: Brigitte, 11 mois après," *Libération* (21 March 1977), 4.

20. Martine Storti, "Histoire d'un viol: L'avocat de son agresseur: 'Ce n'est pas la répression qui va améliorer les rapports entre les hommes et les femmes,'" *Libération* (21 March 1977), 4.

take advantage of immigrant misery [*les marchands du sommeil*] . . . the left has used the justice system, and rightly so." Yet again, the model of antiracist activism both undermined and authorized feminist choices.[21]

In response to the Brigitte case, letters to the editors of *Libération* and *Nouvel observateur* also focused on the Arab question, reminding critics that "the only time a rapist faces condemnation is when he is an immigrant."[22] A group of feminists wrote, "From the very depths of our despair, we feel guilty for sending these poor guys, victims of 'the imperialism of the dick,' into the somber jails of bourgeois justice." Despite their mockery, they reminded readers that, like "the movement" in general, they proposed "to ask that rapes be punished, quite simply," through publicity rather than jail. Posters that would inform neighbors about the identity and crimes of condemned rapists were one of their suggestions.[23]

By mid-April, more responses to the Brigitte case sounded the deep links between the Arab question and that of rape. Many sought to maneuver between rape as bodily experience and its metaphorical politics. A woman wrote to urge feminists "to also take responsibility for the fact that our experience produces contradictions." She highlighted her own reactions, such as "that which makes me hate the immigrant who attacks me because I'm a woman," but also, that "which leads me to stand beside him when, simply because of his dark skin color, he is the one who is subjected to the rape of the pig-cops." "Rape," then, is the term she chose to describe the "shakedown and interrogation in the subway" of such men by police officers: rape in metaphorical terms, suffered by the "immigrant [with] dark skin," set alongside actual sexual violence, presented as coming from the same (figurative) man.[24]

Ahmed Ben Charoud linked his own experience—"immigrant . . . young . . . lost . . ."—to that of Eshak. But he addressed himself to Brigitte—"I feel sorry for you, I feel sorry for your body for being on the same trajectory as ours"—even as he blamed France for the way it had treated "this immigrant whom you sent up to the Assize [court]," who "finally ended at the bottom, as it was obvious would happen ever since he was reduced to a number at the ONI [National Office of Immigration]." Ben

21. Marielle Righini, "'Nous ne sommes pas des procureurs': Celles que dénoncent la justice répressive doivent-elles y faire appel pour stigmatiser le viol?" *Nouvel observateur* 646 (28 March 1977), 52–53.

22. Françoise, 8è, "Courrier: Réponse à Maitre Koskas," *Libération*, (29 March 1977), 2; Nicole, "Ce sont les violeurs qui font le jeu du pouvoir,"*Libération* (24 March 1977), 2.

23. "Courrier: Une commission 'viol' dans le 8e," *Libération* (29 March 1977), 2.

24. "Courrier: A propos du viol: Histoire d'une réunion," *Libération* (20 April 1977), 2.

Charoud's analysis was an effort to map out the complexity of the situation, which still put the metaphorical rape his kind suffered at the hands of France on the same plane as the physical violence to which Eshak had subjected Brigitte. Yet he closed with the assertion, ". . . your cry is, despite it all, ours."[25] A less nuanced Maghrebi perspective also reappeared, as *Libération* published "A Letter from Mohamed on Rape and Racism." The letter's author argued, "My immigrant brothers . . . are the protagonists chosen and accused (by women, by the justice system, by the press) in these Stone-Age dramas of daily life that we name rape." The letter writer sought to place this in the context of the history of Western imperialism. "Who raped whom first? It's too easy to forget that in efforts to act in good conscience." He insisted that the metaphor of colonial rape offered more insight and deserved more attention than any specific act of sexual violence. His focus on "conscience" was also telling.[26]

Sexual Revolutionaries Confront Antirape Campaigns

Guy Hocquenghem, the philosopher and radical gay activist, had already published an even more violent and metaphor-rich condemnation of the trial of Youri Eshak. In a short piece he returned repeatedly to the Arab identity of the accused, whom he portrayed as the victim of a desire for "vengeance" on the part of the "girlfriends" of Brigitte: "leftists, feminists" who "summoned the police, dragged an Arab through the mud—it turns out he is Egyptian." Castigating "their hysterical and condemnatory chorus," he defined them as being "without pity." "He's an Arab? All the better; his punishment will be even more spectacular." (A revised version of this article that appeared the following fall added one more reminder that "the accused" was "an Arab student.") The battle over "intentions," and over who had a "good conscience"—with feminists insisting they had no intention to seek "vengeance" or to target "Arab men"—revealed how intense the disagreements had become.[27]

By 1977, Hocquenghem and other activist gay men associated with "revolutionary homosexuality" regularly targeted feminists as enemies of their struggle. They decried antirape activism as fundamentally antisexual,

25. "Courrier: Solitude," *Libération* (15 April 1977), 2.
26. Mohamed, "Un viol en cache toujours un autre. Une lettre de Mohamed sur le viol et le racisme," *Libération* (5 April 1977), 7.
27. Hocquenghem, "V-I-O-L," *Libération* (29 March 1977), 7; republished with short introduction in Hocquenghem, *La dérive homosexuelle*, 127–134.

a critique that others on the left would take up. The philosopher's fall 1977 book *La dérive homosexuelle* proclaimed in its prelude, "In response to the liberation of morality, to pornography, to the homosexual wave, leagues of women against rape propose a new puritanism."[28] Hocquenghem had leveled a similar critique in an article in the 1973 "Three Billion Perverts," where he recounted the exasperation of "a buddy . . . to always have to hear the girls say they are tired of being hit on." The way he framed his comments helps make visible why the Arab aspect of the rape debate later drew such attention from gay male sex radicals. It connected quite directly to ongoing reflections about sodomy that had absorbed so many of them, notably Hocquenghem. "Of course," he wrote in 1973, "in Morocco and Algeria we had seen guys who were utterly unhinged when they saw a girl walk by; they would yell: 'I'm going to bite your ass, I will rape you or kill you.'" Even as he recognized that "it might sometimes be necessary to repress men like that," what was crucial in his view was to recognize why they acted that way. Rather than attributing their behavior to misogyny or patriarchy, Hocquenghem argued, "It's because they don't know what they really want. What they want is the intense pleasure of orgasm [*c'est jouir*]."[29] It was an analysis that centered on the problem of embodied subjectivity and its relationship to power and domination. The premise was the same as that anchoring his celebration of anal sex: Precisely because it was linked to shame and its seemingly necessary metaphoric relationship to power, sodomy opened up possibilities both of connection and pleasure that a repressive and racist society denied. "When women set themselves in opposition to male desire," he claimed in 1977, they rejected "fags" and, above all, "their taste for sex with a brutal edge, for the phallus."[30] He argued that while feminists were mistakenly focused on patriarchy, they were in fact complicit with society in acting to impede the new possibilities offered by "fags."

The specter of Arab men haunted almost every harsh critique from the left of the feminist campaign against rape. In a 1978 screed, the jurist Claude Alzon accused feminists of abandoning any social analysis. "These women prefer [to focus] on Algerian rapists, who offer clear proof of what men are like," he insisted. Rather than justice, what inspired the feminists was that they had "no doubt that the media will show up and make them

---

28. Guy Hocquenghem, prelude, *La dérive homosexuelle*, 12.
29. Hocquenghem, "Drague et amour," in *La dérive homosexuelle*, 103–108.
30. Hocquenghem, "La violence des marges," in *La dérive homosexuelle*, 125–126.

262 / Chapter Nine

even more well known."[31] Alzon targeted those feminists who had sought to bring rapes to trial but who rejected the use of prison or similar penalties to punish condemned rapists. "In the trial of the Algerian worker, hypocrisy reached its peak," he wrote, maintaining that it was visible in their efforts to propose alternative penalties that did not involve prison, and which he said "would allow feminists to leave with a good conscience while allowing Algerians, when they rape, to avoid getting twenty years." In Alzon's view, such feminists offered "the spectacle, the most dishonorable kind there is, of generosity."[32] The recurrent presence of the Arab man in juridical, political, and media treatment of the rape question sharpened the intensity of such disputes even as it reshaped them.

"Sexual Misery Alone Does Not Explain Rape": Feminist Responses to Far-Left Critics

The Arab question altered feminist responses to leftists, as female militants grew increasingly disgusted by male leftists' efforts to avoid any real discussion of rape as an act of violence against women. In the fall of 1977, for example, *Rouge* published a photo of a poster set up by feminist activists outside the Orléans courthouse, which read, "Sexual misery alone does not explain rape."[33] On a special episode of the television program *Reports from the big screen: Questions around Rape*, a feminist lawyer explained that in the rape trials in which she was involved, "it's not about immigrants haunted by sexual misery; in the sum total of my cases, I have one Moroccan, and he was born in Tours."[34] Writing a few months later in a feminist magazine, an activist complained about the constant deployment of the "immigrant worker; he's the one they always point to in order to back up the sexual misery argument."[35] Yet in conjunction with arguments that the "immigrant" and "rape" questions needed to be pulled apart, many other

31. Claude Alzon, *Femme mythifiée, femme mystifiée* (Paris: Presses universitaires de France, 1978), 285. One of the few strong critiques of the feminist campaign that did not explicitly accuse feminists of anti-Arab racism was Annie Le Brun, in *Lachez-tout* (Paris: La Sagittaire, 1977). Le Brun did, however, compare feminists negatively to "the homosexuals of the FHAR . . . who proudly proclaim that they have privileged relationships with Arabs, betting on the sexual, social, and political provocation of such a confession in our sweetly racist France. . . ."; 58.

32. Alzon, *Femme mythifiée*, 382–385

33. Photo next to "Aux assises d'Orléans, procès pour viol le 20 octobre," *Rouge* (22–23 Oct. 1977), 8.

34. As transcribed in Marie-Odile Fargier, "Dossiers de l'écran, le viol en question," *Rouge* (18 October 1977), 6.

35. "Une riposte originale," *Histoires d'elles* 4 (March-April 1978), 22.

Figure 21. In October 1977 this photo appeared in *Rouge*, the weekly newspaper of the Revolutionary Communist League (LCR, Trotskyist). Against a backdrop of left-wing debates about the feminist campaign to use trials to change social attitudes toward sexual violence against women, it accompanied an article about one such rape trial in Orléans. The poster says, "Sexual misery alone does not explain rape. It does not in any way excuse it. A rape is when one [human] being seizes power over another." Image and permission to reproduce graciously provided by Rouge/RaDAR.

feminists involved in antirape activism remained concerned about the intersections between their antirape struggle and the Arab question.

Actors from outside "the left," who had no attachment to feminism, quite quickly became involved in this antirape campaign, and this forced feminist antirape activists to recalibrate or rethink their political choices as well as their claims. In late May, for example, the judge in the trial of Youri Eshak rejected the request of Brigitte's lawyer that, because "repression is too resonant with the lives women lead within the family for us to embrace it," the accused should be liberated while he awaited trial.[36] This feminist insight, the lawyer argued, was particularly apt in this case because

36. "Viol: La partie civil demandait la liberté. Le tribunal refuse," *Libération* (21–22 May 1977), 6. For an extended version of this argument about feminist/female recognition of oppression, see Michèle Perrein, "Tant qu'il y aura des violeurs. Patrick Boubé, agresseur de vingt femmes, vient d'être condamné à douze ans de réclusion criminelle par la cour d'assises de Paris. Justice est faite. Mais avec le tranchant du glaive," *F. Magazine* 1 (January 1978), 64–65.

"we know that those who are in prison, including the rapists, are always the same (young people from modest backgrounds or immigrants)." The judge ignored the argument, just as numerous other judges would do over the next several years. The courts did not pay the same attention to feminist efforts to alleviate the repressive effects of judicial actions as they did to requests to shift rape cases from the correctional to the Assizes, or to other reforms that would increase the role of the courts.[37]

A burgeoning discussion in the media, ripe with anti-Arab insinuation, also forced the hand of feminists. In fall 1977, *One in Five*, a late afternoon show on the TV channel Antenne 2 aimed at teenagers, centered its first discussion around a nineteen-year-old woman named Danielle. She described being forcibly kidnapped in Pigalle and then gang-raped in a Châtelet apartment by a group of men who "couldn't really speak French." She raised the specter of the "white slave trade"—an accusation ripe with anti-Arab implications (see chapter 5)—noting that "they then planned to prostitute me."[38] Months earlier, tabloid newspaper reports on rapes at the University of Rouen had drawn the ire of a group of feminist students. The women targeted the media's use of these crimes to "calmly deploy their antiyouth and anti-immigrant racism." An article in the scandal sheet *Spécial dernière*, which they decried using a class-struggle analysis, blamed the rapes, in the students's interpretation, on "immigrant students and thugs who come from the housing projects [*des banlieues*] to rape white women." The feminists complained: "The article is not opposed to rape as a phenomenon but only to rapes committed by those excluded from society." All feminists remained committed to the struggle against rape. Many also remained concerned that the success of antirape campaigns might reinforce certain types of social marginalization.[39]

In October 1977, *Le Monde* published an extended analysis of feminist debates about the fight against rape; the most important disagreement between feminists concerned the "immigrant" question. The journalist Michèle Solat asked rhetorically, "Is it necessary to hope that an immigrant will be put in prison because he raped a woman?" To her own question, she responded: "The general tendency leans to the yes side." Solat docu-

37. For other such cases, see, e.g., Catherine Leguay, "Réportage: Au Mans: Procès pour un débat viol et justice," *Histoires d'elles* 3 (February 1978), 21; and, more broadly, Picq, *Libération des femmes*, 242–243.

38. "Bloc notes: Le viol," segment of *Un sur cinq*, A2 (17:40 on 2 November 1977).

39. Groupe femmes étudiantes de la fac de lettres de Rouen, "Quand '*Spécial Dernière*' s'indigne du viol," *Rouge* (23 March 1977), Bibliothèque Marguerite Durand: Dossier "Viol" 1977.

mented this through an interview with an unnamed member of the left-wing Union of Judges (Syndicat de la Magistrature).[40] In archival records and the diverse publications of multiple feminist groups, however, debates over this question remained intense. This was pointedly the case among those feminists who were also closely engaged with other political groups and causes on the far left. Claire Bataille, writing in *Rouge*, summarized left-ist arguments against the use of courts by raped women: "'You can't really want to send a poor fellow up to the Assize [court].' 'You really should not turn into accomplices of bourgeois justice.' 'It's immigrants, young guys, and workers who'll pay, not the others!'" Bataille's analysis of feminist re-actions differed sharply from that of *Le Monde*. She argued that "there is not a single current within the women's movement that is asking for" this type of punishment.[41]

Feminists Confront the Meaning of Mass-Media Support

Within the MLF, in fact, the debate over the institutional effects of the cam-paign was vibrant, as Carole Roussopoulos revealed in her early 1978 docu-mentary film *Rape*. Its cast of subjects included "Brigitte," whose participa-tion in the trial of her rapist had drawn such attention the previous year; Josyane Moutet, a feminist lawyer who had worked with Brigitte; and others. Their discussion of repression was both fraught and nuanced. It included an effort to think about the tension between, in Moutet's words, the "fact that we don't control the repression" and the recognition that it was only after "the women's movement turned to the Assize Court in rape cases" that "the mass media latched on, for obvious reasons linked to the news cycle and to sales." Moutet's summary was lucid. "It's only since we turned to repres-sion to draw attention to the question of rape, through the [judicial] ma-chine, that people talk about it." For all involved, this posed the question of Arab men. Offscreen voices immediately and defensively recalled that leftist lawyers had also been involved in "putting racists on trial." The argu-ment Moutet developed, however, was more specific. She recounted that she had asked a "woman judge" how she would respond "if what was in play was very specifically the wife of an immigrant worker who came before you because her husband was killed at a construction site after a workplace ac-cident, one that happened because of a boss who wanted to save money."

40. Michèle Solat, "Les féministes et le viol: III. Coment lutter," *Le Monde* (20 October 1977), 12.
41. "La lutte contre le viol: Fonction et limite d'une bataille sur le terrain judicaire," *Rouge* (6 October 1977), 6, in Bibliothèque Marguerite Durand: Dossier "Viol" 1977.

The question was whether to shift the trial from the correctional court to the Assizes: "Would you [the judge] ask me [the lawyer for the victim] to reflect on whether the fact of sending this man [the boss] before whatever court would completely destroy his life?"[42] Once Moutet brought an immigrant woman into a discussion that had previously focused almost wholly on male immigrants, the lawyer claimed, the judge changed her approach. This imaginary woman was reduced to her status as "the wife of an immigrant worker" and was brought up only to deflect claims of racism. The weight of the Arab man in left-wing discussions was such that even feminists turned to Arab women not as subjects in and of themselves, but as a way to get out of a double bind of their own making. Their concerns about anti-Arab racism risked displacing their primary agenda. A metaphorical Arab woman offered reassurance that their cause was just.

Algerian lessons remained potent, on the left and among feminists in particular. In an article in the Communist daily *L'Humanité*, which claimed to contribute to "opening up a big debate" on rape, the author suggested that Gisèle Halimi, in her arguments on behalf of a rape victim, "should evoke . . . the several—many—army attacks that annihilated Algerian villages during the national liberation struggle."[43] When Paul Roussopoulos, husband of and sometime codirector with Carole, wrote to criticize how "the trial of Brigitte had provoked a crisis of conscience on the left and far left," he argued that the critics' "hatred of 'those bourgeois ladies' of the feminist movement" reminded him of the "the paratroopers of [General] Bigeard [during the Algerian war] who professed a ferocious hatred of *'chers professeurs'* [intellectuals]."[44] When Claire Bataille critiqued Trotskyist comrades who claimed that they were not aware that the problem of rape was so serious, or who invoked contemporary sexology to claim that "post-rape trauma . . . doesn't even exist," she angrily compared them to others who denied "the horrific massacres in Vietnam or the use of torture in Algeria." Which to say that many on the left, notably feminists, continued to invoke Algerian lessons. As we have seen, however, there were so many lessons to learn that it became increasingly difficult to maneuver between their multiple implications, to make sense of them together.[45]

42. Carole Roussopoulos, dir., *Le viol: Anne, Corinne, Annie, Brigitte, Josyane, Monique et les autres* (1978).

43. Jean-Marie Cordier, "Viol: L'amorce d'un grand débat,"*L'Humanité* (19 October 1977).

44. "Viol ou violences? 3. Un débat de musée," *Libération* (6 April 1977).

45. Claire Bataille, "Elle a ete violée: 'Vous n'allez pas faire un drame?'" *Rouge* (24 November 1977), in Bibliothèque Marguerite Durand: Dossier "Viol" 1977.

"Rape is Everyday Fascism"

Perhaps unsurprisingly, it was Gisèle Halimi who most directly invoked Algerian histories to address the question of rape. Her September 1977 intervention in one of the first rape trials where she appeared on behalf of a victim received wide attention. It began with an effort to force the audience to recognize that rapists, as a group, "are young men who are no more psychopathic than the majority of young men: they are married, divorced, they have children, they work . . . they are unemployed, average, have banal lives." According to her statement, there was only one other thing most rapists *were not*: "They are not immigrants." It was a clear indication of how concerned the feminist was about the type of men the strategy she championed risked targeting. Yet the heart of her argument was more specific, in the parallels she drew to the trial of the presumed "terrorist" Djamila Boupacha, in which the victim had been the accused. She reminded the audience that she had encountered other rapists: "It was seventeen years ago, they were blond, they were parachutists; the Claudine whom I defended then [Boupacha] was a virgin; she was Muslim, they subjected her to torture, then raped her; that time they used a bottle." The description evoked the horrors of French repression in Algeria. It did so, however, not to identify a cause of current rapes in France, but to insist on the damage rape did, and to show how common it had been for so long. Neither was it meant to suggest that there were particular connections between earlier French imperialism and France in 1977. Instead, she used this history to anchor an analysis of the larger dangers of rape, which held wider implications than those that lessons from Algeria could teach.

In 1974, Maï had used histories of French colonialism in Vietnam and the Antilles to describe rape as "daily imperialism." In tacit opposition, Halimi argued, "Rape is just ordinary fascism; it's everyday fascism." Not only had feminist arguments against rape-as-violence succeeded in displacing antiracist reliance on rape-as-metaphor, but Halimi also disentangled French feminist analysis from the metaphors of empire. Imperialism and colonial violence, this hero of French anticolonialism argued, did *not* have specific lessons to teach feminists about rape. The feminist antirape campaign, however, did have crucial lessons to teach anyone committed to justice and anticolonialism. "When we . . . accept [rape's] existence, we've prepared ourselves for fascism more generally. When we accept the whip for women, we accept that the cudgel can be applied to any oppressed peoples." It was a stark affirmation that feminist antirape campaigns had such important lessons for everyone that this struggle should come first.[46]

Halimi's argument addressed a growing exhaustion among feminists over what particular lessons could be learned from Algerian and other French colonial histories. Feminists of all stripes remained concerned about both anti-Arab racism and the risks of a "repressive" strategy in the fight against rape. Halimi's law office, for example, continued to pursue what a journalist in *Marie-Claire* described as two different approaches to punishing rapists: "Rigor in Bobigny, laxity in Limoges; depending on whether [the rapists] are mighty or miserable." Halimi and her colleagues nevertheless revealed a new certainty among many feminists that their own struggles must not be subsumed by such concerns. Rather than get bogged down in debates with leftists about which types of men might suffer from bringing rapes to court, Halimi told a noontime program on Antenne 2 Television in 1979 that her organization proposed to "reduce penalties by half." All legal penalties, for all crimes, for everyone. "We are not for repression," she said, "but we propose that the penalties for all crimes should be cut in half at the same time." This, rather than worrying only about penalties affecting rapists—or, for that matter, Arab men.[47] Halimi argued that the discussion needed to change so that society as a whole, rather than just women and feminists, dealt with the problems of both rape and repression at the hands of courts or the police.

The choice by many feminists to uncouple their antirape campaign from post-Algerian analyses speaks more to broad French developments than to a specifically feminist agenda. This was visible in this book's earlier "Arab" history of the FHAR, and it will be central to its conclusion. In other words, the very emphasis feminists now put on privileging only feminist concerns lined up with similar developments across the left. "Intersectional" thinking faded because it required thinking in conjunction with anticolonialism.

"The Rapist Shocks People Less Than the Violent Racist": The Feminist Abandonment of the Arab Reference

The Algerian frame had come to seem too heavy. Whereas after 1962, looking to the Maghreb seemed to promise answers to French problems, in the

46. Gisèle Halimi, "Extrait de la plaidoirie de Me Gisèle Halimi [procès de Colmar]," *Rouge* 456 (22 September 1977), 8. See also Luc Bernard, "Colmar: Le procès de la torture et du viol," *Le quotidien de Paris* (21 September 1977).

47. *Midi* (A2, 21 March 1979).

late 1970s it seemed to muddle other political claims. For feminists this was particularly true because of the place occupied by the "Arab man." What emerged in the often thoughtful discussions amongst feminist thinkers was the certainty that, as feminist writer Emmanuèle de Lesseps put it in 1980, "The rapist shocks people less than the violent racist. . . . The left's worthy indignation makes it easy to forget that the 'racist aggressor' is just as likely to be a 'poor guy' as is the rapist." She carefully explained herself, and her references were quite specific. "I am not saying that, emotionally, the bloody massacre of a woman appears less horrible than the bloody massacre of an Arab." To explain the political stakes, she turned to psychology, rather than history. "It is perhaps true that many people, because they all have close relations with women, would be more upset by the former than by the latter. It's exactly the transformation of emotion into political morality that I want to talk about." In a rather remarkable footnote, de Lesseps suggested that racist attacks are seen as political because "those individuals who are victims of racism are generally described as being [male]." This is partially the case, she claimed, because "the majority of immigrant workers are men." Yet it is also, she argued, "because if a woman, no matter her ethnic appearance, is attacked 'for no reason,' most people will suspect it's for 'sexual'—we would say sexist—reasons, and rightly so, the evidence suggests."[48] Her response to Yamina and others was to insist that only sexism, not racism, affected them. This move, wholly exemplary of a new feminist consensus that coalesced around 1979, broke with the consistent efforts of many feminists across the decade to analyze post-decolonization racism together with sexism.

One voice that stood out in this discussion was that of Leïla Sebbar, a feminist writer and activist whose father was Algerian. In 1978, amidst the controversies over feminist antirape campaigns, Sebbar mocked "the tears" of leftist men who had never voiced concern for the victims of rape but now bemoaned the punishments inflicted on convicted rapists. Still, in the next line, she pointed out to readers that, yes, the punishment inflicted on the North African rapists in the trials under discussion was several times more severe than those imposed on "white" and bourgeois men.[49] In her 1978 book *On tue les petites filles* (We Kill Little Girls), Sebbar told of an "Algerian" café owner who viciously mistreated his wife and waitresses, but also of a teenage girl who, to escape blame for a consensual sexual encounter,

48. De Lesseps, "Sexisme et racisme," 101.
49. Leïla Sebbar, "Polémique. Encore le viol: On n'a jamais parlé du VIOL," *Histoires d'elles* 5 (April-May 1978), 9.

"told her father and his wife a story of a gang rape that she had suffered," in which she described her attackers as "North African or Portuguese. Given the way they spoke, I think they were Arabs."[50] In these early texts, Sebbar does not speak as a French woman with Algerian roots; she writes as a feminist, one attentive to how power works in multiple registers in the history of oppression she wants to tell. She describes a world in which colonialism and racism function as does capitalism, and where there are other forms of oppression besides patriarchal sexism, even though the latter is her most pressing concern. She insists that violence against women is more than an ethical story about right and wrong, about intentions or consciences: it is about power and domination. Like so many male "Maghrebi perspectives" from this era, her claims suggest that she had no choice but to think of the specific political claims that most engaged her feminism in conjunction with questions framed by empire, decolonization, and post-decolonization racism. And she did so at the very moment when other feminists made exactly such a choice: to leave the post-decolonization frame to the side.

As early as spring 1977, several male commentators who identified as both pro-feminist and "Arab" also intervened in this discussion. We see this, for example, in letters like the one Ahmed Ben Charoud addressed to "Brigitte," or in the letter from Mustapha Djajam, Ali Ghalem, Mahmoud Zemmouri, Jean Duflot, Pierre Boiron, and Jacqueline Narcy about "the Arab man whose sex organs cut like a knife." *Libération* published the latter under the title "Story of a Guy Who Did Not Want to Fall into Antifeminism."[51] In early 1979, the same newspaper published an unusually candid letter, under the title "Immigrants Who Remain in Solidarity." It began, "We were a group of five friends, who are in solidarity with struggles in general and, most particularly, the one waged by women [and] who went to the 8 p.m. demonstration [against rape] last night. . . . One chick who had been calm came up to one of us. 'Oh, a dude!' And, as she said it, she put her hand on his ass. 'What buttocks! They're beautiful, can I butt-fuck him?' She mimes coitus. She was immediately imitated by a dozen other girls who were just waiting for the spark." As reported, the gestures and statements mimicked sexist men, but did so in particular ways that over the course of the 1970s had often been linked to Arab men: from sodomy to sexual harassment in the street. The letter, signed by "Nour, Pascal, Kamel, Lakhdar, Pascal," also recounted other incidents at the march before concluding, "Now we are asking ourselves if our physical appear-

50. Leïla Sebbar, *On tue les petites filles* (Paris: Stock, 1978), 66, 243–244.
51. "Courrier: Solitude," *Libération* (15 April 1977), 2; Mustapha Djajam et al., "Courrier."

ance (because we are Arabs) doesn't explain something. Under the cover of feminism, a racism that claims to be antimale revealed its true face: typical racism, the same as that of cops and bosses, an anti-immigrant racism."[52] The letter seems to have received no response. Many feminists remained concerned with racism in general, and with anti-Arab racism in particular. Yet the growing frustration many of these same women experienced in the face of leftist critiques had rendered it difficult for them to hear these new voices and, more importantly, to consider their own feminist battles in tandem with Arab questions.

This history helps to explain some of the specifically French results of what was a shared transnational effort by feminists across the West to think about and fight rape. In France, as numerous scholars of feminism have noted, the far and new lefts of the 1980s and early 1990s became strikingly unwelcome to feminist activism. So, too, did academic discussions, notably among French academics who publicly identified with the left.[53] Some have argued that aspects of this particular post-1979 isolation of feminists in France shaped French discussion of the 2011 "DSK Affair" (when Dominique Strauss-Kahn, a prominent Socialist politician, faced charges of raping an African immigrant woman who worked as a cleaner in his high-end New York City hotel).[54] Since 2001, some feminists have participated in French political campaigns that pathologize "Muslim" cultural traits and people as the primary or unique source of misogynist, sexist, or homophobic attitudes in France. In turn, certain antiracist militants have turned to histories of imperial complicity to explain why "white feminists" are incapable of grappling with post-decolonization and antiracist critiques. The intense engagement in the 1970s of many French feminists with such critiques suggests a more complicated and less easily remedied genealogy for contemporary ideological conflicts.

52. Des immigrés toujours solidaires Nour, Pascal, Kamel, Lakhdar, Pascal, "Topographie d'une agression caractérisée," *Libération* (14 March 1979), 19.

53. This was very visible in the 1995 debate that took place in the pages of the influential journal *Le débat* between the American feminist historian of France Joan W. Scott and the French historian of the 1789 Revolution and republicanism Mona Ozouf. See esp. Éric Fassin, "L'empire du genre," *L'homme* 187 (2008), 375–392.

54. Christine Delphy et al., "Genre à la française? Débat entre Christine Delphy et Pascale Molinier, animé par Isabelle Clair et Sandrine Rui," *Sociologie* 3, no. 3 (2012), 299–316; Sarah Jacob-Wagner, "Le débat sur le féminisme 'à la française' dans le contexte de l'affaire DSK," *Actes du colloque étudiant féministe* (Laval: Université Laval, 2013), accessible online.

The Erotics of Algerian
Difference, 1979/2016

When Mexico sends its people, they're not sending their best . . . They're sending people that have lots of problems, and they're bringing those problems with [sic] us. They're bringing drugs. They're bringing crime. They're rapists.

—Donald J. Trump (2015)[1] لو صو ,

Throughout the 1960s and 1970s, French people grappled with what contemporaries named the sexual revolution, which upended potent presumptions about how sex, sexuality, and gender should be organized and lived. In their attempts to make sense of these changes, many activists and commentators consistently invoked Algerian histories and spoke of Arab men, and they did so from widely varied perspectives. The Algerian revolution had forced the image of the heroic Algerian man into French discussions, and post–May '68 interest in the category of the "immigrant worker" and the promise of "the Arab revolution" gave this model new life through the 1970s. Across these years, references to the Algerian revolution had offered tools to French left-wing radicals, approaches and arguments that had already defeated the same powerful, imperialist, and capitalist state and system that they aspired to change. The heroic Algerian man, the newest incarnation of revolutionary resistance, had embodied that post-decolonization vision. By 1979, "Arab" models had lost much of their cachet. Intense debates within the left about how to respond to concerns about male sexual violence against women and girls exemplified and intensified this devel-

---

1. Michelle Ye Hee Lee, "Donald Trump's false comments connecting Mexican immigrants and crime," *Washington Post*, July 8, 2015.

opment. Algerian lessons now sowed discord, even as they still entranced French right-wing extremists.

Something sputtered to a close in the late 1970s. Yet the coordinates that "the Arab man" had oriented in French understandings since 1962 did not go away. Many French people continued to think with and invoke the erotics of Algerian difference. What disappeared was a deeply historicized and explicitly political version of "Arabophile" Orientalism; the model of the heroic Algerian man was no longer invoked as a source of solutions to problems for the French left, especially for sex radicals and feminists or, indeed, for France. By 1979, more broadly, the particular post-1962 focus on men rather than women and, in that discussion, on masculinity rather than effeminacy had blurred. It did so in conjunction with the reemergence of the place of women and female sexuality as the organizing coordinates around which Western discussions of the so-called Orient turned. The question of Islam, too, emphatically surged back into French debates, which now included references to a threatening "Islamic revolution" far more frequently than they did to any type of inspirational "Arab revolution."

In part because of this dynamic, the post-1962 demonization of Arab men on the far right continued to grow in force, but also in new directions. In the mid-1960s, ultranationalist intellectuals had theorized the utility of "awakening" French people to the threat of "Arab invasion," with a particular focus on the menace of sexual victimization. These same rallying cries did not only prove usable in discussions that centered on women, female sexuality, and Islam; after 1979 they opened up new connections to political movements and intellectuals with roots in the post-1968 new left. By 1989, the first of many public controversies around the so-called Muslim veil would see these rhyzomes germinate; they continue to blossom today.

To clarify some of the connections between then and now, the following pages will first sketch how, in early 1979, French discussions of Iran displaced questions of Arabs onto concerns about Islam. This shift in focus fortuitously opened escape routes out of the conundrums inspired by "the Arab man" that had so troubled leftist debates. Current debates among historians about the late 1970s, European politics, and "history," the next section proposes, need to take this history of 1979 into account. The final pages turn to very recent developments on the French far right, to suggest how attention to 1979 as a tipping point makes visible the ways in which some newly influential ultranationalists—notably the writer Renaud Camus and the politician Marine Le Pen—have successfully synthesized post-1962 and post-1968 concerns.

1979: From the "Arab" to the "Islamic" Revolution

French responses to the victory of the Iranian revolution, and the establishment of the Islamic Republic of Iran that quickly followed it, recircuited sexualized Orientalist themes in France. Shortly after the 11 February 1979 collapse of the regime of Shah Reza Pahlavi, the revolutionary leadership embraced restrictions on women's public liberties as well as the violent repression of homosexuality. This, at least, was how French descriptions at the time interpreted Iranian developments: this interpretation sparked a debate that helped place Islam (and not, in theory, "Arabs") at the center of many French discussions. A 9 March 1979 article in *Libération* informed readers that "fifty thousand Iranian women took to the streets to stop the Revolution from sending them back to the Middle Ages." The protest had taken place on 8 March (International Women's Day) in Teheran, Iran's capital. "The impressive success of their demonstration," *Libération* noted, "came despite attacks from Muslim fanatics, whose slogan captures their philosophy: '[Wear] the veil or [suffer] a beating.'" The author of the article immediately made clear the extensive implications of what was happening: "This moral order . . . also includes summary executions of deviants, homosexuals among others." These were terms that resonated with lessons that sexual liberationists had celebrated over the course of the 1970s.[2]

In the French press, what was immediately at stake in Iran's takeover by "revolutionary" Islam was liberty of self-expression for women and homosexuals, for the rights and possibilities that, in France, radical feminist and gay rights organizations had forced into public debate since 1968. Most of the key reforms that ultimately would end legal discrimination against homosexuality or women, or even define rape as a crime against the victim (rather than against male honor), had yet to become part of French law. Still, by 1979, the time already had come for French feminists, gay liberationists, and their allies to teach the Iranians rather than to learn from them, or at least to use French lessons to identify which Iranians to support. In mid-March, *Libération* announced a Parisian protest against what was happening in Iran: "The route followed will be symbolic, as it will go from the plaza in front of Notre Dame (departure 6 p.m.) to the [Paris] Mosque." Symbolically, this would allow the demonstrators "to criticize at least two religions, the Catholic version being no more liberatory for

2. M. A. Iran: "Le foulard ou la raclée," *Libération* (9 March 1979), 1. On the following, see esp. Janet Afary and Kevin B. Anderson, *Foucault and the Iranian Revolution: Gender and the Seductions of Islamism* (Chicago: University of Chicago Press, 2010), 106–137.

women than the Muslim."[3] The front page of the first issue of *Le Gai pied*, a new magazine that targeted gay readers, announced that "some 700 women and 300 homosexuals (female and male) . . . protested against the 'new Islamic law' that sends women back to their ancestral oppression and invokes religion to condemn homosexuals." The marchers had embraced a campy rallying cry that joined Arabic and French catchphrases: "Inch'allah [if God wills it], gay gay gay, the homos will be saved." The broader target of monotheistic religions in general motivated the chant "Priests, mullahs [a term for Shi'a Muslim clergy], same struggle [*même combat*]." It was a clear effort to speak across boundaries rather than reinforce them. Despite the work done to focus on religion in general, the larger discussion quickly narrowed in on Islam.[4]

The criticisms of Islam that coalesced in early 1979 immediately resituated certain references to Algeria. Numerous French commentators on Iran noted that the FLN's revolution, too, had been Islamic in inspiration, even if post-1962 observers had largely ignored this aspect (it had been central to French anti-FLN propaganda during the war). Just days after the Shah fled Iran, a feminist journalist turned to recent history to argue that "everywhere that the Koran has triumphed in conjunction with a nationalist revolution (Algeria, Iraq, Libya)," the freedoms Stéphanie Gallicher associated with both modernity and feminist struggles had disappeared, as the new regimes imposed new or stricter limitations on women.[5] Writing two months later, an editorial in a feminist publication regretted that "we rediscover, in an exacerbated fashion here in Iran, the unfortunately classic situation where women, who nourished a revolution with their energies, become its first victims." The article gave one example of this "classic situation": Algeria.[6] "The Arab revolution" had been a source of inspiration for the French far left and feminists in the 1970s, notably via invocations of Algeria. The argument that Arab developments now needed to be reinterpreted as Muslim explained why distance was necessary.

By mid-March, Kate Millett organized an international group of well-known feminists—including a number of French women such as Simone de Beauvoir—for an emergency trip to Iran. Millett, the internationally ac-

3. "Symbole: Ce soir à Paris manifestation de solidarite avec les femmes iraniennes," *Libération* (16 March 1979), 8.

4. "Être homo en Iran, c'est partir les pieds devant," *Le Gai pied* 1 (April 1979), 1.

5. Stéphanie Gallicher, "Le voile retombera-t-il sur les Iraniennes?" *F. Magazine* 13 (February 1979), 48–49.

6. "'Le vêtement de la révolution pour les femmes, c'est le voile': Iran," *Le temps des femmes* 4 (May 1979), 8–10.

claimed American author of *Sexual Politics* (1970), did so in response to an invitation from Iranian women, and against a backdrop of Western concerns.[7] On their return to Paris, the feminist journalist Marie Odile Delacour sharply criticized Millett's analysis of the situation of women in Iran, a critique she grounded in the observation that "this was [Millett's] first stay in an Islamic country. For a Western woman, this encounter with Islam always produces an astonishing shock." In Delacour's reading, Millett's failure to take account of this "shock" explained "an overly 'simplistic' interpretation, overly reductive." She argued that Millett had ignored the radically different situation that Islam created. When a French journalist at the Paris press conference had asked, "What do Iranian women think of Islam?" Millett shot back: "What do you think of Christianity?" Millett's suggestion that the situation women faced in Teheran could be paralleled with what they faced in Paris rang with the slogans of the Notre Dame de Paris to Paris Mosque protests. Delacour found such equivalences wanting; she believed that Islam explained what was going wrong for women in Iran, as it did in other places, too. She singled out Algeria. Delacour argued against relativistic generalities, and for a recognition that certain dangers mattered more. Her analysis recalls Gisèle Halimi's warning, which the lawyer had made in a different context, that "When we accept the whip for women, we accept that the cudgel can be applied to any oppressed peoples." (The left-wing and feminist lawyer was referring to the general phenomenon of fascism, of course, and not Islam.)[8]

This urgent discussion centering on women and Islam overlapped with one about Islam and homosexuality, also tethered to Iranian events. In mid-March, Marc Kravetz, *Libération*'s reporter in Iran, took to the daily's pages to comment on what he termed an "odd demonstration" that, as his newspaper had earlier announced, had taken place on 16 March 1979, "from Notre Dame de Paris to the big Mosque." French demonstrators had proclaimed, Kravetz wrote, "their 'support' for the 'struggle of Iranian women' and protested against the situation the new Iranian regime imposes on women and the 'public executions of homosexuals.'" Kravetz

7. On this trip, see Claudine Mulard, "Téhéran, mars 1979, avec caméra et sans voile," *Les Temps modernes* 5 (2010), 161–177.

8. Marie Odile Delacour, "Kate Millett (se) raconte . . . ," *Libération* (26 March 1979), 16; Halimi, "Extrait de la plaidoirie." Two years later, Delacour would coauthor a book on "the Grenoble Affair," a 1979 trial for pimping (with Germaine Aziz, *Cinq femmes à abattre* [Paris: Stock 2, 1981]). She then coedited the writings of Isabelle Eberhardt, a European female adventurer in late-nineteenth-century Algeria and the Sahara (with her husband, Jean-René Huleu).

chose his scare quotes carefully. In a footnote to the last sentence, he informed readers that "news reports from Iranian sources do not describe the execution of 'homosexuals' per se but of men charged with homosexual pimping and sexual violence."[9] In a letter in response to Kravetz, author "The Token Radical Fairy, Lola Steel" remarked sarcastically, "I took part in the demonstration in support of Iranian women because I had heard about the 'public execution of homosexuals'; but it turns out I had it all wrong because, from what [Kravetz] knows, there have only been executions of men charged with homosexual pimping." Lola's critique of the claims Kravetz made was anchored in identity, a particular knowledge that, she implied, the journalist could not access. "In this case, we're out of luck, we faggots, because Kravetz is going to have a tough time finding an Iranian fairy willing to talk to him." Or perhaps, Lola averred, the journalist was unwilling to do what was necessary to get to the truth—"unless he visits the parks [to cruise for male sexual partners]; but that investigation might be too in-depth for him." It was clear to "we faggots," Lola insisted, that playing with terms missed what was at stake.[10] In late May, Libération journalist Annette Lévy-Willard reported that "two people have been condemned to die by the Islamic Revolutionary Court in Teheran. Yet again. And immediately executed, last Sunday. Their crime? Sodomy." In her analysis, "This time, yet again, the pretext was some vague history of the rape of adolescent boys just as with the first condemnation and the first execution. Rape or pedophilia, it's sodomy that is punishable by death in Iran. Or homosexuality." To understand and to resist, Lévy-Willard suggested, it was necessary to speak clearly and truthfully. "Since this revolution began, nine homosexuals have been executed by firing squad. And the threat has become more pressing, since five executions have taken place over the last four days."[11] Kravetz, with his emphasis on how Iranian explanations highlighted rape, pimps, and pederasty, embedded them in multiple late-1970s French discussions. These discussions, as this book has suggested, had fixated on complicated and difficult definitions and raised many questions about claims anchored in identities. In the face of reports from Iran, the intense effort in which so many feminists and "revolutionary homosexuals" had engaged—and still did, in early 1979—to grapple with the

9. Marc Kravetz, "Une mission d'information féministe en Iran aujourd'hui," Libération (19 March 1979), 7.

10. La pédale radicale de service, Lola Steel, "En Iran autant qu'ailleurs," Libération (28 March 1979), 19.

11. Annette Lévy-Willard, "2 homosexuels fusillés à Teheran," Libération (29 May 1979), 7.

complicated intersection of empire, racism, and the struggle for liberation withered. Iran brought clarity. "Occident" or "Orient," freedom or feudalism, which side were you on?

"Death to the Traitor": Foucault, the Islamic Revolution, and the French Left

It was therefore hardly surprising that the French left's early-1979 unease about Iranian developments focused on Michel Foucault. The philosopher was one of the numerous leftist intellectuals who, before the fall of the Shah, had been entranced by what the Iranian revolution seemed to reveal about the world. His take garnered particular attention, as the Italian newspaper *Corriere della sera* sent him to report on events, and what he wrote circulated widely. In the broadest terms, what interested the author of *La volonté de savoir* (*The Will to Know*), as he told two journalists who interviewed him in late 1978, was that the Iranians "have a different regime of truth than ours." This mattered because "ours . . . is quite specific, even though it has become quasi-universal." From this perspective, the political upheaval in Iran revealed a different way to analyze the world—arguments, approaches, forms of action—which might offer even those situated in the so-called West new ways to think. "Regime of truth" was a category Foucault often used to insist on the particularities and the limits—chronological and geographic, but also social—of the ways of determining truth and falsehood that his historical work sought to map.[12] There was, this approach emphasizes, more than one "regime of truth," in the present just as in the past (and as there would be in the future). In this interview, as so often elsewhere, Foucault identified two such regimes, alongside the one he claimed to recognize during his brief 1978 visit to Iran. In the ancient world, he said, "the Greeks had theirs." In the present day, he proposed, "the Arabs of the Maghreb have another one."[13] By early 1979, however, political and philosophical claims linked to such regimes of truth—especially that of "the Arabs of the Maghreb," which had been

12. Ian Almond, *The New Orientalists: Postmodern Representations of Islam from Foucault to Baudrillard* (London: IB Tauris, 2007), 22–41. See also Behrooz Ghamari-Tabrizi, "'When Life Will No Longer Barter Itself:' In Defense of Foucault on the Iranian Revolution," in *A Foucault for the 21st Century: Governmentality, Biopolitics and Discipline in the New Millennium*, ed. Sam Binkley and Jorge Capetillo (New Castle, UK: Cambridge Scholars Publishing, 2009), 270–290.

13. Claire Brière and Pierre Blanchet, "L'esprit d'un monde sans esprit: Entretien avec Michel Foucault," in *Iran: La révolution au nom de Dieu* (Paris: Seuil, 1979), 227–241.

oft invoked in post-1962 left-wing debates—no longer had much place in France.

In August 1979, Foucault explained to a journalist for a Lebanese newspaper that it was important to make comparisons between the "uprisings of homosexuals in the United States" and the "massive uprisings that can happen in a Third World country." Foucault insisted that while such a comparison "can seem ridiculous . . . I would say no, it is not ridiculous." He did so even as France's Iran debate still raged, and arguments that the Islamic revolution was best understood in terms of its rejection of the rights of homosexuals and women had come to dominate discussions on the left. As he stated, one role of the intellectual is "to demonstrate how much the reality we live in, which they tell us is obvious and straightforward, is actually fragile." Others disagreed.[14]

In early April 1979, an article by the philosopher Guy Hocquenghem in the newspaper *Libération* reported that Foucault had been "attacked in his home," a "beating" that Hocquenghem blamed on the context: in the heat of an intense debate "among intellectuals and in the press . . . about Iran," Hocquenghem deduced, "something has gone decidedly wrong." It seems not to be true that Foucault was beaten up in April 1979, at least not in the conditions this article describes. Still, the report of a physical attack on Foucault because of his analyses of the Iranian revolution is a striking metaphor for the end of the history that this book analyzes. Hocquenghem referenced a particularly cutting attack against Foucault and others who had shown sympathy for the Iranian revolution in the left-wing *Le matin de Paris*, which had the outraged title "What Could Philosophers Be Thinking?"[15] Hocquenghem's article in *Libération* grouped the broader attacks on Foucault's writings on Iran under the title "Death to the Traitor." For the radical gay philosopher, what drove the critics was "something that doesn't necessarily have a direct connection to the 'content' of [Foucault's] claims" about Iran, "but which is more in the domain of a generalized— even hysterical—guilt trip, which makes it impossible to exchange information, to discuss." References to history, in Hocquenghem's interpretation of the attacks on Foucault, could no longer be a means to open new possibilities to think. "Any reflection on this subject [the Iranian revolution]," instead, required "immediate judgment on charges of treason and

---

14. Foucault, "Il ne peut pas y avoir de sociétés sans soulèvements."

15. Claudie and Jacques Broyelle, "A quoi rêvent les philosophes ?" *Le matin* 646 (24 March 1979), 13.

of countertreason before the docket of History."[16] Even if no real blood was shed, this war of words suggests how the quite peripheral involvement of France and some French intellectuals in the Iranian revolution further marginalized efforts to think with the very densely entwined history of Algeria and France.

When the "Muslim Woman" Displaced the "Arab Man"

In broad strokes, we might say that early-1979 French discussions about "Muslim women" and about "sodomy that is punishable by death in Iran . . . or homosexuality," made it easier to let leftist confusion about "the Arab man" fade from view. For example, it became easier to separate discussions of the "uprisings of homosexuals in the United States" from those about the "massive uprisings that can happen in a Third World country," despite the tight links that previous commentators had noted. Over the course of the 1960s and 1970s, attention to Arab men had constantly summoned French histories, notably those linked to Algeria, as this book has detailed. To speak of Islam, and especially of "Muslim women," offered grounds seemingly clear of inconvenient histories of colonial domination, racist violence, and the suffering of the "immigrant worker" or "the colonized." This was inaccurate, but this is how it seemed. It seemed that way in part because, as far-right reactions to May '68 and leftist responses to feminist antirape activism showed, it remained easy to dismiss the political importance of women's actions and histories—and also in part because it had become less important to take imperialism and anticolonialism seriously.[17]

Between Heroes and Victims: 1979 and the Writing of History

The disappearance of Arab models from French efforts to challenge traditional sexual and gender norms coincided with the late 1970s crisis in Western Third-Worldism.[18] Many historians link the latter to a crisis of rev-

---

16. Guy Hocquenghem, "Tabassage. Haro sur le traître: Michel Foucault agressé à son domicile," *Libération* (4 April 1979), 8.

17. On the subsequent emergence of the "Islamic veil" in French debates, see Joan W. Scott, *The Politics of the Veil* (Princeton, NJ: Princeton University Press, 2007). Jim House identifies a similar shift in French discussions of the massacre of Algerian civilians by the French police in Paris at the end of the Algerian war, an event that took place around 17 October 1961. See Jim House and Neil MacMaster, *Paris 1961. Algerians, State Terror and Memory* (Oxford, UK: Oxford. University Press, 2006), 280–295.

18. In France, the 1983 book *Le Sanglot de l'homme blanc: Tiers-Monde, culpabilité, haine de soi* (*The Tears of the White Man: Compassion as Contempt*) (Paris: Seuil, 1983) came to em-

olutionary politics writ large. Radical Western observers had drawn inspiration from anticolonial militancy and, most particularly, the anticolonial "revolutionary nationalisms" that victorious movements in Algeria, Cuba, and Vietnam had embraced. Yet such utopian projects lost traction on the left, notably in late-1970s France. For French historian Henry Rousso, this helps explain a concurrent shift in why European people looked to the past. "The anti-Nazi or anticolonial struggle foregrounded, in the past, the figure of the hero (and thus of the martyr, the person who dies for a cause and sacrifices for the community)," he argues. How different it is today, in his view, when histories of the recent past "foreground the figure of the victim." Rousso insists that "the change in register is significant," for the shift in focus from hero to victim reveals—very much in the manner of what Hocquenghem saw at play around Iran and Foucault in April 1979—a "move from a political reading of the past to a moral reading." The sexual history of the "disappearance" of the heroic Algerian man adds density and detail to Rousso's argument, as does the new attention that reactions to the Iranian revolution catalyzed about the "Muslim woman" and martyred homosexuals in French and European discussions.[19] In a move parallel to Rousso's, a number of Anglophone historians of France recently have identified 1977 as a turning point when the goal of revolution shifted definitively to a focus on "human rights" or "ethics," which took individual possibilities, rather than any collective aspirations, as the ultimate horizon that should guide political action.[20] Late–Cold War claims about Soviet and Communist "barbarism" and disillusionment with "revolutionary Third Worldism" have focused scholarship on these questions. Yet concerns and responses that emerged in opposition to Iran's triumphant

---

blematize the public discrediting of this movement. Its author was Pascal Bruckner, who had first come to public attention with the 1977 essay on the sexual revolution *Le nouveau désordre amoureux*, which he coauthored with Alain Finkielkraut (see chapter 7).

19. Henry Rousso, "Les dilemmes d'une mémoire européenne," *Recherches* (2009), 203–221.

20. See, e.g., Bourg, *From Revolution to Ethics*; Michael Scott Christofferson, *French Intellectuals against the Left: The Anti-Totalitarian Moment of the 1970s* (New York: Berghahn, 2004); Robert Horvath, "'The Solzhenitsyn Effect': East European Dissidents and the Demise of the Revolutionary Privilege," *Human Rights Quarterly* 29 (2007), 879–907, which draws particular attention to intellectuals' responses to Soviet dissident Alexandr Solzhenitsyn's recently translated *The Gulag Archipelago, 1918–1956* (*L'Archipel du Goulag, 1918–1956: Essai d'investigation littéraire*, trans. Geneviève Johannet [Paris: Seuil, 1974]). On the crisis of "Third-Worldism," see esp. Samuel Moyn, *The Last Utopia: Human Rights in History* (Cambridge, MA: Belknap Press/ Harvard University Press, 2010); also, Eleanor Davey, "French Adventures in Solidarity: Revolutionary Tourists and Radical Humanitarians," *European Review of History: Revue européenne d'histoire* 21, no. 4 (2014), 577–595.

"Islamic revolution," which engaged debates around questions of sex, gender, and sexuality, also demand attention. These discussions absorbed broad publics as well as intellectuals from all sides. It is also noteworthy that 1979 French criticisms of Islam sparked by developments in Iran have proven more durable than those that other French critics at the time made in response to the Gulag or post-decolonization mass killings in places like Cambodia or Nigeria. This is in part because, in the post–Cold War world, Islam has emerged as the touchstone for multiple explanations of supposed threats to France, the West, and beyond. Orientalist links to aberrant male sexuality, in particular, continue to obsess public discussions. In 2016, two murderous rampages committed in the name of the "Islamic State" (known variously as ISIS, ISIL, or Daesh)—one in June against a gay nightclub in Orlando, Florida, the other on 14 July (Bastille Day) against a family-friendly celebration in Nice, France—made this brutally clear. The firestorm of public anguish saw both murderers quickly labeled "closeted homosexuals," "bisexuals," and, in the French case, a prostitute for gay men. Communism or, more broadly, nonreligious "utopian politics" now musters less venom, as well as less enthusiasm.

"The Arab Invasion" and the Post-1979 Far Right

Even as new left horizons seemed to fade from the French imagination and quickly lost their Arab colors, visions of dark clouds—more specifically, the threat of darker peoples—assaulting "wholly white" France grew newly important. The post-1962 debate mapped in this book had been structured by two distinct and reductive positions, both of which claimed that meaningful differences between "the French" and "Arabs" could make sense of an ongoing upheaval that sexual questions catalyzed. Proclamations that the Arab man could point the way towards more liberated ways of living sex became difficult to imagine after 1979. This was not the case for warnings that the Arab man incarnated sexual dangers. The second position continued to stir intensely detailed fantasies as well as extreme political projects and acts. In May 2013, to take one over-the-top example, the ultranationalist theorist and writer Dominique Venner committed suicide. As explained in the first chapter of this book, Venner had founded *Europe-action* and had proposed that "masculine humanism" should ground the post-1962 reinvention of ultranationalist politics. On 22 May 2013, *Le Monde* reported that Venner "shot himself in the mouth with an automatic pistol in the middle of the day on Tuesday, just in front of the altar of Notre Dame de Paris Cathedral." In a blog post titled "The Demo of 26 May [2013] and Heidegger," published hours before this tragedy, Venner mistakenly predicted that what he ballyhooed as his martyrdom would add new depth to the mass French movement to stop the extension of marriage rights to same-sex couples. (This movement had adopted the name "The Demo for All," a play on "Marriage for All," the title of the law extending marriage rights to gay and lesbian couples). He also hoped that it would convince those engaged in this movement that they must do everything necessary to stop "Afro-Maghrebi immigration." Even beyond the marriage question, Venner's final blog post warned, "The 'Big Replacement' of the population of France and of Europe, which the writer Renaud Camus has alerted us to, is a far more catastrophic danger for our future."[21] Venner had long been panic-stricken by the supposed perils that Arabs posed to the "white race" and, most acutely, how these traps were connected to the social organization of gender and sexuality. His pre-suicide rant echoed fears registered by the far right that had coalesced in the aftermath of Algerian independence. Camus, as discussed in chapter 4, had first gained notoriety as a gay literary sensation with the publication of his novel *Tricks*, which detailed dozens of sexual encounters between the narrator and a variety of other men. Roland Barthes had hailed *Tricks* as revelatory of a new way of living sex, made possible by the sexual revolution. By 2013, some of Camus' more recent writings had inspired far-right and ultranationalist politics in France and elsewhere in Europe. Camus wrote and campaigned in favor of a deeply rooted white French people, their rich culture, and European civilization, and against the forces of cultural relativism and the "colonization" by outsiders that together threatened to pollute these precious heirlooms. Fear of Islam, Muslims, Maghrebis, and Africans, as well as Jews, are central themes in his writings.

By 2013, Renaud Camus embodied a new post-1979 synthesis among French ultranationalists. Venner's blog post can be read as an effort to hand the torch of the "nationalist revolution" to Camus—the theorist of "masculine humanism" passing the flame to the gay male theorist of the "Big Replacement," a flame stoked by the blood Venner spilled at the altar of Notre Dame Cathedral. It is a writerly scenario that echoes the contemporaneous messy takeover by Marine Le Pen of the political party her father created. Aside from Venner, the other emblematic figure of a far-right generation defined by the fight for French Algeria and against "May '68" was the far more widely known Jean-Marie Le Pen. Venner and fellow in-

21. http://www.lemonde.fr/politique/article/2013/05/22/suicide-de-dominique-venner-un-appel-au-sacrifice-pour-cambadelis_3415157_823448.html, accessed 28 April 2016. See also http://www.dominiquevenner.fr/2013/05/la-manif-du-26-mai-et-heidegger/, accessed 16 September 2014.

tellectuals of the "nationalist revolution" disdained Le Pen, even though their thematic similarities were striking, as has been foregrounded in this book. Both Venner and Jean-Marie Le Pen have now left the center stage of the far-right scene, with as much of a fracas as they could muster, although only Venner did so by choice. The theorist carefully crafted his tragic suicide. The term "politics of spectacle," so associated with French post-'68 politics, accurately describes father Le Pen's clownlike efforts to resist his marginalization and, in 2015, his expulsion from the National Front, the party he founded and led from 1972 until 2011. Yet it was his daughter who used the spectacle to take what her father had built and yet present herself as a new beginning for ultranationalist politics. In this, Marine Le Pen—a pro-gay, unmarried, "modern" woman who wrested control of the National Front from her father—and Renaud Camus together symbolize a new far-right generation. Their generation of 1979 relies on "European roots" and a fear of Islam to integrate post-1962 and post-1968 concerns into a new "feminist" and "gay-friendly" synthesis.[22]

A French "National Liberation Front Has Begun Already to Organize the Resistance"

In late January 2016, Renaud Camus spoke at a press conference to publicize a banned Parisian protest. The goal of the protest, which organizers named "Unhinged Cutthroats, Out of Control . . . Drive Islamists from France," was solidarity with Pegida, a group that had formed in Germany in early 2015 to stop the "Islamization" of Europe. Camus sought to comfort those who had not been able to take to the streets. "A National Liberation Front," he reassured anti-Muslim French people, "has begun already to organize the resistance" within France. His reference point was the Algerian FLN, which in November 1954 had embraced armed struggle—and "revolution"—to win Algerian independence. Camus was making the comparison "merely in jest," a journalist from the right-wing *Le Figaro* reassured its readers. No anti-Muslim French organization or project comparable to

22. On Le Pen's use of pro-gay and feminist arguments, see Sylvain Crépon, *Les faux-semblants du Front national: Sociologie d'un parti politique* (Paris: Presses de Sciences Po, 2015). On the larger phenomenon of what some scholars term "sexual nationalism," see, for France, Mehammed Amadeus Mack, *Sexagon: Muslims, France, and the Sexualization of National Culture* (New York: Fordham University Press, 2016); and, in theoretical terms, Puar, *Terrorist Assemblages*. On "gay-friendliness," see the work of Sylvie Tissot, e.g., "Un quartier gay-friendly? Ethnographie du Marais hétérosexuel," talk presented at the workshop "La sexualité et la Cinquième République / Sex and France since 1958," Johns Hopkins University, Baltimore, 20 September 2013.

the FLN existed.[23] This Camus episode, however, suggests the durable importance of the history this book has explored.

For many French people from widely diverse horizons, their dense Algerian past remains vivid. In multiple depictions, as in Camus's proclamations, that past is wildly distorted. Those people still assaulted by post-1962 understandings and terms about "Arab men" and sex, can often find it difficult to respond. This can be especially true for those people in France who are now often termed "Muslims" or "of Muslim culture." Part of what makes it difficult for them to respond is that so many earlier analyses of this intersection by commentators of Maghrebi origin, some of which are discussed in this book, gained so little traction. The 1960s and 1970s had offered new possibilities to people with biographical ties to the Maghreb to intervene in French discussions, and some seized these opportunities. They had, this book shows, been enjoined to speak about Arab men and sex. Still, their insistent commentary sometimes unsettled this ambient discourse, and merits critical attention. This missing intellectual patrimony has become even more difficult to access, now that post-1979 arguments about "Islam" and "Muslims" have made examinations of previous French claims about "Arabs" more difficult to parse. This book is an attempt to clarify one crucial aspect of France's Algerian history, to show why it mattered and why it faded from memory, and to do so in ways that speak to current concerns, which echo far beyond France.

A History of the Present / The Artists Already in Movement

This book thus brings historical scholarship to bear on a quite frustrating discussion, but one that has inspired several important recent interventions, notably from artists. From a perspective somewhat outside of France and Algeria, for example, the Austrian director Michael Haneke's French film *Caché* (2005) turns around the reemergence in contemporary France of an episode of anti-Algerian violence during the Algerian war. Through this prism, *Caché* delves into intimacy, childhood fantasy, and nightmares. It details how the mere presence of an Algerian boy/man still has the power to upend French domesticity and to inspire violent rage, as well as other responses that allow the film's characters to avoid grappling with the rich humanity of the Arab, who must die.

The gay French novelist Edouard Louis, to take a second example, relies

23. http://www.lefigaro.fr/actualite-france/2015/01/21/01016–20150121ARTFIG00263-en -france-si-pegida-fait-rever-certains-il-peine-a-rassembler.php.

on *autofiction* (autobiographical fiction) to delve into similar themes in *Histoire de la violence* (History of Violence, 2016), although he foregrounds questions of sex and homosexuality that Haneke leaves implicit. In his novel, Louis recounts his own rape at the hands of a young man from Algeria whom he met on Christmas Eve at Place de la République (Republic Square). The novelist's effort to take seriously the history and desires of "Réda," the character who rapes "Edouard Louis," resonates with the 1970s histories of Maï and "Brigitte" sketched out in this book. Like those histories, it is a response to the ambient potency of "anti-Arab" stereotypes.

The novel *Meursault, contre-enquête* (*The Meursault Investigation*, 2013), by the Algerian writer Kamel Daoud, offers a final example. In this international best seller, Daoud reimagines Albert Camus's *The Stranger* from the point of view of the brother and family of "the Arab"—his name, we learn, was Moussa Ould el-Assasse—who died on a beach at the hands of the existentialist classic's main character. Daoud revisits, among other topics, a foundational episode in the imaginary "war over masculinity" that had structured so many discussions during the Algerian war and since. His novel returns repeatedly to questions of desire, both sexual and amorous. Its condemnation of murder sidelines divisions between French and Algerian to focus on how this colonial tragedy affects love and human connections and makes it more difficult to get to greater truths. "The crime permanently compromises love and the possibility to love," says Haroun, the narrator, describing the murder he has committed. "Ever since, the body of each woman's body that I have encountered has very quickly lost its sensuality, its capacity to create in me the illusion of wholeness."

Each of these works sparked much critical reaction, which was overwhelmingly laudatory, and each garnered substantial audiences. The last two were best sellers, and their authors the topic of much public discussion and controversy. All three works avoid presenting their protagonists as either heroes or victims. All three also chart connections between past and present. Haneke, Louis, and Daoud each trace durable links between France and Algeria, and do so in ways that speak beyond the borders of both countries. They are part of a vigorous conversation, one from which scholars can learn, and one on which this book—anchored in archives, discourses, and often faceless actors—has drawn in an effort to analyze a foreign past while paying careful attention to how it shapes actual lives.[24]

24. Edouard Louis, *Histoire de la violence* (Paris: Seuil, 2016); Kamel Daoud, *Meursault, contre-enquête* (Arles: Editions Actes Sud, 2014), 101. I am indebted to Saïd Gahia for his work on *Caché*.

ACKNOWLEDGMENTS

A special thanks to the people at University of Chicago Press who have made the English version of this book possible, especially Doug Mitchell, Kyle Adam Wagner, Tyler McGauhey, Renaldo Migaldi, and Margaret Hivnor-Labarbera, as well as those at éditions Payot in Paris who brought the French version to fruition, above all the extraordinary Christophe Guias and Clément Baude but also Emmanuelle Roederer, Renaud Paquette, and Dominique Desfontaines. There are so many other people who as colleagues, interlocuters, and friends made this book possible. However partial, any list must include: Henry Abelove, Nada Alfiouni, Sarah al-Matari, Farid Azfar, Beth Bailey, Nora Bendaouadji, Omar Benlaâla, Eva Bischoff, Will Bishop, Jennifer Boittin, Julian Bourg, Catherine Brun, Elizabeth Buettner, Melissa K. Byrnes, Juliette Cadiot, Vincent Casanova, George Chauncey, Laryssa Chomiak, Joshua Cole, Nathan Connolly, Jean-Philippe Dedieu, Habiba Djahnine, Laurence Bertrand Dorléac, Kevin Durst (Casablanca Films), Natalie Elder, Didier Eribon, Giulia Fabbiano, Éric Fassin, Constance de Font-Reaulx, Saïd Gahia, Françoise Gaspard, Stéphane Gérard, David Halperin, Daniel Hendrickson, Dagmar Herzog, Katie Hindmarch-Watson, Antoine Idier, Caroline Izambert, Nicolas Jabko, Julian Jackson, Richard Kaye, Seth Koven, Rémi Labrusse, Tarek Lakhrissi, Élisabeth Lebovici, Gildas Le Dem, Tim Madesclaire, Viktoria Metschl, Stuart Michaels, Lydie Moudileno, Jacques Neefs, Tan Hoang Nguyen, Katrin Pahl, Robert Parks, Kevin Passmore, Bruno Perreau, Christelle Rabier, Malika Rahal, Zahia Rahmani, Michal Raz, Akim Reinhardt, Camille Robcis, Marina Rustow, Manuela Salcedo, Olivier Samour, Tiphaine Samoyault, Sandrine Sanos, Joan Wallach Scott, Claude Servan-Schreiber, Daniel Sherman, Michael Sibalis, Marc Siegel, Bonnie G. Smith, Leonard Smith, Lionel Soukaz, Sarah A. Stein, Judith Surkis, Christelle Taraud, Pierre Tévanian,

Sylvie Tissot, Mathieu Trachman, Marion von Osten, and Michelle Zancarini-Fournel.

Innumerable public and workshop discussions were also of particular importance, especially with graduate students in New Brunswick, San Diego, Paris, Ithaca, Marseille, New Haven, Ann Arbor, New York, and Cardiff. To my own graduate students, endless thanks: Sara Rahnama, Simone Gamali Stewart, Nathan Marvin, Tara Tran, Yuval Tal, Thera Naiman, David Attali, Jilene Chua, and Faisal Abu al-Hassan. I am particularly grateful to the support offered by the Institut méditerranéen de recherches avancés/l'IMéRA in Marseille, where I finished the manuscript. For their generous support and the intellectual ferment that each nourishes, I also thank the Department of Sciences Politiques at the Université Paris 8 and the ENS-rue d'Ulm, as well as the History Department, Program for the Study of Women, Gender, and Sexuality, and the Krieger School of Arts and Sciences at Johns Hopkins University. Finally, big love to my family and to Raphael Reyes.

BIBLIOGRAPHY

PUBLISHED PRIMARY SOURCES

Ahmed, *Une vie d'Algérien, est-ce que ça fait un livre que les gens vont lire?* Paris: Seuil, 1973.

Ajar, Emile [Romain Gary]. *La vie devant soi.* Paris: Mercure de France, 1975.

Alleg, Henri. *La question.* Paris: Minuit, 1958.

Alzon, Claude. *Femme mythifiée, femme mystifiée.* Paris: Presses universitaires de France, 1978.

Anonymous. "1-face à face Marthe Richard Joël Le Tac," *Il* no. 4 (January 1979), 2–6.

———. "Les boudoirs clandestins militaires," *Voix de France et du monde* (1948), 58–60.

———. "Il est commandant des pompiers; il viole une femme: 15 jours de prison," *Rouge* (9 February 1977).

———. "Jean-Marie Le Pen: Je ne ménage pas Marine, je la respecte,'" *France-soir* (18 April 2011).

———. "Même une innocente n'est pas à l'abri de la traite des Blanches," *Noir et blanc* (7 December 1962), 808–809.

———. "Des prostituées au tribunal de Grenoble." *Croissance des jeunes nations,* nos. 107–118 (1971), 85.

———. "La Prostitution," *Le crapouillot* 10 (1950), 48–52.

———. "Le Troufion 49 respecte les soldates mais les spahis ont des fatmas à la caserne." *Samedi-soir* (12 March 1949), 8.

———. "Même une innocente n'est pas à l'abri de la traite des Blanches," *Noir et blanc* (7 December 1962), 808–809.

Aron, Jean-Paul, and Roger Kempf. *Le pénis et la démoralisation de l'Occident.* Paris: Bernard Grasset, 1978.

Bastiani, Ange. *Les mauvais lieux de Paris.* Paris: André Balland, 1968.

Baudry, Pierre. "Figuratif, matériel, excrémentiel," *Cahiers du cinéma* 238–239 (May–June 1972), 75–82.

Belkacemi, Mohamed. *Belka.* Paris: Fayard, 1974.

Benayoun, Robert. "Le tango par qui le scandale arrive." *Le point,* no. 12 (11 December 1972), 8.

Bercoff, André. "Prostitution: La lutte finale?" *L'express,* no. 1175 (14 January 1974), 38–40.

Bernard, Luc. "Colmar: Le proces de la torture et du viol." *Quotidien de Paris* (21 September 1977).

Berque, Jacques. *Le Maghreb entre deux guerres.* Paris: Seuil, 1970.

———. "Recent Research on Racial Relations: The North of Africa." *International Social Science Journal* 13, no. 2 (1961), 177–196.

Bertolino, Jean. *Les Trublions.* Paris: Stock, 1969.

Bidault, Georges. *D'une résistance à l'autre.* Paris: Les Presses du siècle, 1965.

Billard, Pierre. "Un enfer nommé désir," *Journal de dimanche* (17 December 1972), 17.

Bizard, Léon Clément. *La vie des filles.* Paris: Grasset, 1934.

Bordeux, Gérard. "La révolte de Peggy (20 ans) fait découvrir un 'réseau de vice.'" *France-soir* (23 November 1963).

Bory, Jean-Louis. "Huis clos sur un matelas: Quand l'amour physique retrouve l'innocente sauvagerie des jeux enfantins." *Nouvel observateur,* no. 424 (23 December 1972), 59.

Boudjedra, Rachid. *La Répudiation.* Paris: Denoël, 1969.

———. *The Repudiation.* Translated by Golda Lambrova. Colorado Springs, CO: Three Continents Press, 1995.

———. *Topographie idéale pour une aggression caractérisée* (Paris: Denoël, 1975),

Boulin, Bertrand. *Au secours des enfants perdus.* Paris: Edition Guy Authier, 1975.

Boumaza, Béchir, Mustapha Francis, Benaïssa Souami, and Moussa Khebaïli. *La gangrène.* Paris: Minuit, 1959.

Brière, Claire, and Pierre Blanchet. "L'esprit d'un monde sans esprit: Entretien avec Michel Foucault" in Brière and Blanchet, *Iran: La révolution au nom de Dieu.* Paris: Seuil, 1979.

Brownmiller, Susan. *Against Our Will: Men, Women, and Rape* (New York: Simon and Schuster, 1975).

———. *Le Viol* (Paris: Stock, 1976).

Broyelle, Claudie, and Jacques Broyelle. "A quoi rêvent les philosophes?" *Le matin,* no. 646 (24 March 1979), 13.

Bruckner, Pascal. "Délivrez-nous du sexe." *Le débat,* no. 3 (1981), 89–105.

Bruckner, Pascal, and Alain Finkielkraut. *Le nouveau désordre amoureux: Essai.* Paris: Seuil, 1977.

Camus, Renaud. *Tricks: 33 Récits.* Paris: Mazarine, 1979.

———. *Tricks: 45 Récits.* Definitive edition. Paris: POL, 1988.

Camus, Renaud, and Tony Duparc, *Travers: Roman.* Paris: Hachette, 1978.

Castaing, Michel. "Au Sénat: La commission des lois adopte plusieurs amendements tendant à renforcer la répression du proxénétisme." *Le Monde* (13 June 1975), 14.

———. "La prostitution aujourd'hui comme hier II: Un 'mal nécessaire' pour qui?" *Le Monde* (15 March 1973), 10.

Chabalier, Hervé. "1. Notre racisme quotidian."*Le matin de Paris* (10 May 1977), 16–18.

Chapier, Henri. "'Le dernier tango à Paris': Pour une révolution des sentiments." *Combat* (14 December 1972), 6.

Chauvet, Louis. "Le dernier tango à Paris." *Le Figaro* (16 December 1972), 29.

Chevalier, Louis. *Les ruines de Subure: Montmartre, de 1939 aux années 80.* Paris: Robert Laffont, 1985.

Chraibi, Driss. *Le passé simple.* Paris: Denoël, 1954.

Christitch, Kosta. "La lutte contre le proxénétisme a Paris: Devant les mesures répressives la plupart des hôtels ont décidé de fermer leur porte a la prostitution." *Le Monde* (26 March 1968), 12.

Collomb, Henri, and P. Robert. "Le thème de l'homosexualité chez le Nord-Africain musulman." *Annales médico-psychologiques* (1958), 531–534.

Copi. *Le bal des folles*. Paris: Christian Bourgois, 1977.

———. *Les quatres jumelles, suivi de La tour de la Défense*. Paris: Christian Bourgois, 1974 [1999].

Cordelier, Jeanne. *La Dérobade*. Paris: Hachette littérature, 1976.

Cordier, Jean-Marie. "Viol: L'amorce d'un grand débat." *L'Humanité* (19 October 1977).

Coutaz, Bernard. "Des filles parmi tant d'autres." In Marie-Thérèse Boutin, Bernard Coutaz, Marc Oraison y Otros, eds, *Les "filles" victimes des hommes*. Special Issue of *Moissons nouvelles* 27 (1960), 17–20.

Crist, Judith. "Last Tango,' but Not the Last Word." *New York Magazine* (5 February 1973), 34–35.

Cypel, Sylvain. "A French Clown's Hateful Gesture." *New York Times* (23 January 2014), 27.

Daoud, Kamel. *Meursault, contre-enquête*. Arles: Editions Actes Sud, 2014.

Dallayrac, Dominique. *Dossier homosexualité*. Paris: Robert Laffont, 1968.

———. *Dossier prostitution*. Paris: Robert Laffont, 1966.

———. *Les Maladies vénériennes: Interviewes, enquêtes et documentation*. With the collaboration of Geneviève Tuduri. Editions Publications premieres, 1971.

Daniel, Marc, and André Baudry. *Les homosexuels*. Paris: Casterman, 1973.

De Gasperi, Anne. "Bertolucci: 'Un poème sur la sexualité.'" *Le Figaro* (16 December 1972), 29.

De Lesseps, Emmanuèle. "Sexisme et racisme: "Ce n'est rien, c'est une femme qui se noie." *Questions féministes*, no. 7 (February 1980), 95–102.

Deleuze, Gilles. "Lettre à Michel Cressole," *La quinzaine littéraire* 161 (1 April 1973), 17–19.

———. "Lettre à un critique sévère," in, Deleuze, *Pourparlers*: 11–23. Paris: Minuit, 1990.

Deleuze, Gilles, and Félix Guattari. *Capitalisme et schizophrénie*: Volume 1. *L' anti-Œdipe*. Paris: Minuit, 1972.

Delpêche, René. *L'hydre aux mille têtes: Un document sur la prostitution à Paris*. Paris: Editions Karolus, 1961.

Dermenghem, Emile. Le pays d'Abel: *Le Sahara des Ouled Naïl, des larbaa et des amour*. Paris: Gallimard, 1960.

Deslandes, André. *Le soleil gris*. Paris: Gallimard, 1962.

Duburg, François. "Tout! Ou rien?" *Lutte ouvrière* (4 May 1970), 13.

Durban, Pierre. *La psychologie des prostituées*. Paris: Librairie Maloine 1969.

Duron, Michel. "Le dernier tango à Pairs (Une débauche de talent)." *Canard enchaîné* (20 December 1972).

Duvert, Tony. *Journal d'un innocent*. Paris: Minuit, 1976.

Eck, Marcel. *Sodome, essai sur l'homosexualité*. Paris: Fayard, 1966.

Editors. "A propos de la demission de Pierre Baudry." *Cahiers du cinéma*, no. 245–246 (1973), 88–90.

Editors. "Et pourtant, elle tourne." *Lettres nouvelles* 51 (July-August 1957), 178.

Ellul, Jacques. "Le viol et le desir." *Le Monde* (3 January 1978), 2.

Esslin, Martin. *The Theatre of the Absurd* (London: Taylor & Francis, 1968).

F., Br. "Le gala houleux de la prostitution: Trois mille personnes aux assises nationales." *Le Monde* (20 November 1975).

Fargier, Marie-Odile. "Dossiers de l'écran, le viol en question." *Rouge* (18 October 1977), 6.

Figueras, André. *Les origines étranges de la Ve République.* Paris: Les presses du Mail, 1962.

Fouletier-Smith, Nicole M. "Les Nord-Africains en France: Réalités et représentations littéraires." *French Review* 51, no. 5 (April 1978), 683–691.

Front homosexuel d'action révolutionnaire. *Rapport contre la normalité.* Paris: Champs Libres, 1971.

Genet, Jean. *Les paravents.* Décines, France: M. Barbezat, 1961.

Glady, Simon. "Les paravants de Genet: Vent d'histoire et inversion des valeurs." *Aux écoutes du monde* (14 April 1966), 31.

Glazounov, Gabriel. "Opprimées oppressantes: Le livre de l'oppression des femmes." *Politique hebdo* (nouvelle formule), no. 6 (1971), 20.

———. "Révolutionnaires par la bande? Suffit-il de se faire sodomiser par un Arabe pour être Marxiste-léniniste?" *Politique hebdo* (nouvelle formule), no. 6 (1971), 26.

Goytisolo, Juan. *Realms of Strife: The Memoirs of Juan Goytisolo, 1957–1982.* Translated by Peter Bush. San Francisco: North Point Press, 1990.

Grall, Xavier. *La génération du djebel.* Paris: Éditions du Cerf, 1962.

———. "Une moisson algérienne." *Le cri du monde,* no. 13 (December 1967), 52–53.

Granotier, Bernard. *Les travailleurs immigrés en France.* 5th ed. Paris: François Maspero, 1979.

Groult, Benoîte. *Ainsi soit-elle.* Paris: Grasset, 1975.

Groupe de libération homosexuel, politique et quotidian. *Dossier de presse sur l'homosexualité.* Éditions librairie de la Jonquière, 1977.

Grunfeld, Jean-Francois. *J'emporterai pas ma coquille d'escargot à la pointe de mes souliers: Roman.* Paris: Le Sagittaire, 1979.

Guénin, Pierre. *Le sexe à trois faces.* Paris: Éditions SAN, 1975.

Guyotat, Pierre. *Carnets de bord, Vol. 1 (1962–1969).* Edited by Valérian Lallement. Paris: Lignes & Manigestes, 2005.

———. *Tombeau pour cinq cent mille soldats, sept chants.* Paris: éditions Gallimard, 1967.

———. *Vivre.* Paris: Denoel, 1984.

Halimi, Gisèle. "Extrait de la plaidoirie de Me Gisèle Halimi [procès de Colmar]." *Rouge* (22 September 1977), 8.

———, ed. *Viol, le procès d'Aix-en-Provence.* Preface by Gisèle Halimi. Paris: Gallimard, 1978.

Hanisch, Carol. "Problèmes actuels: Éveil de la conscience féminine. Le 'personnel est aussi 'politique.'" *Partisans,* no. 54–55 (July-Oct. 1970), 61–64.

Hocquenghem, Guy. *L'amour en relief.* Paris: Albin Michel, 1982.

———. *La Beauté du métis: Réflexions d'un francophobe.* Paris: Ramsay, 1979.

———. *La Colère de l'agneau.* Paris: Albin Michel, 1986.

"Je m'appelle Guy Hocquenghem: J'ai 25 ans . . ." *Nouvel observateur,* no. 374 (10 January 1972), 32–33.

———. *Love in Relief.* Translated by Michael Whisler. New York: SeaHorse Press, 1986.

Jamet, Fabienne. *One two two (122, rue de Provence).* Paris: Olivier Orban 1975.

Kael, Pauline. "The Current Cinema: Tango." *New Yorker* 48, no. 36 (28 October 1972), 130–138.

Khelifa, Messamah. "La Goutte d'Or." *Esprit* nouvelle série, no. 3 (March 1979), 15–22.

Khelil, Mohand. *L'exil kabyle: Essai d'analyse du vécu des migrants.* Paris: L'Harmattan, 1979.

Krafft-Ebing, Richard. *Psychopathia sexualis, avec recherches spéciales sur l'inversion sexuelle.*

Translation from the 8th German edition by Émile Laurent and Sigismond Csapo. Paris: Carré, 1895.

Kunstlé, Marc, and Jean-Claude Lamy. *Notre-Dame des Esclandres*. Paris: Presses de la Cité, 1973.

Internationale situationniste de Strasbourg. *De la Misère en Milieu Etudiant: Considérée sous ses aspects économique, politique, psychologique, sexuel et notamment intellectuel et de quelques moyens pour y remédier*. Strasbourg: L' Internationale situationniste, 1967.

Lacroix, Hugo. "Columbarium neon." *Cahiers critiques de la littérature*, no. 2 (December 1976), 45–55.

Lanoux, Armand. *Paris en forme de Coeur*. Paris: Fayard, 1965.

———. *La Physiognomie de Paris*. Paris: Fayard, 1954.

Lantier, Jacques (pseud.). *La cité magique: Sexualité et magie en Afrique noire*. Paris: Fayard, 1972.

Lartéguy, Jean. *Les centurions*. Paris: Presses de la Cité, 1960.

Le Brun, Annie. *Lachez-tout*. Paris: La Sagittaire, 1977.

Le Vaillant, Yvon. "La guerre des gangs sur la côte: Mais à Nice, le milieu est souvent de droite." *Nouvel observateur* (6 May 1965), 13–15.

Louis, Edouard. *Histoire de la violence*. Paris: Seuil, 2016.

Mabire, Jean. *Les Hors-la-loi*. Paris: Robert Laffont, 1968.

Maï. "Un viol si ordinaire, un impérialisme si quotidian." *Les Temps modernes*, no. 333–334 (1974), 1872–1889.

Mauriac, Claude. "Brando comme on ne l'avait jamais vu." *L'express*, no. 1118 (11 December 1972), 103.

Mauriac, François. *Bloc Notes*, Vol. 4, 1965–1967. Paris: Seuil, 1993.

Maurin, Francois. "Au seuil de l'abîme: Le dernier tango à Paris." *L'Humanité* (16 December 1972), 6.

Mazeran, Jean-Claude. "Non, mon film n'est pas pornographique,' affirme le metteur en scène." *Le journal de dimanche* (17 December 1972), 17.

Mellen, Joan. "Sexual Politics and 'Last Tango in Paris.'" *Film Quarterly* 26, no. 3 (1973), 9–19.

Mercier, Jean-Maurice. "'Hitler avait raison: Des attentats contre des cafés nord-africains aux souvenirs de Nazisme." *Le Monde* (23 November 1969).

Millett, Kate. *La politique du mâle*. Translated by Elisabth Gile. Paris: Stock, 1971.

———. *Sexual Politics*. New York: Doubleday, 1970.

Mollard, Georges-Richard. "La prostitution en France, aujourd'hui: Un signe de mépris, un temps d'hypocrisie." *La revue nouvelle*, no. 4 (April 1974): 712–726.

Monod, Jean. Les Barjots: Essai d'ethnologie des bandes de jeunes. Paris: Juilliard, 1968.

Montaldo, Jean. *Les corrompus*. Paris: La Table ronde, 1971.

Mortemart, Germaine. *Les passions acquises: Quand le troisième sexe n'a plus de légende*. Lyon: Self-published, 1964.

Navarre, Yves. "Les dernières clientes: Pièce en deux actes et 21 scènes," in Navarre, *Theatre 2*, 139–224. Paris: Flammarion, 1976.

Nevers, Jean. "VII. Les filles à soldats de Fréjus." *Qui? Police*, no. 62 (28 August 1947), 4–5.

Perrault, Gilles. *Les parachutistes*. Paris: Seuil, 1961.

Piaitier, Jacqueline. "La loi de 1946 a-t-elle porté atteinte à la prostitution? III: Les organisateurs du marché." *Le Monde* (5 September 1957).

Philipon, Odette. *Esclavage sexuel, torture, amour*. Paris: Téqui, 1976.

Porthault, Pierre. *Être ou ne plus être*. Paris: Self-published, 1971.

Revel, Renaud. "Nouvelle crise à France-soir: Pougatchev, qui veut du trash, menace de virer le patron de la rédaction." Immédias. Le blog de Renaud Revel (11 August 2010), accessed 15 September 2014. http://blogs.lexpress.fr/media/2010/08/11/nouvelle_crise_a_france_soir_p/.

Roberti, Jacques. *Maisons de société: Choses vues*. Paris: Fayard, 1927.

Rothenbourg, Marcia, Margaret Stephenson, Gille Wittig, and Monique Wittig. "Combat pour la libération de la femme: Par delà la libération-gadget, elles découvrent la lutte des classes." *L'idiot international*, no. 6 (May 1970), 16.

Roussel, André. "Les problèmes de Santé publique posés par la migration des travailleurs." *Bulletin de l'INSERM* 21, no. 5 (1966), 1121–1138.

Saâdi, Yacef. *Souvenirs de la bataille d'Alger: Décembre 1956–septembre 1957*. Paris: René Julliard, 1962.

Sacotte, Marcel. *La prostitution*. Paris: Buchet/Chastel, 1959.

Saladin (Slimane Zeghidour, pseud.). *Les migrations de Djeha: Les nouveaux immigrés*. Claix: Éditions la pensée sauvage, 1979.

Salah, Ali. *Communauté algérienne dans le département du Nord*. Lille: Éditions universitaire, 1973.

Samuels, Victor J. *The Anal Compulsion in Homosexuality*. North Hollywood, CA: Brandon House, 1968.

Sandier, Gilles. "Un théâtre d'agression." *Magazine littéraire*, no. 27 (March 1969),10–15.

Scelles, Jean. "Contre la traite des femmes." *Le Monde* (27–28 September 1959), 13.

———. "Les filles de France alimentent les "maisons"en Afrique du Nord." *Moissons nouvelles*, no. 9 (October-December 1953), 3.

———. "La psychologie des travailleurs manuels nord-africains en France, 2e partie." *Bulletin Auxilia* supplément (March-April 1960), 4.

Scelles, Jean, et al. "Proposition tendant à inviter le Gouvernement à fermer en Algérie les maisons dites de tolérance en y appliquant effectivement la loi du 13 avril 1946 et à développer le dépistage et le traitement des maladies vénériens contagieux et la rééducation des prostituées." Annexe n° 164, Assemblée de l'Union Française, 1951 (session of 22 May 1951), 2,465.

———. "Proposition tendant à renforcer la lutte contre le proxénétisme en Algérie." Annexe n° 223, Assemblée de l'Union Française, 1951 (session of 30 August 1951), 3.

Sebbar, Leïla. *On tue les petites filles*. Paris: Stock, 1978.

Service départemental des renseignements généraux. "Photocopie d'un tract qui circule actuellement à Alger; n. 11067 RG.I" (Algiers, 28 November 1961), 1+tract, in Archives nationales d'outre-mer, Aix-en-Provence, France: 91/3F/59.

Situationist International. *On the Poverty of Student Life: A Consideration of Its Economic, Political, Sexual, Psychological and Notably Intellectual Aspects and of a Few Ways to Cure It*. New York: Situationist International, 1967.

Solat, Michèle. "Les féministes et le viol. III. Coment lutter." *Le Monde* (20 October 1977), 12.

Tallenay, Jean-Louis. "'Le dernier tango à Paris': Triste voyeurism." *Télérama* (20 December 1972), 73.

Venner, Dominique. *Pour une critique positive*. Paris: Saint-Juste, 1964.

Vitale, Bruno Roger. "Arab Revolt." *One* 6 (1958), 1–9.

Vivien, Robert-André. "Le proxénétisme nord africain et la rébellion algérienne: 100 million de francs de contribution au terrorisme!" In *Solution au problème de la prostitution.* Lille: Éditions SLEL, 1960.

Zemmour, Eric. *Le suicide français.* Paris: Albin Michel, 2014.

TELEVISION BROADCASTS

"Bloc note: Viol." *Un sur cinq,* Channel 2, broadcast 1 November 1977.

"Comment peut-on être raciste." *Mi-Figue, mi-raison,* Channel 2, broadcast 13 June 1979.

"Gisèle Halimi." *Midi,* Channel 2, broadcast 21 March 1979.

"La lutte contre le proxénétisme a Paris." *Journal télévisé de 20h,* Channel 2, broadcast 24 June 1973.

"Marseille: Les nouveaux gangsters." *Cinq colonnes à la une,* Channel 2, (broadcast 1 February 1963.

"Marthe Richard et la réouverture des 'maisons closes.'"*Journal télévisé de 20h,* Channel 2, broadcast 8 August 1973.

Midi, Channel 2, broadcast 21 March 1979.

"Mise au point: Le racisme et les migrants (1ère partie)." 3rd Channel, broadcast 7 January 1973.

Les paroles et les actes. France 2, 23 June 2011.

"La prostitution est elle nécessaire?" *De vive voix,* Channel 1, broadcast 3 February 1976.

"La prostitution: Rouvrir les maisons closes?" *Les dossiers de l'écran,* A2, broadcast 13 March 1979.

"Le racisme, 1e partie." *Faire face,* Channel 1, broadcast 11 September 1961.

"Le racisme, 2e partie." *Faire face,* Channel 1, broadcast 15 September 1961.

"Le racisme ou les migrants (1ere partie)." *Mise au point,* Channel 3, broadcast 7 January 1973.

"Le racisme ou les migrants (2e partie)." *Mise au point,* Channel 3, broadcast 28 January 1973.

"Suite affaire de Marseille." *Journal télévisé de 20h,* Channel 2, broadcast 27 August 1973.

"Les travailleurs étrangers." *Journal télévisé de 20h,* Channel 2, broadcast 14 August 1970.

"Les travailleurs immigrés." *Dossiers de l'écran,* Channel 2, broadcast 21 November 1978.

"Le viol." *Journal télévisé de 20h,* Channel 1, broadcast 14 November 1978.

"Un flic et les prostituées." *Journal télévisé de 20h,* Channel 2, broadcast 24 June 1973.

"Un samedi à la goutte d'Or," director Yves Laumet, Channel 2, broadcast 29 May 1978.

FILMS

Les ambassadeurs. Directed by Naceur Ktari, 1976.

Le bougnoul. Directed by Daniel Moosmann, 1975.

Caché. Directed by Michael Haneke, 2005.

Le dernier tango à Paris. Directed by Bernardo Bertolucci, 1972.

Diabolo Menthe. Directed by Diane Kurys, 1977.

Dupont Lajoie. Directed by Yves Boisset, 1975.

L'enterrement de Mahmoud Al Hamchari. Directed by Carole and Paul Roussopoulos, 1973.

Le Fhar. Directed by Carole Roussopoulos, 1971.

Le juge et les immigrés. Directed by Carole Roussopoulos, 1980.

Kate Millett parle aux féministes de la prostitution. Directed by Carole Roussopoulos, 1975.

Le viol: Anne, Corinne, Annie, Brigitte, Josyane, Monique et les autres. Directed by Carole Roussopoulos, 1978.

Lip I Monique et christiane. Directed by Carole Roussopoulos, 1973.

Lip VI. Directed by Carole Roussopoulos, 1976.

Lip V Monique et Christiane. Directed by Carole Roussopoulos, 1976.

Maso et miso vont en bateau. Directed by Nadja Ringart, Carole Roussopoulos, and Delphine Seyrig, aka Les Insoumuses, 1975.

Munich. Directed by Carole Roussopoulos, 1972.

Prends 10000 balles et casse toi. Directed by Mahmoud Zemmouri, 1981.

Les prostituées de Lyon parlent. Directed by Carole Roussopoulos, 1975.

Race d'ép. Directed by Lionel Soukaz, 1979.

Soleil des hyènes. Directed by Ridha Behi, 1976.

Tino. Directed by Lionel Soukaz with Guy Hocquenghem, 1985.

Y a qu'à pas baiser. Directed by Carole Roussopoulos, 1973.

ARCHIVES CONSULTED

Archives de la Préfecture de Police de Paris, Paris, France (APP)

B/A 407-8
B/A 1689
DB 412
H/A 19-21

Archives départementales de la Bouche du Rhône, Marseille, France (ADBdR)

38 J/1-93
38 J/1
1650 W 1
137 W 687
208 W 3

Archives Ville de Paris (AvP)

Pérotin: 101/77/2-1 and 2; 101/77/3-7l 101/77/4- 29; 101/77/11-61 to 64.

Bibliothèque de documentation internationale contemporaine, Nanterre, France (BDIC)

(Fonds Assia Melamed) F delta rés. 696/22/1-3
(Fonds Cahiers de mai/Immigrés) F delta rés. 578/8/travailleurs immigres 1968-1975, 1-10
(Fonds Daniel Guérin) F delta 721/15/1
(Fonds Daniel Guérin) F delta 721/15/3
(Fonds Immigration en France) F delta rés. 705/1/ 3
(Fonds Immigration en France) F delta rés. 705/1/ 2
(Fonds Liliane KANDEL) F delta rés. 704
(Fonds Vive la Révolution/Archives Françoise Picq) F delta rés. 612/16

Bibliotheque Marguerite Durand, Paris

Dossiers "Viol" 1976, 1977, 1978

Centre d'accueil et de recherche des Archives nationales, Paris, France (CARAN)

F/1A /5015
4AG/532

Centre des archives contemporaines, Fontainebleau, France (CAC)

19771141/ 17
19770317/1; 19800273/61; 19800273/254; 19810568 /18; 19810202/1; 19810201/4; 19860269/10; 19860269/11; 19870056 /19-20; 19930317/16-17; 19950493 /8; 19950493 /6; 19960405/11; 19960134/12; 19960405 /1; 19960134/6

Institut Mémoires de l'édition contemporaine, Caen, France (IMEC)
ABN 32.3 FHAR (Front homosexuel d'action revolutionnaire)
COP 7 (Fonds Copi)
COP 9.3 (Fonds Copi)
GTR (Fonds Guattari) File Sur l'interdiction du numéro de *Recherches*: "Trois milliards de pervers"
GTR (Fonds Guattari) 58.29
GTR 58.30 (Fonds Guattari) Recherches réunion juidique
HAC 8745 (Fonds Hachette Livre): 5GE
RCF 53 (Fonds Christiane Rochefort)
SEL 3721.2 Marcel Marnat (Fonds Le Seuil)
SEL 3743.6 (Fonds Le Seuil)

Papiers Nelly Rouget (private collection)

Service historique de la Défénse, Vincennes, France (SHD)
1H/1735/1

PERIODICALS

Actuel (1970–1975)
Actuel: Le mensuel des années 80 (1979–1980)
L'antinorm (1972–1975)
Arcadie: Revue littéraire et scientifique (1954–1956, 1962, 1968–1975)
Les cahiers du GRIF (1973–1979)
Cahiers de Sexologie clinque (1975–1980)
Le crapouillot (1967–1972)
Don (1975–1976), became *Icognito magazine* (1977–1978)
Ecrits de Paris (1966–1970)
Femmes et mondes (1966–1979)
F. Magazine (1978–1980)
France-observateur (1961–1963), became *Nouvel observateur* (1968–1979)
Le Gai pied (1979–1980)
Gaycontacts (1978–1979)
Gay magazine (1978)
Histoires d'elles (1977–1980)
In magazine masculin (1972–1975), became *In magazine* (1975–1978)
Interlopes (1977–1979)
Libération (1973–1979)
Marie Claire (1976–1979)
Minute (1962–1969)
Moissons nouvelles (1962–1966)
Nous, les hommes (1970–1974); became *Hommes* (1974–1979)
Nouvel accord (1973–1974)
Olympe: Revue naturiste et sportive (1968–1978)
Pan! (1971–1975)
Paris-jour (1962–63)
Partisans (1968–1972)
Les pétroleuses (1974–1976)
Plexus (1979–1980)
Politique-hebdo (nouvelle formule) (1970–1972)

Rivarol (1962–1970)

Sexpol: Sexologie politique (1975–1979)

Spartacus: For Gay Men (1980)

Spartacus International Gay Guide (1973, 1975, 1977–1980)

Le temps des femmes (1978–1980)

Tout! (1970–1971)

Union (1971–1981)

SECONDARY SOURCES

Abelove, Henry. "New York City Gay Liberation and the Queer Commuters." In Henry Abelove, *Deep Gossip*, 70–88. Minneapolis: University of Minnesota Press, 2005.

———. "Some Speculations on the History of Sexual Intercourse during the Long Eighteenth Century in England." *Genders*, no. 6 (1989), 125–30.

Afary, Janet, and Kevin B. Anderson. *Foucault and the Iranian Revolution: Gender and the Seductions of Islamism.* Chicago: University of Chicago Press, 2010.

Aissaoui, Rabah. *Immigration and National Identity: North African Political Movements in Colonial and Postcolonial France.* New York: Palgrave Macmillan, 2009.

Aldrich, Robert. *Colonialism and Homosexuality.* London: Routledge, 2008.

———. *The Seduction of the Mediterranean: Writing, Art and Homosexual Fantasy.* London: Routledge, 2002.

Algazy, Joseph. *L'extrême-droite en France de 1965 à 1984.* Paris: L'Harmattan, 1989.

Ali, Tariq, and Susan Watkins. *1968: Marching in the Streets.* New York: Free Press, 1998.

Alloula, Malek. *The Colonial Harem.* Minneapolis: University of Minnesota Press, 1986.

———. *Le harem colonial: Images d'un sous-érotisme.* Paris: Slatkine, 1981.

Almond, Ian. *The New Orientalists: Postmodern Representations of Islam from Foucault to Baudrillard.* London: IB Tauris, 2007.

Altman, Dennis. *The Homosexualization of America.* Boston: Beacon Press, 1982.

Ambroise-Rendu, Anne-Claude. *Histoire de la pédophilie: XIXe–XXIe siècles.* Paris: Fayard, 2014.

———. "Un siècle de pédophilie dans la presse (1880–2000): Accusation, plaidoirie, condamnation." *Le temps des médias* 1, no. 1 (2003), 31–41.

Amrane-Minne, Danièle Djamila. *Les femmes dans la guerre d'Algérie.* Paris: Karthala, 1994.

André, Marc. "Des Algériennes à Lyon. 1947–1974." PhD diss., Université Paris 4, 2014. http://www.theses.fr/2014PA040033.

Anonymous, "Le dernier tango à Paris: La critique," *L'avant-scène cinéma*, no. 133 (February 1973), 57–58.

Audigier, François. "Le Gaullisme d'ordre des années 68." *Vingtième siècle: Revue d'histoire*, no. 116 (2012), 53–68.

Bailey, Beth. *Sex in the Heartland.* Cambridge, MA: Harvard University Press, 1999.

Bar-On, Tamir. *Where Have All the Fascists Gone?* Aldershot: Ashgate, 2007.

Barthes, Roland. *Roland Barthes.* Paris: Seuil, 1975.

———. *Sade, Fourier, Loyola.* Paris: Seuil, 1971.

———. *Sade, Fourier, Loyola.* Translated by Richard Miller. New York: Hill and Wang, 1976.

Bellil, Samira, Josée Stoquart, and Guy Birenbaum. *Dans l'enfer des tournantes.* Paris: Gallimard, 2003.

Ben Jelloun, Tahar. *La plus haute des solitudes: Misère sexuelle d'émigrés Nord-Africains.* Paris: Seuil, 1977.

Bennington, Geoffrey, and Jacques Derrida. *Jacques Derrida*. Chicago: University of Chicago Press, 1999.

Benoit, Christian. *Le soldat et la putain: Histoire d'un couple inseparable*. Paris: Edition Pierre de Taillac, 2013.

Bentahar, Mekki. *Les Arabes en France*. Rabat: Société Marocaine des Editions Réunis, 1979.

Bergeron, Francis, and Philippe Vilgier. *De Le Pen à Le Pen: Une histoire des nationaux et des nationalistes sous la ve république*. Paris: Dominique Martin Morin, 1985.

Bernard, Bernard. *Les clercs de 68*. Paris: Presses universitaires de France, 2003.

Berry, David. "'Workers of the World, Embrace!' Daniel Guérin, the Labour Movement and Homosexuality." *Left History*, no. 9 (2004), 11–43.

Berry, John, et al. "Diane Kurys," In Yvonne Tasker, ed., *Fifty Contemporary Film Directors*, 219–227. London: Routledge, 2010.

Bertrand-Dorléac, Laurence. "L'histoire croquée sur le vif." *Vingtieme siecle: Revue d'histoire*, no. 27 (1990): 110–11.

Blanchard, Emmanuel. "Le mauvais genre des Algériens." *Clio: Histoire, femmes et sociétés*, no. 27 (2008): 209–224.

———. *La police parisienne et les Algériens, 1944–1962*. Paris: Nouveau Monde, 2011.

Bloom, Joshua, and Waldo E. Martin. *Black against Empire: The History and Politics of the Black Panther Party*. Berkeley: University of California Press, 2013.

Boone, Joseph A. *The Homoerotics of Orientalism*. New York: Columbia University Press, 2014.

Borrillo, Daniel, and Eric Fassin, eds. *Au-delà du PaCS: L'expertise familiale à l'épreuve de l'homosexualité*. Presses universitaires de France, 2001.

Bourg, Julian, ed. *After the Deluge: New Perspectives on the Intellectual and Cultural History of Postwar France*. Lanham, MD: Lexington Books, 2004.

———. "Les contributions accidentelles du marxisme au renouveau des droits de l'homme en France dans l'après-68." *Actuel Marx* 32, no. 2 (2002), 125–138.

———. *From Revolution to Ethics: May 1968 and Contemporary French Thought*. Montreal: McGill-Queen's University Press-MQUP, 2007.

Branche, Raphaëlle. "Des viols pendant la guerre d'Algérie." *Vingtième siècle: Revue d'histoire*, no. 75 (September 2002).

———. *La guerre d'Algérie: Une histoire apaisée?* Paris: Seuil, 2005.

———. "La masculinité à l'épreuve de la guerre sans nom." *Clio: Histoire, femmes et sociétés*, no. 20 (2004): 111–22.

———. "La sexualité des appelés en Algérie." In Jean-Charles Jauffret, ed., *Des hommes et des femmes en guerre d'Algérie*, 402–415. Paris: Autrement, 2003.

———. "La torture pendant la guerre d'Algérie." In Mohammed Harbi and Benjamin Stora, eds., *La guerre d'Algérie, 1954–2004: La fin de l'amnésie*, 381–402. Paris: Robert Laffont, 2004.

———. *La torture et l'armée pendant la guerre d'Algérie, 1954–1962*. Paris: Gallimard, 2001.

Bristow, Edward J. *Prostitution and Prejudice: The Jewish Fight against White Slavery, 1870–1939*. Oxford: Clarendon Press, 1982.

Brun, Catherine. "Guerre couilles coupées," in Catherine Brun and Todd Shepard, eds., *Guerre d'Algérie: Le sexe outrage*, 141–159. Paris: CNRS éditions, 2016.

———. *Pierre Guyotat, essai biographique*. Paris: Flammarion, 2015.

Brunet, Jean-Paul. *Police contre FLN: Le drame d'octobre 1961*. Paris: Flammarion, 1999.

Burgnard, Sylvie. "Se regrouper, se rendre visibles, s'affirmer: L'expérience des mouvements homosexuels à Genève dans les années 1970." *Genre, sexualité & société*, no. 3 (2010).

Byrne, Jeffrey James. *Mecca of Revolution: Algeria, Decolonization, and the Third World Order.* New York: Oxford University Press, 2016.

Campbell, Caroline. *Political Belief in France, 1927–1945: Gender, Empire, and Fascism in the Croix de Feu and Parti Social Français.* Baton Rouge, LA: LSU Press, 2015.

Camus, Jean-Yves, and Nicolas Lebourg, eds. *Les droites extrêmes en Europe.* Paris: Éditions du Seuil, 2015.

Canaday, Margot. *The Straight State: Sexuality and Citizenship in Twentieth-Century America.* Princeton, NJ: Princeton University Press, 2009.

Cardon, Patrick. "'Histoire d'une revue: Le fléau social (1972–1974). Le mariage des situs et des pédés,'" 1999. http://semgai.free.fr/contenu/textes/p_Cardon_Fleau_social .html, accessed 25 October 2014.

Caserio, Robert L., Lee Edelman, Judith Halberstam, José Esteban Muñoz, and Tim Dean. "The Antisocial Thesis in Queer Theory." *PMLA* 121, no. 3 (2006), 819–28.

Cervulle, Maxime. "French Homonormativity and the Commodification of the Arab Body." *Radical History Review* 2008, no. 100 (2008), 171–79.

Chambers, Ross. "Pointless Stories, Storyless Points: Roland Barthes between 'Soirees de Paris' and 'Incidents.'" *L'esprit createur* 34, no. 2 (1994), 12–30.

Charpier, Frédéric. *Génération Occident.* Paris: Seuil, 2014.

Chauncey, George. *Gay New York: Gender, Urban Culture, and the Making of the Gay Male World, 1890–1940.* New York: Basic Books, 1994.

Chauvin, Sébastien. "Les aventures d'une 'alliance Objective': Quelques moments de la relation entre mouvements homosexuels et mouvements féministes au XXe siècle." *L'homme et la société*, no. 4 (2005): 111–30.

Chiroux, René. *L'extrême-droite sous la Ve République.* Paris: Librairie générale de droit et de jurisprudence, 1974.

Christofferson, Michael Scott. *French Intellectuals against the Left: The Antitotalitarian Moment of the 1970s.* New York: Berghahn Books, 2004.

Churchill, David S. "Transnationalism and Homophile Political Culture in the Postwar Decades." *GLQ: A Journal of Lesbian and Gay Studies* 15, no. 1 (2009), 31–66.

Cline, Sharon Elise. "Feminité à la Francaise: Femininity, Social Change and French National Identity: 1945–1970." PhD diss., University of Wisconsin–Madison, 2008.

Corbin, Alain. *Les filles des noces.* Paris: Aubier Montagne, 1978.

———. *Women for Hire: Prostitution and Sexuality in France after 1850.* Translation by Alan Sheridan. Cambridge, MA: Harvard University Press, 1990.

Coston, Henry. *Dictionnaire de la politique française.* Vol. 1. Paris: Publications Henry Coston/Librairie française, 1967.

Courrière, Yves. *La guerre d'Algérie: Les fils de la Toussaint.* Vol. 1. 4 vols. Paris: Fayard, 1968.

———. *La guerre d'Algérie. Les feux du désespoir: La fin d'un empire.* Vol. 4. 4 vols. Fayard, 1971.

———. *La guerre d'Algérie. Le temps des léopards.* Vol. 2. 4 vols. Paris: Fayard, 1969.

———. *La guerre d'Algérie. L'heure des colonels.* Vol. 3. 4 vols. Paris: Fayard, 1970.

Crépon, Sylvain. *Les faux-semblants du Front national: Sociologie d'un parti politique.* Paris: Presses de Sciences po, 2015.

Crouzières-Ingenthron, Armelle. *Le double pluriel dans les romans de Rachid Boudjedra.* Paris: Editions l'Harmattan, 2001.

Dard, Olivier, and Michel Grunewald. *Charles Maurras et l'étranger, l'étranger et Charles Maurras: L'action française–culture, politique, societé II.* Vol. 2. Bern: Peter Lang, 2009.

Dargelos, Bertrand. "Genèse d'un problème social. Entre moralisation et médicalisation: La lutte antialcoolique en France (1850–1915)." *Lien social et politiques*, no. 55 (2006), 67–75.

Davey, Eleanor. "French Adventures in Solidarity: Revolutionary Tourists and Radical Humanitarians." *European Review of History: Revue européenne d'histoire* 21, no. 4 (2014), 577–95.

Dean, Carolyn J. *The Frail Social Body: Pornography, Homosexuality, and Other Fantasies in Interwar France.* Berkeley: University of California Press, 2000.

D'Eaubonne, Françoise. "Le FHAR, origines et illustrations." *La Revue h* 2 (1996), 18–30.

De Becker, Raymond. *L'érotisme d'en face.* Paris: J. J. Pauvert, 1964.

Delage, Pauline. "Après l'année zéro. Histoire croisée de la lutte contre le viol en France et aux États-Unis." *Critique internationale*, no. 70 (2016), 21–35.

De Lesseps, Emmanuèle. "Sexisme et Racisme." *Questions Féministes*, no. 7 (1980), 95–102.

Deleuze, Gilles. "Lettre à un critique sévère." *Pourparlers 1972* 1990 (1990), 11–23.

Deleuze, Gilles, and Michel Foucault. "Intellectuals and Power." In Gilles Deleuze, *Desert Islands and Other Texts*, trans. M. Taormina (New York: Semiotext[e], 2004), 205–213.

———. "'Les intellectuels et le pouvoir': Entretien de Michel Foucault avec Gilles Deleuze." *L'arc*, no. 49 (1972), 3–10.

Delphy, Christine, Pascale Molinier, Isabelle Clair, and Sandrine Rui. "Genre à la Française? Débat entre Christine Delphy et Pascale Molinier, animé par Isabelle Clair et Sandrine Rui." *Sociologie* 3, no. 3 (2012), 299–316.

Delpla, François, and Jean-Gabriel Foucaud. "Les communistes français et la sexualité (1932–1938)." *Le mouvement social*, no. 91 (1975), 121–152.

D'Emilio, John. "Capitalism and Gay Identity." In Ann Snitow, Christine Stansell, and Sharon Thompson, eds., *Powers of Desire: The Politics of Sexuality*, 100–113. New York: Monthly Review Press, 1997.

D'Hauteville, Laure. "Algériens: Feu la liberté de circulation." *Plein droit*, no. 29–30 (1995), 29–30.

Dine, Philip. *Images of the Algerian War: French Fiction and Film, 1954–1992.* New York: Oxford University Press, 1994.

Dobry, Michel. *Le mythe de l'allergie française au fascisme.* Paris: Albin Michel, 2003.

Donald, Stephanie Hemelryk. "Tang Wei Sex, the City and the Scapegoat in Lust, Caution." *Theory, Culture & Society* 27, no. 4 (2010), 46–68.

Donovan, James Michael. *Juries and the Transformation of Criminal Justice in France in the Nineteenth and Twentieth Centuries.* Chapel Hill: University of North Carolina Press, 2010.

Dreyfus-Armand, Geneviève, Robert Frank, Marie-Françoise Lévy, and Michelle Zancarini-Fournel, eds. *Les années 68: Le temps de la contestation.* Brussels: Editions complexe, 2000.

Droit, R. P., and A. Gallien. *La réalité sexuelle. Une enquête en France: Des femmes et des hommes disent les difficultés quotidiennes de leur vie sexuelle.* Paris: Robert Laffont, 1974.

Duprat, François. *Les mouvements d'extrême-droite en France depuis 1944.* Paris, Albatros, 1972.

Duranton-Crabol, Anne-Marie. "'Combat' et la guerre d'Algérie." *Vingtieme siecle: Revue d'histoire*, no. 40 (1993), 86–96.

———. "La 'Nouvelle droite' entre printemps et automne, 1968–1986." *Vingtieme siecle: Revue d'histoire*, no. 17 (1988): 39–49.

———. *Visages de la Nouvelle droite: Le GRECE et son histoire*. Paris: Presses de Sciences po, 1988.

Durban, Pierre. *La psychologie des prostitutées*. Paris: Maloine, 1969.

Duriez, Bruno, ed. *Les Catholiques dans la République, 1905–2005*. Editions de l'atelier, 2005.

Editors. "Introducing History of the Present." *History of the Present* 1, no. 1 (2011), 1–4.

Eribon, Didier. *Réflexions sur la question gay*. Paris: Fayard, 1999.

Fanon, Frantz. ""Le 'syndrome Nord Africain.'" In *Pour la révolution Africaine: Ecrits politiques*, 13–25. Paris: François Maspero, 1964.

Fassin, Eric. "L'empire du genre." *L'homme*, no. 187 (2008): 375–392.

———. "Good cop, bad cop modèle et contre-modèle américains dans le discours libéral français depuis les années 1980." *Raisons politiques*, no. 1 (2001), 77–87.

Fichte, Hubert. "Interview with Jean Genet." *Gay Sunshine Interviews* 1 (1978): 67–94.

Flamant, Françoise. *À tire d'elles: Itinéraires de féministes radicales des années 1970*. Rennes: Presses universitaires de Rennes, 2007.

Fontaine, Darcie. *Decolonizing Christianity: Religion and the End of Empire in France and Algeria*. Cambridge: Cambridge University Press, 2016.

Fortin, Andrée. "Amour et Utopie." *Nuit blanche*, no. 12 (1984): 46–49.

Foucault, Michel. *Histoire de la sexualité*. Volume 1. *La volonté de savoir*. Parirs: Gallimard, 1976.

———. *The History of Sexuality, Volume I: An Introduction*. Translated by Robert Hurley. New York: Pantheon, 1978.

———. "La Scène de la philosophie (1978)." In *Dits et écrits*, Vol. 3, 571–595. Paris: Gallimard, 1994.

———. "The Stage of Philosophy: A conversation between Michel Foucault and Moriaki Watanabe," Translated by Rosa Eidelpes and Kevin Kennedy. *New York Magazine of Contemporary Art and Theory* 1, no. 15 (2014), http://www.ny-magazine.org/PDF/The _Stage_of_Philosophy.html.

Foucault, Michel, interviewed by Farès Sassine. "Il ne peut pas y avoir de sociétés sans soulèvements (August 1979)." *Revue Rodéo* no. 2 (2013), 34–56.

Fougeyrollas-Schwebel, Dominique. "Controverses et anathèmes au sein du féminisme français des années 1970." *Cahiers du genre*, no. 2 (2005), 13–26.

François, Stéphane and Nicolas Lebourg, "Dominique Venner et le renouvellement du racisme." Fragments sur les temps présents (23 May 2013), http://tempspresents .com/2013/05/23/dominique-venner-renouvellement-racisme-stephane-francois -nicolas-lebourg/, accessed 5 October 2014.

Frémeaux, Jacques. *La France et l'Algérie en guerre: 1830–1870, 1954–1962*. Paris: Economica, 2002.

Freud, Sigmund. "Reflections upon War and Death." In *Character and Culture*, ed. Philip Rieff, 107–133. New York: Collier Books, 1963.

Furlough, Ellen. "Packaging Pleasures: Club Méditerranée and French Consumer Culture, 1950–1968." *French Historical Studies* 18, no. 1 (1993), 65–81.

Gamari-Tabrizi, Behrooz. "When Life Will No Longer Barter Itself: In Defense of Foucault on the Iranian Revolution." In Sam Binkley and Jorge Capetillo, eds., *A Foucault for the 21st Century: Governmentality, Biopolitics and Discipline in the New Millennium*: 270–290. New Castle, UK: Cambridge Scholars Publishing, 2009.

Garcia, Sandrine. "Expertise scientifique et capital militant." *Actes de la recherche en sciences sociales*, no. 158 (2005), 96–115.

Gaspard, Françoise. *A Small City in France: A Socialist Mayor Confronts Neofascism*. Translated by Arthur Goldhammer. Cambridge, MA: Harvard University Press, 1995.

Gastaud, Yvan. *L'immigration et l'opinion en France sous la Ve République*. Paris: Seuil, 2000.

———. "Français et immigrés à l'épreuve de la crise (1973–1995)." *Vingtième siècle: Revue d'histoire*, no. 84 (2004), 107–118 .

Gautier, Jean-Paul. *La restauration nationale: Un mouvement royaliste sous la 5e République*. Paris: Editions syllepse, 2002.

Genosko, Gary. "The Figure of the Arab in Three Billion Perverts.'" *Deleuze Studies* 1, no. 1 (2007), 60–78.

Georgi, Frank. "Le moment Lip dans l'histoire de l'autogestion en France." *Semaine sociale Lamy*, no. 1631 (19 May 2014).

Giami, Alain. "Misère, Répression et Libération Sexuelles." *Mouvements*, no. 20 (2002), 23–29.

———."Therapies of Sexual Liberation: Society, Sex and Self." In Alain Giami and Gert Hekma, eds., *Sexual Revolutions*, 155–172. Basingstoke, UK: Palgrave, 2014.

Giami, Alain, and Gert Hekma, eds. *Sexual Revolutions*. Basingstoke, UK: Palgrave, 2014.

Giudice, Fausto. *Arabicides: Une chronique française, 1970–1991*. Paris: La Découverte, 1992.

Glissant, Edouard. *Le discours Antillais*. Paris: Seuil, 1981.

Gordon, Daniel A. "'Il est recommande aux étrangers de ne pas participer': Les étrangers expulses en mai-juin 1968." *Migrations Societé*, no. 87 (2003), 45–65.

———. *Immigrants and Intellectuals: May '68 and the Rise of Anti-Racism in France*. Pontypool, UK: Merlin Press, 2012.

Guénif-Souilamas, Nacira. "En un combat douteux: Concurrence pour la conformation sexuée des Français d'ascendance migrante et coloniale." *Revue eEuropéenne des migrations internationales* 21, no. 2 (2005), 91–109.

Guénif-Souilamas, Nacira, and Éric Macé, *Les féministes et le garçon arabe*. La Tour d'Aigues, France: Éditions de l'Aube, 2004.

Guillochon, Mary B. "Prostitution and Sexuality in Lyon, 1938–1956." PhD diss., State University of New York at Binghamton, 2011.

Gunther, Scott Eric. *The Elastic Closet: A History of Homosexuality in France, 1942–Present*. New York: Palgrave Macmillan, 2009.

Guyotat, Pierre. *Carnets de Bord*. Vol. 1. Paris: Lignes & Manifestes, 2005.

Haas, Ron. "Guy Hocquenghem and the Cultural Revolution in France after May 1968." In Julian Bourg, ed., *After the Deluge: New Perspectives on the Intellectual and Cultural History of Postwar France*, 175–200. Lanham, MD: Lexington Books, 2004.

Hajjat, Abdellali. "Les comités Palestine (1970–1972): Aux origines du soutien de la cause palestinienne en France." *Revue d'études palestiniennes*, no. 98 (2006), 74–92.

Halperin, David M. *How to Be Gay*. Cambridge, MA: Harvard University Press, 2012.

———. *How to Do the History of Homosexuality*. Chicago: University of Chicago Press, 2004.

Hardy, Michel Serge. *De la morale au moral des troupes ou l'histoire des BMC, 1918–2004*. Paris: Lavauzelle, 2004.

Haroun, Ali. *La septième wilaya: La guerre du FLN en France, 1954–1962*. Paris: Seuil, 1986.

Harvey, Keith. *Intercultural Movements: American Gay in French Translation*. New York: Routledge, 2014.

Harvey, Simmons. *The French Front National: The Extremist Challenge to Democracy.* Boulder, CO: Westview Press, 1996.

Hayes, Jarrod. *Queer Nations: Marginal Sexualities in the Maghreb.* Chicago: University of Chicago Press, 2000.

Heineman, Elizabeth. "The Hour of the Woman: Memories of Germany's 'Crisis Years' and West German National Identity." In Hanna Schlissler, eds., *The Miracle Years: A Cultural History of West Germany, 1949–1968,* 21–56 Princeton, NJ: Princeton University Press, 2001.

Hennig, Jean Luc. *Les garçons de passe: Enquête sur la prostitution masculine.* Paris: Editions Libres Hallier, 1978.

Henry, Coston. *Dictionnaire de la politique française.* Paris: Librairie française, 1967.

Herzog, Dagmar. *Sex after Fascism: Memory and Morality in Twentieth-Century Germany.* Princeton, NJ: Princeton University Press, 2007.

———. *Sexuality in Europe: A Twentieth-Century History.* Cambridge: Cambridge University Press, 2011.

———. "Syncopated Sex: Transforming European Sexual Cultures." *American Historical Review* 114, no. 5 (2009), 1287–1308.

Hilderbrand, Lucas. "A Suitcase Full of Vaseline, or Travels in the 1970s Gay World." *Journal of the History of Sexuality* 22, no. 3 (2013), 373–402.

Hocquenghem, Guy. *La dérive homosexuelle.* Paris: Editions universitaires / Jean-Pierre Delarge, 1977.

Horvath, Robert. "'The Solzhenitsyn Effect': East European Dissidents and the Demise of the Revolutionary Privilege." *Human Rights Quarterly* 29, no. 4 (2007), 879–907.

Hosek, Jennifer Ruth. "'Subaltern Nationalism' and the West Berlin Anti-Authoritarians." *German Politics & Society,* no. 26 (2008), 57–81.

Houlbrook, Matt. *Queer London: Perils and Pleasures in the Sexual Metropolis, 1918–1957.* Chicago: University of Chicago Press, 2005.

House, Jim, and Neil MacMaster. *Paris 1961: Algerians, State Terror, and Memory.* Oxford, UK: Oxford University Press, 2006.

Huyssen, Andreas. "Mass Culture as Woman: Modernism's Other." In Huyssen, *After the Great Divide,* 44–62. Bloomington: Indiana University Press, 1986.

Idier, Antoine. "Les vies de Guy Hocquenghem: Sociologie d'une trajectoire à l'intersection des champs politiques, culturels et intellectuels français des années 1960 aux années 1980." PhD diss., Université d'Amiens, 2015.

Jackson, Julian. *Living in Arcadia: Homosexuality, Politics, and Morality in France from the Liberation to AIDS.* Chicago: University of Chicago Press, 2009.

Jacob-Wagner, Sarah. "Le débat sur le féminisme 'à la française' dans lLe cContexte de l'affaire DSK." In *Actes du colloque étudiant féministe.* Laval: Université Laval, 2013.

Jappe, Anselm. *Guy Debord.* Berkeley: University of California Press, 1999.

Jauffret, Jean-Charles, ed. *Des hommes et des femmes en guerre d'Algérie.* Paris: Autrement, 2003.

Jobs, Richard Ivan. *Riding the New Wave: Youth and the Rejuvenation of France after the Second World War.* Stanford, CA: Stanford University Press, 2007.

Johnson, David K. *The Lavender Scare: The Cold War Persecution of Gays and Lesbians in the Federal Government.* Chicago: University of Chicago Press, 2009.

Katz, Ethan B. *The Burdens of Brotherhood: Jews and Muslims from North Africa to France.* Cambridge, MA: Harvard University Press, 2015.

Kaye, Richard A. "Writers: Guy Hocquenghem. a New French Connection." *Advocate,* no. 406 (10 October 1984), 42–43.

Kitzinger, Jenny. "Media Coverage of Sexual Violence against Women and Children." In Karen Ross and Carolyn M. Byerly, eds., *Women and Media: International Perspectives*, 13–38. Oxford, UK: Blackwell, 2004.

Kuby, Emma. "From the Torture Chamber to the Bedchamber: French Soldiers, Antiwar Activists, and the Discourse of Sexual Deviancy in the Algerian War (1954–1962)." *Contemporary French Civilization* 38, no. 2 (2013), 131–153.

LaCapra, Dominick. *Writing History, Writing Trauma*. Baltimore: Johns Hopkins University Press, 2014.

Lacoste-Dujardin, Camille. *Des mères contre les femmes: Maternité et patriarcat au Maghreb*. Paris: La Découverte, 2013.

Laqueur, Thomas W. *Solitary Sex: A Cultural History of Masturbation*. New York: Zone Books, 2003.

Laubier, Claire. *The Condition of Women in France: 1945 to the Present–A Documentary Anthology*. London: Routledge, 2003.

Laurens, Sylvain. *Une politisation feutrée: Les hauts fonctionnaires et l'immigration en France (1962–1981)*. Paris: Belin, 2009.

Liskenne, Anne. *L'Algérie indépendante: L'ambassade de Jean-Marcel Jeanneney (juillet 1962–janvier 1963)*. Paris: Armand Colin, 2015

Lyons, Amelia. *The Civilizing Mission in the Metropole: Algerian Families and the French Welfare State during Decolonization*. Stanford, CA: Stanford University Press, 2013.

MacDonald, Scott. "Confessions of a Feminist Porn Watcher." *Film Quarterly*, 36, no. 3 (Spring 1983), 10–17.

Macey, David. "The Algerian with the Knife." *Parallax* 4, no. 2 (1998), 159–167.

———. *The Lives of Michel Foucault: A Biography*. New York: Vintage Books, 1995.

Mack, Mehammed Amadeus. *Sexagon: Muslims, France, and the Sexualization of National Culture*. New York: Fordham University Press, 2016.

MacMaster, Neil. *Colonial Migrants and Racism: Algerians in France, 1900–62*. London: Macmillan, 1997.

Mancini, Jean Gabriel. *Prostitutes and Their Parasites*. London: Elek Books, 1963.

Mangeot, Philippe, and George Chauncey. "De l'autre côté du placard." *Vacarme*, no. 1 (2004), 4–12.

Marcus, Herbert. *One-Dimensional Man: Studies in the Ideology of Advanced Industrial Society*. Boston: Beacon Press, 1964.

Marshall, Bill. *Guy Hocquenghem: Beyond Gay Identity*. Durham, NC: Duke University Press, 1997.

Martel, Frédéric. *The Pink and the Black: Homosexuals in France since 1968*. Translated by Jane-Marie Todd. Stanford, CA: Stanford University Press, 1999.

Massad, Joseph A. *Desiring Arabs*. Chicago: University of Chicago Press, 2008.

———. "Re-Orienting Desire: The Gay International and the Arab World." *Public Culture* 14, no. 2 (2002), 361–385.

Mathews, Timothy. *Literature, Art and the Pursuit of Decay in Twentieth-Century France*. Cambridge: Cambridge University Press, 2005.

Mathieu, Lilian. "An Ambiguous Compassion: Policing and Debating Prostitution in Contemporary France." *Sexuality Research and Social Policy* 9, no. 3 (2012), 203–211.

———. "Débat d'étudiants avec des prostituées à l'université de Lyon II en avril 1976." *Clio: Femmes, genre, histoire*, no. 17 (2003), 175–185.

———. *La fin du tapin: Sociologie de la croisade pour l'abolition de la prostitution*. Paris: François Bourin, 2014.

———. *Mobilisations de prostituées*. Paris: Belin, 2001.

———. *Sociologie de la prostitution*. Paris: La Découverte, 2015.

———. "Une mobilisation improbable: L'occupation de l'église Saint-Nizier par les prostituées Lyonnaises." *Revue française de sociologie* (1999), 475–499.

Maugère, Amélie. *Les politiques de la prostitution: Du Moyen âge au XXIe siècle. thèse pour le doctorat eEn science politique de 'Université de Versailles-Saint-Quentin-en-Yveline présentée et soutenue publiquement le 27 octobre 2008*. Paris: Dalloz, 2009.

Mauriac, Claude. *Mauriac et fils*. Paris: B. Grasset, 1986.

Mayeur, Jean Marie. *Catholicisme social et démocratie chrétienne: Principes romains, expériences françaises*. Paris: Cerf, 1986.

McGrogan, Manus. "Militants sans Frontières? Fusions and Frictions of US Movements in Paris, 1970." *Contemporary French Civilization* 39, no. 2 (2014), 197–222.

Meyers, Mark. "Feminizing Fascist Men: Crowd Psychology, Gender, and Sexuality in French Antifascism, 1929–1945." *French Historical Studies* 29, no. 1 (2006), 109–142.

Michard, Henri. "La délinquance des jeunes en France." *Notes et études documentaires* 3987–3988 (1973), 24–25.

Michéa, Jean-Claude. *L'empire du moindre mal: Essai sur la civilisation libérale*. Paris: Editions Climats / Flammarion, 2010.

Michel, Andrée. *Les travailleurs algériens en France*. Paris: CNRS, 1956.

Mills-Affif, Édouard. *Filmer les immigrés: Les représentations audiovisuelles de l'immigration à la télévision française*. Brussels: De Boeck Supérieur, 2004.

Minces, Juliette. *Travailleurs étrangers en France*. Paris: Seuil, 1973.

Montuori, Alfonso. "Edgar Morin: A Partial Introduction." *World Futures* 60, no. 5–6 (2004), 349–355.

Morin, Edgar, ed. *La rumeur d'Orléans*. Paris: Seuil, 1969.

———. *La rumeur d'Orléans: Edition complétée avec la rumeur d'Amiens (de Claude Fischler)*. Paris: Seuil, 1970.

Mort, Frank. ———. "The Ben Pimlott Memorial Lecture 2010: The Permissive Society Revisited." *Twentieth Century British History* 22, no. 2 (2011), 269–298.

———. *Capital Affairs: London and the Making of the Permissive Society*. New Haven: Yale University Press, 2009.

———. *Dangerous Sexualities: Medico-Moral Politics in England since 1830*, 2nd ed. London: Routledge, 2000.

Moyn, Samuel. *The Last Utopia*. Cambridge, MA: Harvard University Press, 2010.

Mulvey, Laura. "Visual Pleasure and Narrative Cinema." *Screen* 16, no. 3 (1975), 6–18.

Murat, Laure. *La loi du genre: Une histoire culturelle du "troisième sexe."* Paris: Fayard, 2006.

Murray, Ros. "Raised Fists: Politics, Technology, and Embodiment in 1970s French Feminist Video Collectives." *Camera Obscura: Feminism, Culture, and Media Studies* 31, no. 1 (91) (2016), 93–121.

Ouvrard, Lucile. *La prostitution: Analyse juridique et choix de politique criminelle*. Paris: L'Harmattan, 2000.

Passmore, Kevin. "'Class Gender and Populism: The Parti Populaire Français in Lyon, 1936–40." In Nicholas Atkin and Frank Tallett, eds., *The Right in France*, 183–214. London: IB Tauris, 2004.

———. *The Right in France from the Third Republic to Vichy*. Oxford, UK: Oxford University Press, 2013.

Pavard, Bibia. *Si je veux, quand je veux: Contraception et avortement dans la société française (1956–1979)*. Rennes: Presses universitaires de Rennes, 2012.

Pedersen, Jean Elisabeth. "Regulating Abortion and Birth Control: Gender, Medicine, and

Republican Politics in France, 1870–1920." *French Historical Studies* 19, no. 3 (1996), 673–698.

Perrier, Aurelie Evangeline. "Intimate Matters: Negotiating Sex, Gender and the Home in Colonial Algeria," PhD diss., Georgetown University, 2014.

Pervillé, Guy. "Antiracisme, décolonisation de l'Algérie et immigration algérienne en France." *Cahiers de la Méditerranée* 61, no. 1 (2000), 121–130.

Petitfils, Jean-Christian. *L'extrême droite en France*. Paris: Presses universitaires de France, 1983.

Picq, Françoise. *Libération des femmes: Les années-mouvement*. Paris: Seuil, 1993.

Pierre, Simon, Jean Gondonneau, Lucien Mironer, and Anne-Marie Dourlen-Rollier. *Rapport sur le comportement sexuel des Français*. Paris: Julliard/Charron, 1972.

Pipon, Colette. *Et on tuera tous les affreux:Le féminisme au risque de la misandrie (1970–1980)*. Rennes: Presses universitaires de Rennes, 2013.

Pollak, Michael. "Les vertus de la banalité." *Le débat*, no. 3 (1981), 132–143.

Preciado, Beatriz. *Testo junkie: Sexe, drogue et biopolitique*. Paris: Grasset & Fasquelle, 2008.

Puar, Jasbir. *Terrorist Assemblages: Homonationalism in Queer Times*. Durham, NC: Duke University Press, 2007.

Rabinow, Paul. "Book Review: Working in Paris." *Dialectical Anthropology*, no. 3 (1978), 361–364.

Rashkin, Esther. "Sex, Sadism, Encrypted Loss and Encrypted History in Last Tango in Paris." *Parallax* 15, no. 1 (2009), 55–66.

Reich, Wilhelm. *L'irruption de la morale sexuelle: Étude des origines du caractère compulsif de la morale sexuelle*. Translated by Pierre Kamnitzer. Paris: Payot, 1972.

Revenin, Régis. *Une histoire des garçons et des filles: Amour, genre, sexualité dans la France d'après-guerre*. Paris: Vendémiaire, 2015.

Richlin, Amy. "Eros Underground: Greece and Rome in Gay Print Culture, 1953-65." *Journal of Homosexuality* 49, no. 3-4 (2005), 421–461.

Robcis, Camille. "Catholics, the 'Theory of Gender,' and the Turn to the Human in France: A New Dreyfus Affair?" *Journal of Modern History* 87, no. 4 (2015), 892–923.

———. "Liberté, Égalité, Hétérosexualité: Race and Reproduction in the French Gay Marriage Debates." *Constellations* 22, no. 3 (2015), 447–461.

———. *The Law of Kinship: Anthropology, Psychoanalysis, and the Family in France*. Ithaca, NY: Cornell University Press, 2013.

Roberts, Mary Louise. *What Soldiers Do: Sex and the American GI in World War II France*. Chicago: University of Chicago Press, 2013.

Robson, Kathryn. "The Subject of Rape: Feminist Discourses on Rape and Violability in Contemporary France." *French Cultural Studies* 26, no. 1 (2015), 45–55.

Rodinis, Giuliana Toso. *Fêtes et défaites d'éros dans l'oeuvre de Rachid Boudjedra*. Paris: L'Harmattan, 1994.

Roditi, Edouard. *De l'homosexualité*. Paris: SEDIMO, 1962.

Ross, Kristin. *Fast Cars, Clean Bodies: Decolonization and the Reordering of French Culture*. Cambridge, MA: MIT Press, 1996.

———. *May '68 and Its Afterlives*. Chicago: University of Chicago Press, 2008.

Roth-Bettoni, Didier. *L'homosexualité au cinéma*. Paris: Musardine, 2007.

Rousso, Henry. "12: Les dilemmes d'une mémoire européenne." *Recherches* (2009), 203–221.

———. *Le syndrome de Vichy*. Paris: Seuil, 1987.

Saada, Emmanuelle. *Empire's Children: Race, Filiation, and Citizenship in the French Colonies*. Translated by Arthur Goldhammer. Chicago: University of Chicago Press, 2011.

Saadia-et-Lakhdar (Salima Sahraoui-Bouaziz, known as "Saadia," and Rabah Bouaziz, known as "Lakhdar"). *L'aliénation colonialiste et la résistance de lLa famille Algérienne*. Lausanne: La Cité, 1961.

Sahraoui-Bouaziz, Salima ("Saadia") and Rabah Bouaziz ("Lakhdar"). *L'aliénation colonialiste et la résistance de la famille Algérienne*. Re-edition. Algiers: Casbah éditions, 2014.

Said, Edward. *Orientalism*. New York: Pantheon, 1978.

——. *L'Orientalisme: L'OrientcCréé par l'Occident*. Translated by Catherine Malamoud. Paris: Seuil, 1980.

Salah, Ali. *La communauté algérienne: Étude sur l'immigration algérienne dans le département du Nord, 1945–1972*. Lille: Université de Lille III, 1973.

Samoyault, Tiphaine. *Roland Barthes*. Paris: Seuil, 2015.

Sanos, Sandrine. *The Aesthetics of Hate: Far-Right Intellectuals, Antisemitism, and Gender in 1930s France*. Stanford, CA: Stanford University Press, 2012.

Sartre, Jean Paul. *Saint Genet: Comédien et martyr*. Paris: Gallimard, 1952.

Sassine, Farès. "Foucault en l'entretien," http://fares-sassine.blogspot.fr/2014/08/foucault-en-lentretien.html, accessed 17 May 2016.

Schor, Ralph. *L'opinion française et les étrangers en France, 1919–1939*. Paris: Publications de la Sorbonne, 1985.

Scott, Joan Wallach. *Only Paradoxes to Offer: French Feminists and the Rights of Man*. Cambridge, MA: Harvard University Press, 2009.

——. *The Politics of the Veil*. Princeton, NJ: Princeton University Press, 2009.

Sebbar, Leïla. *On tue les petites filles*. Paris: Stock, 1978.

Sedgwick, Eve Kosofsky. *Epistemology of the Closet*. Berkeley: University of California Press, 1990.

Seidman, Michael. *The Imaginary Revolution: Parisian Students and Workers in 1968*. New York: Berghahn Books, 2004.

——. "The Pre-May 1968 Sexual Revolution." *Contemporary French Civilization* 25, no. 1 (2001), 20–41.

Shepard, Todd. "Algeria, France, Mexico, UNESCO: A Transnational History of Anti-Racism and Decolonization, 1932–1962." *Journal of Global History* 6, no. 2 (2011), 273–297.

——. "Algerian Nationalism, Zionism, and French Laïcité: A History of Ethnoreligious Nationalisms and Decolonization." *International Journal of Middle East Studies* 45, no. 3 (2013), 445–467.

——. "Comment et pourquoi éviter le racisme: Causes, effets, culture, 'seuils de tolérance' ou résistances? Le débat français entre 1954 et 1976." *Arts & Sociétés: Lettre du séminaire* 51 (March 2013), http://www.artsetsocietes.org/f/f-index51.html, accessed 12 May 2014.

——. "Decolonization and the Republic." In Edward Berenson, Vincent Duclert, and Christophe Prochasson, eds., *The French Republic: History, Values, Debates*: 252–261. Ithaca, NY: Cornell University Press, 2011.

——. "L'extrême droite et 'mai 68': Une obsession d'Algérie et de virilité." *Clio: Femmes, genre, histoire*, no. 29 (2009), 37–57.

——. "'History Is Past Politics'? Archives, 'Tainted Evidence,' and the Return of the State." *American Historical Review* 115, no. 2 (2010), 474–483.

——. *The Invention of Decolonization: The Algerian War and the Remaking of France*. 2nd Edition. Ithaca, NY: Cornell University Press, 2008.

———. "Making French and European Coincide: Decolonization and the Politics of Comparative and Transnational Histories." *Ab Imperio* 2007, no. 2 (2007), 339–360.

———. "'Something Notably Erotic': Politics, 'Arab Men,' and Sexual Revolution in Post-Decolonization France, 1962–1974." *Journal of Modern History* 84, no. 1 (2012), 80–115.

———. "What Drew Foucault to Sodomy." Foucaultblog, http://www.fsw.uzh.ch/foucaultblog/issue/131/what-drew-foucault-to-sodomy, accessed 10 March 2016.

Shield, Andrew D. J. "'Suriname–Seeking a Lonely, Lesbian Friend for Correspondence': Immigration and Homo-Emancipation in the Netherlands, 1965–79." *History Workshop Journal*, 78, no. 1 (Autumn 2014), 246–264.

Sibalis, Michael. "L'arrivée de la libération gay en France: Le Front homosexuel d'action révolutionnaire (FHAR)." *Genre, Sexualité & Société*, no. 3 (2010), 2–17.

———. "Urban Space and Homosexuality: The Example of the Marais, Paris' Gay Ghetto.'" *Urban Studies* 41, no. 9 (2004), 1739–1758.

Simon, Jacques. *L'immigration algérienne en France de 1962 à nos jours.* Paris: L'Harmattan, 2002.

Slade, Joseph W. "Recent Trends in Pornographic Films." *Society* 12, no. 6 (1975), 77–84.

Spencer, Ian R. G. *British Immigration Policy since 1939: The Making of Multi-Racial Britain.* London: Routledge, 2002.

Spivak, Gayatri Chakravorty. *Can the Subaltern Speak?* In Cary Nelson and Lawrence Grossberg, eds., *Marxism and the Interpretation of Culture,* 271–313. Urbana: University of Illinois Press, 1988.

Stoler, Ann Laura. *Carnal Knowledge and Imperial Power: Race and the Intimate in Colonial Rule.* Berkeley: University of California Press, 2002.

Stora, Benjamin. *Algeria, 1830–2000: A Short History.* Translated by Jane Marie Todd. Ithaca, NY: Cornell University Press, 2004.

———. *La gangrène et l'oubli: La mémoire de la guerre d'Algérie.* Paris: La Découverte, 1998.

———. *Le transfert d'une mémoire: De l'Algérie française au racisme anti-arabe.* Paris: La Découverte, 1999.

Storti, Martine. *Je suis une femme, pourquoi pas vous?* Paris: Michel de Maule, 2010.

Stryker, Susan. "An Introduction to Transgender Studies." In Susan Stryker and Stephen Whittle, eds., *The Transgender Studies Reader,* 1–17. New York: Routledge, 2006.

Surkis, Judith. "Ethics and Violence: Simone de Beauvoir, Djamila Boupacha, and the Algerian War." *French Politics, Culture & Society* 28, no. 2 (2010), 38–55.

———. *Sexing the Citizen: Masculinity and Morality in France, 1870–1920.* Ithaca, NY: Cornell University Press, 2006.

Taguieff, Pierre-André. "La stratégie culturelle de la 'nouvelle droite' en France (1968–1983)." In Antoine Spire, ed., *Vous avez dit fascismes?,* 13–152. Paris: Editions Montalba, 1984.

Talbott, John E. *The War without a Name: France in Algeria, 1954–1962.* New York: Alfred A. Knopf, 1980.

Tamagne, Florence. "Paris: 'Resting on Its Laurels'?" In Jennifer V. Evans, Matt Cook, eds., *Queer Cities, Queer Cultures: Europe Since 1945:* 240–260. London: Bloomsbury, 2014.

Taraud, Christelle. *La prostitution coloniale: Algérie, Tunisie, Maroc, 1830–1962.* Paris, Payot, 2003.

Thébaud, Françoise. "Le privé est politique: Féminismes des années 1970." In Michel Pigenet and Danielle Tartakowsky, eds., *Histoire des mouvements sociaux en France: De 1814 à nos jours,* 509–520. Paris: La Découverte, 2014.

Tissot, Sylvie. "Un quartier gay-friendly? Ethnographie du Marais hétérosexuel," talk presented at the workshop "La sexualité et la Cinquième République / Sex and France since 1958," Johns Hopkins University, Baltimore, 20 September 2013.

Traub, Valerie. *Thinking Sex with the Early Moderns.* Philadelphia: University of Pennsylvania Press, 2015.

Vidal, Gore. "Some Jews and the Gays. A Reply." *The Nation* (14 November 1981), 489–497.

Vigarello, Georges. *Histoire du Viol, XVIe–XXe siècle.* Paris: Seuil, 1998.

Vigna, Xavier. "Une émancipation des invisibles? Les ouvriers immigrés dans les grèves de mai-juin 68." In Ahmed Boubeker and Abdellali Hajjat, eds., *Histoire politique des immigrations (post) coloniales, France, 1920–2008,* 85–94. Paris: Édition Amsterdam, 2008.

Vinen, Richard C. *Bourgeois Politics in France, 1945–1951.* Cambridge: Cambridge University Press, 2002.

———. "The End of an Ideology? Right-Wing Antisemitism in France, 1944–1970." *Historical Journal* 37, no. 2 (1994), 365–388.

Virgili, Fabrice. *La France virile: Des femmes tondues la Libération.* Paris: Payot, 2000.

———. "Viol (histoire du)." In *Dictionnaire de la violence,* 1423–1429. Paris: Michela Marzano Paris, 2011.

Waitt, Gordon, and Kevin Markwell. *Gay Tourism: Culture and Context.* New York: Routledge, 2006.

Walker, Muriel. "Pour une lecture narratologique d'Histoire d'O." *Études Littéraires* 33, no. 1 (2001), 149–168.

Walkowitz, Judith R. *City of Dreadful Delight: Narratives of Sexual Danger in Late-Victorian London.* Chicago: University of Chicago Press, 1992.

———. *Prostitution and Victorian Society: Women, Class, and the State.* Cambridge: Cambridge University Press, 1982.

Watson, Molly McGregor. "The Trade in Women: 'White Slavery' and the French Nation, 1899–1939." PhD diss., Stanford University, 1999.

Weiss, Gillian. *Captives and Corsairs: France and Slavery in the Early Modern Mediterranean.* Stanford, CA: Stanford University Press, 2011.

Wetsel, David. "Copi (Pseud. of Raúl Damonte; Argentina; 1941–1987)." In David William Foster, ed., *Latin American Writers on Gay and Lesbian Themes: A Bio-Critical Sourcebook,* 116–121. Westport, CT: Greenwood Press, 1994.

White, Edmund. *Genet: A Biography.* New York: Vintage, 1993.

Wieviorka, Annette. *L'ère du témoin.* Paris: Plon, 1998.

Wildenthal, Lora. *The Language of Human Rights in West Germany.* Philadelphia: University of Pennsylvania Press, 2012.

Zancarini-Fournel, Michelle. Conclusion to Geneviève Dreyfus-Armand, Robert Frank, Marie-Françoise Lévy, and Michelle Zancarini-Fournel, eds., *Les années 68: Le temps de la contestation* (Paris: Complexe, 2000).

———. "La question immigrée après 68." *Plein droit,* no. 2 (2002), 3–7.

abortion, 75n25, 77, 216, 227, 246–47, 254–55. *See also* feminism

Actuel, 171

Ahmed, *Une Vie d'Algérien* (1973), 113–15

Al-Din, Isma'il Waliy, *Hammam al-Malatili* (1970), 210

Algazy, Joseph, 58

Algeria: "Algeria is France"/"*Algérie française*," 20, 55, 57, 60, 153, 163; conscientious objection and, 81; Franco-Algerian rapport, 31–32, 129; French Algeria, 7, 19–21, 36, 50–55, 163 (*see also* far right; "nostalgeria"); French racism and, 239; gender relations in, 34, 111, 261; homosexuality and, 61, 64, 97n2, 111, 113; invocations of, 8; *Last Tango in Paris* and, 212, 214–15; masculinized, 33, 39; as "the Mecca of revolutionaries," 5; nationalistes/nationaux and, 8n11; oppression of women in, 275–76; pied noir repatriates from, 20, 182; post-1962 rape in, 35; prostitution and, 133, 139–40, 148–49, 161, 186–87 (*see also* prostitution); relationship to France, 9–10; as sexually repressive, 108; sexual tourism and, 120–21; traffic in women and, 132, 183–84, 186, 188–89; as woman, 32–33

Algerian independence, 1, 3, 10n14, 16, 18–20, 29, 33, 134, 140, 152, 159–60, 183, 185–87, 200–202, 205, 218, 255, 283–84

Algerian invasion. *See* Arab invasion

Algerian men. *See* Arab men

Algerian National Liberation Front (FLN), 5, 29–30, 35, 39, 44, 50, 55, 61, 65, 69, 79, 82, 113, 146–53, 159, 163–64, 172, 192, 201–3, 234, 255, 275, 284–85

Algerian revolution (1954–1962): "Algerian war," 4n6; anti-colonial activism and, 9, 200, 206; Arab revolution and, 5, 82–83; crisis of masculinity and, 25, 30–31, 35, 92; erotics of, 2; feminism and, 246–47, 249, 268; heroic Algerian man and, 11–12, 272–73, 281; literature and, 2; new left and, 55, 69–71, 80–83, 272; public discussions of, 4; sexual revolution and, 1, 9, 14, 69–70, 77, 88, 137–39 (*see also* Homosexual Front for Revolutionary Action); social plague laws and, 137–38; veiled woman and, 12. *See also* Algerian National Liberation Front (FLN)

Algerians: anti-Algerian racism, 58, 80, 239–40, 244; anti-Algerian violence, 59–60, 80, 231, 235, 239, 280n17, 285 (*see also* Ali, Djellali Ben; Secret Army Organization); associations with criminality, 37, 39, 153, 235–36 (*see also* pimps; proxenetism; rape); erotics of Algerian difference, 9, 18, 96, 105, 124, 129, 273; as foreigners, 11, 20–21, 32, 36n35; as French, 32, 137–38, 140–41n13, 144, 155, 230n9, 232; homosociality and, 109–10; immigration, 10n15, 21–23, 39, 41, 57, 59, 167,